taste of home

healthy
COOking

2011
annual
recipes

tasteofhome

2011 Healthy Cooking
Annual Recipes

©2011 Reiman Media Group, LLC
5400 S. 60th St., Greendale WI 53129

Taste of Home is a registered trademark
of The Reader's Digest Association, Inc.

International Standard Book Number (10):
0-89821-862-4

International Standard Book Number (13):
978-0-89821-862-2

International Standard Serial Number:
1944-7736

Printed in U.S.A.
13 5 7 9 10 8 6 4 2

Cover Photography:
Photographer: Dan Roberts
Food Stylist: Kathryn Conrad
Set Stylists: Dee Dee Jacq, Grace Natoli Sheldon

Pictured on the Front Cover:
Biscuit-Topped Shepherd's Pies (p. 108);
Mexicali Chicken (p. 135); Makeover Peanut Butter Cup
Cheesecake (p. 242); and Hawaiian Beef Sliders (p. 118).

Pictured on the Back Cover:
Gingered Spaghetti Salad (p. 89); Candy Bar Cupcakes (p. 252);
Omelet Tortilla Wraps (p. 83); and Asparagus with Tarragon
Lemon Sauce (p. 228).

To order additional copies of this book,
or to purchase other Taste of Home
books and products, visit
ShopTasteofHome.com

Vice President, Editor in Chief
Catherine Cassidy

Vice President, Executive Editor/Books
Heidi Reuter Lloyd

Creative Director
Howard Greenberg

Food Director
Diane Werner, RD

Senior Editor/Books
Mark Hagen

Associate Book Editor
Ellie Martin Cliffe

Associate Creative Director
Edwin Robles, Jr.

Art Director
Gretchen Trautman

Editor/Healthy Cooking
Mary Spencer

Food Editor/Healthy Cooking
Peggy Woodward, RD

Content Production Manager
Julie Wagner

Layout Designer
Nancy Novak

Proofreader
Linne Bruskewitz

Recipe Asset System Manager
Coleen Martin

Recipe Testing and Editing
Taste of Home Test Kitchen

Food Photography
Taste of Home Photo Studio

Administrative Assistant
Barb Czysz

_____

North American Chief Marketing Officer
Lisa Karpinski

Vice President/Book Marketing
Dan Fink

Creative Director/Creative Marketing
James Palmen

The Reader's Digest Association, Inc.

President and Chief Executive Officer
Mary G. Berner

President, North American Affinities
Suzanne M. Grimes

Contents

With 17 chapters to consider, the 2011 edition of *Healthy Cooking Annual Recipes* makes it easier than ever to find the perfect dish for any menu or occasion and still keep your commitment to eating right!

Family Favorites

With *Healthy Cooking Annual Recipes*, it's a cinch to put satisfying all-time classics on the table...no matter how busy your day is. Best of all, no one will suspect they're eating lighter. Just ask Food Editor Peggy Woodward.

As a busy working mom, I know the importance of getting dinner on the table fast, but as a registered dietitian, I want those dinners to be healthy, too. I also know that no matter what I prepare, it has to be tasty and satisfying. That's why I'm so excited to bring you this edition of *Healthy Cooking Annual Recipes*.

Packed with more than 480 recipes and tips plus hundreds of full-color photos, this handy cookbook makes it a snap to find the perfect dish. Every delicious recipe pares down calories, fat and/or sodium without sacrificing flavor! Even my husband has no clue that he's eating healthy because he is too busy asking for second helpings!

Best of all, every recipe includes a full set of Nutrition Facts as well as Diabetic Exchanges when applicable, so I'm always well aware of what I'm serving. In addition, all of the recipes were tested and approved by the professionals at the Test of Home Test Kitchen, guaranteeing that everything will turn out perfect.

Speaking of which, whipping up recipes from *Healthy Cooking Annual Recipes* is a breeze. In fact, there are prep/cook guidelines with every dish, so I can plan my time in the kitchen accordingly. For those extra-busy nights, I turn to any of the 150+ lifesavers that are ready in just 30 minutes—or less! (To learn more, see the box titled "30-Minute Specialties" at the far right.) And don't forget to check out the "Dinner in 30" chapter on page 88. It features nothing but half-hour entrees!

I love how everything in this book comes together with healthful ingredients I usually have on hand or can simply pick up at my local supermarket. There's no running to specialty stores or buying expensive items I won't likely use again. What could be easier?

But just because these foods are made with heart-smart ingredients and whip together quickly, doesn't mean they lack the satisfying goodness your family craves. Flip through the following pages and you'll find low-calorie takes on all of your favorites. Whether you're in the mood for pizza, meat loaf, mashed potatoes or even strudel, this popular cookbook always has you covered.

Cooking for a special diet? Check out the At-a-Glance Icons, highlighting items particularly low in fat, sodium and carbs. You might also want to consider recipes such as Lactose-Free Spinach Lasagna (p. 188), Gluten-Free Brownies (p. 243) and Low-Fat Carrot Cake (p. 232). They're perfect for all of your family members—whether they have a food intolerance or not.

If you need a fast supper on a hectic weeknight or if you're looking for a decadent treat for someone on a special diet, you are sure to find the right recipe within this fantastic collection. Because with *Healthy Cooking Annual Recipes 2011*, you can satisfy everyone at your table and still keep your commitment to eating right!

Peggy Woodward, RD

Food Editor, *Healthy Cooking*

Nutrition Facts Nuggets

Nutritional Guidelines

Every recipe in *Healthy Cooking Annual Recipes* fits the lifestyle of a health-conscious cook. The recipes represent a variety of foods that will fit into any meal plan that is within the standards of the USDA's "My Pyramid Plan" for moderately active adults (see box below). The target nutritional content of recipes, on a per-serving basis, is:

- 400 calories (or less)
- 12 grams of fat (or less)
- 1,000 mg sodium (or less)
- 100 mg cholesterol (or less)

How We Calculated the Nutrition Facts

- Whenever a choice of ingredients is given in a recipe (such as 1/3 cup of sour cream or plain yogurt), the first ingredient listed is always the one calculated in the Nutrition Facts.
- When a range is given for an ingredient (such as 2 to 3 teaspoons), we calculate the first amount given.
- Only the amount of marinade absorbed during preparation is calculated.
- Garnishes listed in recipes are generally included in our calculations.

Diabetic Exchanges

All recipes in this book have been reviewed by a registered dietitian. Diabetic Exchanges are assigned to recipes in accordance with guidelines from the American Diabetic and American Dietetic associations. The majority of recipes in *Healthy Cooking Annual Recipes* are suitable for diabetics.

Special Diet Indicators

To help those on restricted diets easily find dishes to suit their needs, we clearly indicate recipes that are low in carbohydrates, fat or sodium or those that contain no meat. You'll find these colored special diet indicators after the recipe title where appropriate:

F One serving contains 3 grams or less of fat

S One serving contains 140 milligrams or less of sodium

C One serving contains 15 grams or less of carbohydrates

M Appetizers, salads, savory breads, side dishes and entrees that contain no meat

30-Minute Specialties

The kitchen clock is ticking, but you want to serve a meal that's not loaded with fat and calories.

Between driving home from work, picking up the kids from school, and dealing with homework and extracurricular activities, there's not much time to cook. Don't turn to fast food...look at your copy of *Healthy Cooking Annual Recipes*!

The 2011 edition of this popular series features more than 450 recipes—including 159 that are table-ready in just half an hour or less! Finding these effortless favorites is easy. Simply turn to the recipe indexes, starting on page 262. All of the items that can be ready in 30 minutes are clearly marked with a small purple dot.

The next time you're in a time crunch, consider Sausage Pizza (p. 157), Black Bean Chicken with Rice (p. 101), Favorite Skillet Lasagna (p. 137) or Pork Chops with Apricot Sauce (p. 228). They're each ready in a half-hour.

Need a quick dessert that trims back calories? Try Mock Apple Strudel (p. 260), Berry-Marshmallow Trifle (p. 247) or Chocolate Biscuit Puffs (p. 256). They come together in no time. You'll find all of these speedy sensations and more in this edition of *Healthy Cooking Annual Recipes*.

DAILY NUTRITION GUIDE

	Women 25-50	Women over 50	Men 50-65
CALORIES	2,000	1,800	2,400
FAT	67 g or less	60 g or less	80 g or less
SATURATED FAT	22 g or less	20 g or less	27 g or less
CHOLESTEROL	300 mg or less	300 mg or less	300 mg or less
SODIUM	2,400 mg or less	2,400 mg or less	2,400 mg or less
CARBOHYDRATES	300 g	270 g	360 g
FIBER	20-30 g	20-30 g	20-30 g
PROTEIN	50 g	45 g	60 g

This chart is only a guide. Requirements vary, depending on age, weight, height and amount of activity.
Children's dietary needs vary as they grow.

APRICOT-RICOTTA STUFFED CELERY

VEGGIE PINWHEEL APPETIZERS

HEALTHY SNACK MIX

Starters & Snacks

Whether you need a bite to pass for a casual party or an impressive appetizer for your holiday buffet, this chapter has you covered! Beverages, snack mixes and sweets round out the low-calorie offerings found here.

Apricot-Ricotta Stuffed Celery F S C M

PREP/TOTAL TIME: 15 min. YIELD: about 2 dozen

DOROTHY REINHOLD • MALIBU, CALIFORNIA

This healthful protein filling can double as a dip for sliced apples. I often make it ahead, so kids can help themselves to an after-school snack.

3	dried apricots
1/2	cup part-skim ricotta cheese
2	tsp. brown sugar
1/4	tsp. grated orange peel
1/8	tsp. salt
5	celery ribs, cut into 1-1/2-in. pieces

1. Place apricots in a food processor. Cover and process until finely chopped. Add the ricotta cheese, brown sugar, orange peel and salt; cover and process until blended. Stuff or pipe into celery. Chill until serving.

Nutrition Facts: 1 piece equals 12 calories, trace fat (trace saturated fat), 2 mg cholesterol, 25 mg sodium, 1 g carbohydrate, trace fiber, 1 g protein. **Diabetic Exchange:** Free food.

Healthy Snack Mix

PREP: 15 min. BAKE: 1 hour + cooling
YIELD: 3-1/2 qt.

MELISSA HANSEN • ROCHESTER, MINNESOTA

Party mix has always been a tradition in our home. I lightened my mom's recipe, replacing margarine with heart-healthy olive oil. No one even noticed.

3	cups Corn Chex
3	cups Rice Chex
3	cups Wheat Chex
3	cups Multi Grain Cheerios
1	cup salted peanuts
1-1/2	cups pretzel sticks
1/3	cup olive oil
4	tsp. Worcestershire sauce
1	tsp. seasoned salt
1/8	tsp. garlic powder

1. In a large bowl, combine the cereals, peanuts and pretzels. In a small bowl, combine the remaining ingredients; pour over the cereal mixture and toss to coat.

2. Transfer to two 15-in. x 10-in. x 1-in. baking pans coated with cooking spray. Bake at 250° for 1 hour, stirring every 15 minutes. Cool completely on wire racks. Store in an airtight container.

Nutrition Facts: 3/4 cup equals 150 calories, 8 g fat (1 g saturated fat), 0 cholesterol, 310 mg sodium, 19 g carbohydrate, 2 g fiber, 4 g protein. **Diabetic Exchanges:** 1-1/2 starch, 1-1/2 fat.

Veggie Pinwheel Appetizers

PREP TIME: 20 min. + chilling YIELD: 32 appetizers

BEVERLY JONES • CAMBRIDGE, MARYLAND

My son, Tyler, loves these and even asked me to make them for his school party instead of cupcakes! Now his classmates love them, too, and I make them for every party. To keep it easy, I usually get the veggies from the grocery store's salad bar.

1	pkg. (8 oz.) reduced-fat cream cheese
2	Tbsp. Vidalia onion salad dressing
1/2	cup finely chopped fresh broccoli
1/4	cup grated carrot
1/4	cup finely chopped red onion
1/2	tsp. dill weed
4	whole wheat tortillas (8 in.)

1. In a small bowl, beat cream cheese and salad dressing until blended. Stir in the broccoli, carrot, onion and dill weed. Spread over tortillas. Roll up tightly; wrap in plastic wrap. Refrigerate for at least 2 hours. Unwrap and cut each into eight slices.

Nutrition Facts: 1 piece equals 40 calories, 2 g fat (1 g saturated fat), 5 mg cholesterol, 56 mg sodium, 4 g carbohydrate, trace fiber, 1 g protein.

Have leftover tortillas? Let tortillas dry on racks until brittle, then **crumble into pieces** to use in soups or salads in place of crackers and croutons.

Creamy Radish Dip F C

PREP/TOTAL TIME: 10 min. YIELD: 1-1/2 cups

TERRI CHATFIELD • HAMILTON, OHIO

This Scandinavian dish is one of our favorite spring appetizers. We use homegrown onions and radishes. The best part is that the dip only calls for four ingredients! I can whip it up in no time, which is great when unexpected company drops by.

> 1 cup chopped radishes
> 1/2 cup reduced-fat sour cream
> 4 green onions, sliced
> 1/2 tsp. salt

Rye crackers

1. In a small bowl, combine the radishes, sour cream, onions and salt. Serve on crackers.

Nutrition Facts: 1/4 cup (calculated without crackers) equals 33 calories, 2 g fat (1 g saturated fat), 7 mg cholesterol, 219 mg sodium, 3 g carbohydrate, 1 g fiber, 2 g protein.

Chilly-Day Hot Cocoa Mix F S

PREP/TOTAL TIME: 15 min.
YIELD: 10 servings (2-1/2 cups hot chocolate mix)

MARIE WIERSMA • ST. JOHNS, MICHIGAN

Here's a great way to chase the chills when winter winds blow. Not only does it taste great, but the easy-to-assemble mix is a perfect gift for teachers, friends, neighbors and anyone you'd like to surprise with a gift during the holidays.

> 2 cups nonfat dry milk powder
> 6 Tbsp. baking cocoa
> 5 Tbsp. confectioners' sugar
> 5 Tbsp. sugar

EACH SERVING:
> 1/2 cup hot fat-free milk
> 1/2 cup hot water

1. In a small airtight container, combine the milk powder, cocoa, confectioners' sugar and sugar. Store in a cool dry place for up to 2 months. For each serving, place 1/4 cup mix in a mug; stir in hot milk and water until blended.

Nutrition Facts: 1 cup equals 137 calories, trace fat (trace saturated fat), 5 mg cholesterol, 127 mg sodium, 25 g carbohydrate, 1 g fiber, 10 g protein. **Diabetic Exchanges:** 1 fat-free milk, 1/2 starch.

CHILLY-DAY HOT COCOA MIX

CREAMY RADISH DIP

CRUNCHY VANILLA WALNUTS

Crunchy Vanilla Walnuts S C

PREP: 10 min. **BAKE:** 35 min. **YIELD:** 4-1/3 cups

GABRIELE OSBORN • RANCHO SANTA FE, CALIFORNIA

A source of omega-3s and B vitamins, walnuts are always a hit at my house. Featuring coriander, cinnamon, nutmeg and allspice, this change-of-pace version is oh-so delicious.

1/3	cup sugar
1/4	tsp. salt
1/4	tsp. ground coriander
1/4	tsp. ground cinnamon
1/4	tsp. ground nutmeg
1/4	tsp. ground allspice
1/8	tsp. pepper
4	cups walnut halves
2	Tbsp. canola oil
1	tsp. vanilla extract

1. In a small bowl, combine the first seven ingredients; set aside. In a large bowl, combine the walnuts, oil and vanilla. Add sugar mixture; toss to coat.

2. Transfer to a 15-in. x 10-in. x 1-in. foil-lined baking pan coated with cooking spray. Bake at 325° for 35 minutes, stirring occasionally. Cool completely. Store in an airtight container.

Nutrition Facts: 1/3 cup equals 243 calories, 22 g fat (2 g saturated fat), 0 cholesterol, 46 mg sodium, 10 g carbohydrate, 2 g fiber, 5 g protein.

Makeover Nutty Monkey Malts F

PREP/TOTAL TIME: 5 min. **YIELD:** 5 servings

HEALTHY COOKING TEST KITCHEN

Say good-bye to guilt with this no-fuss take on an all-time favorite. You can get all the flavor of a classic diner milk shake with only a fraction of the calories and fat if you follow this recipe. Flavored with peanut butter and bananas, it's one treat that kids of all ages will go crazy for!

1/4	cup fat-free milk
1	small banana, cut into chunks
1/4	cup chocolate malted milk powder
2	Tbsp. reduced-fat creamy peanut butter
2	cups fat-free frozen chocolate yogurt

Whipped cream, optional

1. In a blender, combine the milk, banana, malted milk powder and peanut butter. Cover and process for 10 seconds or until smooth. Add frozen yogurt. Cover and process 10 seconds longer or until blended. Stir if necessary. Pour into chilled glasses; garnish with whipped cream if desired. Serve immediately.

Nutrition Facts: 1/2 cup (calculated without whipped cream) equals 203 calories, 3 g fat (1 g saturated fat), 1 mg cholesterol, 190 mg sodium, 39 g carbohydrate, 3 g fiber, 8 g protein.

Chocolate Cheesecakes S C

PREP: 15 min. **BAKE:** 10 min. + chilling **YIELD:** 2 dozen

SHARON VALENTA • WESTCHESTER, ILLINOIS

Try this bite-sized chocolaty treat that's rich, creamy and guaranteed to satisfy any sweet tooth.

24	miniature vanilla wafers *or* gingersnap cookies
1	pkg. (8 oz.) reduced-fat cream cheese

Sugar substitute equivalent to 1/2 cup sugar

1/2	cup semisweet chocolate chips, melted and cooled
1	tsp. vanilla extract
1	egg, lightly beaten
1/3	cup heavy whipping cream
4	tsp. confectioners' sugar

Chocolate curls, optional

1. Place wafers flat side down in paper-lined miniature muffin cups; set aside.

2. In a small bowl, beat cream cheese and sugar substitute until smooth. Add chocolate chips and vanilla; mix well. Add egg; beat on low speed just until combined. Spoon about 1 Tbsp. into each cup.

3. Bake at 350° for 10-12 minutes or just until set. Cool completely on a wire rack. Cover and refrigerate for 1 hour.

4. In a small bowl, beat cream until it begins to thicken. Add confectioners' sugar; beat until stiff peaks form. Top cheesecakes with whipped cream mixture; garnish with chocolate curls if desired.

Nutrition Facts: 1 cheesecake (calculated without chocolate curls) equals 65 calories, 5 g fat (3 g saturated fat), 20 mg cholesterol, 50 mg sodium, 5 g carbohydrate, trace fiber, 2 g protein. **Diabetic Exchange:** 1 fat.

Buttermilk Dill Dip F C M

PREP/TOTAL TIME: 15 min. **YIELD:** 1 cup

BETSY KING • DULUTH, MINNESOTA

This light, flavorful dip brings protein and perks up fresh sliced veggies in a hurry.

- 1/2 cup buttermilk
- 4 oz. fat-free cream cheese
- 3 green onions, finely chopped
- 1/4 cup finely chopped green pepper
- 3 Tbsp. snipped fresh dill *or* 1 Tbsp. dill weed
- 4-1/2 tsp. horseradish sauce
- 1/8 tsp. garlic powder
- Assorted fresh vegetables

1. In a small bowl, beat buttermilk and cream cheese until blended. Stir in the onions, pepper, dill, horseradish sauce and garlic powder. Chill until serving. Serve with vegetables.

Nutrition Facts: 1/4 cup (calculated without vegetables) equals 68 calories, 2 g fat (trace saturated fat), 9 mg cholesterol, 228 mg sodium, 6 g carbohydrate, trace fiber, 5 g protein. **Diabetic Exchanges:** 1/2 starch, 1/2 fat.

Party Shrimp F S C

PREP: 15 min. + marinating **BROIL:** 10 min.
YIELD: 2-1/2 dozen

KENDRA DOSS • KANSAS CITY, MISSOURI

This is such a flavorful appetizer, you won't need a dipping sauce. Even those who claim they don't like shellfish rave about these shrimp. It's such an easy recipe, I enjoy serving it at all sorts of parties and get-togethers.

- 1 Tbsp. olive oil
- 1-1/2 tsp. brown sugar
- 1-1/2 tsp. lemon juice
- 1 garlic clove, thinly sliced
- 1/2 tsp. paprika
- 1/2 tsp. Italian seasoning
- 1/2 tsp. dried basil
- 1/4 tsp. pepper
- 1 lb. uncooked large shrimp, peeled and deveined

1. In a large resealable plastic bag, combine the first eight ingredients. Add the shrimp; seal bag and turn to coat. Refrigerate for 2 hours. Drain and discard marinade.

2. Place shrimp on an ungreased baking sheet. Broil 4 in. from the heat for 6-8 minutes or until shrimp turn pink, turning once.

Nutrition Facts: 1 shrimp equals 14 calories, trace fat (trace saturated fat), 18 mg cholesterol, 18 mg sodium, trace carbohydrate, trace fiber, 2 g protein. **Diabetic Exchange:** Free food.

Uncooked shrimp will have shells that range in color from gray to pink. Fresh shrimp should have a **firm texture** with a mild aroma.

PARTY SHRIMP

BUTTERMILK DILL DIP

Cinnamon Granola Bars [S]

PREP: 15 min. BAKE: 15 min. + cooling YIELD: 1 dozen

JESSICA VANLANINGHAM • COCKEYSVILLE, MARYLAND

I make these at least once a week for my husband, David. He takes one in his lunch every week and never gets tired of them. I love providing him with something so healthy to munch on that doesn't taste low-fat.

- 1/4 cup butter, softened
- 1 cup packed brown sugar
- 1 egg
- 2 Tbsp. ground flaxseed
- 2 Tbsp. honey
- 2 cups old-fashioned oats
- 1 cup all-purpose flour
- 1 tsp. ground cinnamon
- 1/2 tsp. baking soda
- 1/2 cup raisins

1. In a large bowl, beat butter and brown sugar until crumbly, about 2 minutes. Add egg; beat well. Stir in flax and honey. In a small bowl, combine the oats, flour, cinnamon and baking soda; stir into creamed mixture just until blended. Gently stir in raisins.

2. Press into an 11-in. x 7-in. baking dish coated with cooking spray. Bake at 350° for 14-18 minutes or until set and edges are lightly browned. Cool on a wire rack. Cut into bars.

Nutrition Facts: 1 bar equals 231 calories, 6 g fat (3 g saturated fat), 28 mg cholesterol, 94 mg sodium, 43 g carbohydrate, 2 g fiber, 4 g protein.

CINNAMON GRANOLA BARS

Frappe Mocha

PREP: 5 min. + freezing YIELD: 2 servings

BEVERLY COYDE • GASPORT, NEW YORK

Using coffee ice cubes add body to this refreshing drink. What a treat!

- 1 tsp. instant coffee granules
- 1/4 cup boiling water
- 1 cup milk
- 4-1/2 tsp. chocolate syrup
- 1/2 cup crushed ice

Whipped topping and additional chocolate syrup, optional

1. In a small bowl, dissolve coffee granules in water. Pour into an ice cube tray; freeze.

2. In a blender, combine the milk, chocolate syrup and coffee ice cubes. Cover and process until smooth. Add crushed ice; blend. Pour into chilled glasses; serve immediately. Garnish with whipped topping and additional chocolate syrup if desired.

Nutrition Facts: 1 cup (calculated without garnishes) equals 114 calories, 4 g fat (3 g saturated fat), 17 mg cholesterol, 67 mg sodium, 15 g carbohydrate, trace fiber, 4 g protein.

Orange Fruit Cups [F][S]

PREP/TOTAL TIME: 20 min. YIELD: 4 servings

SUSAN WIENER • SPRING HILL, FLORIDA

This is always a favorite with children who come to visit. It's a wonderful snack that is healthy, fast and easy to make.

- 2 medium navel oranges, halved
- 1 small apple, chopped
- 1 small banana, sliced
- 1/4 cup plain yogurt
- 1/4 tsp. ground cinnamon

Additional ground cinnamon, optional

ORANGE FRUIT CUPS

1. Using a paring or grapefruit knife and spoon, scoop out pulp from oranges, leaving a shell. Separate orange sections and chop; transfer to a small bowl.

2. Add the apple, banana, yogurt and cinnamon. Fill orange shells with fruit mixture. Sprinkle with additional cinnamon if desired. Serve immediately.

Nutrition Facts: 1/2 cup fruit equals 80 calories, 1 g fat (trace saturated fat), 2 mg cholesterol, 8 mg sodium, 19 g carbohydrate, 3 g fiber, 2 g protein. **Diabetic Exchange:** 1 fruit.

Parmesan Popcorn F C

PREP/TOTAL TIME: 10 min. **YIELD:** 2 qts.

BETSY KING • DULUTH, MINNESOTA

Give popcorn a new twist with this fun and tasty recipe. It's great for watching movies or as an on-the-go snack. Kids and adults alike are sure to gobble it up.

 8 cups air-popped popcorn
 2 Tbsp. reduced-fat butter, melted
 2 Tbsp. grated Parmesan cheese

 1/4 tsp. salt
 1/4 tsp. dried oregano
 1/8 tsp. garlic salt

1. Place popcorn in a large bowl. Drizzle with butter. Combine the remaining ingredients; sprinkle over popcorn and toss to coat.

Nutrition Facts: 1 cup equals 49 calories, 2 g fat (1 g saturated fat), 5 mg cholesterol, 146 mg sodium, 7 g carbohydrate, 1 g fiber, 2 g protein. **Diabetic Exchange:** 1/2 starch.

When making a popcorn treat, remember that 1 cup of unpopped kernels equals about 8 cups of popped popcorn. Don't **pre-salt the kernels** before popping as this can toughen the popcorn.

SPINACH CHEESE TRIANGLES

Spinach Cheese Triangles F S C M

PREP: 40 min. **BAKE:** 10 min. **YIELD:** 4 dozen

SHERRI MELOTIK • OAK CREEK, WISCONSIN

Filled with three kinds of cheese and lots of spinach, these light little bites pack a delectable punch. Friends and family will think you fussed, but these starters come together quickly, making them prefect for hurried holidays.

1/3	cup finely chopped onion
1	Tbsp. butter
1	pkg. (10 oz.) frozen chopped spinach, thawed and squeezed dry
1	cup grated Parmesan cheese
3/4	cup shredded part-skim mozzarella cheese
3	Tbsp. crumbled feta cheese
2	eggs, lightly beaten
2	Tbsp. soft bread crumbs
1/4	tsp. salt
1/4	tsp. pepper
12	sheets phyllo dough (14 in. x 9 in.)

Butter-flavored cooking spray

1. In a large skillet, saute onion in butter until tender. Stir in spinach; cook over medium-low heat just until spinach is wilted. Transfer to a large bowl; add the cheeses, eggs, bread crumbs, salt and pepper. Set aside.

2. Place one sheet of phyllo dough on a work surface with a long side facing you. (Keep remaining phyllo covered with plastic wrap to prevent it from drying out.) Spray sheet with butter-flavored spray; cut into four 9-in. x 3-1/2-in. strips.

3. Place 1 Tbsp. filling on lower corner of each strip. Fold dough over filling, forming a triangle. Fold triangle up, then fold triangle over, forming another triangle. Continue folding, like a flag, until you come to the end of the strip.

4. Spritz end of dough with spray and press onto triangle to seal. Turn triangle and spritz top with cooking spray. Repeat with remaining phyllo and filling.

5. Place triangles on baking sheets coated with cooking spray. Bake at 375° for 10-12 minutes or until golden brown.

Nutrition Facts: 1 appetizer equals 30 calories, 2 g fat (1 g saturated fat), 12 mg cholesterol, 71 mg sodium, 2 g carbohydrate, trace fiber, 2 g protein.

Cucumber Punch F S C

PREP: 10 min. + chilling
YIELD: 25 servings (4-3/4 qt.)

RENEE OLSON • KENDRICK, IDAHO

I first tasted this at a ladies' luncheon, and it was the most unusual, refreshing drink I'd had. I've served it numerous times since and always get requests for the recipe.

- 2 medium cucumbers
- 3 cups water
- 1 can (12 oz.) frozen lemonade concentrate, thawed
- 2 liters diet ginger ale, chilled
- 4-1/2 cups diet grapefruit *or* citrus soda, chilled

1. With a zester or fork, score cucumbers lengthwise; cut widthwise into thin slices. In a large pitcher, combine water and lemonade concentrate; add cucumbers. Cover and refrigerate overnight.

2. Just before serving, transfer cucumber mixture to a punch bowl; stir in ginger ale and grapefruit soda.

Nutrition Facts: 3/4 cup equals 29 calories, trace fat (trace saturated fat), 0 cholesterol, 15 mg sodium, 7 g carbohydrate, trace fiber, trace protein. **Diabetic Exchange:** 1/2 starch.

Broccoli Fritters C M

PREP: 20 min. **COOK:** 10 min./batch **YIELD:** 6 servings

TRACY EUBANKS • EWING, KENTUCKY

These cute cakes offer a fun and kid-friendly way to use up broccoli. They're tasty as a side dish paired with any meat, or you can serve them with salsa and a dollop of fat-free sour cream for a festive appetizer.

- 1 bunch broccoli, cut into florets
- 2 eggs, lightly beaten
- 2 egg whites, lightly beaten
- 1/3 cup grated Parmesan cheese
- 2 Tbsp. all-purpose flour
- 1/2 tsp. salt
- 1/2 tsp. garlic powder
- 1/2 tsp. pepper
- 2 Tbsp. canola oil

Salsa, optional

1. Place broccoli in a steamer basket; place in a small saucepan over 1 in. of water. Bring to a boil; cover and steam for 3-4 minutes or until crisp-tender. Coarsely chop broccoli and set aside.

2. In a large bowl, combine the eggs, egg whites, cheese, flour, salt, garlic powder and pepper. Stir in the broccoli.

3. Heat 1 Tbsp. oil in a large nonstick skillet over medium heat. Drop batter by 2 heaping Tbsp.fuls into oil; press lightly to flatten. Cook in batches for 3-4 minutes on each side or until golden brown, using remaining oil as needed. Drain on paper towels. Serve with salsa if desired.

Nutrition Facts: 2 fritters (calculated without salsa) equals 129 calories, 8 g fat (2 g saturated fat), 74 mg cholesterol, 334 mg sodium, 8 g carbohydrate, 3 g fiber, 8 g protein. **Diabetic Exchanges:** 1 medium-fat meat, 1 vegetable, 1 fat.

CUCUMBER PUNCH

BROCCOLI FRITTERS

Antipasto Kabobs F C

PREP: 30 min. + marinating **YIELD:** 12 kabobs

KENDRA DOSS • KANSAS CITY, MISSOURI

This is one elegant, easy recipe people really seem to like at every party. I found a marinade recipe that wasn't so heavy on olive oil and modified it to my taste. The kabobs are a snap to assemble. You don't even need to turn on the oven.

1	cup refrigerated cheese tortellini
1/2	cup balsamic vinegar
1/4	cup grated Parmesan cheese
1/4	cup minced fresh basil
2	Tbsp. Dijon mustard
1	Tbsp. olive oil
2	tsp. honey
1/4	tsp. pepper
1	can (14 oz.) water-packed artichoke hearts, rinsed and drained
1	large green pepper, cut into 1-in. pieces
1	cup grape tomatoes
1	cup pitted ripe olives
1/4	lb. thinly sliced deli ham, cut into 1-in. strips
12	wooden skewers (6 in.)

1. Cook tortellini according to package directions.

2. Meanwhile, in a large resealable plastic bag, combine the vinegar, cheese, basil, mustard, oil, honey and pepper. Add the artichokes, green pepper, tomatoes, olives and ham. Drain and rinse tortellini in cold water; add to bag. Seal bag and turn to coat. Refrigerate for 4 hours or overnight.

3. Drain and discard marinade. For each kabob, thread tortellini, artichokes, green pepper, tomatoes, olives and folded ham onto a skewer.

Nutrition Facts: 1 kabob equals 90 calories, 3 g fat (1 g saturated fat), 9 mg cholesterol, 356 mg sodium, 11 g carbohydrate, 1 g fiber, 5 g protein.

Presto Chocolate Dessert Dip F S

PREP/TOTAL TIME: 10 min. **YIELD:** 1/2 cup

KAREN OWEN • RISING SUN, INDIANA

This fun and fancy dessert dip is ideal for special occasions and doubles nicely for get-togethers with friends. But, it tastes so wonderful, you'll have a hard time sharing it at all!

1/4	cup reduced-fat sour cream
2	Tbsp. honey
2	Tbsp. baking cocoa
1/4	tsp. vanilla extract

Assorted fresh fruit *and/or* cubed angel food cake

1. In a small bowl, combine the sour cream, honey, cocoa and vanilla. Cover and refrigerate until serving. Serve with fruit and/or cake.

Nutrition Facts: 1/4 cup (calculated without fruit and cake) equals 121 calories, 3 g fat (2 g saturated fat), 10 mg cholesterol, 21 mg sodium, 22 g carbohydrate, 1 g fiber, 3 g protein. **Diabetic Exchanges:** 1-1/2 starch, 1/2 fat.

ANTIPASTO KABOBS

PRESTO CHOCOLATE DESSERT DIP

IRRESISTIBLE GRILLED SHRIMP WITH FRUIT SALSA

Irresistible Grilled Shrimp with Fruit Salsa F C

PREP: 20 min. + marinating **GRILL:** 5 min.
YIELD: 8 servings (1-1/4 cups salsa)

AGNES WARD • STRATFORD, ONTARIO

These skewers are super lean and scrumptious—especially when dipped in the fresh fruit salsa. My guests rave about the salsa's sweet heat and the shrimp's party-pretty look.

- 3 Tbsp. reduced-sodium soy sauce
- 2 Tbsp. brown sugar
- 2 Tbsp. lime juice
- 1 Tbsp. olive oil
- 1 Tbsp. ketchup
- 2 garlic cloves, minced
- 1 tsp. ground coriander
- 1/2 tsp. ground cumin
- 1 lb. uncooked large shrimp, peeled and deveined

FRUIT SALSA:

- 1 medium tart apple, peeled and cut into wedges
- 3/4 cup orange segments
- 2 Tbsp. lime juice
- 2 green onions, cut into 2-in. pieces
- 1 Tbsp. minced fresh mint *or* 1 tsp. dried mint
- 1 tsp. sugar
- 1/2 tsp. crushed red pepper flakes

1. In a large resealable plastic bag, combine the first eight ingredients. Add the shrimp; seal bag and turn to coat. Refrigerate for 30 minutes.

2. Meanwhile, place salsa ingredients in a food processor; cover and process until finely chopped. Transfer to a small bowl. Chill until serving.

3. Drain and discard marinade. Using long-handled tongs, moisten a paper towel with cooking oil and lightly coat the grill rack. Thread shrimp onto three metal or soaked wooden skewers. Grill shrimp, covered, over medium heat or broil 4 in. from the heat for 5-8 minutes or until shrimp turn pink, turning once. Serve with salsa.

Nutrition Facts: 3 shrimp with about 2 Tbsp. salsa equals 78 calories, 1 g fat (trace saturated fat), 69 mg cholesterol, 150 mg sodium, 7 g carbohydrate, 1 g fiber, 10 g protein. **Diabetic Exchanges:** 1 lean meat, 1/2 starch.

CRISPY CARIBBEAN VEGGIE WRAPS

Crispy Caribbean Veggie Wraps F C M

PREP: 40 min. **BAKE:** 15 min. **YIELD:** 22 appetizers

MARY BETH HARRIS-MURPHREE • TYLER, TEXAS

Filled with a sweet potato mixture, these delicious wraps are great for vegetarians, and they're relatively high in fiber, too. Served with salsa, they are sure to disappear from appetizer trays fast.

1	medium sweet potato
1/2	cup canned black beans, rinsed and drained
1/4	cup chopped red onion
2	Tbsp. minced fresh cilantro
1	Tbsp. lime juice
1	tsp. salt
1	tsp. ground cumin
1	tsp. chopped jalapeno pepper
1	garlic clove, minced
22	wonton wrappers

Cooking spray

1-1/2 cups salsa

1. Scrub and pierce sweet potato; place on a microwave-safe plate. Microwave, uncovered, on high for 12-14 minutes or until tender, turning once. When cool enough to handle, cut the potato in half. Scoop out the pulp discarding shell; place pulp in a small bowl and mash. Stir in the beans, onion, cilantro, lime juice, salt, cumin, jalapeno and garlic.

2. Lightly brush water over all four edges of one wonton wrapper. (Keep remaining wrappers covered with a damp paper towel until ready to use.) Spread 1 Tbsp. filling along one edge of wrapper; roll up tightly. Repeat with remaining wrappers and filling.

3. Place seam side down on a baking sheet coated with cooking spray. Lightly spritz wraps with cooking spray. Bake at 375° for 15 minutes or until golden brown. Serve warm with salsa.

Editor's Note: This recipe was tested in a 1,100-watt microwave. When cutting hot peppers, disposable gloves are recommended. Avoid touching your face.

Nutrition Facts: 1 wrap with about 1 Tbsp. salsa equals 42 calories, trace fat (trace saturated fat), 1 mg cholesterol, 230 mg sodium, 8 g carbohydrate, 1 g fiber, 1 g protein. **Diabetic Exchange:** 1/2 starch.

Chocolate Zucchini Snack Cake

PREP: 20 min. **BAKE:** 30 min. + cooling
YIELD: 18 servings

MARGO SEEGRIST • SHELTON, WASHINGTON

I like to make this when the zucchini in my garden gets ahead of me. It's a great way to get children to eat their veggies because, after all, who doesn't like a bite of decadent chocolate cake? The next time you give some zucchini to a friend, considering handing them this recipe, too!

1/3	cup butter, softened
1-1/4	cups sugar
2	eggs
1/2	cup buttermilk
1/3	cup unsweetened applesauce
2	oz. semisweet chocolate, melted
1	tsp. vanilla extract
2-1/4	cups all-purpose flour
1-1/2	tsp. baking powder
1	tsp. salt
1/4	tsp. baking soda
2	cups shredded zucchini
2	tsp. confectioners' sugar

1. In a large bowl, beat butter and sugar until crumbly, about 2 minutes. Add eggs; mix well. Beat in the buttermilk, applesauce, chocolate and vanilla. Combine the flour, baking powder, salt and baking soda; beat into butter mixture just until moistened. Stir in zucchini.

2. Transfer to a 13-in. x 9-in. baking dish coated with cooking spray. Bake at 350° for 30-35 minutes or until a toothpick inserted near the center comes out clean. Cool on a wire rack. Sprinkle with confectioners' sugar.

Nutrition Facts: 1 piece equals 172 calories, 5 g fat (3 g saturated fat), 33 mg cholesterol, 223 mg sodium, 29 g carbohydrate, 1 g fiber, 3 g protein. **Diabetic Exchanges:** 2 starch, 1 fat.

Makeover Hot Pizza Dip

PREP/TOTAL TIME: 25 min. **YIELD:** about 4 cups

TRISHA KRUSE • EAGLE, IDAHO

This standout makeover from the Healthy Cooking Test Kitchen, has less than half the saturated fat and way fewer calories than the original recipe. It's hard to believe it's light. I promise it will be a guaranteed hit at your next gathering!

1	pkg. (8 oz.) fat-free cream cheese
1-1/2	tsp. Italian seasoning
1	cup (4 oz.) shredded part-skim mozzarella cheese, *divided*
1/2	cup grated Parmigiano-Reggiano cheese, *divided*
1	small sweet red pepper, chopped
1/4	cup chopped sweet onion
1	tsp. olive oil
1	garlic clove, minced
1	can (8 oz.) pizza sauce

4	oz. sliced turkey pepperoni, chopped
1	can (2-1/4 oz.) sliced ripe olives, drained
1	French bread baguette (10-1/2 oz.), cut into 1/4-in. slices, toasted

1. In a small bowl, beat cream cheese and Italian seasoning until smooth; spread into a 9-in. microwave-safe pie plate. Sprinkle with 1/2 cup mozzarella cheese and 1/4 cup Parmigiano-Reggiano cheese.

2. In a small nonstick skillet, saute pepper and onion in oil until tender. Add garlic; cook 1 minute longer. Spoon over cheeses. Spread pizza sauce over pepper mixture. Sprinkle with remaining cheeses, pepperoni and olives.

3. Microwave, uncovered, at 70% power for 5-7 minutes or until cheese is melted. Serve with toasted baguette slices.

Editor's Note: This recipe was tested in a 1,100-watt microwave.

Nutrition Facts: 1/4 cup dip with 4 baguette slices equals 154 calories, 6 g fat (2 g saturated fat), 16 mg cholesterol, 466 mg sodium, 17 g carbohydrate, 2 g fiber, 9 g protein.

If you don't have any **Italian seasoning** on hand, simply blend together 1/4 teaspoon each of dried basil, thyme, rosemary and oregano for every teaspoon of Italian seasoning called for in a recipe.

MAKEOVER HOT PIZZA DIP

Phyllo Fruit Tart

PREP: 15 min. BAKE: 5 min. + cooling YIELD: 8 servings

HEALTHY COOKING TEST KITCHEN

Always impressive on a buffet table, this elegant treat tastes as fantastic as it looks. Try it for a bridal shower or ladies' lunch. You can also try it with a wonderful topping of mixed berries.

- 1 Tbsp. butter, melted
- 1 Tbsp. canola oil
- 8 sheets phyllo dough (14 in. x 9 in.)
- 1 pkg. (8 oz.) fat-free cream cheese
- 3 Tbsp. confectioners' sugar
- 1 cup reduced-fat whipped topping
- 1 can (11 oz.) mandarin oranges, drained
- 4 kiwifruit, peeled and sliced
- 1-1/2 cups sliced fresh strawberries
- 1 oz. white baking chocolate, melted

1. In a small bowl, combine butter and oil. Place one sheet of phyllo dough on a work surface; brush evenly with butter-oil mixture. Repeat with seven more sheets of phyllo, brushing each layer and stacking on previous sheet. (Keep remaining phyllo dough covered with waxed paper to prevent it from drying out.)

2. Place phyllo dough on a baking sheet. Bake at 400° for 5-7 minutes or until golden. Cool on a wire rack.

3. In a small bowl, beat cream cheese and confectioners' sugar until smooth; fold in whipped topping. Gently spread over cooled crust. Arrange fruits over cream cheese layer; drizzle with chocolate.

Nutrition Facts: 1 piece equals 183 calories, 6 g fat (3 g saturated fat), 7 mg cholesterol, 222 mg sodium, 26 g carbohydrate, 3 g fiber, 6 g protein. **Diabetic Exchanges:** 1 starch, 1 fat, 1/2 fruit.

Spicy Chunky Salsa F S C M

PREP: 1-1/2 hours PROCESS: 15 min./batch
YIELD: 8 pints

DONNA GOUTERMONT • JUNEAU, ALASKA

Here's a delectable way to use up a summer bounty of garden-fresh tomatoes, onions, peppers and cilantro. Vinegar adds delightful tang to this sweet salsa. You'll love its flavor, but for more heat, leave in some of the hot pepper seeds.

- 6 lbs. tomatoes
- 3 large green peppers, chopped
- 3 large onions, chopped
- 2 cups white vinegar
- 1 large sweet red pepper, chopped
- 1 can (12 oz.) tomato paste
- 4 jalapeno peppers, seeded and chopped
- 2 serrano peppers, seeded and chopped
- 1/2 cup sugar
- 1/2 cup minced fresh cilantro
- 1/2 cup bottled lemon juice
- 3 garlic cloves, minced
- 4 tsp. ground cumin
- 3 tsp. salt
- 2 tsp. dried oregano
- 1 tsp. hot pepper sauce

1. In a large saucepan, bring 8 cups water to a boil. Using a slotted spoon, place tomatoes, a few at a time, in boiling water for 30-60 seconds. Remove each tomato and immediately plunge in ice water. Drain and pat dry. Peel and finely chop tomatoes to measure 9 cups. In a stockpot, combine the tomatoes and remaining ingredients. Bring to a boil. Reduce heat; simmer, uncovered, for 30 minutes or until slightly thickened.

2. Carefully ladle hot mixture into hot 1-pint jars, leaving 1/2-in. headspace. Remove air bubbles; wipe rims and adjust lids. Process for 15 minutes in a boiling-water canner.

Editor's Note: When cutting hot peppers, disposable gloves are recommended. Avoid touching your face. The processing time listed is for altitudes of 1,000 feet or less. For altitudes up to 3,000 feet, add 5 minutes; 6,000 feet, add 10 minutes; 8,000 feet, add 15 minutes; 10,000 feet, add 20 minutes.

Nutrition Facts: 1/4 cup equals 25 calories, trace fat (trace saturated fat), 0 cholesterol, 117 mg sodium, 6 g carbohydrate, 1 g fiber, 1 g protein. **Diabetic Exchange:** 1/2 starch.

PHYLLO FRUIT TART

ROASTED VEGETABLE DIP

Roasted Vegetable Dip F S C M

PREP: 15 min. **BAKE:** 25 min. + cooling
YIELD: 2-1/2 cups

SARAH VASQUES • MILFORD, NEW HAMPSHIRE

Roasting brings out the best flavor in red pepper, onion and zucchini, making this appetizer a great way to use your garden bounty. Blended with cream cheese, the vegetables make a delicious dip perfect on crackers. You can even try it as a spread on lean turkey sandwiches.

- 2 large sweet red peppers, cut into 1-in. pieces
- 1 large zucchini, cut into 1-in. pieces
- 1 medium onion, cut into 1-in. pieces
- 1 Tbsp. olive oil
- 1/2 tsp. salt
- 1/4 tsp. pepper
- 1 pkg. (8 oz.) reduced-fat cream cheese

Assorted crackers

1. Place the red peppers, zucchini and onion in a 15-in. x 10-in. x 1-in. baking pan coated with cooking spray. Combine the olive oil, salt and pepper; drizzle over vegetables and toss to coat. Bake, uncovered, at 425° for 25-30 minutes or until tender, stirring occasionally. Cool to room temperature.

2. Place cream cheese and vegetables in a food processor; cover and process until blended. Chill until serving. Serve with crackers.

Nutrition Facts: 2 Tbsp. (calculated without crackers) equals 44 calories, 3 g fat (2 g saturated fat), 8 mg cholesterol, 110 mg sodium, 3 g carbohydrate, 1 g fiber, 2 g protein.

Maple-Glazed Snack Mix

PREP: 10 min. **BAKE:** 45 min. + cooling
YIELD: 7-1/2 cups

CYNTHIA NORRIS • WINNETKA, CALIFORNIA

I haven't met a kid yet that doesn't love this mix! My three children especially enjoy it for snacks during the school year.

- 2 cups Corn Chex
- 2 cups Rice Chex
- 2 cups Honey-Nut Cheerios
- 1 cup miniature pretzels
- 1/2 cup pecan halves, coarsely chopped
- 1/3 cup maple syrup
- 1 Tbsp. butter
- 1 tsp. vanilla extract

1. In a large bowl, combine the cereals, pretzels and pecans. In a small microwave-safe dish, combine maple syrup and butter. Cover and microwave on high for 45 seconds or until butter is melted. Stir in vanilla. Pour over cereal mixture and toss to coat.

2. Transfer to a 15-in. x 10-in. x 1-in. baking pan coated with cooking spray. Bake at 250° for 45 minutes, stirring every 15 minutes. Cool on a wire rack. Store in an airtight container.

Editor's Note: This recipe was tested in a 1,100-watt microwave.

Nutrition Facts: 1/2 cup equals 104 calories, 4 g fat (1 g saturated fat), 2 mg cholesterol, 141 mg sodium, 17 g carbohydrate, 1 g fiber, 2 g protein. **Diabetic Exchanges:** 1 starch, 1/2 fat.

ON-THE-GO SNACK MIX

On-the-Go Snack Mix S

PREP/TOTAL TIME: 10 min. YIELD: 7 cups

LEAH FIRESTONE • SCOTTDALE, PENNSYLVANIA

*Since there's no baking required, this savory snack mix is really
a simple treat to make. Plus, it's also healthy and tasty. If you
want a snack that delivers protein and a few vitamins and
minerals, this will do it.*

3	cups Wheat Chex
1/2	cup blanched almonds
1/2	cup unsalted peanuts
1/2	cup lightly salted cashews
1/2	cup chopped pecans
1/2	cup fat-free miniature pretzels
1/2	cup raisins
1/2	cup milk chocolate M&M's
1/4	cup dried banana chips
1/4	cup dried cranberries

1. In a large bowl, combine all ingredients. Store in
an airtight container.

Nutrition Facts: 1/2 cup equals 217 calories, 13 g fat (3 g
saturated fat), 1 mg cholesterol, 93 mg sodium, 23 g
carbohydrate, 3 g fiber, 5 g protein.

Garlic Artichoke Dip F C M

PREP: 25 min. + chilling YIELD: 2-1/2 cups

LISA VARNER • CHARLESTON, SOUTH CAROLINA

*This chilled dip is quite delicious, lower in fat and offers
almost effortless and time-saving preparation.*

1	large onion, chopped
1/2	tsp. dried oregano
1/2	tsp. dried thyme
2	Tbsp. olive oil
5	garlic cloves, minced
1	can (15 oz.) white kidney *or* cannellini beans, rinsed and drained
1	can (14 oz.) water-packed artichoke hearts, rinsed and drained
1	Tbsp. lemon juice
1/2	tsp. salt
1/8	tsp. cayenne pepper

Assorted fresh vegetables *and/or* baked pita chips

1. In a small nonstick skillet, saute the onion,
oregano and thyme in oil until onions tender. Add
garlic; cook 1 minute longer. Remove from the heat;
cool slightly.

2. In a food processor, combine the beans, artichokes, lemon juice, salt, cayenne and onion mixture; cover and process until pureed.

3. Transfer to a small bowl. Cover and refrigerate at least 2 hours before serving. Serve with vegetables and/or pita chips.

Nutrition Facts: 1/4 cup (calculated without vegetables and chips) equals 81 calories, 3 g fat (trace saturated fat), 0 cholesterol, 271 mg sodium, 11 g carbohydrate, 2 g fiber, 3 g protein. **Diabetic Exchanges:** 1 vegetable, 1/2 starch, 1/2 fat.

Smoked Salmon Cucumber Canapes F S C

Opts

PREP: 25 min. + chilling YIELD: about 3-1/2 dozen

JUDY GREBETZ • RACINE, WISCONSIN

This is one appetizer I'm always asked to bring to parties. It's make-ahead convenient, pretty and a winner.

2	medium cucumbers, peeled
4	oz. smoked salmon, flaked
2	Tbsp. lemon juice
1	Tbsp. finely chopped onion
1	Tbsp. capers, drained
1	Tbsp. minced fresh parsley
1/2	tsp. Dijon mustard
1/8	tsp. pepper

1. Cut cucumbers in half lengthwise; remove and discard seeds. In a small bowl, combine the remaining ingredients. Spoon into cucumber halves.

2. Wrap in plastic wrap. Refrigerate for 3-4 hours or until filling is firm. Cut into 1/2-in. slices.

Nutrition Facts: 1 canape equals 6 calories, trace fat (trace saturated fat), 1 mg cholesterol, 27 mg sodium, 1 g carbohydrate, trace fiber, 1 g protein. **Diabetic Exchange:** Free food.

Lime Cilantro Hummus C M

PREP/TOTAL TIME: 20 min. YIELD: 3 cups

KIMBERLY GRUSENDORF • MEDINA, OHIO

Enjoy this fun dip with crackers or veggies or on your favorite sandwich or burger. To make it smoother, add a bit more olive oil. If you prefer a more rustic texture, decrease the oil a little.

2	cans (15 oz.) garbanzo beans or chickpeas, rinsed and drained
1	cup coarsely chopped cilantro leaves
1/2	cup lime juice
1/4	cup water
3	Tbsp. olive oil
4	garlic cloves, halved
1-1/2	tsp. grated lime peel
1	tsp. garlic salt
1/2	tsp. cayenne pepper

Assorted fresh vegetables *or* crackers

1. In a food processor, combine garbanzo beans, cilantro, lime juice, water, oil, garlic, lime peel, garlic salt and cayenne; cover and process until blended. Serve with vegetables or crackers.

Nutrition Facts: 1/4 cup (calculated without vegetables or crackers) equals 100 calories, 5 g fat (trace saturated fat), 0 cholesterol, 244 mg sodium, 12 g carbohydrate, 3 g fiber, 3 g protein. **Diabetic Exchanges:** 1 starch, 1 fat.

LIME CILANTRO HUMMUS

SMOKED SALMON CUCUMBER CANAPES

PEACHY CHICKEN SALAD

APPLE SALAD WITH MAPLE-MUSTARD VINAIGRETTE

CONFETTI COUSCOUS SALAD

Salads

Peachy Chicken Salad

PREP/TOTAL TIME: 10 min. YIELD: 4 servings

RADELLE KNAPPENBERGER • OVIEDO, FLORIDA

This is a very healthy and simple salad to make; even my non-cooking husband can whip it together in minutes. We've served this to friends over the years, and they always ask us to share the recipe.

- 2 cups cubed cooked chicken breast
- 2 medium peaches, coarsely chopped
- 1/2 cup chopped walnuts
- 1/2 cup fat-free mayonnaise
- 1/4 cup raisins
- 1 tsp. curry powder
- 1 pkg. (5 oz.) spring mix salad greens

1. In a small bowl, combine the first six ingredients. Divide salad greens among four plates; top each with 1/2 cup chicken salad.

Nutrition Facts: 1/2 cup chicken salad with 2 cups salad greens equals 277 calories, 12 g fat (1 g saturated fat), 57 mg cholesterol, 295 mg sodium, 19 g carbohydrate, 3 g fiber, 26 g protein. **Diabetic Exchanges:** 3 lean meat, 1-1/2 fat, 1 starch.

Confetti Couscous Salad

PREP/TOTAL TIME: 30 min. YIELD: 6 servings

SUZANNE KESEL • COHOCTON, NEW YORK

Bursting with color and flavor, this delightful side dish will take any entree up a notch.

- 1 cup reduced-sodium chicken broth
- 1 cup uncooked couscous
- 1 can (15 oz.) black beans, rinsed and drained
- 3/4 cup frozen corn, thawed
- 1 medium sweet red pepper, chopped
- 6 green onions, chopped
- 1/4 cup minced fresh cilantro

DRESSING:
- 2 Tbsp. plus 1 tsp. olive oil
- 2 Tbsp. lime juice
- 1-1/2 tsp. red wine vinegar
- 1/2 tsp. ground cumin
- 1/4 tsp. salt
- 1/4 tsp. pepper

Pine nuts, optional

1. In a large saucepan, bring broth to a boil. Stir in couscous. Remove from the heat; cover and let stand for 5-10 minutes or until broth is absorbed.

2. Fluff with a fork. Stir in the beans, corn, red pepper, onions and cilantro. In a small bowl, whisk the oil, lime juice, vinegar, cumin, salt and pepper. Drizzle over salad and toss to coat. Sprinkle with the pine nuts if desired.

Nutrition Facts: 3/4 cup (calculated without pine nuts) equals 245 calories, 6 g fat (1 g saturated fat), 0 cholesterol, 335 mg sodium, 41 g carbohydrate, 5 g fiber, 9 g protein.

Apple Salad with Maple-Mustard Vinaigrette [F] [S] [C] [M]

PREP/TOTAL TIME: 15 min.
YIELD: 16 servings (3/4 cup each)

BETH DAUENHAUER • PUEBLO, COLORADO

This seasonal salad will be a hit at any large gathering. It's also easy for family dinners; just halve the recipe.

- 9 cups torn mixed salad greens
- 2 large tart apples, chopped
- 1 small red onion, thinly sliced
- 1/3 cup chopped walnuts, toasted

DRESSING:
- 1/4 cup thawed frozen apple juice concentrate
- 2 Tbsp. cider vinegar
- 2 Tbsp. canola oil
- 2 Tbsp. maple syrup
- 2 Tbsp. spicy brown mustard
- 1/4 tsp. salt
- 1/8 tsp. pepper

1. In a large bowl, combine the salad greens, apples, onion and walnuts. In a small bowl, whisk the dressing ingredients. Drizzle over salad; toss to coat.

Nutrition Facts: 3/4 cup equals 68 calories, 3 g fat (trace saturated fat), 0 cholesterol, 71 mg sodium, 9 g carbohydrate, 2 g fiber, 1 g protein. **Diabetic Exchanges:** 1/2 starch, 1/2 fat.

Crunchy Broccoli Salad C

PREP/TOTAL TIME: 20 min. YIELD: 10 servings

JESSICA CONREY • CEDAR RAPIDS, IOWA

Growing up, I never liked broccoli, but I'm hooked on this salad's light, sweet taste. It gives broccoli a whole new flavor.

8	cups fresh broccoli florets
1	bunch green onions, thinly sliced
1/2	cup dried cranberries
3	Tbsp. canola oil
3	Tbsp. seasoned rice vinegar
2	Tbsp. sugar
1/4	cup sunflower kernels
3	bacon strips, cooked and crumbled

1. In a large bowl, combine the broccoli, onions and cranberries. In a small bowl, whisk the oil, vinegar and sugar; drizzle over broccoli and toss to coat. Chill until serving. Sprinkle with sunflower kernels and bacon.

Nutrition Facts: 1 serving (3/4 cup) equals 121 calories, 7 g fat (1 g saturated fat), 2 mg cholesterol, 233 mg sodium, 14 g carbohydrate, 3 g fiber, 3 g protein. **Diabetic Exchanges:** 1 vegetable, 1 fat, 1/2 starch.

Quinoa Wilted Spinach Salad S M

PREP/TOTAL TIME: 30 min. YIELD: 10 servings

SHARON RICCI • MENDON, NEW YORK

Get all the nutritious benefits of quinoa, spinach and cranberries paired with the crunchy texture of nuts in this easy and scrumptious salad. A light, flavorful dressing splashed with citrus tops off everything!

1	cup quinoa, rinsed
2	cups water
1	pkg. (6 oz.) fresh baby spinach, torn
1/2	cup dried cranberries

DRESSING:
- 3 Tbsp. olive oil
- 2 Tbsp. orange juice
- 1 Tbsp. red wine vinegar
- 1 Tbsp. maple syrup
- 1 garlic clove, minced
- 1/2 tsp. salt
- 1/8 tsp. pepper
- 1 green onion, finely chopped
- 1/2 cup chopped pecans, toasted

1. In a small saucepan, bring quinoa and water to a boil. Reduce heat; cover and simmer for 12-15 minutes or until water is absorbed. Remove from the heat; fluff with a fork. Cover and let stand for 10 minutes.

2. In a large bowl, combine the warm quinoa, spinach and cranberries. For dressing, in a small bowl, whisk the oil, orange juice, vinegar, maple syrup, garlic, salt and pepper. Stir in onion. Pour over quinoa mixture; toss to coat. Sprinkle with pecans.

Editor's Note: Look for quinoa in the cereal, rice or organic food aisle.

Nutrition Facts: 3/4 cup equals 171 calories, 9 g fat (1 g saturated fat), 0 cholesterol, 136 mg sodium, 20 g carbohydrate, 2 g fiber, 3 g protein.

Spinach Orzo Salad

PREP/TOTAL TIME: 30 min. **YIELD:** 10 servings

DONNA BARDOCZ • HOWELL, MICHIGAN

This incredibly tasty salad couldn't be any simpler to put together, and since it feeds a bunch, you won't have to double the recipe for potlucks or picnics. Chill it for about an hour to bring out all the fresh flavors.

- 1 pkg. (16 oz.) orzo pasta
- 1 pkg. (6 oz.) fresh baby spinach, finely chopped
- 3/4 cup crumbled feta cheese
- 3/4 cup finely chopped red onion
- 3/4 cup reduced-fat balsamic vinaigrette
- 1/2 tsp. dried basil
- 1/4 tsp. white pepper
- 1/4 cup pine nuts, toasted

1. Cook orzo according to package directions. Drain and rinse in cold water.

2. In a large bowl, combine the spinach, cheese, onion and orzo. In a small bowl, combine the vinaigrette, basil and pepper. Pour over orzo; toss to coat. Chill until serving. Just before serving, stir in pine nuts.

Nutrition Facts: 3/4 cup equals 249 calories, 7 g fat (2 g saturated fat), 5 mg cholesterol, 235 mg sodium, 38 g carbohydrate, 2 g fiber, 9 g protein.

Orzo can usually be substituted for rice in many recipes. Nutritionally speaking, **orzo and rice** contain similar amounts of fat, sugar, carbohydrates and even sodium when compared ounce for ounce.

SPINACH ORZO SALAD

QUINOA WILTED SPINACH SALAD

Roasted Pear Salad  M

PREP: 15 min. BAKE: 15 min. + cooling YIELD: 4 servings

HEALTHY COOKING TEST KITCHEN

Oven-roasted pears are tossed with crispy greens, dried cranberries and nuts. Sweetened with a touch of honey, the creamy dressing adds even more pear flavor.

- 2 medium pears, halved and cored
- 4 tsp. olive oil, *divided*
- 2 Tbsp. cider vinegar
- 1 tsp. water
- 1 tsp. honey
- 1/4 tsp. salt
- 1/8 tsp. white pepper
- 1 pkg. (10 oz.) mixed baby salad greens
- 1 cup watercress sprigs
- 1/4 cup chopped hazelnuts, toasted
- 1/4 cup dried cranberries

1. In a small bowl, toss pears with 1 tsp. oil. Place in a 15-in. x 10-in. x 1-in. baking pan coated with cooking spray. Bake at 400° for 10 minutes. Turn pears over; bake 5-7 minutes longer or until golden and tender.

2. When cool enough to handle, peel pears. Thinly slice two pear halves lengthwise and set aside. Place remaining pear halves in a blender. Add the vinegar, water, honey, salt and white pepper; cover and process until smooth. While processing, gradually add the remaining oil in a steady stream.

3. In a large bowl, toss the salad greens, watercress, hazelnuts and cranberries. Arrange reserved pear slices on top; drizzle with dressing.

Nutrition Facts: 1 serving equals 174 calories, 9 g fat (1 g saturated fat), 0 cholesterol, 178 mg sodium, 24 g carbohydrate, 5 g fiber, 3 g protein.

Makeover Cleo's Potato Salad

PREP: 30 min. COOK: 20 min.
YIELD: 16 servings (3/4 cup each)

JOAN HALLFORD • NORTH RICHLAND HILLS, TEXAS

This recipe is perfect for large gatherings, and now with this healthy version, I can enjoy it all summer long.

- 6 large potatoes
- 6 bacon strips, diced
- 1/4 cup sugar
- 1 Tbsp. all-purpose flour
- 1/2 cup water
- 1 egg, lightly beaten
- 2 cups fat-free Miracle Whip
- 3 Tbsp. cider vinegar
- 1/2 cup heavy whipping cream, whipped
- 2 medium celery ribs, sliced
- 2 hard-cooked eggs, chopped
- 1 Tbsp. grated onion
- 1 tsp. celery seed
- 1/2 tsp. salt

1. Scrub and cube potatoes; place in a Dutch oven and cover with water. Bring to a boil. Reduce heat; cover and cook for 15-20 minutes or until tender. Drain and cool to room temperature.

2. Meanwhile, in a small saucepan, cook bacon over medium heat until crisp. Using a slotted spoon, remove to paper towels; drain, reserving 1 Tbsp. drippings. Add sugar and flour to the pan; stir in water until blended. Cook and stir over medium-high heat until thickened and bubbly.

MAKEOVER CLEO'S POTATO SALAD

ROASTED PEAR SALAD

3. Remove from the heat. Stir a small amount of hot mixture into egg; return all to the pan, stirring constantly. Bring to a gentle boil; cook and stir for 2 minutes. Remove from the heat and cool completely. Stir in Miracle Whip and vinegar. Fold in cream.

4. In a large bowl, combine the potatoes, celery, eggs, onion, celery seed and salt. Add dressing and bacon; stir until blended. Chill until serving.

Nutrition Facts: 3/4 cup equals 215 calories, 6 g fat (3 g saturated fat), 53 mg cholesterol, 407 mg sodium, 33 g carbohydrate, 2 g fiber, 5 g protein. **Diabetic Exchanges:** 2 starch, 1 fat.

Spinach Salad with Penne C M

PREP/TOTAL TIME: 25 min. **YIELD:** 9 servings

LYNNELL LOWNEY • WAUNAKEE, WISCONSIN

Loaded with fresh greens, this delightful pasta salad fits the season perfectly.

    1   cup uncooked whole wheat penne pasta
    1   pkg. (6 oz.) fresh baby spinach
  3/4   cup grated Parmesan cheese
  3/4   cup reduced-fat balsamic vinaigrette
  1/3   cup pine nuts, toasted
    8   fresh basil leaves, thinly sliced

1. Cook pasta according to package directions; drain and rinse in cold water.

2. In a large bowl, combine the spinach, cheese, vinaigrette, pine nuts, basil and the pasta. Serve the salad immediately.

Nutrition Facts: 3/4 cup equals 144 calories, 8 g fat (2 g saturated fat), 6 mg cholesterol, 269 mg sodium, 13 g carbohydrate, 2 g fiber, 7 g protein. **Diabetic Exchanges:** 1 vegetable, 1 fat, 1/2 starch.

Small, elongated and ivory-colored, pine nuts have a soft texture and buttery flavor. Frequently used in salads, sauces and Italian entrees, pine nuts are often toasted to enhance their delightfully earthy flavor.

GREEN SALAD WITH TANGY BASIL VINAIGRETTE

Green Salad with Tangy Basil Vinaigrette C M

PREP/TOTAL TIME: 15 min. YIELD: 4 servings

KRISTIN RIMKUS • SNOHOMISH, WASHINGTON

My tart and tangy dressing turns a basic salad into something special. It works for weeknight dining but is good enough for company and pairs perfectly with just about anything.

3	Tbsp. white wine vinegar
4-1/2	tsp. minced fresh basil
4-1/2	tsp. olive oil
1-1/2	tsp. honey
1/4	tsp. salt
1/8	tsp. pepper
6	cups torn mixed salad greens
1	cup cherry tomatoes, halved
2	Tbsp. shredded Parmesan cheese

1. In a small bowl, whisk the first six ingredients until blended. In a large bowl, combine salad greens and tomatoes. Drizzle with vinaigrette; toss to coat. Sprinkle with cheese.

Nutrition Facts: 1 cup equals 89 calories, 6 g fat (1 g saturated fat), 2 mg cholesterol, 214 mg sodium, 7 g carbohydrate, 2 g fiber, 3 g protein. **Diabetic Exchanges:** 1 vegetable, 1 fat.

Cilantro Blue Cheese Slaw F C

PREP/TOTAL TIME: 25 min. YIELD: 8 servings

CHRISTI DALTON • HARTSVILLE, TENNESSEE

A zesty dressing, crisp cabbage, fresh cilantro and a jalapeno pepper make this recipe a runaway hit! Serve the slaw as a side dish to any meal, or use it to top your favorite fish taco recipe instead of lettuce and the usual toppings.

8	cups shredded cabbage
1	small red onion, halved and thinly sliced
1/3	cup minced fresh cilantro
1	jalapeno pepper, seeded and minced
1/4	cup crumbled blue cheese
1/4	cup fat-free mayonnaise
1/4	cup reduced-fat sour cream
2	Tbsp. rice vinegar
2	Tbsp. lime juice
1	garlic clove, minced
1	tsp. sugar
1	tsp. grated lime peel
3/4	tsp. salt
1/2	tsp. coarsely ground pepper

1. In a large bowl, combine the cabbage, onion, cilantro and jalapeno. In a small bowl, combine the remaining ingredients; pour over salad and toss to coat.

Editor's Note: When cutting hot peppers, disposable gloves are recommended. Avoid touching your face.

Nutrition Facts: 3/4 cup equals 63 calories, 2 g fat (1 g saturated fat), 6 mg cholesterol, 362 mg sodium, 9 g carbohydrate, 3 g fiber, 3 g protein. **Diabetic Exchanges:** 1 vegetable, 1/2 fat.

Flank Steak Salad C

PREP: 25 min. + marinating **GRILL:** 15 min. + standing
YIELD: 8 servings

JENNIFER HUNSAKER • ROY, UTAH

This beautiful salad combines perfectly marinated flank steak with a tasty homemade dressing for a satisfying meal that's sure to please.

- 2 Tbsp. lime juice
- 2 Tbsp. reduced-sodium soy sauce
- 3 garlic cloves, minced
- 2 tsp. minced fresh gingerroot
- 1 beef flank steak (2 lbs.)

VINAIGRETTE:
- 2 Tbsp. plus 2 tsp. white vinegar
- 1 Tbsp. reduced-sodium soy sauce
- 1 tsp. ketchup
- 3 Tbsp. chopped onion
- 1 Tbsp. sugar
- 1 small garlic clove, peeled and halved
- 1/2 tsp. minced fresh gingerroot
- 1/4 tsp. salt
- 1/4 tsp. pepper
- 3 Tbsp. canola oil
- 1 bunch romaine, torn
- 1 cup grape tomatoes

1. In a large resealable plastic bag, combine the lime juice, soy sauce, garlic and ginger; add the beef. Seal bag and turn to coat; refrigerate for 8 hours or overnight.

2. Drain beef and discard marinade. Using long-handled tongs, moisten a paper towel with cooking oil and lightly coat the grill rack. Grill beef, covered, over medium heat or broil 4 in. from the heat for 6-8 minutes on each side or until meat reaches desired doneness (for medium-rare, a meat thermometer should read 145°; medium, 160°; well-done, 170°). Let stand for 10 minutes. To serve, thinly slice across the grain.

3. Meanwhile, in a blender, combine the vinegar, soy sauce, ketchup, onion, sugar, garlic, ginger, salt and pepper; cover and process until pureed. While processing, gradually add oil in a steady stream.

4. Place romaine and tomatoes in a large bowl. Drizzle with vinaigrette; toss to coat. Divide among eight plates; top with steak.

Nutrition Facts: 1 cup salad with 3 oz. cooked beef equals 237 calories, 14 g fat (4 g saturated fat), 54 mg cholesterol, 270 mg sodium, 5 g carbohydrate, 1 g fiber, 23 g protein. **Diabetic Exchanges:** 3 lean meat, 1 vegetable, 1 fat.

Balsamic-Salmon Spinach Salad C

PREP/TOTAL TIME: 20 min. **YIELD:** 2 servings

KAREN1969 • TASTE OF HOME ONLINE COMMUNITY

This main-dish salad is really healthy, and it's a cinch to make after a hard day at work.

- 1 salmon fillet (6 oz.)
- 2 Tbsp. reduced-fat balsamic vinaigrette, *divided*
- 3 cups fresh baby spinach
- 1/4 cup cubed avocado
- 1 Tbsp. chopped walnuts, toasted
- 1 Tbsp. sunflower kernels, toasted
- 1 Tbsp. dried cranberries

1. Drizzle salmon with 1 Tbsp. vinaigrette. Place on a broiler pan coated with cooking spray. Broil 3-4 in. from the heat for 10-15 minutes or until fish flakes easily with a fork. Cut salmon into two pieces.

2. Meanwhile, in a large bowl, toss spinach with remaining vinaigrette. Divide between two plates. Top each with half of the salmon, avocado, walnuts, sunflower kernels and cranberries.

Nutrition Facts: 1 serving equals 283 calories, 19 g fat (3 g saturated fat), 50 mg cholesterol, 219 mg sodium, 9 g carbohydrate, 3 g fiber, 21 g protein. **Diabetic Exchanges:** 2 medium-fat meat, 2 fat, 1 vegetable.

BALSAMIC-SALMON SPINACH SALAD

Pecan Sweet Potato Salad M 5 pts

PREP: 40 min. + chilling YIELD: 12 servings

PATRICIA SWART • GALLOWAY, NEW JERSEY

A new twist on an old favorite, this tasty, easy-to-make sweet potato salad is sure to be the talk of your next party.

6	to 7 large sweet potatoes (about 5 lbs.), peeled and cut into 1-in. cubes
4	celery ribs, chopped
2	green onions, thinly sliced
1	cup fat-free mayonnaise
1/2	cup reduced-fat sour cream
2/3	cup chopped pecans, toasted

1. Place sweet potatoes in a Dutch oven and cover with water. Bring to a boil. Reduce heat; cover and cook for 10-15 minutes or just until tender. Drain. Transfer to a large bowl; cool to room temperature. Stir in celery and green onions.

2. In a small bowl, combine mayonnaise and sour cream. Gently stir into potato mixture. Cover and refrigerate for several hours or overnight. Just before serving, sprinkle with pecans.

Nutrition Facts: 3/4 cup equals 184 calories, 6 g fat (1 g saturated fat), 5 mg cholesterol, 188 mg sodium, 30 g carbohydrate, 4 g fiber, 3 g protein. **Diabetic Exchanges:** 2 starch, 1 fat.

Minty-Watermelon Cucumber Salad F S C M

PREP/TOTAL TIME: 20 min.
YIELD: 16 servings (3/4 cup each)

ROBLYNN HUNNISETT • GUELPH, ONTARIO

Capturing the fantastic flavors of summer, this refreshing, beautiful salad truly shines at picnics and potlucks.

8	cups cubed seedless watermelon
2	medium English cucumbers, halved lengthwise and sliced
6	green onions, chopped
1/4	cup minced fresh mint
1/4	cup olive oil
1/4	cup balsamic vinegar
1/2	tsp. salt
1/2	tsp. pepper

1. In a large bowl, combine the watermelon, cucumbers, onions and mint. In a small bowl, whisk the oil, vinegar, salt and pepper. Pour over watermelon mixture; toss to coat. Serve immediately or cover and refrigerate for up to 2 hours.

Nutrition Facts: 3/4 cup equals 60 calories, 3 g fat (trace saturated fat), 0 cholesterol, 78 mg sodium, 9 g carbohydrate, 1 g fiber, 1 g protein. **Diabetic Exchanges:** 1/2 fruit, 1/2 fat.

Four-Fruit Salad F S C M

PREP: 15 min. + chilling
YIELD: 12 servings (3/4 cup each)

KRISTIN RIMKUS • SNOHOMISH, WASHINGTON

With a honey glaze and a hint of mint, this fresh fruit medley captures the mouthwatering flavors folks crave.

PECAN SWEET POTATO SALAD

FOUR-FRUIT SALAD

4 cups fresh raspberries
4 medium plums, coarsely chopped
4 medium apricots, coarsely chopped
2 medium peaches, coarsely chopped
2 Tbsp. minced fresh mint
2 Tbsp. honey

1. In a large bowl, combine the first five ingredients. Drizzle with honey and toss to coat. Refrigerate the mixture until chilled.

Nutrition Facts: 3/4 cup equals 55 calories, trace fat (trace saturated fat), 0 cholesterol, trace sodium, 13 g carbohydrate, 4 g fiber, 1 g protein. **Diabetic Exchange:** 1 fruit.

Seafood & Shells Salad F

PREP/TOTAL TIME: 30 min. YIELD: 13 servings

ROSALEE RAY • LANSING, MICHIGAN

My family asks for this salad often during the summer months. Packed with garden-fresh vegetables and succulent seafood, it has become a favorite.

2 cups uncooked small pasta shells
3 pkg. (8 oz. *each*) imitation crabmeat

1 lb. cooked small shrimp, peeled and deveined
1/4 cup finely chopped sweet onion
1/4 cup finely chopped celery
3 Tbsp. *each* finely chopped green, sweet red and yellow pepper
3 Tbsp. minced fresh parsley
2 Tbsp. snipped fresh dill *or* 2 tsp. dill weed
1-1/2 cups fat-free mayonnaise
2 Tbsp. lemon juice
1/4 tsp. salt
1/4 tsp. pepper

1. Cook pasta according to package directions; drain and rinse in cold water.

2. In a large bowl, combine the crab, shrimp, onion, celery, peppers, parsley and dill. Stir in pasta. In a small bowl, combine the mayonnaise, lemon juice, salt and pepper. Pour over salad and toss to coat. Chill until serving.

Nutrition Facts: 3/4 cup equals 164 calories, 2 g fat (trace saturated fat), 62 mg cholesterol, 612 mg sodium, 22 g carbohydrate, 1 g fiber, 14 g protein. **Diabetic Exchanges:** 2 lean meat, 1-1/2 starch.

WILD RICE SALAD

Wild Rice Salad M

PREP: 15 min. **COOK:** 55 min. + chilling
YIELD: 15 servings (2/3 cup each)

BARBARA SCHULTE • PAYSON, ARIZONA

Nutty, fruity and packed with flavor, this make-ahead dish is a wholesome side for a wide variety of entrees.

3	cups water
2	cups uncooked wild rice
2	cups finely chopped dried apricots
2	cups dried cherries
1	cup chopped walnuts
1/2	cup olive oil
1/3	cup lemon juice
2	Tbsp. maple syrup
1-1/2	tsp. salt

1. In a large saucepan, bring water and rice to a boil. Reduce heat; cover and simmer for 45-50 minutes or until rice is tender. Drain if necessary. Transfer to a large bowl; cool completely.

2. Meanwhile, place apricots in a small bowl; cover with boiling water. Let stand for 5 minutes; drain.

Stir the apricots, cherries and walnuts into rice. In a small bowl, whisk the oil, lemon juice, maple syrup and salt. Pour over rice mixture and mix well. Refrigerate for at least 30 minutes.

Nutrition Facts: 2/3 cup equals 293 calories, 12 g fat (1 g saturated fat), 0 cholesterol, 234 mg sodium, 44 g carbohydrate, 3 g fiber, 5 g protein.

Makeover Creamy Cranberry Salad S

PREP: 15 min. + chilling
YIELD: 12 servings (2/3 cup each)

ALEXANDRA LYPECKY • DEARBORN, MICHIGAN

This luscious makeover takes a longtime family favorite and makes it even better. With just a fourth of the original's saturated fat but all of the creamy flavor, everyone will find room for it.

3	cups fresh or frozen cranberries, thawed and coarsely chopped
1	can (20 oz.) unsweetened crushed pineapple, drained
2	cups miniature marshmallows
1	medium apple, chopped

Sugar substitute equivalent to 1/2 cup sugar

1/8 tsp. salt

1 carton (8 oz.) frozen reduced-fat whipped topping, thawed

1/4 cup chopped walnuts

1. In a large bowl, combine the cranberries, pineapple, marshmallows, apple, sugar substitute and salt. Cover and refrigerate overnight.

2. Just before serving, fold in whipped topping and walnuts.

Editor's Note: This recipe was tested with Splenda no-calorie sweetener.

Nutrition Facts: 2/3 cup equals 133 calories, 4 g fat (2 g saturated fat), 0 cholesterol, 29 mg sodium, 24 g carbohydrate, 2 g fiber, 1 g protein. **Diabetic Exchanges:** 1 starch, 1/2 fruit, 1/2 fat.

Bulgur Greek Salad

PREP: 20 min. + standing YIELD: 12 servings

JENNIFER ANDRZJEWSKI • GRIZZLY FLATS, CALIFORNIA

I've tried to start eating healthier, and this recipe is wonderful and so versatile. The ingredients are easy to find...and to have on hand at all times.

1-1/2 cups bulgur

3 cups boiling water

1/4 cup plus 2 Tbsp. lemon juice, *divided*

1 tsp. salt, *divided*

1-1/4 cups cubed cooked chicken breast

1-1/4 cups chopped cucumber

1/2 cup cherry tomatoes, halved

1/3 cup Greek olives

1/4 cup minced fresh parsley

1/4 cup roasted sweet red peppers, drained and chopped

1/4 cup chopped red onion

3 Tbsp. minced fresh basil

3 Tbsp. olive oil

1/4 tsp. dried oregano

1/4 tsp. pepper

1/8 tsp. cayenne pepper

1/4 cup crumbled feta cheese

1. Place bulgur in a small bowl. Stir in the water, 1/4 cup lemon juice and 1/2 tsp. salt. Cover and let stand for 30 minutes or until most of the liquid is absorbed. Drain well.

2. In a large bowl, combine the chicken, cucumber, tomatoes, olives, parsley, red peppers, onion and basil. Stir in bulgur.

3. In a small bowl, whisk the oil, oregano, pepper, cayenne and remaining lemon juice and salt. Pour over bulgur mixture; toss to coat. Sprinkle with cheese.

Nutrition Facts: 2/3 cup equals 137 calories, 5 g fat (1 g saturated fat), 12 mg cholesterol, 313 mg sodium, 16 g carbohydrate, 4 g fiber, 7 g protein. **Diabetic Exchanges:** 1 starch, 1 lean meat, 1/2 fat.

MAKEOVER CREAMY CRANBERRY SALAD

BULGUR GREEK SALAD

Apricot Orange Vinaigrette §C

PREP/TOTAL TIME: 5 min. YIELD: about 3/4 cup

DIANA RIOS • LYTLE, TEXAS

This sweet and tangy citrus dressing perks up any salad, lending appeal to even a simple blend of mixed greens.

> 1/4 cup apricot preserves
> 2 Tbsp. orange juice
> 2 Tbsp. rice vinegar
> 2 Tbsp. canola oil
> 1 Tbsp. water
> 1/8 tsp. salt

Dash pepper

1. Place all ingredients in a jar with a tight-fitting lid; shake well. Cover and refrigerate until serving.

Nutrition Facts: 2 Tbsp. equals 78 calories, 5 g fat (trace saturated fat), 0 cholesterol, 55 mg sodium, 10 g carbohydrate, trace fiber, trace protein. **Diabetic Exchanges:** 1 fat, 1/2 starch.

Homemade Ranch Dressing Mix C

PREP/TOTAL TIME: 5 min.
YIELD: 4 batches (about 3/4 cup)

HEALTHY COOKING TEST KITCHEN

Used as both a mix for a dip and a salad dressing, this tongue-tingling ranch mix is both tasty and versatile.

> 1/3 cup buttermilk blend powder
> 1/4 cup dried parsley flakes
> 2 Tbsp. dried minced onion
> 2 tsp. salt
> 2 tsp. garlic powder

ADDITIONAL INGREDIENTS FOR SALAD DRESSING:
> 1 cup reduced-fat mayonnaise
> 1 cup plus 6 Tbsp. buttermilk

ADDITIONAL INGREDIENTS FOR DIP:
> 2 cups (16 oz.) reduced-fat sour cream

1. Combine the first five ingredients. Store in an airtight container in a cool dry place for up to 1 year.

For salad dressing: In a small bowl, whisk the mayonnaise, buttermilk and 3 Tbsp. mix. Refrigerate for at least 1 hour. Yield: about 2 cups.

For dip: In a small bowl, combine sour cream and 3 Tbsp. mix. Refrigerate for at least 2 hours. Serve with assorted crackers and fresh vegetables. Yield: about 2 cups.

Nutrition Facts–Ranch Salad Dressing: 2 Tbsp. equals 62 calories, 5 g fat (1 g saturated fat), 7 mg cholesterol, 219 mg sodium, 3 g carbohydrate, trace fiber, 1 g protein.

Nutrition Facts–Ranch Dip: 2 Tbsp. equals 42 calories, 3 g fat (2 g saturated fat), 10 mg cholesterol, 73 mg sodium, 2 g carbohydrate, trace fiber, 2 g protein.

Zucchini "Linguine" Salad C M

PREP: 30 min. + chilling YIELD: 6 servings

LILY JULOW • GAINESVILLE, FLORIDA

This idea came to me from a recipe I saw for zucchini cut into noodle-like strips and dressed with a creamy sauce.

> 5 medium zucchini
> 3/4 tsp. salt, *divided*

APRICOT ORANGE VINAIGRETTE

ZUCCHINI "LINGUINE" SALAD

1 large sweet red pepper, julienned
1 large tomato, seeded and cut into thin strips
1/2 cup thinly sliced sweet onion
3 Tbsp. olive oil
2 Tbsp. cider vinegar
1/4 cup minced fresh parsley
1-1/2 tsp. minced fresh oregano or 1/2 tsp. dried oregano
1/4 tsp. pepper
Shredded Parmesan cheese, optional

1. Cut the ends off of each zucchini. Using a cheese slicer or vegetable peeler, cut zucchini into thin lengthwise strips. Cut zucchini on all sides, as if peeling a carrot, until the seeds become visible. Discard seeded portion or save for another use. Cut zucchini strips into 1/4-in. widths.

2. Place in a strainer; sprinkle with 1/2 tsp. salt and gently toss to coat. Let stand for 15 minutes. Gently shake strainer. Drain zucchini on paper towels and pat dry.

3. Transfer to a large bowl; add the red pepper, tomato and onion. In a small bowl, whisk the oil, vinegar, parsley, oregano, pepper and remaining salt. Pour over zucchini mixture and toss to coat. Cover and refrigerate for at least 30 minutes before serving. Sprinkle with cheese if desired.

Nutrition Facts: 3/4 cup equals 100 calories, 7 g fat (1 g saturated fat), 0 cholesterol, 254 mg sodium, 9 g carbohydrate, 3 g fiber, 2 g protein. **Diabetic Exchanges:** 1 vegetable, 1 fat.

Mediterranean Tuna Salad

PREP/TOTAL TIME: 25 min. YIELD: 4 servings

RENEE NASH • SNOQUALMIE, WASHINGTON

In spite of a long list of ingredients, this salad is very quick to prepare. You'll love the fresh flavors.

1 can (15 oz.) garbanzo beans or chickpeas, rinsed and drained
3 celery ribs, chopped
1 small sweet red pepper, chopped
4 green onions, chopped
2 Tbsp. olive oil
2 Tbsp. balsamic vinegar
2 Tbsp. spicy brown mustard
1/2 tsp. dried basil
1/4 tsp. salt
1/4 tsp. pepper
2 cans (5 oz. *each*) white water-packed tuna
4 cups shredded lettuce
1/2 cup crumbled feta or blue cheese, optional

1. In a large bowl, combine the beans, celery, red pepper and onions. In a small bowl, whisk the oil, vinegar, mustard, basil, salt and pepper. Pour over bean mixture; toss to coat. Gently stir in tuna. Serve over lettuce. Sprinkle with cheese if desired.

Nutrition Facts: 1-1/2 cups tuna salad with 1 cup shredded lettuce (calculated without cheese) equals 282 calories, 11 g fat (2 g saturated fat), 30 mg cholesterol, 682 mg sodium, 23 g carbohydrate, 6 g fiber, 23 g protein. **Diabetic Exchanges:** 3 lean meat, 1 starch, 1 vegetable, 1 fat.

BLT-AND-MORE SALAD

BLT-and-More Salad [C]

PREP/TOTAL TIME: 20 min YIELD: 4 servings

PAULA MARCHESI • LENHARTSVILLE, PENNSYLVANIA

*I created this when my husband and I were looking for
something quick, yet different. The blend of flavors is
wonderful, and I make it often. It's simply the best!*

1-1/2 cups yellow cherry tomatoes, halved
1-1/2 cups cherry tomatoes, halved
   1/3 cup cubed avocado
     2 bacon strips, cooked and crumbled
     2 Tbsp. fat-free sour cream
     2 Tbsp. fat-free mayonnaise
     2 Tbsp. fat-free milk
     1 garlic clove, minced
   1/2 tsp. dill weed
Dash *each* salt and pepper
   1/3 cup crumbled goat cheese
     2 Tbsp. pine nuts
     4 Bibb lettuce leaves

1. In a small bowl, combine the tomatoes, avocado
and bacon. In another small bowl, whisk the sour
cream, mayonnaise, milk, garlic, dill, salt and pepper;
pour over salad. Gently toss to coat. Sprinkle with
cheese and pine nuts. Serve immediately in lettuce
leaves.

Nutrition Facts: 3/4 cup equals 129 calories, 8 g fat (3 g
saturated fat), 17 mg cholesterol, 236 mg sodium, 10 g
carbohydrate, 3 g fiber, 6 g protein. **Diabetic Exchanges:**
1 high-fat meat, 1 vegetable.

Berry Chicken Salad [C]

PREP/TOTAL TIME: 20 min. YIELD: 4 servings

WENDY BALL • BATTLE CREEK, MICHIGAN

*Bright berries and creamy goat cheese make this colorful salad
a new twist on an all-time classic. No matter how you look at
it, it's a true winner! Ideal on its own, the salad could also
work as a sandwich filler on whole wheat bread.*

     4 boneless skinless chicken breast halves
        (4 oz. *each*)
   1/4 tsp. salt
   1/4 tsp. pepper
     1 pkg. (6 oz.) fresh baby spinach
     1 cup fresh raspberries
     1 cup halved fresh strawberries
   2/3 cup crumbled goat cheese
     3 Tbsp. chopped pecans, toasted
   1/4 cup prepared fat-free raspberry vinaigrette

1. Sprinkle chicken with salt and pepper. Grill
chicken, covered, over medium heat or broil 4 in.
from the heat for 4-7 minutes on each side or until
juices run clear.

2. In a large bowl, combine the spinach, raspberries,
strawberries, cheese and pecans. Divide among four
serving plates. Slice chicken and arrange over spinach
mixture; drizzle with vinaigrette.

Nutrition Facts: 1-1/2 cups salad with 1 chicken breast half and
1 Tbsp. dressing equals 268 calories, 12 g fat (4 g saturated fat),
86 mg cholesterol, 391 mg sodium, 15 g carbohydrate, 5 g
fiber, 28 g protein. **Diabetic Exchanges:** 4 lean meat, 1
vegetable, 1 fat, 1/2 fruit.

Teriyaki Chicken Salad with Poppy Seed Dressing

PREP: 30 min. + marinating **GRILL:** 10 min.
YIELD: 6 servings

CATHLEEN LEONARD • WOODBRIDGE, CALIFORNIA

I've made this salad so often and shared it with many people. It's originally from my good friend's daughter, and we always receive compliments on how wonderful the light fruit flavors come alive with the poppy seed dressing.

- 1   cup honey teriyaki marinade
- 1   lb. boneless skinless chicken breasts
- 6   cups torn romaine
- 3   medium kiwifruit, peeled and sliced
- 1   can (20 oz.) unsweetened pineapple chunks, drained
- 1   can (11 oz.) mandarin oranges, drained
- 2   celery ribs, chopped
- 1   medium sweet red pepper, chopped
- 1   medium green pepper, chopped
- 1   cup fresh raspberries
- 1   cup sliced fresh strawberries
- 3   green onions, chopped
- 1/2 cup salted cashews
- 1/3 cup reduced-fat poppy seed salad dressing

1. Place marinade in a large resealable plastic bag; add the chicken. Seal bag and turn to coat; refrigerate for 8 hours or overnight. Drain and discard marinade.

2. Grill chicken, covered, over medium heat for 5-7 minutes on each side or until a meat thermometer reads 170°.

3. Slice chicken. Divide the romaine, kiwi, pineapple, oranges, celery, peppers, raspberries and strawberries among six plates; top with chicken. Sprinkle with green onions and cashews. Drizzle with salad dressing.

Nutrition Facts: 1 serving equals 361 calories, 11 g fat (2 g saturated fat), 42 mg cholesterol, 761 mg sodium, 49 g carbohydrate, 7 g fiber, 20 g protein. **Diabetic Exchanges:** 2 lean meat, 1-1/2 starch, 1-1/2 fat, 1 vegetable, 1 fruit.

Shrimp Spinach Salad C

PREP/TOTAL TIME: 20 min. **YIELD:** 4 servings

JAMIE LARSON • DODGE CENTER, MINNESOTA

Shrimp and garlic are sauteed in butter then set atop a bed of spinach in this no-fuss salad. Almonds, tomatoes and a squeeze of lemon finish off this beauty.

- 2   Tbsp. butter
- 1   lb. uncooked medium shrimp, peeled and deveined
- 3   garlic cloves, minced
- 2   Tbsp. minced fresh parsley
- 4   cups fresh baby spinach
- 3/4 cup cherry tomatoes, halved
- 1/4 cup sliced almonds, toasted
- 1   medium lemon
- 1/4 tsp. salt
- 1/4 tsp. pepper

1. In a large nonstick skillet over medium heat, melt butter. Add the shrimp. Cook and stir for 3-4 minutes or until shrimp turn pink. Add garlic and parsley; cook 1 minute longer. Remove from the heat.

2. Place spinach in a salad bowl. Top with tomatoes, almonds and shrimp mixture. Squeeze the juice from the lemon; drizzle over the salad. Sprinkle with the salt and pepper.

Nutrition Facts: 1 cup equals 201 calories, 10 g fat (4 g saturated fat), 153 mg cholesterol, 350 mg sodium, 6 g carbohydrate, 2 g fiber, 21 g protein. **Diabetic Exchanges:** 3 lean meat, 1-1/2 fat, 1 vegetable.

TERIYAKI CHICKEN SALAD WITH POPPY SEED DRESSING

SHRIMP SPINACH SALAD

CURRY CHICKEN SOUP

TURKEY CHILI WITH PENNE

CURRIED CHICKEN PANINIS

Soups & Sandwiches

Just because you're watching your weight doesn't mean you have to turn down a classic soup-and-sandwich pairing. Turn here when you need a savory soup and piled-high sandwich that keep fat and calories at bay!

Curried Chicken Paninis

PREP/TOTAL TIME: 20 min. YIELD: 4 servings

MICHAELA ROSENTHAL • WOODLAND HILLS, CALIFORNIA

Serve the leftover chutney with chicken or pork tenderloin or with fat-free cream cheese as a fast cracker spread.

    2 cups cubed cooked chicken breast
  1/4 cup chopped celery
  1/4 cup fat-free mayonnaise
  3/4 tsp. curry powder
  1/4 tsp. grated lemon peel
    8 slices whole wheat bread
  1/3 cup mango chutney
    1 cup watercress *or* fresh arugula
    2 Tbsp. butter, softened

1. In a small bowl, combine the first five ingredients.

2. Spread four bread slices with chutney. Layer each with 1/2 cup chicken salad and 1/4 cup watercress; top with remaining bread. Spread outsides of sandwiches with butter.

3. Cook on a panini maker or indoor grill for 3-4 minutes or until bread is browned.

Nutrition Facts: 1 sandwich equals 389 calories, 10 g fat (5 g saturated fat), 71 mg cholesterol, 705 mg sodium, 44 g carbohydrate, 4 g fiber, 28 g protein. **Diabetic Exchanges:** 3 starch, 3 lean meat, 1-1/2 fat.

Makeover Tuna Melt Bites

PREP/TOTAL TIME: 25 min. YIELD: 4 servings

HEALTHY COOKING TEST KITCHEN

For a healthier take on this diner special, our Test Kitchen updated to tinier "tuna melt bites," pumped up nutrition with whole wheat buns, slashed fat by substituting fat-free mayo and reduced-fat cheese, and added tomato and spinach on top. Give these a try!

    2 cans (5 oz. *each*) light water-packed tuna, drained and flaked
    1 celery rib, finely chopped
  1/2 cup fat-free mayonnaise
  1/4 cup shredded carrot
    1 Tbsp. lemon juice

  1/4 tsp. pepper
    4 whole wheat hot dog buns, split
    2 plum tomatoes, sliced
    3 slices reduced-fat cheddar cheese, quartered
  1/2 cup fresh baby spinach

1. In a small bowl, combine the first six ingredients; set aside. Place hot dog buns cut side up on an ungreased baking sheet. Broil 4-6 in. from the heat for 2-3 minutes or until golden brown.

2. Spoon tuna mixture over bottom halves; top with tomato and cheese slices. Broil 1-2 minutes longer or until cheese is melted. Top with spinach. Replace bun tops. Secure with toothpicks; cut each of the sandwiches into thirds.

Nutrition Facts: 3 mini sandwiches equals 274 calories, 6 g fat (3 g saturated fat), 34 mg cholesterol, 806 mg sodium, 29 g carbohydrate, 5 g fiber, 27 g protein.

Berry Turkey Sandwich

PREP/TOTAL TIME: 5 min. YIELD: 2 servings

EDWARD MEYER • ARNOLD, MISSOURI

Sliced fresh strawberries, Swiss cheese and a nutty cream cheese spread make this turkey sandwich different. Try it on whole wheat, oatmeal or sunflower seed bread. It's tasty and simple to put together.

    4 slices whole wheat bread
    2 lettuce leaves
    2 slices reduced-fat Swiss cheese
  1/4 lb. thinly sliced deli turkey breast
    4 fresh strawberries, sliced
    2 Tbsp. reduced-fat spreadable cream cheese
    2 tsp. finely chopped pecans

1. On two slices of bread, layer with lettuce, cheese, turkey and strawberries. Combine cream cheese and pecans; spread over remaining bread. Place over the strawberry slices.

Nutrition Facts: One sandwich equals 356 calories, 10 g fat (3 g saturated fat), 39 mg cholesterol, 932 mg sodium, 39 g carbohydrate, 5 g fiber, 28 g protein.

Taco Salad Wraps

PREP/TOTAL TIME: 25 min. YIELD: 2 servings

MARLENE ROBERTS • MOORE, OKLAHOMA

These change-of-pace Southwestern wraps will be a hit the next time you need a quick lunch or dinner.

- 1/4 lb. lean ground beef (90% lean)
- 1/3 cup plus 2 Tbsp. salsa, *divided*
- 1/4 cup chili beans, drained
- 1-1/2 tsp. Worcestershire sauce
- 1 tsp. onion powder
- 1 tsp. chili powder
- 1/8 tsp. garlic powder
- Pepper to taste
- 2 flour tortillas (8 in.), warmed
- 1/3 cup shredded lettuce
- 1 plum tomato, chopped
- 2 Tbsp. shredded cheddar cheese
- 6 baked tortilla chip scoops, coarsely crushed

1. In a small nonstick skillet, cook beef over medium heat until no longer pink; drain. Stir in 1/3 cup salsa, beans, Worcestershire sauce, onion powder, chili powder, garlic powder and pepper. Bring to a boil; reduce heat and simmer, uncovered, for 5 minutes.

2. Spoon meat mixture onto each tortilla. Layer with lettuce, tomato, cheese, crushed tortilla chips and remaining salsa; roll up.

Nutrition Facts: 1 wrap equals 345 calories, 10 g fat (4 g saturated fat), 35 mg cholesterol, 764 mg sodium, 42 g carbohydrate, 5 g fiber, 20 g protein.

Butternut Squash & Pear Soup

PREP: 1-1/4 hours COOK: 45 min. YIELD: 9 servings

SARAH VASQUES • MILFORD, NEW HAMPSHIRE

Pears give this harvest soup a pleasant sweetness and lovely velvety finish, while curry and ginger provide delightful flavor.

- 1 medium butternut squash (about 3 lbs.)
- 1 medium onion, chopped
- 2 Tbsp. canola oil
- 1 Tbsp. curry powder
- 2 garlic cloves, minced
- 2 tsp. minced fresh gingerroot
- 1 tsp. salt
- 4 cups reduced-sodium chicken broth
- 4 medium pears, peeled and chopped
- 1/2 cup heavy whipping cream
- Balsamic vinegar and snipped chives, optional

1. Cut squash in half; discard seeds. Place squash cut side down in a 15-in. x 10-in. x 1-in. baking pan coated with cooking spray. Bake at 400° for 40-50 minutes or until tender. Cool slightly; scoop out pulp and set aside.

2. In a Dutch oven, saute onion in oil until tender. Add the curry, garlic, ginger and salt; cook 1 minute longer. Stir in the broth, pears and squash. Bring to a boil. Reduce heat; simmer, uncovered, for 30 minutes. Cool slightly.

3. In a blender, process soup in batches until smooth. Return all to the pan; add cream and heat through. Top with balsamic vinegar and chives if desired.

Nutrition Facts: 3/4 cup equals 190 calories, 8 g fat (3 g saturated fat), 18 mg cholesterol, 527 mg sodium, 29 g carbohydrate, 7 g fiber, 4 g protein. **Diabetic Exchanges:** 2 starch, 1 fat.

TACO SALAD WRAPS

BUTTERNUT SQUASH & PEAR SOUP

Chicken Barley Soup

PREP: 20 min. **COOK:** 45 min. **YIELD:** 6 servings

PATRICIA RANDALL • NEWTON, KANSAS

With chicken, barley and a host of delicious veggies, this is a yummy way to beat winter's chill. The leeks add an unexpected twist to the soup.

- 1 lb. boneless skinless chicken breasts, cut into 3/4-in. pieces
- 2 Tbsp. canola oil, *divided*
- 2 cups chopped leeks (white portion only)
- 1 celery rib, thinly sliced
- 1 carrot, thinly sliced
- 2 cups sliced fresh mushrooms
- 1 garlic clove, minced
- 2 cans (14-1/2 oz. *each*) reduced-sodium chicken broth
- 2-1/4 cups water
- 1 bay leaf
- 1/2 tsp. dried thyme
- 1/4 tsp. salt
- 1/4 tsp. pepper
- 1/2 cup quick-cooking barley

1. In a Dutch oven, brown chicken in 1 Tbsp. oil. Remove and set aside.

2. In the same pan, saute the leeks, celery and carrot in remaining oil for 4 minutes. Add mushrooms and garlic; cook 2 minutes longer. Stir in the broth, water, bay leaf, seasonings and chicken. Bring to a boil. Reduce heat; cover and simmer for 15 minutes.

3. Stir in barley and return to a boil. Reduce heat; cover and simmer for 10-12 minutes or until barley and vegetables are tender. Discard bay leaf.

Nutrition Facts: 1 cup equals 218 calories, 7 g fat (1 g saturated fat), 42 mg cholesterol, 550 mg sodium, 19 g carbohydrate, 4 g fiber, 21 g protein. **Diabetic Exchanges:** 2 lean meat, 1 starch, 1 vegetable, 1 fat.

Turkey-White Bean Soup ⓕ

PREP: 20 min. **COOK:** 40 min. **YIELD:** 6 servings (2 qt.)

MARY RELYEA • CANASTOTA, NEW YORK

Packed with veggies, turkey and nutrition, this hearty soup will warm 'em up right down to their toes. For an extra-special touch, top the soup with shredded Parmesan cheese.

- 2 garlic cloves, minced
- 2 tsp. olive oil
- 1/2 tsp. dried rosemary, crushed
- 1/4 tsp. crushed red pepper flakes
- 1 can (28 oz.) whole tomatoes in puree, cut up
- 1 can (14-1/2 oz.) reduced-sodium chicken broth
- 1 pkg. (6 oz.) fresh baby spinach, cut into thin strips
- 2 cups shredded carrots
- 2 cans (15 oz. *each*) white kidney *or* cannellini beans, rinsed and drained
- 1-1/2 cups cubed cooked turkey breast

Shredded Parmesan cheese, optional

1. In a large saucepan over medium heat, cook garlic in oil for 1 minute. Add rosemary and pepper flakes; cook 1 minute longer.

2. Stir in the tomatoes, broth, spinach and carrots. Bring to a boil. Reduce heat; cover and simmer for 15 minutes. Stir in beans and turkey; return to a boil. Reduce heat; cover and simmer 10 minutes longer. Serve with cheese if desired.

Nutrition Facts: 1-1/3 cups (calculated without cheese) equals 233 calories, 3 g fat (trace saturated fat), 30 mg cholesterol, 893 mg sodium, 32 g carbohydrate, 9 g fiber, 20 g protein.

Potluck Sloppy Joes

PREP: 30 min. **COOK:** 15 min. **YIELD:** 12 servings

RICK BOLTE • MONTCLAIR, CALIFORNIA

For a change of pace, I suggest swapping out the green pepper in these comforting sloppy joes for an Anaheim pepper if available. Anaheim peppers are longer and lighter in color than green bell peppers, and they add a tiny bite, which is just perfect for those who like a little kick in their food.

- 3 lbs. lean ground turkey
- 3 celery ribs, chopped
- 2 medium onions, chopped
- 1 large green pepper, chopped
- 1-3/4 cups ketchup
- 1 can (8 oz.) no-salt-added tomato sauce
- 3 Tbsp. all-purpose flour
- 3 Tbsp. sugar
- 3 Tbsp. cider vinegar
- 1 Tbsp. prepared mustard
- 12 whole wheat hamburger buns, split and toasted

1. In a large nonstick skillet, cook the turkey, celery, onions and pepper over medium heat until meat is no longer pink; drain.

2. Stir in the ketchup, tomato sauce, flour, sugar, vinegar and mustard. Bring to a boil. Reduce heat; cover and simmer for 10-15 minutes or until heated through. Spoon 2/3 cup turkey mixture onto each bun.

Nutrition Facts: 1 sandwich equals 360 calories, 11 g fat (3 g saturated fat), 90 mg cholesterol, 785 mg sodium, 41 g carbohydrate, 4 g fiber, 24 g protein. **Diabetic Exchanges:** 3 lean meat, 2-1/2 starch.

Open-Faced Meatball Sandwiches

PREP: 30 min. COOK: 10 min. YIELD: 8 servings

KAREN BARTHEL • NORTH CANTON, OHIO

My husband and I love classic meatball subs, but I wanted to create a version that's fast to fix after a long day. This recipe always comes together in a snap, and the meatballs are very freezer-friendly as well.

1/4	cup egg substitute
1/2	cup soft bread crumbs
1/4	cup finely chopped onion
2	garlic cloves, minced
1/2	tsp. onion powder
1/2	tsp. dried oregano
1/2	tsp. dried basil
1/4	tsp. pepper

Dash salt

1-1/4	lbs. lean ground beef (90% lean)
2	cups garden-style pasta sauce
4	hoagie buns, split
2	Tbsp. shredded part-skim mozzarella cheese

Shredded Parmesan cheese, optional

1. In a large bowl, combine the first nine ingredients. Crumble beef over mixture and mix well. Shape into 40 meatballs. In a large skillet coated with cooking spray, brown meatballs in batches; drain.

2. Place meatballs in a large saucepan. Add pasta sauce; bring to a boil. Reduce heat; cover and simmer for 10-15 minutes or until meat is no longer pink. Spoon meatballs and sauce onto bun halves; sprinkle with mozzarella and Parmesan cheese if desired.

Nutrition Facts: 1 sandwich (calculated without Parmesan cheese) equals 277 calories, 10 g fat (4 g saturated fat), 47 mg cholesterol, 506 mg sodium, 28 g carbohydrate, 3 g fiber, 20 g protein.

Asian Chicken Salad Wraps

PREP/TOTAL TIME: 25 min. YIELD: 6 servings

JASON BRANNON • CONWAY, ARKANSAS

Loaded with chicken, cabbage and carrots, these wraps feature a fantastic homemade dressing. They'll be a yummy, nutritious lunch or dinner any time of year.

3	cups shredded cooked chicken breasts
4	green onions, finely chopped
1	cup finely shredded cabbage
1/2	cup shredded carrot

DRESSING:

3	Tbsp. seasoned rice vinegar
3	Tbsp. canola oil
2	Tbsp. honey
1	Tbsp. water
1	garlic clove, halved
3/4	tsp. minced fresh gingerroot
1/4	tsp. coarsely ground pepper
1	cup fresh cilantro leaves
6	lettuce leaves
6	whole wheat tortillas (8 in.), room temperature

1. In a large bowl, combine the chicken, green onions, cabbage and carrot. For dressing, in a small food processor, combine the vinegar, oil, honey, water, garlic, ginger and pepper. Cover and process until blended. Add cilantro; cover and process until chopped. Pour over chicken mixture; toss to coat.

2. Place a lettuce leaf on each tortilla; top with chicken mixture. Roll up tightly.

Nutrition Facts: 1 wrap equals 370 calories, 13 g fat (1 g saturated fat), 60 mg cholesterol, 503 mg sodium, 34 g carbohydrate, 3 g fiber, 26 g protein.

ASIAN CHICKEN SALAD WRAPS

OPEN-FACED MEATBALL SANDWICHES

Italian Lentil Soup F M

PREP: 15 min. **COOK:** 40 min. **YIELD:** 6 servings (2 qt.)

MARYBETH GESSELE • GASTON, OREGON

Lentils, like beans, are part of the legume family and add cholesterol-reducing fiber to this no-fuss soup.

1	medium onion, chopped
1	Tbsp. olive oil
2	garlic cloves, minced
3-1/4	cups water
1	can (14-1/2 oz.) vegetable broth
1	cup dried lentils, rinsed
1	medium carrot, shredded
1	small green pepper, finely chopped
1	tsp. dried oregano
1/2	tsp. dried basil
1/4	tsp. crushed red pepper flakes, optional
1	can (14-1/2 oz.) no-salt-added diced tomatoes
1	can (6 oz.) tomato paste
1	Tbsp. lemon juice
2	cups cooked brown rice

1. In a Dutch oven, saute onion in oil until tender. Add garlic; cook 1 minute longer. Add the water, broth, lentils, carrot, green pepper, oregano, basil and pepper flakes if desired. Bring to a boil. Reduce heat; cover and simmer for 20-25 minutes or until lentils are almost tender.

2. Stir in the tomatoes, tomato paste and lemon juice. Bring to a boil. Reduce heat; cover and simmer 10 minutes longer or until lentils are tender. Serve with the rice.

Nutrition Facts: 1-1/3 cups with 1/3 cup rice equals 269 calories, 3 g fat (trace saturated fat), 0 cholesterol, 383 mg sodium, 48 g carbohydrate, 14 g fiber, 13 g protein.

Turkey Chili with Penne

PREP: 25 min. **COOK:** 1 hour **YIELD:** 12 servings

PATRICIA BURK • NORTH CANTON, OHIO

This recipe easily turns into a vegetarian dish by leaving out the meat or replacing it with soy crumbles. A topping of goat cheese makes this hearty chili stand out from others.

1-1/2	lbs. extra-lean ground turkey
1	tsp. olive oil
3	celery ribs, chopped
3	large carrots, sliced
1	medium onion, chopped
1	poblano pepper, seeded and finely chopped
1/2	cup marsala wine *or* reduced-sodium chicken broth
1	can (28 oz.) diced tomatoes, undrained
2	cans (one 15 oz., one 8 oz.) tomato sauce
1	can (4 oz.) chopped green chilies
1	Tbsp. chili powder
1	Tbsp. honey
3-1/2	cups uncooked whole wheat penne pasta
2	cans (15 oz. *each*) black beans, rinsed and drained
8	oz. fresh goat cheese, cut into 12 slices

1. In a Dutch oven, cook turkey in oil over medium heat until no longer pink. Stir in the celery, carrots, onion, pepper and wine; cook until the vegetables are tender.

2. Stir in the tomatoes, tomato sauce, chilies, chili powder and honey. Bring to a boil. Reduce heat; simmer, uncovered, for 1 hour or until thickened.

3. Meanwhile, cook pasta according to pkg. directions. Stir beans into chili; heat through. Drain pasta; spoon 1/2 cup into each serving bowl. Spoon chili over pasta; top with cheese.

Nutrition Facts: 1 cup chili with 1/2 cup pasta and 2/3 oz. cheese equals 343 calories, 4 g fat (2 g saturated fat), 35 mg cholesterol, 642 mg sodium, 48 g carbohydrate, 9 g fiber, 27 g protein.

ITALIAN LENTIL SOUP

TURKEY CHILI WITH PENNE

New Orleans-Style Subs

PREP: 30 min. BROIL: 5 min. YIELD: 12 servings

SHANNON LEE DENNEY • MILWAUKEE, WISCONSIN

This satisfying muffuletta-style sandwich contains loads of meat and cheese. The chopped olive spread makes it a true New Orleans classic.

1-1/3 cups giardiniera

2/3 cup chopped pitted green olives

2/3 cup pitted ripe olives

2 loaves (1 lb. *each*) unsliced French bread

1/4 cup fat-free Italian salad dressing

1/2 lb. thinly sliced deli ham

1/2 lb. thinly sliced deli turkey

1/2 lb. sliced reduced-fat provolone cheese

1/2 lb. thinly sliced deli roast beef

1/2 lb. sliced reduced-fat Colby-Monterey Jack cheese

2 medium tomatoes, sliced

2 cups shredded lettuce

1 large red onion, thinly sliced and separated into rings

1. Place giardiniera and olives in a food processor; cover and process until coarsely chopped. Set aside.

2. Cut bread in half lengthwise; carefully hollow out top and bottom of loaves, leaving 1/2-in. shells (discard removed bread or save for another use). Place on two large baking sheets. Broil 4-6 in. from the heat for 3-4 minutes or until toasted. Brush bottom halves with dressing; layer with ham, turkey and provolone cheese. Spread top halves with olive mixture; layer with roast beef and Colby-Monterey Jack cheese.

3. Broil 2-3 minutes longer or until cheese is melted. Layer bottom halves with tomatoes, lettuce and onion; replace tops. Cut each loaf into six slices.

Nutrition Facts: 1 slice equals 336 calories, 11 g fat (5 g saturated fat), 46 mg cholesterol, 1,368 mg sodium, 32 g carbohydrate, 2 g fiber, 27 g protein.

Italian Turkey Sloppy Joes

PREP: 15 min. **COOK:** 45 min. **YIELD:** 8 servings

CHARLENE CHAMBERS • ORMOND BEACH, FLORIDA

Everyone seems to love my take on sloppy joes. For a change, I often fix them with ground chicken instead of ground turkey and use fresh parsley and oregano.

- 1 pkg. (19-1/2 oz.) hot Italian turkey sausage links, casings removed
- 1 lb. extra-lean ground turkey
- 1 medium green pepper, chopped
- 1 small onion, chopped
- 4 garlic cloves, minced
- 2 cans (8 oz. *each*) no-salt-added tomato sauce
- 2 Tbsp. no-salt-added tomato paste
- 1 Tbsp. chili powder
- 2 tsp. dried parsley flakes
- 1 tsp. dried oregano
- 8 whole wheat hamburger buns, split
- 3/4 cup shredded part-skim mozzarella cheese
- 1/4 cup shredded Parmesan cheese

1. In a Dutch oven, cook the sausage, turkey, pepper and onion over medium heat until meat is no longer pink. Add garlic; cook 1 minute longer. Drain. Stir in the tomato sauce, tomato paste and seasonings. Bring to a boil. Reduce the heat; cover and simmer meat mixture for 30 minutes.

2. Spoon 3/4 cup turkey mixture onto each bun; sprinkle with cheeses.

Nutrition Facts: 1 sandwich equals 348 calories, 12 g fat (3 g saturated fat), 72 mg cholesterol, 775 mg sodium, 30 g carbohydrate, 5 g fiber, 33 g protein. **Diabetic Exchanges:** 4 medium-fat meat, 2 starch, 1 vegetable.

Spicy Chicken Tomato Pitas

PREP/TOTAL TIME: 30 min. **YIELD:** 4 servings

CORI COOPER • BOISE, IDAHO

This is a terrific recipe. It cooks up quickly, too, which is always a big bonus. A sizzling blend of Southwest tastes with a bright splash of lemon, this one's a crowd-pleaser!

TOMATO RELISH:
- 4 medium tomatoes, seeded and chopped
- 1 small onion, chopped
- 1/4 cup minced fresh parsley
- 1/4 cup lemon juice
- 1 Tbsp. olive oil
- 1 tsp. ground coriander
- 1 tsp. ground cumin
- 1/4 tsp. crushed red pepper flakes

CHICKEN PITAS:
- 1 Tbsp. ground cumin
- 1 Tbsp. paprika
- 1-1/2 tsp. dried oregano
- 1-1/2 tsp. ground coriander
- 1/2 tsp. crushed red pepper flakes
- 1/4 tsp. salt
- 4 boneless skinless chicken breast halves (4 oz. *each*)
- 8 whole wheat pita pocket halves

1. Combine the relish ingredients; chill until serving.

2. Combine the cumin, paprika, oregano, coriander, pepper flakes and salt; rub over both sides of chicken. Grill chicken, covered, over medium heat or broil 4 in. from the heat for 4-7 minutes on each side or until juices run clear.

3. Slice chicken. Fill each pita half with chicken and tomato relish.

Nutrition Facts: 2 filled pita halves equals 383 calories, 9 g fat (2 g saturated fat), 63 mg cholesterol, 558 mg sodium, 47 g carbohydrate, 9 g fiber, 32 g protein.

Pea Soup with Mushroom Cream Sauce

PREP: 25 min. **COOK:** 15 min. **YIELD:** 6 servings

SALLY SIBTHORPE • SHELBY TOWNSHIP, MICHIGAN

Fresh garden peas combine with a hint of basil for a delightfully light spring soup. A unique mushroom drizzle adds extra depth to this beautiful dish.

1/2	lb. sliced baby portobello mushrooms, *divided*
1	Tbsp. butter
1/4	cup chopped onion
1	garlic clove, minced
1/2	cup half-and-half cream
3	Tbsp. sherry *or* reduced-sodium chicken broth
1	Tbsp. minced fresh thyme *or* 1 tsp. dried thyme
3/4	tsp. salt, *divided*
5	cups fresh *or* frozen peas, *divided*
3	cups reduced-sodium chicken broth
2	Tbsp. lemon juice
4-1/2	tsp. minced fresh basil *or* 1-1/2 tsp. dried basil

1. Set aside 3 Tbsp. mushrooms for garnish. In a large skillet, saute remaining mushrooms in butter until tender.

2. Add onion and garlic to skillet; saute until tender. Stir in the cream, sherry, thyme and 1/4 tsp. salt. Bring to a boil. Reduce heat; simmer, uncovered, for 2 minutes. Cool slightly. Transfer to a blender; process until smooth. Set aside.

3. In a Dutch oven, combine 4-1/2 cups peas, chicken broth and remaining salt. Bring to a boil. Reduce heat; simmer, uncovered, for 4 minutes or until peas are tender. Stir in lemon juice and basil; heat through. Transfer to a blender; process in batches until blended.

4. Ladle soup into serving bowls; top with mushroom cream sauce. Garnish with reserved mushrooms and remaining peas.

Nutrition Facts: 3/4 cup soup with 2 Tbsp. sauce equals 169 calories, 5 g fat (3 g saturated fat), 15 mg cholesterol, 612 mg sodium, 22 g carbohydrate, 7 g fiber, 10 g protein. **Diabetic Exchanges:** 1-1/2 starch, 1 fat.

Day After Easter Soup

PREP: 25 min. **COOK:** 45 min.
YIELD: 9 servings (2-1/4 qt.)

SUSAN WILSON • MILWAUKEE, WISCONSIN

Every spring I wait impatiently for the asparagus crop to arrive so I can make my cream of asparagus soup. One year I added the leftovers from Easter, and it turned into this hit that has since become a spring tradition.

2	medium leeks (white portion only), chopped
2	Tbsp. butter
2	Tbsp. all-purpose flour
1	carton (32 oz.) vegetable broth
1	cup water
1	Tbsp. minced fresh parsley
1	tsp. herbes de Provence
1	tsp. minced chives
1/2	tsp. celery seed
1/4	tsp. ground nutmeg
1	lb. fresh asparagus, trimmed
5	medium red potatoes, peeled and cut into 1/2-in. cubes
1-1/2	cups cubed fully cooked lean ham
1-1/4	cups half-and-half cream
3	Tbsp. shredded Gruyere *or* Swiss cheese

1. In a large saucepan, saute leeks in butter until tender. Stir in flour until blended. Gradually add the broth, water, parsley, herbes de Provence, chives, celery seed and nutmeg. Bring to a boil; cook and stir for 2 minutes or until thickened.

2. Cut tips off asparagus and set aside. Cut stalks into 1/2-in. pieces; add to pan. Reduce heat; cover and simmer for 10-15 minutes or until asparagus is tender. Cool slightly.

3. In a blender, process soup in batches until smooth. Return all to pan. Stir in potatoes. Bring to a boil. Reduce heat; cover and simmer for 10 minutes. Stir in asparagus tips; cover and simmer 5-8 minutes longer or until vegetables are tender. Stir in ham and cream; heat through. Sprinkle with cheese.

Editor's Note: Look for herbes de Provence in the spice aisle.

Nutrition Facts: 1 cup equals 207 calories, 8 g fat (5 g saturated fat), 35 mg cholesterol, 824 mg sodium, 24 g carbohydrate, 2 g fiber, 9 g protein.

DAY AFTER EASTER SOUP

Open-Faced Chicken Salad Sandwiches

PREP/TOTAL TIME: 25 min. **YIELD:** 6 servings

CHRISTINA BALDWIN • COVINGTON, LOUISIANA

These uniquely flavored chicken sandwiches, with their sweet-tangy-tart combo of ingredients, are absolutely delectable. Enjoy this recipe as it is or, even better, use a panini press and fix it as a normal sandwich—it works fabulously.

- 3 cups cubed cooked chicken breast
- 3 celery ribs, finely chopped
- 1 cup fat-free mayonnaise
- 1 small onion, finely chopped
- 1/2 cup dried cranberries
- 1/4 cup chopped pecans
- 2 Tbsp. white wine vinegar
- 2 Tbsp. Creole mustard
- 1 Tbsp. lemon juice
- 1/4 tsp. pepper
- 6 slices sourdough bread
- Butter-flavored cooking spray
- 3/4 cup sugar-free apricot preserves
- 6 slices Brie cheese (1/2 oz. *each*)

1. In a large bowl, gently combine the first 10 ingredients. Place bread slices on a baking sheet; spritz with butter-flavored cooking spray. Broil 4 in. from the heat for 2-3 minutes or until golden brown.

2. Spread preserves over untoasted sides of bread slices. Top each with 2/3 cup chicken salad and a slice of cheese. Broil 2-3 minutes longer or until the cheese is melted.

Nutrition Facts: 1 sandwich equals 381 calories, 12 g fat (4 g saturated fat), 72 mg cholesterol, 780 mg sodium, 46 g carbohydrate, 3 g fiber, 28 g protein.

OPEN-FACED CHICKEN SALAD SANDWICHES

Sweet Potato & Black Bean Chili Ⓜ

PREP: 25 min. **COOK:** 35 min. **YIELD:** 8 servings (2 qt.)

JOY PENDLEY • ORTONVILLE, MICHIGAN

My whole family enjoys this chili, but my daughter especially loves it. I like to make it because it's so easy and very flavorful.

- 3 large sweet potatoes, peeled and cut into 1/2-in. cubes
- 1 large onion, chopped
- 1 Tbsp. olive oil
- 2 Tbsp. chili powder
- 3 garlic cloves, minced
- 1 tsp. ground cumin
- 1/4 tsp. cayenne pepper
- 2 cans (15 oz. *each*) black beans, rinsed and drained
- 1 can (28 oz.) diced tomatoes, undrained
- 1/4 cup brewed coffee
- 2 Tbsp. honey
- 1/2 tsp. salt
- 1/4 tsp. pepper
- 1/2 cup shredded reduced-fat Monterey Jack cheese *or* reduced-fat Mexican cheese blend

1. In a nonstick Dutch oven coated with cooking spray, saute sweet potatoes and onion in oil until crisp-tender. Add the chili powder, garlic, cumin and cayenne; cook 1 minute longer. Stir in the beans, tomatoes, coffee, honey, salt and pepper.

2. Bring to a boil. Reduce heat; cover and simmer for 30-35 minutes or until sweet potatoes are tender. Sprinkle with cheese.

Nutrition Facts: 1 cup chili with 1 Tbsp. cheese equals 252 calories, 4 g fat (1 g saturated fat), 5 mg cholesterol, 554 mg sodium, 47 g carbohydrate, 9 g fiber, 10 g protein.

Garbanzo Bean Burgers Ⓜ

PREP: 25 min. **COOK:** 10 min. **YIELD:** 6 servings

BEREA RIDER • EAST POINT, KENTUCKY

These meatless burgers are totally awesome. I think I'd rather have one than any cheeseburger at a restaurant. They really rock! Need I say more?

- 1 can (15 oz.) garbanzo beans *or* chickpeas, rinsed and drained
- 3 Tbsp. water
- 1 tsp. lemon juice
- 1 cup dry bread crumbs
- 1 egg
- 1 tsp. Italian seasoning
- 1/2 tsp. garlic powder
- 1/2 tsp. onion powder
- Dash crushed red pepper flakes
- 2 Tbsp. canola oil
- 6 whole wheat hamburger buns, split and toasted
- 6 slices reduced-fat process American cheese product
- Dill pickle slices, fat-free mayonnaise and ketchup, optional

1. Place the beans, water and lemon juice in a food processor; cover and process until blended. Transfer to a large bowl. Add the bread crumbs, egg and seasonings and mix well. Shape into six patties.

2. In a large skillet, cook patties in oil in batches for 3-4 minutes on each side or until lightly browned. Serve on buns with cheese. Top with pickle slices, mayonnaise and ketchup if desired.

Nutrition Facts: 1 burger (calculated without optional ingredients) equals 346 calories, 11 g fat (2 g saturated fat), 40 mg cholesterol, 641 mg sodium, 48 g carbohydrate, 7 g fiber, 15 g protein.

Curry Chicken Soup

PREP: 20 min. **COOK:** 15 min. **YIELD:** 4 servings

JANE HACKER • MILWAUKEE, WISCONSIN

Despite the longer ingredient list, this yummy soup is simple and fast. What a fantastic way to get your veggies!

1/2	lb. boneless skinless chicken breast, cut into 1/2-in. cubes
3	tsp. canola oil, *divided*
3/4	cup chopped onion
1/2	cup chopped carrot
1/2	cup chopped celery
1/2	cup chopped green pepper
1	cup chopped peeled apple
2	Tbsp. all-purpose flour
1/4	tsp. salt
2	cans (14-1/2 oz. *each*) reduced-sodium chicken broth
1/4	cup tomato paste
2 to 3	tsp. curry powder
1	tsp. ground ginger
1/4 to 1/2	tsp. crushed red pepper flakes
2	Tbsp. minced fresh parsley

1. In a large saucepan coated with cooking spray, cook chicken in 1 tsp. oil for 4-5 minutes or until no longer pink. Remove chicken and set aside.

2. In the same saucepan, saute the onion, carrot, celery and green pepper in remaining oil for 4 minutes. Add apple; cook 2 minutes longer. Combine flour and salt. Sprinkle over vegetable mixture; cook and stir for 1 minute. Gradually stir in broth and tomato paste. Bring to a boil; cook and stir 1-2 minutes longer or until slightly thickened.

3. Stir in the curry, ginger and pepper flakes. Return chicken to saucepan and bring to a boil. Reduce heat; simmer, uncovered, for 8-10 minutes or until the vegetables are tender. Sprinkle with parsley.

Nutrition Facts: 1-1/2 cups equals 183 calories, 5 g fat (1 g saturated fat), 31 mg cholesterol, 752 mg sodium, 19 g carbohydrate, 4 g fiber, 16 g protein. **Diabetic Exchanges:** 2 lean meat, 2 vegetable, 1/2 starch, 1/2 fat.

Cajun Catfish Sandwiches

PREP/TOTAL TIME: 25 min. **YIELD:** 4 servings

SHAUNIECE FRAZIER • LOS ANGELES, CALIFORNIA

This spicy bistro-style sandwich makes such an effortless summertime supper. Serve it alongside your favorite vegetable side dish and enjoy.

- 3/4 tsp. seasoned pepper
- 1/2 tsp. chili powder
- 1/2 tsp. cayenne pepper
- 1/4 tsp. seasoned salt
- 4 catfish fillets (4 oz. *each*)
- 2 tsp. olive oil, *divided*
- 2 green onions, chopped
- 3 garlic cloves, minced
- 1/2 cup fat-free mayonnaise
- 4 French *or* kaiser rolls, split and toasted
- 4 romaine leaves

1. Combine the seasoned pepper, chili powder, cayenne and seasoned salt; sprinkle over fillets. In a large skillet, cook fillets in 1 tsp. oil for 4-6 minutes on each side or until fish flakes easily with a fork. Remove and keep warm.

2. In the same skillet, saute onions and garlic in remaining oil until tender. Remove from the heat; stir in mayonnaise. Spread over rolls; top each with a romaine leaf and fillet. Replace tops.

Nutrition Facts: 1 sandwich equals 373 calories, 14 g fat (3 g saturated fat), 56 mg cholesterol, 710 mg sodium, 37 g carbohydrate, 3 g fiber, 24 g protein.

Sausage Pizza Soup

PREP: 10 min. **COOK:** 25 min. **YIELD:** 4 servings

BETH SHERER • MILWAUKEE, WISCONSIN

Here's a healthy take on ooey-gooey sausage pizza. You won't believe something so comforting could be so light.

- 1/2 lb. Italian turkey sausage links, casings removed
- 1 medium zucchini, sliced
- 1 cup sliced fresh mushrooms
- 1 small onion, chopped
- 1 can (14-1/2 oz.) no-salt-added diced tomatoes
- 1 cup water
- 1 cup reduced-sodium chicken broth
- 1 tsp. dried basil
- 1/4 tsp. pepper

Minced fresh basil and crushed red pepper flakes, optional

1. In a large saucepan, cook the sausage, zucchini, mushrooms and onion over medium heat until meat is no longer pink; drain. Add the tomatoes, water, broth, dried basil and pepper. Bring to a boil. Reduce heat; simmer, uncovered, for 15 minutes. Sprinkle with fresh basil and pepper flakes if desired.

Nutrition Facts: 1 cup equals 128 calories, 5 g fat (1 g saturated fat), 34 mg cholesterol, 528 mg sodium, 9 g carbohydrate, 3 g fiber, 12 g protein. **Diabetic Exchanges:** 2 vegetable, 1 medium-fat meat.

Lightened-Up Pasta Fagioli Soup

PREP: 20 min. **COOK:** 40 min.
YIELD: 6 servings (2-1/4 qt.)

CINDIE KITCHIN • GRANTS PASS, OREGON

After trying pasta fagioli at a popular restaurant, I was determined to make it at home, only healthier. It turns out mine was a big hit! Loaded with veggies, it is such a simple way to boost nutrition and fiber at mealtime.

- 1 lb. lean ground turkey
- 1 large onion, chopped
- 2 celery ribs, chopped
- 2 medium carrots, sliced
- 1 garlic clove, minced
- 3 cups water
- 1 can (16 oz.) kidney beans, rinsed and drained
- 2 cans (8 oz. *each*) no-salt-added tomato sauce
- 1 can (14-1/2 oz.) no-salt-added diced tomatoes, undrained
- 1 Tbsp. dried parsley flakes
- 2 tsp. reduced-sodium beef bouillon granules
- 1/2 tsp. dried oregano
- 1/2 tsp. dried basil
- 1/4 tsp. pepper
- 2 cups shredded cabbage
- 1 cup fresh *or* frozen cut green beans (1-in. pieces)
- 1/2 cup uncooked elbow macaroni

1. In a Dutch oven coated with cooking spray, cook the turkey, onion, celery and carrots over medium heat until meat is no longer pink. Add garlic; cook 1 minute longer. Add the water, beans, tomato sauce, tomatoes, parsley, bouillon, oregano, basil and pepper. Bring to a boil. Reduce heat; cover and simmer for 20 minutes.

2. Add the cabbage, green beans and macaroni; cover and simmer 8-10 minutes longer or until the vegetables and macaroni are tender.

Nutrition Facts: 1-1/2 cups equals 276 calories, 7 g fat (2 g saturated fat), 60 mg cholesterol, 379 mg sodium, 33 g carbohydrate, 8 g fiber, 21 g protein. **Diabetic Exchanges:** 2 starch, 2 lean meat.

Mango Shrimp Pitas

PREP: 15 min. + marinating **GRILL:** 10 min.
YIELD: 4 servings

BEVERLY OFERRALL • LINKWOOD, MARYLAND

Mango, ginger and curry combine with a splash of lime juice to coat this juicy, grilled shrimp. Stuffed in pitas, the shrimp combo makes for an easy-to-hold, fabulous entree! You could also serve it on a bed of rice.

- 1/2 cup mango chutney
- 3 Tbsp. lime juice
- 1 tsp. grated fresh gingerroot
- 1/2 tsp. curry powder
- 1 lb. uncooked large shrimp, peeled and deveined
- 2 pita breads (6 in.), halved
- 8 Bibb *or* Boston lettuce leaves
- 1 large tomato, thinly sliced

1. In a small bowl, combine the chutney, lime juice, ginger and curry. Pour 1/2 cup marinade into a large resealable plastic bag; add the shrimp. Seal bag and turn to coat; refrigerate for at least 15 minutes. Cover and refrigerate remaining marinade.

2. Drain and discard marinade. Thread shrimp onto four metal or soaked wooden skewers. Using long-handled tongs, moisten a paper towel with cooking oil and lightly coat the grill rack. Grill shrimp, covered, over medium heat or broil 4 in. from the heat for 6-8 minutes or until shrimp turn pink, turning frequently.

3. Fill pita halves with lettuce, tomato and shrimp; spoon reserved chutney mixture over filling.

Nutrition Facts: 1 filled pita half equals 230 calories, 2 g fat (trace saturated fat), 138 mg cholesterol, 410 mg sodium, 29 g carbohydrate, 1 g fiber, 22 g protein. **Diabetic Exchanges:** 3 lean meat, 2 starch.

MANGO SHRIMP PITAS

LIGHTENED-UP PASTA FAGIOLI SOUP

Curried Parsnip Soup F

PREP: 15 min. **COOK:** 35 min. **YIELD:** 6 servings

JULIE MATHIESON • BRISTOL, TENNESSEE

My mum used to make this recipe at home in England, where parsnips are more widely used than here. It's very aromatic and has a nice bite from the curry and pepper.

- 1 large onion, chopped
- 1 large carrot, chopped
- 1 Tbsp. butter
- 1 lb. parsnips, peeled and chopped
- 2 cans (14-1/2 oz. *each*) reduced-sodium chicken broth
- 1 tsp. curry powder
- 1/4 tsp. salt
- 1/4 tsp. pepper
- 1 cup fat-free milk

1. In a large saucepan, saute onion and carrot in butter until onion is tender. Add parsnips; cook 2 minutes longer. Stir in broth and seasonings. Bring to a boil. Reduce heat; cover and simmer for 12-15 minutes or until parsnips are tender.

2. Cool slightly. In a blender, process soup in batches until smooth. Return all to the pan; stir in milk and heat through.

Nutrition Facts: 1 cup equals 113 calories, 2 g fat (1 g saturated fat), 6 mg cholesterol, 513 mg sodium, 20 g carbohydrate, 5 g fiber, 5 g protein. **Diabetic Exchanges:** 1 starch, 1/2 fat.

Turkey Wraps with Maple Mustard Dressing

PREP/TOTAL TIME: 30 min. **YIELD:** 4 servings

MICHELLE FRATI • MANORVILLE, NEW YORK

These came about when I needed to make a meal with the few ingredients I had in my fridge. Now they're a favorite.

- 8 fresh asparagus spears
- 4 tsp. stone-ground mustard
- 1 Tbsp. fat-free mayonnaise
- 1 Tbsp. maple syrup
- 4 whole wheat tortilla (8 in.), warmed
- 1/2 lb. sliced deli turkey
- 1/2 medium ripe avocado, peeled and sliced
- 2 turkey bacon strips, diced and cooked
- 1 cup shredded lettuce
- 1/8 tsp. pepper

1. In a large skillet, bring 3 cups water to a boil. Add asparagus; cover and cook for 2-4 minutes. Drain and immediately place asparagus in ice water. Drain and pat dry.

2. Combine the mustard, mayonnaise and syrup; spread over each tortilla. Layer with turkey, avocado, bacon, lettuce and asparagus. Sprinkle with pepper. Roll up and secure with toothpicks.

Nutrition Facts: 1 wrap equals 288 calories, 9 g fat (1 g saturated fat), 28 mg cholesterol, 894 mg sodium, 32 g carbohydrate, 5 g fiber, 18 g protein.

Italian Tortellini Soup

PREP: 15 min. **COOK:** 25 min. **YIELD:** 8 servings (2 qt.)

GILDA LESTER • MILLSBORO, DELAWARE

You can pick up everything for this hearty soup at the supermarket on the way home, then put it together in minutes. To save more time, purchase sliced mushrooms. Serve with crusty bread and salad greens.

CURRIED PARSNIP SOUP

TURKEY WRAPS WITH MAPLE MUSTARD DRESSING

1/2	lb. sliced fresh mushrooms
2	tsp. olive oil
4-1/2	cups water
1	can (14-1/2 oz.) no-salt-added diced tomatoes, undrained
3	Tbsp. grated Romano cheese
5	tsp. sodium-free chicken bouillon granules
1	Tbsp. prepared pesto
1	jar (7 oz.) roasted sweet red peppers, drained
1	pkg. (9 oz.) refrigerated cheese tortellini

GARNISH:

8	thin slices prosciutto *or* deli ham
8	tsp. grated Romano cheese

1. In a Dutch oven, saute mushrooms in oil until tender. Add the water, tomatoes, cheese, bouillon and prepared pesto.

2. Place peppers in a food processor; cover and process until blended. Add to mushroom mixture and bring to a boil. Reduce the heat; cover and simmer for 10 minutes.

3. Stir in the tortellini; return to a boil. Cook for 7-9 minutes or until tender, stirring occasionally. Cut the prosciutto into thin strips; garnish each individual serving with 1 slice prosciutto and 1 tsp. cheese. Serve immediately.

Nutrition Facts: 1 cup equals 201 calories, 8 g fat (3 g saturated fat), 32 mg cholesterol, 609 mg sodium, 20 g carbohydrate, 2 g fiber, 12 g protein. **Diabetic Exchanges:** 1 starch, 1 medium-fat meat, 1 vegetable.

Plum Chicken Wraps

PREP/TOTAL TIME: 20 min. **YIELD:** 4 servings

JENNIFER MICHALICEK • PHOENIX, ARIZONA

Dinner's a wrap with this easy, nutritious recipe that's loaded with the fruity flavors of pineapple and plum. It makes a sweet-and-sour chicken handheld specialty that is hard to beat any time of the year.

1	can (8 oz.) unsweetened crushed pineapple, drained
1/3	cup plum sauce
1	Tbsp. rice vinegar
1/2	tsp. sesame oil
2	cups cubed cooked chicken breast
1/2	cup chopped green onions
1/4	cup salted cashews
2	medium fresh plums, sliced
12	Boston or Bibb lettuce leaves

1. In a large saucepan, combine the pineapple, plum sauce, vinegar and oil. Cook and stir over medium heat for 5 minutes.

2. Stir in the chicken, green onions and cashews; heat through. Remove from the heat; stir in plums. Place 1/3 cup chicken mixture on each lettuce leaf. Fold lettuce over filling.

Nutrition Facts: 3 filled wraps equals 298 calories, 8 g fat (2 g saturated fat), 54 mg cholesterol, 237 mg sodium, 32 g carbohydrate, 2 g fiber, 23 g protein. **Diabetic Exchanges:** 3 lean meat, 1-1/2 fruit, 1 fat, 1/2 starch.

SESAME GREEN BEANS

DIJON VEGGIES WITH COUSCOUS

HERB-TOPPED STUFFED TOMATOES

Side Dishes

Take vegetables to new heights with the flavorful assortment of side dishes found here. Let items such as Thai-Style Green Beans, Nutty Gingered Carrots and Sesame Snap Peas add a bit of flair to your menu!

Herb-Topped Stuffed Tomatoes M

PREP/TOTAL TIME: 25 min. YIELD: 4 servings

MARY RELYEA • CANASTOTA, NEW YORK

This simple treatment perfectly complements the fresh taste of tomatoes. Serve it as a side dish to any entree or as a fresh summer appetizer.

- 1 cup chopped onion
- 1 garlic clove, minced
- 1 Tbsp. plus 2 tsp. butter, *divided*
- 1/4 cup plus 1 Tbsp. seasoned bread crumbs
- 2 Tbsp. grated Parmesan cheese
- 4 large tomatoes, halved
- 1 Tbsp. chopped fresh basil
- 1 Tbsp. minced fresh parsley

1. In a small skillet, saute onion and garlic in 1 Tbsp. butter until tender. Melt remaining butter. In a small bowl, combine the onion mixture, bread crumbs, cheese and melted butter. Spoon 2 Tbsp. onto each tomato half.

2. Place on a baking sheet. Broil 8 in. from the heat for 4-5 minutes or until lightly browned. Sprinkle with basil and parsley. Serve immediately.

Nutrition Facts: 2 halves equals 143 calories, 7 g fat (4 g saturated fat), 15 mg cholesterol, 247 mg sodium, 19 g carbohydrate, 3 g fiber, 4 g protein.

Sesame Green Beans F C M

PREP/TOTAL TIME: 30 min. YIELD: 6 servings

NOELLE MYERS • GRAND FORKS, NORTH DAKOTA

With Asian-inspired flair, this treatment for green beans is simply wonderful with light dishes such as marinated and grilled salmon. The colors also make it nice for holiday menus, so it's one dish you'll turn to all year long.

- 1 lb. fresh green beans, trimmed
- 1 medium sweet red pepper, julienned
- 1 Tbsp. sesame seeds
- 1 Tbsp. rice vinegar
- 1 Tbsp. sesame oil
- 1 Tbsp. reduced-sodium soy sauce

- 1/4 tsp. salt
- 1/4 tsp. pepper

1. Place beans and red pepper in a 15-in. x 10-in. x 1-in. baking pan coated with cooking spray. Combine the remaining ingredients. Drizzle over vegetables; stir to coat.

2. Bake, uncovered, at 425° for 20-25 minutes or until beans are tender, stirring once.

Nutrition Facts: 2/3 cup equals 55 calories, 3 g fat (trace saturated fat), 0 cholesterol, 205 mg sodium, 7 g carbohydrate, 3 g fiber, 2 g protein. **Diabetic Exchanges:** 1 vegetable, 1/2 fat.

Sweet & Sour Carrots F M

PREP/TOTAL TIME: 30 min. YIELD: 6 servings

DELORES ROMYN • STRATTON, ONTARIO

I wanted to try serving carrots differently, and everyone raved over these. You'll love the combination of flavors and colors.

- 1 lb. medium carrots, cut into 1-in. slices
- 1 medium green pepper, cut into 1-in. chunks
- 1 can (20 oz.) unsweetened pineapple chunks, undrained
- 1/4 cup sugar
- 1 Tbsp. cornstarch
- 1/2 tsp. salt
- 2 Tbsp. cider vinegar
- 2 Tbsp. reduced-sodium soy sauce

1. Place 1 in. of water and carrots in a large saucepan. Bring to a boil. Reduce heat; cover and simmer for 7-9 minutes or until crisp-tender. Add green pepper. Cover and cook 3 minutes longer or until tender. Drain and set aside.

2. Drain pineapple, reserving juice; add enough water to the juice to measure 3/4 cup. Set pineapple aside. In a large saucepan, combine the sugar, cornstarch and salt. Stir in the pineapple juice mixture, vinegar and soy sauce until smooth. Bring to a boil. Cook and stir for 2 minutes or until thickened and bubbly. Stir in the reserved carrots and pineapple; heat through.

Nutrition Facts: 2/3 cup equals 123 calories, trace fat (trace saturated fat), 0 cholesterol, 459 mg sodium, 30 g carbohydrate, 3 g fiber, 1 g protein. **Diabetic Exchanges:** 1 vegetable, 1 fruit, 1/2 starch.

Honey Mustard Carrots F M

PREP/TOTAL TIME: 20 min. YIELD: 10 servings

TRISHA KRUSE • EAGLE, IDAHO

Wonderful color and flavor make fresh carrots a standout side dish for almost any entree you serve to loved ones.

- 4 pkg. (10 oz. *each*) julienned carrots
- 1/2 cup honey
- 1/4 cup honey mustard
- 4 tsp. butter
- 1/2 tsp. salt

1. Place 1 in. of water in a large saucepan; add carrots. Bring to a boil. Reduce heat; cover and simmer for 3-4 minutes or until crisp-tender. Drain and set aside.

2. In a small saucepan, combine the remaining ingredients. Bring to a boil; cook and stir for 2-3 minutes or until slightly thickened. Pour over carrots; heat through.

Nutrition Facts: 1/2 cup equals 125 calories, 2 g fat (1 g saturated fat), 4 mg cholesterol, 259 mg sodium, 28 g carbohydrate, 3 g fiber, 1 g protein. **Diabetic Exchanges:** 2 vegetable, 1 starch, 1/2 fat.

Spiced Rhubarb Sauce F C

PREP: 20 min. COOK: 50 min. YIELD: 2-1/2 cups

KARA HAWKE • POLK, PENNSYLVANIA

Served here with pork chops, this unique sauce adds bold flavor to just about any cut of pork. The sweet-savory relish-like sauce is also a perfect complement to any variety of roasted, baked or grilled poultry.

- 4 cups chopped fresh or frozen rhubarb, thawed
- 2 large onions, chopped
- 1 medium green pepper, chopped
- 3/4 cup packed brown sugar
- 3/4 cup cider vinegar
- 1/4 cup reduced-sodium soy sauce
- 2 tsp. steak seasoning
- 1 garlic clove, minced
- 1/2 tsp. celery seed
- 1/2 tsp. ground coriander
- 1/2 tsp. ground cinnamon
- 1/2 tsp. ground allspice

1. In a large saucepan, combine all ingredients. Bring to a boil. Reduce heat; simmer, uncovered, for 45-50 minutes or until thickened. Serve warm with chicken or pork. Refrigerate leftovers.

Editor's Note: If using frozen rhubarb, measure rhubarb while still frozen, then thaw completely. Drain in a colander, but do not press liquid out. This recipe was tested with McCormick's Montreal Steak Seasoning. Look for it in the spice aisle.

Nutrition Facts: 2 Tbsp. equals 48 calories, trace fat (trace saturated fat), 0 cholesterol, 195 mg sodium, 11 g carbohydrate, 1 g fiber, 1 g protein. **Diabetic Exchange:** 1 starch.

Quinoa Pilaf M

5 PP ✓

PREP/TOTAL TIME: 30 min. YIELD: 4 servings

SONYA FOX • PEYTON, COLORADO

I created this recipe after tasting quinoa at a local restaurant. I really enjoy rice pilaf, but I don't usually have time to make it. This quick-cooking side is a tasty alternative.

- 1 medium onion, chopped
- 1 medium carrot, finely chopped
- 1 tsp. olive oil
- 1 garlic clove, minced
- 1 can (14-1/2 oz.) reduced-sodium chicken broth *or* vegetable broth
- 1/4 cup water
- 1/4 tsp. salt
- 1 cup quinoa, rinsed

HONEY MUSTARD CARROTS

QUINOA PILAF

1. In a small nonstick saucepan coated with cooking spray, cook onion and carrot in oil for 2-3 minutes or until crisp-tender. Add garlic; cook 1 minute longer. Stir in the broth, water and salt; bring to a boil.

2. Stir in quinoa; return to a boil. Reduce heat; cover and simmer for 12-15 minutes or until liquid is absorbed. Remove from the heat; let stand for 5 minutes. Fluff with a fork.

Editor's Note: Look for quinoa in the cereal, rice or organic food aisle.

Nutrition Facts: 3/4 cup equals 198 calories, 4 g fat (trace saturated fat), 0 cholesterol, 434 mg sodium, 35 g carbohydrate, 4 g fiber, 8 g protein. **Diabetic Exchanges:** 2 starch, 1/2 fat.

Feta Zucchini Pancakes S C M

2PPV

PREP/TOTAL TIME: 25 min. YIELD: 8 pancakes

DIANA JOHNSON • AUBURN, WASHINGTON

Fun and flavorful, these rustic veggie pancakes make a wonderfully versatile side dish. They're also a great solution for what to do with all your extra zucchini!

1	cup shredded zucchini
1/4	cup panko (Japanese) bread crumbs
2	green onions, chopped
1	egg
3	Tbsp. minced fresh parsley
1	Tbsp. snipped fresh dill
1	garlic clove, minced
1/4	cup crumbled feta cheese
3	tsp. olive oil, *divided*

1. In a sieve or colander, drain zucchini, squeezing to remove excess liquid. Pat dry. In a small bowl, combine the zucchini, bread crumbs, onions, egg, parsley, dill, garlic and cheese.

2. Heat 1-1/2 tsp. oil in a large nonstick skillet over medium-low heat. Drop the batter by heaping tablespoonfuls into oil; press lightly to flatten. Fry in batches until golden brown on both sides, using remaining oil as needed.

Nutrition Facts: 2 pancakes equals 91 calories, 6 g fat (2 g saturated fat), 57 mg cholesterol, 104 mg sodium, 5 g carbohydrate, 1 g fiber, 4 g protein. **Diabetic Exchanges:** 1 fat, 1/2 starch.

When a recipe calls for green onions, it can be easier and faster to cut them with a **kitchen scissors** than with a knife. If the recipe calls for quite a few, grab a bunch of onions at one time and snip away. This saves time washing a cutting board, too.

Herbed Fennel and Onion C

PREP/TOTAL TIME: 30 min. **YIELD:** 3 servings

MEGHANN MINTON • PORTLAND, OREGON

Wondering what to do with those fennel bulbs you brought home from the market? Try them in this aromatic and savory side dish that's so rich, no one will guess it's healthy. Vinegar adds a slight tang.

- 1 large sweet onion, halved and sliced
- 1 medium fennel bulb, halved and cut into 1/2-in. slices
- 1 Tbsp. olive oil
- 1 cup reduced-sodium chicken broth
- 1 Tbsp. minced fresh sage *or* 1 tsp. dried sage leaves
- 2 tsp. minced fresh rosemary *or* 1/2 tsp. dried rosemary, crushed
- 2 tsp. balsamic vinegar
- 1/4 tsp. salt
- 1/4 tsp. pepper

1. In a large skillet, saute onion and fennel in oil until crisp-tender. Add the broth, sage and rosemary. Bring to a boil; cook until broth is evaporated.

2. Remove from the heat; stir in the vinegar, salt and pepper.

Nutrition Facts: 1/2 cup equals 109 calories, 5 g fat (1 g saturated fat), 0 cholesterol, 437 mg sodium, 15 g carbohydrate, 3 g fiber, 3 g protein. **Diabetic Exchanges:** 2 vegetable, 1 fat.

Pear Cranberry Sauce F S

PREP: 10 min. **COOK:** 15 min. + chilling **YIELD:** 3 cups

DEB WILLIAMS • PEORIA, ARIZONA

Pears and ginger turn a classic side into something spectacular. Best of all, it calls for just a moment of hands-on work.

- 1 pkg. (12 oz.) fresh *or* frozen cranberries
- 2 medium pears, peeled and cubed
- 1 cup sugar
- 3/4 cup water
- 1 to 2 tsp. minced fresh gingerroot
- 1/4 tsp. ground cinnamon
- 1/8 tsp. salt

1. In a large saucepan, combine all ingredients. Cook over medium heat until berries pop, about 15 minutes. Transfer to a small bowl; refrigerate until chilled.

Nutrition Facts: 1/4 cup equals 94 calories, trace fat (trace saturated fat), 0 cholesterol, 25 mg sodium, 24 g carbohydrate, 2 g fiber, trace protein. **Diabetic Exchanges:** 1 starch, 1/2 fruit.

Parsnips & Turnips Au Gratin

PREP: 20 min. **BAKE:** 15 min. **YIELD:** 8 servings

PRISCILLA GILBERT • INDIAN HARBOUR BEACH, FLORIDA

This is a delicious variation on au gratin that features something besides potatoes. I sometimes substitute rutabaga for the turnips. It's a well-guarded recipe in my collection. Until now that is!

1-1/2 lbs. parsnips, peeled and sliced
1-1/4 lbs. turnips, peeled and sliced
   1 can (10-3/4 oz.) reduced-fat reduced-sodium condensed cream of celery soup, undiluted
   1 cup fat-free milk
1/2 tsp. pepper
   1 cup (4 oz.) shredded sharp cheddar cheese
1/2 cup panko (Japanese) bread crumbs
   1 Tbsp. butter, melted

1. Place parsnips and turnips in a large saucepan; cover with water. Bring to a boil. Reduce heat; simmer, uncovered, for 5-7 minutes or until crisp-tender.

2. Meanwhile, in a small saucepan, combine the soup, milk and pepper. Bring to a boil; remove from the heat. Stir in cheese until melted.

3. Drain vegetables; transfer to an 11-in. x 7-in. baking dish coated with cooking spray. Pour sauce over vegetables.

4. Combine the bread crumbs and butter; sprinkle over the top. Bake, uncovered, at 400° for 15-20 minutes or until vegetables are tender and crumbs are golden brown.

Nutrition Facts: 3/4 cup equals 189 calories, 7 g fat (4 g saturated fat), 21 mg cholesterol, 309 mg sodium, 27 g carbohydrate, 4 g fiber, 7 g protein. **Diabetic Exchanges:** 1 starch, 1 high-fat meat, 1 vegetable.

Lemon Beans With Prosciutto C

PREP/TOTAL TIME: 25 min. YIELD: 6 servings

LORI WIESE • HUMBOLDT, MINNESOTA

There's nothing ordinary about these green beans. Prosciutto and white wine make them decadent and special.

   8 thin slices prosciutto *or* deli ham, julienned
   2 tsp. olive oil
1/2 cup white wine *or* reduced-sodium chicken broth
1/4 cup lemon juice
   2 Tbsp. butter
1-1/2 lbs. fresh green beans, trimmed

1. In a large nonstick skillet coated with cooking spray, cook prosciutto in oil over medium heat until crisp. Remove to paper towels with a slotted spoon; drain.

2. In the same skillet, combine the wine, lemon juice and butter. Bring to a boil. Reduce heat; simmer, uncovered, for 5-6 minutes or until sauce is reduced by half.

3. Meanwhile, place beans in a large saucepan and cover with water. Bring to a boil. Cover and cook for 4-7 minutes or until crisp-tender; drain. Add beans to skillet; toss to coat. Sprinkle with prosciutto just before serving.

Nutrition Facts: 3/4 cup equals 127 calories, 8 g fat (3 g saturated fat), 27 mg cholesterol, 397 mg sodium, 8 g carbohydrate, 3 g fiber, 7 g protein. **Diabetic Exchanges:** 1 lean meat, 1 vegetable, 1 fat.

Easy Sauteed Spinach F C M

PREP/TOTAL TIME: 20 min. YIELD: 4 servings

HEALTHY COOKING TEST KITCHEN

Here's a light, lively side to complement almost any entree you put on the table. A little Test Kitchen know-how helps to dress up everyday spinach with garlic, onion, a lick of sherry and a sprinkling of pine nuts.

   1 small onion, finely chopped
   1 garlic clove, minced
   2 pkg. (6 oz. *each*) fresh baby spinach
   3 Tbsp. sherry *or* reduced-sodium chicken broth
1/4 tsp. salt
1/8 tsp. pepper
   1 Tbsp. pine nuts

1. In a large nonstick skillet coated with cooking spray, saute onion until tender. Add garlic; cook 1 minute longer. Stir in the spinach, sherry, salt and pepper; cook and stir for 4-5 minutes or until spinach is wilted. Sprinkle with pine nuts.

Nutrition Facts: 1/2 cup equals 47 calories, 1 g fat (trace saturated fat), 0 cholesterol, 216 mg sodium, 5 g carbohydrate, 2 g fiber, 3 g protein. **Diabetic Exchange:** 1 vegetable.

> Minced garlic that you can buy, garlic that's been finely chopped by hand and garlic that's been put through a press can all be used **interchangeably** in recipes. Choose whichever is easiest and most convenient for you.

EASY SAUTEED SPINACH

Broccoli-Cauliflower Cheese Bake C M

3 pts

PREP: 35 min. BAKE: 20 min. YIELD: 16 servings

JENN TIDWELL • FAIR OAKS, CALIFORNIA

Creamy mozzarella and Swiss cheeses create the base for these tasty veggies, while a hint of cayenne pepper gives them a kick guests will adore.

7	cups fresh cauliflowerets
6	cups fresh broccoli florets
3	Tbsp. butter
1/3	cup all-purpose flour
1-1/2	tsp. spicy brown mustard
3/4	tsp. salt
1/4	tsp. ground nutmeg
1/4	tsp. cayenne pepper
1/4	tsp. pepper
3-3/4	cups fat-free milk
1-1/2	cups (6 oz.) shredded part-skim mozzarella cheese, *divided*
1-1/2	cups (6 oz.) shredded Swiss cheese, *divided*

1. Place cauliflower and broccoli in a Dutch oven; add 1 in. of water. Bring to a boil. Reduce heat; cover and simmer for 3-5 minutes or until crisp-tender. Drain; transfer to a 13-in. x 9-in. baking dish coated with cooking spray.

2. In small saucepan, melt butter. Stir in the flour, mustard, salt, nutmeg, cayenne and pepper until smooth; gradually add milk. Bring to a boil; cook and stir for 1-2 minutes or until thickened.

3. Stir in 1-1/4 cups each mozzarella and Swiss cheeses until melted. Pour over vegetables. Bake, uncovered, at 400° for 15-20 minutes or until bubbly. Sprinkle with remaining cheeses. Bake 5 minutes longer or until golden brown.

Nutrition Facts: 3/4 cup equals 132 calories, 7 g fat (4 g saturated fat), 22 mg cholesterol, 252 mg sodium, 9 g carbohydrate, 2 g fiber, 9 g protein. **Diabetic Exchanges:** 1 high-fat meat, 1 vegetable.

BROCCOLI-CAULIFLOWER CHEESE BAKE

Moist Turkey Sausage Stuffing

PREP: 20 min. COOK: 20 min.
YIELD: 16 servings (2/3 cup each)

5 pts

PRISCILLA GILBERT • INDIAN HARBOUR BEACH, FLORIDA

With tangy apricots and turkey sausage, this stuffing is a terrific mix of sweet and savory.

1	pkg. (19-1/2 oz.) Italian turkey sausage links, casings removed
4	celery ribs, chopped
1	large onion, chopped
1-1/2	cups chopped dried apricots
1/4	cup minced fresh parsley
1	Tbsp. minced fresh sage *or* 1 tsp. dried sage
1	tsp. poultry seasoning
1/4	tsp. pepper
3	tsp. sodium-free chicken bouillon granules
3-1/4	cups boiling water
1	pkg. (14 oz.) crushed corn bread stuffing
1	cup fresh *or* frozen cranberries, chopped

1. In a Dutch oven, cook the turkey sausage, celery and onion over medium heat until meat is no longer pink and vegetables are tender; drain. Stir in the apricots, parsley, sage, poultry seasoning and pepper; cook 3 minutes longer.

2. Dissolve bouillon in boiling water; stir into sausage mixture. Stir in corn bread stuffing; cook and stir until liquid is absorbed. Gently stir in cranberries; heat through.

Editor's Note: This recipe makes enough stuffing to stuff a 14-lb. turkey. Bake until a meat thermometer reads 180° for turkey and 165° for stuffing.

Nutrition Facts: 2/3 cup equals 205 calories, 5 g fat (1 g saturated fat), 21 mg cholesterol, 540 mg sodium, 32 g carbohydrate, 3 g fiber, 9 g protein. **Diabetic Exchanges:** 2 starch, 1 lean meat.

Cheddar Mashed Potatoes M

PREP: 35 min. COOK: 10 min.
YIELD: 12 servings (3/4 cup each)

5 pts P

CONNIE BOLL • CHILTON, WISCONSIN

A sweet potato added to the usual Yukon Golds gives these cheesy potatoes a slightly sweet flavor and nice rich color. No one will believe they're lighter.

3-3/4	lbs. Yukon Gold potatoes, peeled and cubed
1	large sweet potato, peeled and cubed
6	garlic cloves, halved
1	cup (8 oz.) reduced-fat sour cream
1	tsp. minced fresh thyme *or* 1/4 tsp. dried thyme
1-1/2	tsp. salt
1/2	tsp. pepper
2	cups (8 oz.) shredded reduced-fat cheddar cheese, *divided*

1. Place potatoes and garlic in a large saucepan and cover with water. Bring to a boil. Reduce heat; cover and cook for 10-15 minutes or until potatoes are tender. Drain.

GRILLED ITALIAN EGGPLANT SLICES

2. In a large bowl, mash potatoes. Stir in the sour cream, thyme, salt, pepper and 1 cup cheese. Transfer to a 3-qt. baking dish coated with cooking spray. Sprinkle with remaining cheese. Bake, uncovered, at 350° for 10-15 minutes or until heated through.

Nutrition Facts: 3/4 cup equals 179 calories, 6 g fat (4 g saturated fat), 19 mg cholesterol, 434 mg sodium, 25 g carbohydrate, 2 g fiber, 8 g protein. **Diabetic Exchanges:** 1-1/2 starch, 1 medium-fat meat.

Grilled Italian Eggplant Slices S C M

PREP/TOTAL TIME: 25 min. **YIELD:** 5 servings

THERESA LASALLE • MIDLOTHIAN, VIRGINIA

What a fabulous way to dress up eggplant! Piled high with herbs, cheese and fresh tomatoes, this fail-proof, grilled side nicely matches a variety of main dishes.

1/4	cup shredded Parmesan cheese
3	Tbsp. lemon juice
2	Tbsp. minced fresh basil
5	tsp. olive oil
3	garlic cloves, minced
1	tsp. minced fresh oregano
1	large eggplant, cut into 10 slices
10	slices tomato
1/2	cup shredded part-skim mozzarella cheese

1. In a small bowl, combine the first six ingredients.

2. Grill eggplant, covered, over medium heat for 3 minutes. Turn slices; spoon Parmesan mixture onto each. Top with tomato; sprinkle with mozzarella cheese. Grill, covered, 2-3 minutes longer or until cheese is melted.

Nutrition Facts: 2 eggplant slices equals 134 calories, 8 g fat (3 g saturated fat), 9 mg cholesterol, 129 mg sodium, 12 g carbohydrate, 4 g fiber, 6 g protein. **Diabetic Exchanges:** 2 vegetable, 1 medium-fat meat.

Makeover Scalloped Pineapple M

PREP: 10 min. **BAKE:** 50 min. **YIELD:** 12 servings

NANCY BROWN • DAHINDA, ILLINOIS

This sweet holiday side dish is buttery, sugary and big on pineapple flavor, but now it's not nearly as bad for you as the original. In fact, you might not want to wait on the holidays.

1/2	cup butter, softened
1-1/2	cups sugar
4	eggs
4	egg whites
2	cans (20 oz. *each*) unsweetened crushed pineapple, undrained
1/2	cup fat-free milk
8	cups cubed bread

1. In a large bowl, beat butter and sugar until crumbly, about 2 minutes. Add eggs and egg whites, one at a time, beating well after each addition. Stir in pineapple and milk; add bread cubes and toss to coat.

2. Transfer to a 13-in. x 9-in. baking dish coated with cooking spray. Bake, uncovered, at 350° for 50-55 minutes or until bread cubes are lightly browned. Serve warm. Refrigerate leftovers.

Nutrition Facts: 1 cup equals 316 calories, 10 g fat (5 g saturated fat), 91 mg cholesterol, 260 mg sodium, 52 g carbohydrate, 1 g fiber, 6 g protein.

Creamed Garden Potatoes and Peas [M]

PREP/TOTAL TIME: 25 min. **YIELD:** 12 servings

JANE UPHOFF • CUNNINGHAM, KANSAS

New potatoes and colorful peas are treated to a creamy sauce for this special side dish.

2	lbs. small red potatoes, quartered
3	cups fresh or frozen peas
1	cup water
2	Tbsp. chopped onion
2	Tbsp. butter
3	Tbsp. plus 1 tsp. all-purpose flour
1-1/2	tsp. salt
1/4	tsp. pepper
2	cups 2% milk
1	cup half-and-half cream

1. Place potatoes in a large saucepan and cover with water. Bring to a boil. Reduce heat; cover and simmer for 8-12 minutes or until tender. Drain.

2. Meanwhile, place peas and water in a small saucepan. Bring to a boil. Reduce heat; cover and simmer for 3-5 minutes or until tender. Drain.

3. In a large saucepan, saute onion in butter until tender. Stir in the flour, salt and pepper until blended; gradually add milk and cream. Bring to a boil; cook and stir for 2 minutes or until thickened. Stir in potatoes and peas; heat through.

Nutrition Facts: 2/3 cup equals 156 calories, 5 g fat (3 g saturated fat), 18 mg cholesterol, 345 mg sodium, 22 g carbohydrate, 3 g fiber, 6 g protein. **Diabetic Exchanges:** 1-1/2 starch, 1 fat.

Sesame Snap Peas [S] [C] [M]

PREP/TOTAL TIME: 15 min. **YIELD:** 8 servings

HEALTHY COOKING TEST KITCHEN

With their fresh taste, these colorful snap peas make an ideal partner for most any entree. Sweet red pepper adds a pop to this sesame-infused favorite.

1-1/2	lbs. fresh sugar snap peas
1	small sweet red pepper, chopped
2	Tbsp. butter
1	Tbsp. sesame seeds, toasted
1	Tbsp. reduced-sodium soy sauce
1/8	tsp. pepper

1. In a large nonstick skillet, saute peas and red pepper in butter until crisp-tender. Stir in the remaining ingredients; heat through.

Nutrition Facts: 3/4 cup equals 70 calories, 4 g fat (2 g saturated fat), 8 mg cholesterol, 105 mg sodium, 7 g carbohydrate, 3 g fiber, 3 g protein. **Diabetic Exchanges:** 1 vegetable, 1/2 fat.

Dijon Veggies With Couscous [M]

PREP: 20 min. **BAKE:** 20 min. **YIELD:** 6 servings

JULIANA DUMITRU • FAIRVIEW PARK, OHIO

Coated in a tangy Dijon sauce, these tasty veggies and fluffy couscous make for a delightful side.

1/2	lb. medium fresh mushrooms, quartered
1	medium zucchini, halved lengthwise and cut into 1/4-in. slices

1	medium sweet red pepper, cut into 1-in. pieces
1/4	cup dry red wine *or* reduced-sodium chicken broth
3	Tbsp. Dijon mustard
2	Tbsp. olive oil
2	garlic cloves, minced
1	tsp. prepared horseradish
1/2	tsp. salt
1/4	tsp. pepper
1	cup water
1	cup uncooked couscous

1. Place an 18-in. x 12-in. piece of heavy-duty foil on a large baking sheet; set aside.

2. In a large bowl, combine the mushrooms, zucchini and red pepper. Combine the wine, mustard, oil, garlic, horseradish, salt and pepper; drizzle over vegetables. Toss to coat; transfer to baking sheet. Top with a second large piece of foil. Bring edges of foil pieces together; crimp to seal, forming a large packet.

3. Bake at 350° for 20-25 minutes or until vegetables are tender.

4. Meanwhile, in a small saucepan, bring water to a boil. Stir in couscous. Remove from the heat; cover and let stand for 5-10 minutes or until water is absorbed. Fluff with a fork. Transfer couscous and vegetables to a large serving bowl; toss to combine.

Nutrition Facts: 1 cup equals 182 calories, 5 g fat (1 g saturated fat), 0 cholesterol, 388 mg sodium, 29 g carbohydrate, 3 g fiber, 6 g protein. **Diabetic Exchanges:** 1-1/2 starch, 1 vegetable, 1 fat.

Garden Risotto F

PREP: 20 min. **COOK:** 25 min. **YIELD:** 8 servings

KENDRA DOSS • KANSAS CITY, MISSOURI

With asparagus, spinach and peas, this simple dish adds spectacular flavor and lots of health benefits from green veggies. Add some Parmesan cheese, and you've got one delectable delight!

1/2	lb. fresh asparagus, trimmed and cut into 3/4-in. pieces
4-1/2	cups reduced-sodium chicken broth
1	medium onion, chopped
2	tsp. olive oil
1-1/2	cups uncooked arborio rice
1/2	cup dry white wine *or* additional reduced-sodium chicken broth
1/2	tsp. salt
1/4	tsp. pepper
3	cups fresh baby spinach
1	cup frozen peas
1/4	cup grated Parmesan cheese

1. Place asparagus in a steamer basket; place in a small saucepan over 1 in. of water. Bring to a boil; cover and steam for 2-3 minutes or until crisp-tender. Set aside.

2. Meanwhile, in a small saucepan, heat broth and keep warm. In a large nonstick skillet coated with cooking spray, saute onion in oil until tender. Add rice; cook and stir for 2-3 minutes. Reduce heat; stir in the wine, salt and pepper. Cook and stir until all of the liquid is absorbed.

3. Add heated broth, 1/2 cup at a time, stirring constantly. Allow the liquid to absorb between additions. Cook just until risotto is creamy and rice is almost tender. (Cooking time is about 20 minutes.)

4. Add the spinach, peas, cheese and reserved asparagus; cook and stir until heated through. Serve immediately.

Nutrition Facts: 3/4 cup equals 203 calories, 2 g fat (1 g saturated fat), 2 mg cholesterol, 539 mg sodium, 36 g carbohydrate, 2 g fiber, 7 g protein.

GARDEN RISOTTO

DIJON VEGGIES WITH COUSCOUS

Sweet Potato Delight F S M

PREP: 25 min. **BAKE:** 30 min. **YIELD:** 10 servings

MARLENE KROLL • CHICAGO, ILLINOIS

My family wouldn't dream of a Thanksgiving dinner without this side dish, but it's great anytime—I serve it once a month. The fluffy texture and subtle orange flavor make it a standout.

4	large sweet potatoes, peeled and quartered
1/2	cup orange marmalade
1/2	cup orange juice
1/4	cup packed brown sugar
1/2	tsp. almond extract
3	egg whites
1/4	cup slivered almonds

1. Place sweet potatoes in a Dutch oven; cover with water. Bring to a boil. Reduce heat; cover and cook for 15-20 minutes or just until tender. Drain potatoes; place in a large bowl and mash. Stir in the orange marmalade, orange juice, brown sugar and extract. Cool slightly.

2. In a small bowl, beat egg whites until stiff peaks form. Fold into sweet potato mixture. Transfer to a 2-1/2-qt. baking dish coated with cooking spray. Sprinkle with almonds. Bake, uncovered, at 350° for 30-35 minutes or until a thermometer reads 160°.

Nutrition Facts: 3/4 cup equals 174 calories, 1 g fat (trace saturated fat), 0 cholesterol, 36 mg sodium, 38 g carbohydrate, 3 g fiber, 3 g protein. **Diabetic Exchange:** 2 starch.

SWEET POTATO DELIGHT

Nutty Gingered Carrots C M

PREP/TOTAL TIME: 30 min. **YIELD:** 6 servings

JEANNE HOLT • SAINT PAUL, MINNESOTA

My mother makes a delicious carrot and onion side dish, but it calls for a whole stick of butter. My lighter version uses only 1 tablespoon and relies on some lively Asian flavors to make up the difference.

1	large onion, chopped
2	tsp. canola oil
1	tsp. minced fresh gingerroot
6	large carrots, sliced
2/3	cup orange juice
1	Tbsp. butter
2	tsp. honey
1	tsp. grated orange peel
1/4	tsp. salt
1/8	tsp. pepper
1/4	cup chopped walnuts, toasted
1	Tbsp. minced fresh parsley

1. In a large skillet, saute onion in oil until tender. Add ginger; cook 1 minute longer. Stir in the carrots, orange juice, butter, honey, orange peel, salt and pepper.

2. Bring to a boil. Reduce heat; cover and simmer for 12-15 minutes or until carrots are tender. Stir in walnuts and sprinkle with parsley.

Nutrition Facts: 2/3 cup equals 122 calories, 7 g fat (2 g saturated fat), 5 mg cholesterol, 163 mg sodium, 15 g carbohydrate, 3 g fiber, 2 g protein. **Diabetic Exchanges:** 2 vegetable, 1 fat.

Summer Squash Medley F C M

PREP/TOTAL TIME: 25 min. **YIELD:** 6 servings

JENNIFER LEIGHTY • WEST SALEM, OHIO

This dish is fantastic as a side, but you can also add some cooked turkey sausage and serve it over rice for a meal.

1	large sweet onion, chopped
1	medium yellow summer squash, chopped
1	large green pepper, chopped
1	Tbsp. olive oil
1	garlic clove, minced
2	large tomatoes, seeded and chopped
1-1/2	tsp. Italian seasoning
1	tsp. salt
1/2	tsp. pepper
1/8	tsp. crushed red pepper flakes, optional

1. In a large nonstick skillet, saute the onion, squash and green pepper in oil until crisp-tender. Add the garlic; cook 1 minute longer. Stir in the tomatoes, Italian seasoning, salt, pepper and pepper flakes if desired; heat through.

Nutrition Facts: 2/3 cup equals 61 calories, 3 g fat (trace saturated fat), 0 cholesterol, 403 mg sodium, 9 g carbohydrate, 2 g fiber, 2 g protein. **Diabetic Exchanges:** 2 vegetable, 1/2 fat.

Green Rice Pilaf

PREP: 35 min. **BAKE:** 15 min. **YIELD:** 6 servings

SHERRI MELOTIK • OAK CREEK, WISCONSIN

With its mild heat and full flavors, this side pairs well with a variety of entrees, especially Southwest or Mexican specialties.

- 1/4 cup finely chopped onion
- 1 Tbsp. canola oil
- 1 cup uncooked long grain rice
- 1 can (14-1/2 oz.) reduced-sodium chicken broth
- 1 can (4 oz.) chopped green chilies
- 1 jalapeno pepper, seeded and chopped
- 1/2 tsp. ground cumin
- 1/4 tsp. garlic powder
- 1/8 tsp. salt
- 1/2 cup shredded part-skim mozzarella cheese
- 1/2 cup minced fresh cilantro

1. In a large saucepan, saute onion in oil until tender. Add the rice; cook and stir for 2 minutes or until lightly browned.

2. Add broth, chilies, jalapeno, cumin, garlic powder and salt. Bring to a boil. Reduce heat; cover and simmer for 12-15 minutes or until liquid is absorbed.

3. Stir in cheese and cilantro. Transfer to a 1-1/2-qt. baking dish coated with cooking spray. Cover and bake at 375° for 14-16 minutes or until rice is tender.

Editor's Note: When cutting hot peppers, disposable gloves are recommended. Avoid touching your face.

Nutrition Facts: 2/3 cup equals 171 calories, 4 g fat (1 g saturated fat), 5 mg cholesterol, 368 mg sodium, 27 g carbohydrate, 1 g fiber, 6 g protein. **Diabetic Exchanges:** 1-1/2 starch, 1 fat.

Thai-Style Green Beans

PREP/TOTAL TIME: 20 min. **YIELD:** 2 servings

CANDACE MCMENAMIN • LEXINGTON, SOUTH CAROLINA

Two for Thai, anyone? Peanut butter and soy and hoisin sauces flavor this quick and fabulous treatment for green beans.

- 1 Tbsp. reduced-sodium soy sauce
- 1 Tbsp. hoisin sauce
- 1 Tbsp. creamy peanut butter
- 1/8 tsp. crushed red pepper flakes
- 1 Tbsp. chopped shallot
- 1 tsp. minced fresh gingerroot
- 1 Tbsp. canola oil
- 1/2 lb. fresh green beans, trimmed

Minced fresh cilantro and chopped dry roasted peanuts, optional

1. In a small bowl, combine the soy sauce, hoisin sauce, peanut butter and red pepper flakes; set aside.

2. In a small skillet, saute shallot and ginger in oil over medium heat for 2 minutes or until crisp-tender. Add green beans; cook and stir for 3 minutes or until crisp-tender. Add reserved sauce; toss to coat. Sprinkle with cilantro and peanuts if desired.

Nutrition Facts: 1 serving (calculated without peanuts) equals 168 calories, 12 g fat (1 g saturated fat), trace cholesterol, 476 mg sodium, 14 g carbohydrate, 4 g fiber, 5 g protein.

RICE AND BARLEY PILAF

Rice and Barley Pilaf

5 ppr.

PREP: 20 min. COOK: 1 hour YIELD: 6 servings

BARB TEMPLIN • NORWOOD, MINNESOTA

With a trio of whole grains, wild and brown rice and barley, this is packed with nutrition. Add half-and-half and Parmesan cheese, and you've got one satisfying pilaf!

3	cups reduced-sodium chicken broth
1/4	cup uncooked wild rice
1/4	cup medium pearl barley
1/4	cup uncooked brown rice
1/2	lb. baby portobello mushrooms, chopped
1	small onion, chopped
1	celery rib, finely chopped
1	Tbsp. butter
1	Tbsp. olive oil
3	garlic cloves, minced
1/4	cup grated Parmesan cheese
1/4	cup half-and-half cream
1/8	tsp. pepper

1. In a large saucepan, combine broth and wild rice. Bring to a boil. Reduce heat; cover and simmer for 10 minutes. Stir in barley and brown rice; cover and simmer for 40-45 minutes or until grains are tender and the liquid is absorbed.

2. Meanwhile, in a large nonstick skillet, saute the mushrooms, onion and celery in butter and oil until tender. Add garlic; cook 1 minute longer. Stir in the rice mixture, cheese, cream and pepper; heat through.

Nutrition Facts: 1/2 cup equals 176 calories, 7 g fat (3 g saturated fat), 13 mg cholesterol, 363 mg sodium, 23 g carbohydate, 3 g fiber, 7 g protein. **Diabetic Exchanges:** 1-1/2 fat, 1 starch, 1 vegetable.

Colorful Broccoli Rice

PREP/TOTAL TIME: 15 min. YIELD: 2 servings

GALE LALMOND • DEERING, NEW HAMPSHIRE

I found this microwave-quick and simple recipe years ago. It's a favorite with many meals. Its buttery flavor and color make it a great side for all kinds of meats.

2/3	cup water
2	tsp. butter
1	tsp. reduced-sodium chicken bouillon granules
1	cup coarsely chopped fresh broccoli
1/2	cup instant brown rice
2	Tbsp. chopped sweet red pepper

1. In a small microwave-safe bowl, combine the water, butter and bouillon. Cover and microwave on high for 1-2 minutes; stir until blended. Add the broccoli, rice and red pepper. Cover and cook 6-7 minutes longer or until broccoli is crisp-tender.

2. Let stand for 5 minutes. Fluff with a fork.

Editor's Note: This recipe was tested in a 1,100-watt microwave.

Nutrition Facts: 1/2 cup equals 136 calories, 5 g fat (2 g saturated fat), 10 mg cholesterol, 197 mg sodium, 20 g carbohydrate, 2 g fiber, 3 g protein. **Diabetic Exchanges:** 1 starch, 1 fat.

Green Beans Provencale F C M

PREP/TOTAL TIME: 30 min. YIELD: 5 servings

PAULA WHARTON • EL PASO, TEXAS

Garlic, tomatoes and olive oil are wonderful ingredients often found in Southern French cooking. In this dish, they complement the green beans perfectly.

- 1 lb. fresh green beans, trimmed and cut into 2-in. pieces
- 4 green onions, sliced
- 2 Tbsp. minced shallot
- 4 garlic cloves, minced
- 2 tsp. minced fresh rosemary or 1/2 tsp. dried rosemary, crushed
- 1 Tbsp. olive oil
- 1-1/2 cups grape tomatoes, halved
- 2 Tbsp. minced fresh or 2 tsp. dried basil
- 1/2 tsp. salt
- 1/4 tsp. pepper

1. Place beans in a steamer basket; place in a large saucepan over 1 in. of water. Bring to a boil; cover and steam for 4-5 minutes or until crisp-tender.

2. Meanwhile, in a large skillet, saute the onions, shallot, garlic and rosemary in oil until vegetables are tender. Add the green beans, tomatoes, basil, salt and pepper; saute 2-3 minutes longer or until heated through.

Nutrition Facts: 3/4 cup equals 70 calories, 3 g fat (trace saturated fat), 0 cholesterol, 248 mg sodium, 10 g carbohydrate, 4 g fiber, 2 g protein. **Diabetic Exchanges:** 2 vegetable, 1/2 fat.

Spinach and Mushrooms C

PREP/TOTAL TIME: 30 min. YIELD: 4 servings

JOYCE FREY • MACKSVILLE, KANSAS

Warm sauteed spinach and fresh, garlicky mushrooms make for a perfect combination that tastes terrific and looks impressive, too. Water chestnuts add a fun crunch.

- 1/2 lb. sliced fresh mushrooms
- 1 Tbsp. butter
- 1 Tbsp. olive oil
- 2 garlic cloves, minced
- 1/4 cup dry white wine or reduced-sodium chicken broth
- 3 Tbsp. Worcestershire sauce
- 1 tsp. minced fresh oregano or 1/2 tsp. dried oregano
- 3/4 tsp. minced fresh thyme or 1/4 tsp. dried thyme
- 1/4 tsp. salt
- 1/4 tsp. pepper
- 1 pkg. (6 oz.) fresh baby spinach
- 1 can (8 oz.) sliced water chestnuts, drained

1. In a large nonstick skillet, saute mushrooms in butter and oil until tender. Add garlic; cook 1 minute longer. Stir in the wine, Worcestershire sauce and seasonings. Bring to a boil. Reduce heat; simmer, uncovered, for 7-8 minutes or until liquid has evaporated.

2. Add spinach; cook and stir until wilted. Stir in water chestnuts; heat through.

Nutrition Facts: 3/4 cup equals 124 calories, 7 g fat (2 g saturated fat), 8 mg cholesterol, 334 mg sodium, 14 g carbohydrate, 3 g fiber, 4 g protein. **Diabetic Exchanges:** 2 vegetable, 1 fat.

Grilled-to-Perfection Potatoes F M

PREP: 15 min. GRILL: 40 min. YIELD: 8 servings

ROBIN JOHNSON • RATTAN, OKLAHOMA

This is a wonderful side for any grilled meat. If you don't want to do both with the grill, just place the potatoes in a dish, cover and bake in the oven.

- 8 medium potatoes, cut into 1-in. cubes
- 2 large onions, halved and sliced
- 2 Tbsp. butter, melted
- 2 garlic cloves, minced
- 1/2 tsp. garlic salt
- 1/2 tsp. pepper

Reduced-fat sour cream, optional

1. In a large bowl, combine the first six ingredients. Divide mixture between two double thicknesses of heavy-duty foil (about 18 in. square). Fold foil around mixture and seal tightly.

2. Grill, covered, over medium heat for 40-45 minutes or until potatoes are tender, turning once. Open foil carefully to allow steam to escape. Serve with sour cream if desired.

Nutrition Facts: 3/4 cup (calculated without sour cream) equals 210 calories, 3 g fat (2 g saturated fat), 8 mg cholesterol, 148 mg sodium, 42 g carbohydrate, 4 g fiber, 5 g protein.

GRILLED-TO-PERFECTION POTATOES

Makeover Crunchy Sweet Potato Casserole S M

PREP: 20 min. BAKE: 35 min. YIELD: 6 servings

SCOTT JONES • TULSA, OKLAHOMA

This makeover recipe keeps all the crunchy texture from toasty pecans and all the healthy sweet potatoes, but half of the saturated fat and cholesterol of the original.

1-3/4	lbs. sweet potatoes (about 3 large), peeled and cut into 2-in. pieces
1/3	cup fat-free milk
1/4	cup egg substitute
1	egg
2	Tbsp. butter, softened
1	tsp. lemon extract
1	tsp. vanilla extract

TOPPING:

2/3	cup packed brown sugar
1/4	cup all-purpose flour
1	Tbsp. cold butter
1/4	cup chopped pecans

1. Place sweet potatoes in a large saucepan and cover with water. Bring to a boil. Reduce heat; cover and cook for 15-20 minutes or until tender. Drain and place in a food processor. Add the milk, egg substitute, egg, butter and extracts; cover and process until smooth. Pour into a 1-1/2-qt. baking dish coated with cooking spray.

2. In a small bowl, combine brown sugar and flour. Cut in butter until crumbly. Sprinkle over sweet potato mixture; sprinkle with pecans. Bake, uncovered, at 350° for 35-40 minutes or until a thermometer reads 160°.

Nutrition Facts: 1/2 cup equals 306 calories, 10 g fat (4 g saturated fat), 51 mg cholesterol, 114 mg sodium, 49 g carbohydrate, 3 g fiber, 5 g protein.

Five-Fruit Compote F S C

PREP/TOTAL TIME: 20 min. YIELD: 6 cups

JEAN ECOS • HARTLAND, WISCONSIN

Bring out the best in your Easter ham or lamb with this fast fruit compote.

2	cans (15 oz. *each*) sliced peaches in juice, drained
1	can (20 oz.) unsweetened pineapple chunks, drained
1	can (20 oz.) reduced-sugar cherry pie filling
2/3	cup chopped dried apricots
2/3	cup chopped dates
1/2	tsp. ground cinnamon

Fully cooked lean ham

1. In a large saucepan, combine the first six ingredients. Bring to a boil. Reduced heat; simmer, uncovered, for 5 minutes, stirring frequently. Serve warm with ham.

Nutrition Facts: 1/4 cup (calculated without ham) equals 57 calories, trace fat (trace saturated fat), 0 cholesterol, 5 mg sodium, 14 g carbohydrate, 2 g fiber, 1 g protein. **Diabetic Exchange:** 1 starch.

Makeover Creamed Corn M

PREP/TOTAL TIME: 30 min. YIELD: 10 servings

TRISHA KRUSE • EAGLE, IDAHO

This scrumptious makeover has all the rich feel and flavor of my original, but it only has about half the calories and about a third of the saturated fat.

4	pkg. (10 oz. *each*) frozen corn, thawed
1	cup half-and-half cream
1/4	cup butter, cubed

MAKEOVER CREAMED CORN

MAKEOVER CRUNCHY SWEET POTATO CASSEROLE

BROCCOLI CHEESE BAKE

2 Tbsp. sugar
2 tsp. salt
1/2 tsp. pepper
1/3 cup all-purpose flour
2 cups fat-free milk
1/2 cup shredded sharp cheddar cheese

1. In a Dutch oven, combine the first six ingredients. Cook and stir over medium heat for 8-10 minutes or until heated through.

2. Combine flour and milk until smooth. Stir into pan. Bring to a boil; cook and stir for 2 minutes or until thickened. Remove from the heat; stir in cheese until melted.

Nutrition Facts: 3/4 cup equals 234 calories, 9 g fat (6 g saturated fat), 31 mg cholesterol, 574 mg sodium, 33 g carbohydrate, 3 g fiber, 8 g protein.

Broccoli Cheese Bake C M

PREP: 20 min. **BAKE:** 25 min. **YIELD:** 4 servings

DEBORAH PATRAUCHUK • SICAMOUS, BRITISH COLUMBIA

Here's a handy and versatile side that's creamy, colorful and bursting with flavor and nutrition. Pair it with almost any entree for a terrific meal.

1-3/4 cups fresh broccoli florets
1 Tbsp. cornstarch
1/8 tsp. salt
Dash pepper
2/3 cup fat-free milk
1 medium onion, chopped
1/2 cup shredded cheddar cheese
2 Tbsp. grated Parmesan cheese

1. Place 1 in. of water and broccoli in a small saucepan; bring to a boil. Reduce heat; cover and simmer for 3-5 minutes or until crisp-tender.

2. Meanwhile, in a small saucepan, combine the cornstarch, salt, pepper and milk until smooth. Bring to a boil; cook and stir for 1 minute or until thickened. Stir in onion and cheddar cheese until cheese is melted. Drain broccoli; stir into cheese sauce.

3. Transfer to a 1-qt. baking dish coated with cooking spray. Sprinkle with Parmesan cheese. Cover and bake at 350° for 25-30 minutes or until vegetables are tender.

Nutrition Facts: 3/4 cup equals 106 calories, 5 g fat (3 g saturated fat), 18 mg cholesterol, 224 mg sodium, 10 g carbohydrate, 2 g fiber, 7 g protein. **Diabetic Exchanges:** 1 high-fat meat, 1 vegetable.

MAKEOVER SAUSAGE & SPINACH PIE

EGGS BENEDICT

MAKEOVER BLUEBERRY FRENCH TOAST

Good Mornings

Get your day off to a healthy start with the eye-opening breakfast items found here. Whether you need something quick before work or a contribution to a friendly brunch, these rise-and-shine delights can't be beat!

Makeover Blueberry French Toast M

PREP: 30 min. + chilling **BAKE:** 55 min.
YIELD: 8 servings (1-1/2 cups sauce)

JOAN HALLFORD • NORTH RICHLAND HILLS, TEXAS

With this luscious makeover from the Healthy Cooking Test Kitchen, I can enjoy all the richness and flavor of my original recipe but with fewer calories and less fat and cholesterol.

- 6 whole wheat hamburger buns
- 1 pkg. (8 oz.) reduced-fat cream cheese
- 1 cup fresh *or* frozen blueberries
- 6 eggs
- 1 cup egg substitute
- 2 cups fat-free milk
- 1/3 cup maple syrup *or* honey

SAUCE:
- 1/2 cup sugar
- 2 Tbsp. cornstarch
- 1 cup grape juice
- 1 cup fresh *or* frozen blueberries

1. Cut buns into 1-in. cubes; place half in a 13-in. x 9-in. baking dish coated with cooking spray. Cut cream cheese into 1-in. cubes; place over buns. Top with blueberries and remaining bun cubes.

2. In a large bowl, beat eggs and egg substitute. Add milk and syrup; mix well. Pour over bun mixture. Cover and refrigerate for 8 hours or overnight.

3. Remove from the refrigerator 30 minutes before baking. Cover and bake at 350° for 30 minutes. Uncover; bake 25-30 minutes longer or until golden brown and center is set.

4. Meanwhile, in a small saucepan, combine sugar and cornstarch; stir in juice until smooth. Bring to a boil over medium heat; cook and stir for 2 minutes. Stir in blueberries. Reduce heat; simmer, uncovered, for 8-10 minutes or until berries burst, stirring occasionally. Serve with French toast.

Nutrition Facts: 1 slice with 3 Tbsp. sauce equals 375 calories, 11 g fat (6 g saturated fat), 180 mg cholesterol, 418 mg sodium, 54 g carbohydrate, 3 g fiber, 16 g protein.

Makeover Sausage & Spinach Pie

PREP: 20 min. **BAKE:** 40 min. + standing
YIELD: 6 servings

CAROL HANEMAN • ST. LOUIS, MISSOURI

Thanks to its flaky crust and savory filling, this sausage and spinach pie is a showstopping entree fit for any time of day. Now that it's lightened up, it's just as delicious as it is good for you!

- 1 frozen deep-dish pie shell
- 1/2 lb. Italian turkey sausage links, casings removed
- 1 cup egg substitute
- 1 pkg. (10 oz.) frozen chopped spinach, thawed and squeezed dry
- 1 cup (4 oz.) shredded part-skim mozzarella cheese
- 2/3 cup reduced-fat ricotta cheese
- 1/8 tsp. pepper

1. Line unpricked pastry shell with a double thickness of heavy-duty foil. Bake at 400° for 4 minutes. Remove foil; bake 4 minutes longer. Remove from the oven; reduce heat to 375°.

2. Meanwhile, in a large nonstick skillet, cook sausage over medium heat until no longer pink; drain. In a large bowl, whisk the egg substitute, spinach, cheeses, pepper and cooked sausage. Pour into crust. Place pie on a baking sheet. Cover the edges loosely with foil.

3. Bake for 40-45 minutes or until a knife inserted near the center comes out clean. Let stand for 10 minutes before cutting.

Nutrition Facts: 1 piece equals 282 calories, 14 g fat (5 g saturated fat), 40 mg cholesterol, 563 mg sodium, 19 g carbohydrate, 1 g fiber, 19 g protein.

You can substitute **2 fresh eggs** for 1/2 cup of egg substitute in your recipes. There might be a slight change in texture, but the results are still great!

Makeover Waffles M

PREP/TOTAL TIME: 25 min. **YIELD:** 10 waffles

CAROL BURGER • PHILLIPS, WISCONSIN

These waffles taste just as terrific as the original recipe—with only half the fat. In other words, dust off that waffle iron because these breakfast sensations are a wonderful way to start your day!

- 1-3/4 cups all-purpose flour
- 3 tsp. baking powder
- 1/2 tsp. salt
- 2 egg yolks
- 1-3/4 cups fat-free milk
- 1/4 cup canola oil
- 1/4 cup unsweetened applesauce
- 2 egg whites

1. In a large bowl, combine the flour, baking powder and salt. In a small bowl, whisk the egg yolks, milk, oil and applesauce. Stir into the dry ingredients just until moistened.

2. In another small bowl, beat egg whites until stiff peaks form. Fold into batter. Bake in a preheated waffle iron according to manufacturer's directions until golden brown.

Nutrition Facts: 2 waffles equals 321 calories, 13 g fat (2 g saturated fat), 84 mg cholesterol, 538 mg sodium, 39 g carbohydrate, 1 g fiber, 10 g protein.

Roasted Red Pepper Omelets C M

PREP/TOTAL TIME: 20 min. **YIELD:** 2 servings

HEALTHY COOKING TEST KITCHEN

Roasted red peppers, Muenster cheese and green onions give this breakfast favorite vibrant color and flavor.

- 3 eggs
- 3 Tbsp. water
- 1/4 tsp. salt
- 1/8 tsp. pepper
- 1/2 cup chopped roasted sweet red peppers
- 1/4 cup shredded Muenster cheese
- 2 green onions, chopped

1. Coat an 8-in. nonstick skillet with cooking spray and place over medium heat. In a small bowl, whisk the eggs, water, salt and pepper. Add half of egg mixture to skillet (mixture should set immediately at the edges).

2. As eggs set, push cooked edges toward the center, letting uncooked portion flow underneath. When the eggs are set, add half of the red peppers, cheese and onions on one side; fold other side over filling. Slide omelet onto a plate. Repeat.

Nutrition Facts: 1 omelet equals 185 calories, 12 g fat (5 g saturated fat), 331 mg cholesterol, 714 mg sodium, 4 g carbohydrate, trace fiber, 13 g protein.

Makeover Apple Coffee Cake

PREP: 20 min. **BAKE:** 40 min. + cooling
YIELD: 12 servings

DENISE SNYDER • LEMOYNE, OHIO

This sugary-topped apple coffee cake is a delicious way to get your family out of bed in the morning. The pros at "Healthy Cooking" lightened the original up, but this makeover version is still scrumptious to the core!

- 1/3 cup butter, softened
- 2/3 cup sugar
- 2 eggs
- 1 tsp. vanilla extract
- 2 cups all-purpose flour
- 1 tsp. baking soda
- 1 cup (8 oz.) reduced-fat sour cream

MAKEOVER WAFFLES

ROASTED RED PEPPER OMELETS

TOPPING:

- 1/3 cup chopped walnuts
- 1/3 cup packed brown sugar
- 2 Tbsp. sugar
- 1 tsp. ground cinnamon
- 2 medium tart apples, peeled and thinly sliced

1. In a large bowl, beat butter and sugar until crumbly, about 2 minutes. Add eggs, one at a time, beating well after each addition. Beat in vanilla. Combine flour and baking soda; add to creamed mixture alternately with sour cream, beating well after each addition (batter will be sticky).

2. In a small bowl, combine the walnuts, sugars and cinnamon. Spread half of the batter into an 11-in. x 7-in. baking dish coated with cooking spray. Top with apples; sprinkle with half of the topping. Gently top with remaining batter and topping.

3. Bake at 350° for 40-45 minutes or until a toothpick inserted near the center comes out clean. Cool on a wire rack.

Nutrition Facts: 1 piece equals 266 calories, 10 g fat (5 g saturated fat), 55 mg cholesterol, 169 mg sodium, 40 g carbohydrate, 1 g fiber, 5 g protein.

Eggs Benedict

PREP: 25 min. COOK: 15 min. YIELD: 8 servings

REBECCA BAIRD • SALT LAKE CITY, UTAH
This mock hollandaise sauce is smooth and creamy and much healthier than the regular version.

- 8 slices Canadian bacon
- 8 eggs

HOLLANDAISE SAUCE:
- 2 Tbsp. all-purpose flour
- 1/4 tsp. salt
- 1/4 tsp. ground mustard
- 1/8 tsp. cayenne pepper
- 1/2 cup fat-free milk
- 1/2 cup fat-free evaporated milk
- 1 egg yolk, lightly beaten
- 1 Tbsp. butter-flavored sprinkles
- 1 Tbsp. lemon juice
- 4 whole wheat English muffins, split and toasted

1. In a nonstick skillet coated with cooking spray, brown bacon on both sides; remove and keep warm.

2. Place 2-3 in. of water in a large skillet with high sides. Bring to a boil; reduce heat and simmer gently. Break cold eggs, one at a time, into a custard cup or saucer; holding the cup close to the surface of the water, slip each egg into water. Cook, uncovered, until whites are completely set and yolks begin to thicken but are not hard, about 4 minutes.

3. Meanwhile, in a small saucepan, combine the flour, salt, mustard and cayenne. Gradually stir in milk and evaporated milk until smooth. Bring to a boil; cook and stir for 1-2 minutes or until thickened. Remove from the heat.

4. Stir a small amount of sauce into egg yolk; return all to the pan, stirring constantly. Bring to a gentle boil; cook and stir for 2 minutes. Remove from the heat; stir in butter-flavored sprinkles and lemon juice.

5. With a slotted spoon, lift each egg out of the water. Top each muffin half with a slice of bacon, an egg and 2 Tbsp. sauce. Serve immediately.

Editor's Note: This recipe was tested with Molly McButter. Look for it in the spice aisle.

Nutrition Facts: 1 serving equals 216 calories, 8 g fat (3 g saturated fat), 252 mg cholesterol, 752 mg sodium, 19 g carbohydrate, 2 g fiber, 17 g protein. **Diabetic Exchanges:** 2 medium-fat meat, 1 starch.

Whole Wheat Pancakes M

PREP/TOTAL TIME: 25 min. **YIELD:** 20 pancakes

LINE WALTER • WAYNE, PENNSYLVANIA

These light, fluffy pancakes seem like a treat. Whole wheat flour and toasted wheat germ make them so filling.

- 2 cups whole wheat flour
- 1/2 cup toasted wheat germ
- 1 tsp. baking soda
- 1/2 tsp. salt
- 2 eggs, lightly beaten
- 3 cups buttermilk
- 1 Tbsp. canola oil

1. In a large bowl, combine the flour, wheat germ, baking soda and salt. In another bowl, whisk the eggs, buttermilk and oil. Stir into dry ingredients just until blended.

2. Pour batter by 1/4 cupfuls onto a hot griddle coated with cooking spray; turn when bubbles form on top. Cook until the second side is golden brown.

Nutrition Facts: 2 pancakes equals 157 calories, 4 g fat (1 g saturated fat), 45 mg cholesterol, 335 mg sodium, 24 g carbohydrate, 4 g fiber, 9 g protein. **Diabetic Exchanges:** 1-1/2 starch, 1 fat.

Makeover Hearty Egg Casserole C

PREP: 20 min. **BAKE:** 35 min. **YIELD:** 12 servings

KRISTINE OCIEPA • MILWAUKEE, WISCONSIN

Here's a down-home breakfast bake that's true to its name. Packed with sausage, veggies, eggs and cheese, this dish will get you going and keep you feeling satisfied.

- 1 lb. bulk pork sausage
- 3/4 cup sliced fresh mushrooms
- 1 small onion, chopped
- 1 pkg. (10 oz.) frozen chopped spinach, thawed and well drained
- 3/4 cup shredded sharp cheddar cheese, *divided*
- 6 eggs
- 1-1/2 cups egg substitute
- 1 cup half-and-half cream
- 1 cup fat-free milk
- 1/4 tsp. ground nutmeg

1. In a large nonstick skillet, cook the sausage, mushrooms and onion over medium heat until meat is no longer pink; drain. Remove from the heat; stir in spinach and 1/2 cup cheese. Transfer to a 13-in. x 9-in. baking dish coated with cooking spray.

2. In a large bowl, beat the eggs, egg substitute, cream, milk and nutmeg. Pour over sausage mixture. Bake, uncovered, at 350° for 35-40 minutes or until a knife inserted near the center comes out clean. Sprinkle with remaining cheese. Let stand for 5 minutes before cutting.

Nutrition Facts: 1 piece equals 195 calories, 14 g fat (6 g saturated fat), 137 mg cholesterol, 332 mg sodium, 5 g carbohydrate, 1 g fiber, 13 g protein.

Cinnamon Mocha Coffee F S

PREP/TOTAL TIME: 20 min. **YIELD:** 6 servings

BERNICE MORRIS • MARSHFIELD, MISSOURI

One snowy day, my neighbor called and invited me over to try a new beverage she'd made. It was delicious! This spiced coffee is a lovely treat any time of year.

- 1/2 cup ground dark roast coffee
- 1 Tbsp. ground cinnamon
- 1/4 tsp. ground nutmeg
- 5 cups water
- 1 cup milk
- 1/3 cup chocolate syrup

1/4 cup packed brown sugar

1 tsp. vanilla extract

Whipped cream, optional

1. In a small bowl, combine the coffee grounds, cinnamon and nutmeg; pour into a coffee filter of a drip coffeemaker. Add water; brew according to manufacturer's directions.

2. In a large saucepan, combine the milk, chocolate syrup and brown sugar. Cook over low heat until sugar is dissolved, stirring occasionally. Stir in the vanilla and brewed coffee. Ladle into mugs; garnish with whipped cream if desired.

Nutrition Facts: 1 cup equals 126 calories, 2 g fat (1 g saturated fat), 6 mg cholesterol, 34 mg sodium, 25 g carbohydrate, 1 g fiber, 3 g protein.

Maple Nut Bagel Spread ⓢⒸⓜ

PREP/TOTAL TIME: 10 min. **YIELD:** 1-1/4 cups

HEALTHY COOKING TEST KITCHEN

You won't believe how easy it is to whip up this creamy, four-ingredient bagel spread. It's also wonderful on toast or English muffins.

1 carton (8 oz.) reduced-fat spreadable cream cheese

3 Tbsp. maple syrup

1/8 tsp. ground cinnamon

1/4 cup finely chopped walnuts, toasted

Bagels, split

1. In a large bowl, beat the cream cheese, syrup and cinnamon until smooth; stir in walnuts. Chill until serving. Serve with bagels.

Nutrition Facts: 2 Tbsp. equals 84 calories, 5 g fat (3 g saturated fat), 11 mg cholesterol, 107 mg sodium, 6 g carbohydrate, trace fiber, 3 g protein. **Diabetic Exchanges:** 1 fat, 1/2 starch.

Baked Eggs with Cheddar and Bacon Ⓒ

PREP/TOTAL TIME: 25 min. **YIELD:** 4 servings

CATHERINE WILKINSON • DEWEY, ARIZONA

These little treats are super-easy to make and perfect for a special breakfast. They're also very nice for a casual dinner. The smoky cheese and bacon elevate eggs to a new level!

4 eggs

4 Tbsp. fat-free milk, *divided*

2 Tbsp. shredded smoked cheddar cheese

2 tsp. minced fresh parsley

1/4 tsp. salt

1/8 tsp. pepper

2 bacon strips

1. Coat four 4-oz. ramekins with cooking spray; break an egg into each dish. Spoon 1 Tbsp. milk over each egg. Combine the cheese, parsley, salt and pepper; sprinkle over tops.

2. Bake, uncovered, at 325° for 12-15 minutes or until whites are completely set and yolks begin to thicken but are not firm.

3. Meanwhile, in a small skillet, cook bacon over medium heat until crisp. Remove to paper towels to drain. Crumble bacon and sprinkle over eggs.

Nutrition Facts: 1 serving equals 107 calories, 7 g fat (3 g saturated fat), 219 mg cholesterol, 319 mg sodium, 1 g carbohydrate, trace fiber, 9 g protein. **Diabetic Exchange:** 1 medium-fat meat.

BAKED EGGS WITH CHEDDAR AND BACON

MAPLE NUT BAGEL SPREAD

Ultimate Fruity Granola ⓢ

PREP: 15 min. BAKE: 20 min. + cooling YIELD: 9 cups

SARAH VASQUES • MILFORD, NEW HAMPSHIRE

Honey, maple syrup and vanilla coat this wonderfully crunchy treat that's fantastic no matter how you serve it—alone, with cold milk or in a yogurt parfait.

5	cups old-fashioned oats
1	cup sliced almonds
1/2	cup sunflower kernels
1/2	cup ground flaxseed
1/2	cup packed brown sugar
1/4	cup maple syrup
1/4	cup honey
2	Tbsp. canola oil
1/2	tsp. salt
1/2	tsp. ground cinnamon
1	tsp. vanilla extract
1/2	cup dried cranberries
1/2	cup dried banana chips
1/2	cup dried apricots, halved

1. In a large bowl, combine the oats, almonds, sunflower kernels and flax. In a small saucepan, combine the brown sugar, maple syrup, honey, oil, salt and cinnamon. Cook and stir over medium heat for 2-3 minutes or until brown sugar is dissolved and mixture is heated through. Remove from the heat; stir in vanilla. Pour over oat mixture and toss to coat.

2. Transfer to a 15-in. x 10-in. x 1-in. baking pan coated with cooking spray. Bake at 350° for 20-25 minutes or until golden brown, stirring every 8 minutes. Cool completely on a wire rack. Stir in dried fruits. Store in an airtight container.

Nutrition Facts: 1/2 cup equals 253 calories, 10 g fat (2 g saturated fat), 0 cholesterol, 86 mg sodium, 38 g carbohydrate, 5 g fiber, 6 g protein. **Diabetic Exchanges:** 2-1/2 starch, 1 fat.

Fruit Smoothies Ⓕ Ⓢ

PREP/TOTAL TIME: 5 min. YIELD: 3 servings

BRYCE SICKICH • NEW PORT RICHEY, FLORIDA

With its combination of fruits, this delicious, quick-to-fix smoothie is a powerhouse of nutrition.

3/4	cup fat-free milk
1/2	cup orange juice
1/2	cup unsweetened applesauce
1	small ripe banana, halved
1/2	cup frozen unsweetened raspberries
7	to 10 ice cubes

1. In a blender, combine all ingredients; cover and process until smooth. Pour into chilled glasses; serve immediately.

Nutrition Facts: 1 cup equals 97 calories, trace fat (trace saturated fat), 1 mg cholesterol, 33 mg sodium, 22 g carbohydrate, 2 g fiber, 3 g protein. **Diabetic Exchange:** 1-1/2 fruit.

FRUIT SMOOTHIES

ULTIMATE FRUITY GRANOLA

COLORFUL CHEESE OMELET

Colorful Cheese Omelet C

PREP/TOTAL TIME: 20 min YIELD: 1 serving

LYNDA O'DELL LYNCH • PORT HURON, MICHIGAN

When I start my day with this omelet, I'm able to go nonstop and know I'm getting valuable nutrients besides.

- 1 egg
- 2 egg whites
- 2 Tbsp. chopped fresh baby spinach
- 1/8 tsp. hot pepper sauce
- 2 Tbsp. chopped sweet red pepper
- 1 green onion, chopped
- 2 Tbsp. shredded cheddar cheese

1. In a small bowl, whisk the egg, egg whites, spinach and pepper sauce; set aside. In a small nonstick skillet coated with cooking spray, saute red pepper and onion until tender. Reduce heat to medium.

2. Add egg mixture to skillet (mixture should set immediately at edges). As eggs set, push cooked edges toward the center, letting uncooked portion flow underneath. When the eggs are set, sprinkle with cheese; fold other side over filling. Carefully slide omelet onto a plate.

Nutrition Facts: 1 omelet equals 167 calories, 9 g fat (5 g saturated fat), 227 mg cholesterol, 276 mg sodium, 4 g carbohydrate, 1 g fiber, 17 g protein. **Diabetic Exchange:** 2 medium-fat meat.

Tropical Yogurt F S

PREP/TOTAL TIME: 5 min. YIELD: 4 servings

HEALTHY COOKING TEST KITCHEN

Plain yogurt becomes a flavorful sensation with help from coconut extract, pineapple and a hint of lime. It's great with granola in the morning or as a low-fat snack during the day.

- 2 cups (16 oz.) reduced-fat plain yogurt
- 1 can (8 oz.) unsweetened crushed pineapple, drained
- 2 tsp. sugar
- 1/4 tsp. coconut extract
- 1/4 tsp. grated lime peel

1. In a small bowl, combine all ingredients. Chill mixture until serving.

Nutrition Facts: 1/2 cup equals 121 calories, 2 g fat (1 g saturated fat), 7 mg cholesterol, 86 mg sodium, 20 g carbohydrate, trace fiber, 7 g protein. **Diabetic Exchanges:** 1 fat-free milk, 1/2 fruit.

VEGETARIAN EGG STRATA

Vegetarian Egg Strata M

PREP: 25 min. + chilling **BAKE:** 45 min. + standing
YIELD: 12 servings

DANNA ROGERS • WESTPORT, CONNECTICUT

I used to make this with turkey or chicken sausage, but adapted it for a vegetarian friend, and it was a huge hit. I serve it with fresh breads or bagels and a big mixed salad featuring arugula, apples and walnuts for brunch. It also works well for lunch, served with tomato bisque.

1	medium zucchini, finely chopped
1	medium sweet red pepper, finely chopped
1	cup sliced baby portobello mushrooms
1	medium red onion, finely chopped
2	tsp. olive oil
3	garlic cloves, minced
2	tsp. minced fresh thyme *or* 1/2 tsp. dried thyme
1/2	tsp. salt
1/4	tsp. pepper
1	loaf (1 lb.) day-old French bread, cubed
2	pkg. (5.3 oz. *each*) fresh goat cheese, crumbled
1-3/4	cups grated Parmesan cheese
6	eggs
2	cups fat-free milk
1/4	tsp. ground nutmeg

1. In a large skillet, saute the zucchini, red pepper, mushrooms and onion in oil until tender. Add the garlic, thyme, salt and pepper; saute 2 minutes longer.

2. In a 13-in. x 9-in. baking dish coated with cooking spray, layer half of the bread cubes, zucchini mixture, goat cheese and Parmesan cheese. Repeat layers.

3. In a small bowl, whisk the eggs, milk and nutmeg. Pour over top. Cover and refrigerate overnight.

4. Remove from the refrigerator 30 minutes before baking. Bake, uncovered, at 350° for 45-50 minutes or until a knife inserted near the center comes out clean. Let stand for 10 minutes before cutting.

Nutrition Facts: 1 piece equals 281 calories, 12 g fat (6 g saturated fat), 140 mg cholesterol, 667 mg sodium, 27 g carbohydrate, 2 g fiber, 17 g protein.

Homemade Granola S

PREP: 15 min. **BAKE:** 20 min. + cooling **YIELD:** 5 cups

NANCY JOHNSON • LAVERNE, OKLAHOMA

If you ask me, this crunchy treat is absolutely fantastic! And with 7 g of protein and 4 g of fiber, the sweet mixture helps fill you up deliciously.

4-1/2	cups old-fashioned oats
1/3	cup sliced almonds
1/4	cup unsweetened apple juice
1/4	cup maple syrup
1	Tbsp. canola oil
2	tsp. ground cinnamon
1/2	tsp. salt
1/2	cup flaked coconut, toasted
1/2	cup raisins

Fat-free milk, optional

1. In a large bowl, combine oats and almonds. In a small saucepan, combine the apple juice, syrup, oil, cinnamon and salt. Cook and stir for 3-4 minutes over medium heat until heated through. Remove from the heat. Pour over oat mixture; stir to coat.

2. Transfer to a 15-in. x 10-in. x 1-in. baking pan coated with cooking spray. Bake at 350° for 20-25 minutes or until crisp, stirring every 10 minutes. Cool completely on a wire rack. Stir in coconut and raisins. Store in an airtight container. Serve granola with milk if desired.

Nutrition Facts: 1/2 cup (calculated without milk) equals 234 calories, 7 g fat (2 g saturated fat), 0 cholesterol, 133 mg sodium, 39 g carbohydrate, 4 g fiber, 7 g protein. **Diabetic Exchanges:** 2-1/2 starch, 1 fat.

Spiced Apple-Grape Juice F S

PREP: 10 min. **COOK:** 1 hour **YIELD:** 8 servings

CLAIRE BEATTIE • TORONTO, ONTARIO

Round out any brunch with this spiced apple drink. Seasoned with cinnamon, cloves and allspice, it will wrap your guests in a tempting aroma as it simmers.

- 4 cups white grape juice
- 3 cups unsweetened apple juice
- 1 cup water
- 2 cinnamon sticks (3 in.)
- 12 whole cloves
- 8 whole allspice

1. In a large saucepan, combine the grape juice, apple juice and water. Place the cinnamon, cloves and allspice on a double thickness of cheesecloth; bring up corners of cloth and tie with string to form a bag. Add to the pan.

2. Bring to a boil. Reduce heat; simmer, uncovered, for 1 to 1-1/2 hours or until flavors are blended. Discard spice bag. Serve warm in mugs.

Nutrition Facts: 3/4 cup equals 121 calories, trace fat (trace saturated fat), 0 cholesterol, 10 mg sodium, 29 g carbohydrate, trace fiber, 1 g protein.

Isaiah's Gingerbread Pancakes with Apple Slaw

PREP: 25 min. **COOK:** 5 min./batch
YIELD: 10 servings (3 cups slaw)

SILVANA NARDONE • BROOKLYN, NEW YORK

Perfect for weekend mornings, these gluten-free pancakes are served with a sweet slaw. I suggest using decaf coffee for kids, and swapping pears for apples to change things up.

- 2 cups gluten-free pancake mix
- 2 Tbsp. brown sugar
- 1 Tbsp. baking cocoa
- 1-1/2 tsp. ground ginger
- 1 tsp. pumpkin pie spice
- 1/2 tsp. baking soda
- 2 eggs, *separated*
- 1 cup rice milk
- 1/2 cup plus 1 Tbsp. brewed coffee, room temperature
- 2 Tbsp. canola oil
- 1 Tbsp. molasses

SLAW:
- 3 medium apples, grated
- 1/2 cup chopped pecans, toasted
- 1/4 cup golden raisins
- 2 Tbsp. lemon juice
- 1 Tbsp. honey

Maple syrup, warmed

1. In a large bowl, combine the first six ingredients. Combine the egg yolks, rice milk, coffee, oil and molasses; add to dry ingredients just until moistened. In a small bowl, beat egg whites on medium speed until stiff peaks form. Fold into batter.

2. Pour batter by scant 1/4 cupfuls onto a hot griddle coated with cooking spray; turn when bubbles form on top. Cook until the second side is golden brown.

3. Meanwhile, in a small bowl, combine the apples, pecans, raisins, lemon juice and honey. Serve with pancakes and syrup.

Editor's Note: Read all ingredient labels for possible gluten content prior to use. Ingredient formulas can change, and production facilities vary among brands. If you're concerned that your brand may contain gluten, contact the company.

Nutrition Facts: 2 pancakes with 1/4 cup slaw (calculated without syrup) equals 225 calories, 8 g fat (1 g saturated fat), 42 mg cholesterol, 231 mg sodium, 36 g carbohydrate, 2 g fiber, 3 g protein. **Diabetic Exchanges:** 1-1/2 starch, 1-1/2 fat, 1/2 fruit.

SPICED APPLE-GRAPE JUICE

ISAIAH'S GINGERBREAD PANCAKES WITH APPLE SLAW

Gluten-Free Breakfast Blintzes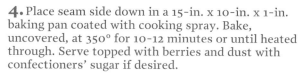

PREP: 30 min. + chilling **BAKE:** 10 min. **YIELD:** 9 servings

LAURA FALL-SUTTON • BUHL, IDAHO

These cheese-filled, berry-topped blintzes taste just as mouthwatering and special as they look. Enjoy!

1-1/2 cups fat-free milk
   3 eggs
   2 Tbsp. butter, melted
  2/3 cup gluten-free all-purpose baking flour
  1/2 tsp. salt

FILLING:
   1 cup (8 oz.) 2% cottage cheese
   3 oz. reduced-fat cream cheese
   2 Tbsp. sugar
  1/4 tsp. almond extract
2-1/4 cups *each* fresh blueberries and raspberries
Confectioners' sugar, optional

1. In a small bowl, combine the milk, eggs and butter. Combine the flour and salt; add to milk mixture and mix well. Cover and refrigerate for 1 hour.

2. Coat an 8-in. nonstick skillet with cooking spray; heat over medium heat. Stir crepe batter; pour 2 Tbsp. into center of skillet. Lift and tilt pan to coat bottom evenly. Cook until top appears dry; turn and cook 15-20 seconds longer. Remove to a wire rack. Repeat with remaining batter, coating skillet with cooking spray as needed. When cool, stack crepes with waxed paper or paper towels in between.

3. In a blender, cover and process cheeses until smooth. Add sugar and extract; pulse until combined. Spread a scant 1 tablespoonful onto each crepe. Fold opposite sides of crepe over filling, forming a bundle.

4. Place seam side down in a 15-in. x 10-in. x 1-in. baking pan coated with cooking spray. Bake, uncovered, at 350° for 10-12 minutes or until heated through. Serve topped with berries and dust with confectioners' sugar if desired.

Editor's Note: Read all ingredient labels for possible gluten content prior to use. Ingredient formulas can change, and production facilities vary among brands. If you're concerned that your brand may contain gluten, contact the company.

Nutrition Facts: 2 blintzes with 1/2 cup fruit (calculated without confectioners' sugar) equals 180 calories, 7 g fat (4 g saturated fat), 88 mg cholesterol, 319 mg sodium, 22 g carbohydrate, 4 g fiber, 9 g protein. **Diabetic Exchanges:** 1 starch, 1 lean meat, 1/2 fruit, 1/2 fat.

Scrambled Egg Poppers

PREP: 15 min. **BAKE:** 25 min. **YIELD:** 8 servings

KATIE WILLIAMS • BLACK CREEK, WISCONSIN

These handy grab-and-go breakfast treats are ideal for busy mornings and sure to be a favorite with kids of all ages.

   2 loaves (1 lb. *each*) frozen whole wheat bread dough, thawed
   8 eggs
  1/2 cup fat-free milk
  1/4 tsp. salt
  1/4 tsp. pepper
  1/2 cup bacon bits, *divided*
  1/2 cup shredded cheddar cheese

1. Divide each loaf into eight pieces. Roll into balls. Place in muffin cups coated with cooking spray. Bake at 350° for 20-25 minutes or until golden brown.

2. Meanwhile, in a large bowl, whisk the eggs, milk, salt and pepper; stir in 1/4 cup bacon bits. Coat a large nonstick skillet with cooking spray and place over medium heat. Add egg mixture to skillet (mixture should set immediately at edges).

3. As eggs set, push cooked edges toward the center, letting uncooked portion flow underneath. When the eggs are set, remove from the heat.

GLUTEN-FREE BREAKFAST BLINTZES

SCRAMBLED EGG POPPERS

OMELET TORTILLA WRAP

4. Using a melon baller, scoop out the center of each roll, leaving a 1/4-in. shell (discard removed bread or save for another use). Spoon 3 Tbsp. cooked egg mixture into each roll. Top with remaining bacon bits and sprinkle with cheese. Bake 2-3 minutes longer or until cheese is melted.

Nutrition Facts: 2 poppers equals 252 calories, 10 g fat (4 g saturated fat), 224 mg cholesterol, 637 mg sodium, 25 g carbohydrate, 3 g fiber, 17 g protein.

Omelet Tortilla Wrap

PREP/TOTAL TIME: 25 min. YIELD: 1 serving

INGRID PARKER • HATTIESBURG, MISSISSIPPI

Here's a hearty, better-for-you breakfast that can be eaten right out of hand. Kids just love it.

- 1 egg
- 2 egg whites
- 2 Tbsp. finely chopped fully cooked lean ham
- 1 green onion, thinly sliced
- 1 Tbsp. chopped sweet red pepper
- 1 Tbsp. fat-free milk
- 2 tsp. chopped seeded jalapeno pepper
- 1/8 tsp. pepper

Dash hot pepper sauce, optional

- 2 Tbsp. shredded reduced-fat Monterey Jack cheese or Mexican cheese blend
- 1 whole wheat tortilla (8 in.), warmed

1. In a small bowl, whisk the egg, egg whites, ham, onion, red pepper, milk, jalapeno, pepper and pepper sauce if desired. Coat a small nonstick skillet with cooking spray and place over medium heat. Add egg mixture to skillet (mixture should set immediately at edges).

2. As eggs set, push cooked edges toward the center, letting uncooked portion flow underneath. When the eggs are set, remove from the heat; sprinkle with cheese. Slide omelet onto tortilla; roll up tightly.

Editor's Note: When cutting hot peppers, disposable gloves are recommended. Avoid touching your face.

Nutrition Facts: 1 wrap equals 322 calories, 12 g fat (4 g saturated fat), 229 mg cholesterol, 701 mg sodium, 26 g carbohydrate, 3 g fiber, 25 g protein.

Test egg dishes containing beaten eggs—like quiche, strata or custard **for doneness** by inserting a knife near the center of the dish. If the knife comes out clean, the eggs are cooked.

QUICK OATMEAL RAISIN PANCAKES

Quick Oatmeal Raisin Pancakes

PREP: 15 min. **COOK:** 10 min./ batch **YIELD:** 12 pancakes

KAREL HURT • CORTEZ, COLORADO

I found this recipe in a newspaper nearly 50 years ago and have used it regularly ever since.

2	cups quick-cooking oats
2	cups buttermilk
1/2	cup egg substitute
2	Tbsp. canola oil
1/2	cup all-purpose flour
2	Tbsp. sugar
1	tsp. baking powder
1	tsp. baking soda
1	tsp. ground cinnamon
1/4	tsp. salt
1/2	cup raisins

1. In a small bowl, combine oats and buttermilk; let stand for 5 minutes. Stir in egg substitute and oil; set aside.

2. In a large bowl, combine the flour, sugar, baking powder, baking soda, cinnamon and salt. Stir in the wet ingredients just until moistened; add raisins.

3. Pour batter by heaping 1/4 cupfuls onto a hot griddle coated with cooking spray; turn when bubbles form on top. Cook until second side is golden brown.

Nutrition Facts: 2 pancakes equals 274 calories, 7 g fat (1 g saturated fat), 3 mg cholesterol, 505 mg sodium, 44 g carbohydrate, 3 g fiber, 10 g protein. **Diabetic Exchanges:** 2 starch, 1 fruit, 1 fat.

Cinnamon Bagels With Crunchy Topping **F**

PREP: 40 min. + rising BAKE: 15 min. YIELD: 1 dozen

KRISTEN STREEPEY • GENEVA, ILLINOIS

Once you get the hang of it, you won't believe how simple it is to make these bakery-quality bagels right in your kitchen.

- 2 Tbsp. active dry yeast
- 1-1/2 cups warm water (110° to 115°)
- 1/4 cup packed brown sugar, *divided*
- 3 tsp. ground cinnamon
- 1-1/2 tsp. salt
- 2-3/4 to 3-1/4 cups all-purpose flour

TOPPING:
- 1/4 cup sugar
- 1/4 cup packed brown sugar
- 3 tsp. ground cinnamon

1. In a large bowl, dissolve yeast in warm water. Add 3 Tbsp. brown sugar, cinnamon and salt; mix well. Stir in enough flour to form a soft dough.

2. Turn onto a lightly floured surface; knead until smooth and elastic, about 6-8 minutes. Place in a bowl coated with cooking spray, turning once to coat the top. Cover and let rise in a warm place until doubled, about 1 hour.

3. Punch dough down. Shape into 12 balls. Push thumb through centers to form a 1-1/2-in. hole. Stretch and shape dough to form an even ring. Place on a floured surface. Cover and let rest for 10 minutes.

4. Fill a Dutch oven two-thirds full with water and remaining brown sugar; bring to a boil. Drop bagels, two at a time, into boiling water. Cook for 45 seconds; turn and cook 45 seconds longer. Remove with a slotted spoon; drain well on paper towels.

5. Combine topping ingredients; sprinkle over bagels. Place 2 in. apart on baking sheets coated with cooking spray. Bake at 400° for 15-20 minutes or until golden brown. Remove to wire racks to cool.

Nutrition Facts: 1 bagel equals 164 calories, trace fat (trace saturated fat), 0 cholesterol, 300 mg sodium, 37 g carbohydrate, 2 g fiber, 4 g protein.

Makeover Hash and Eggs

PREP/TOTAL TIME: 30 min. YIELD: 4 servings

HEALTHY COOKING TEST KITCHEN

Loaded with red potatoes and deli corned beef, our lightened up version of corned beef hash delivers fresh flavors and a dose of fiber. It's so spot on, you'll swear you're in a diner!

- 1 large onion, chopped
- 1 Tbsp. canola oil
- 6 medium red potatoes (about 1-1/2 lbs.), cut into 1/2-in. cubes
- 1/4 cup water
- 3 pkg. (2 oz. *each*) thinly sliced deli corned beef, coarsely chopped
- 1/4 tsp. pepper
- 4 eggs

1. In a large nonstick skillet, saute onion in oil until tender. Stir in potatoes and water. Bring to a boil. Reduce heat; cover and simmer for 15-20 minutes or until potatoes are tender. Stir in corned beef and pepper; heat through.

2. Meanwhile, in a large nonstick skillet coated with cooking spray, fry eggs as desired. Serve with corned beef hash.

Nutrition Facts: 1 cup corned beef hash with 1 egg equals 301 calories, 12 g fat (3 g saturated fat), 239 mg cholesterol, 652 mg sodium, 31 g carbohydrate, 4 g fiber, 18 g protein.

MAKEOVER HASH AND EGGS

CINNAMON BAGELS WITH CRUNCHY TOPPING

Hearty Confetti Breakfast ⓜ

PREP: 35 min. **BROIL:** 5 min. **YIELD:** 4 servings

LORI MERRICK • DANVERS, ILLINOIS

Start your day the right way with a glass of orange juice and this all-in-one potato-and-egg skillet. Or, serve it with iced tea as an easy weeknight dinner.

1	large sweet potato, peeled and cut into 1/2-in. cubes
1	large Yukon Gold potato, cut into 1/2-in. cubes
1	medium red potato, cut into 1/2-in. cubes
1	small onion, finely chopped
3/4	tsp. minced fresh rosemary *or* 1/4 tsp. dried rosemary, crushed
3/4	tsp. minced fresh thyme *or* 1/4 tsp. dried thyme
1/4	tsp. salt
1/4	tsp. pepper
2	tsp. butter
2	tsp. olive oil
4	eggs
1/4	cup shredded Asiago cheese

1. In a 10-in. ovenproof skillet, saute the potatoes, onion and seasonings in butter and oil until vegetables are golden brown and tender. With the back of a spoon, make four wells in the potato mixture; add an egg to each well. Remove from the heat; sprinkle with cheese.

2. Broil 3-4 in. from the heat for 3-4 minutes or until eggs are completely set.

Nutrition Facts: 1 serving equals 297 calories, 11 g fat (4 g saturated fat), 223 mg cholesterol, 262 mg sodium, 37 g carbohydrate, 4 g fiber, 12 g protein. **Diabetic Exchanges:** 2 starch, 1-1/2 fat, 1 medium-fat meat.

Blueberry Orange Blast Ⓕ Ⓢ

PREP/TOTAL TIME: 5 min. **YIELD:** 4 servings

DIANE NEIBLING • OVERLAND PARK, KANSAS

I developed this healthful, pretty smoothie after our annual blueberry-picking trip. As you may know, blueberries are loaded with antioxidants and flavor!

1	cup orange juice
1	cup (8 oz.) vanilla yogurt
1	medium banana, sliced and frozen
1	cup frozen unsweetened blueberries
1/2	cup silken firm tofu

1. In a blender, combine all of the ingredients; cover and process until smooth. Pour into chilled glasses; serve immediately.

Nutrition Facts: 3/4 cup equals 140 calories, 2 g fat (1 g saturated fat), 3 mg cholesterol, 49 mg sodium, 27 g carbohydrate, 2 g fiber, 5 g protein. **Diabetic Exchanges:** 1 fruit, 1/2 reduced-fat milk.

Sage Turkey Sausage Patties Ⓒ

PREP/TOTAL TIME: 30 min. **YIELD:** 12 servings

SHARMAN SCHUBERT • SEATTLE, WASHINGTON

This is a very easy recipe that's full of flavor but cuts salt and saturated fat. Our taste panel loved the aroma of this savory alternative to pork sausage.

1/4	cup grated Parmesan cheese
3	Tbsp. minced fresh parsley *or* 1 Tbsp. dried parsley flakes
2	Tbsp. fresh sage *or* 2 tsp. dried sage leaves
2	garlic cloves, minced
1	tsp. fennel seed, crushed
3/4	tsp. salt
1/2	tsp. pepper
1-1/2	lbs. lean ground turkey
1	Tbsp. olive oil

HEARTY CONFETTI BREAKFAST

SAGE TURKEY SAUSAGE PATTIES

SUNDAY BRUNCH STRATA

1. In a large bowl, combine the first seven ingredients. Crumble turkey over mixture and mix well. Shape into twelve 3-in. patties.

2. In a large skillet coated with cooking spray, cook patties in oil in batches over medium heat for 3-5 minutes on each side or until meat is no longer pink. Drain on paper towels if necessary.

Nutrition Facts: 1 patty equals 104 calories, 6 g fat (2 g saturated fat), 46 mg cholesterol, 227 mg sodium, trace carbohydrate, trace fiber, 11 g protein. **Diabetic Exchanges:** 1 lean meat, 1 fat.

Sunday Brunch Strata M

PREP: 25 min. + chilling **BAKE:** 50 min. + standing
YIELD: 8 servings

SONYA LABBE • SANTA MONICA, CALIFORNIA

Hearty and fresh-tasting, this classic strata makes a wonderful breakfast dish.

- 8 slices whole wheat bread, cubed
- 3 cups sliced fresh mushrooms
- 1 medium red onion, chopped
- 1 Tbsp. olive oil
- 2 garlic cloves, minced
- 8 eggs
- 8 egg whites
- 2 cups fat-free milk
- 1 pkg. (10 oz.) frozen chopped spinach, thawed and squeezed dry
- 2/3 cup shredded Swiss cheese
- 1/2 cup shredded sharp cheddar cheese
- 1 Tbsp. Dijon mustard
- 3/4 tsp. salt
- 1/2 tsp. ground nutmeg
- 1/2 tsp. pepper

1. Place bread cubes in a 13-in. x 9-in. baking dish coated with cooking spray; set aside.

2. In a large skillet, saute mushrooms and onion in oil until tender. Add garlic; cook 1 minute longer. In a large bowl, combine the eggs, egg whites, milk, spinach, cheeses, mustard, salt, nutmeg, pepper and mushroom mixture; pour over top. Cover and refrigerate overnight.

3. Remove from the refrigerator 30 minutes before baking. Bake, uncovered, at 350° for 50-60 minutes or until a knife inserted near the center comes out clean. Let stand for 10 minutes before cutting.

Nutrition Facts: 1 piece equals 277 calories, 12 g fat (5 g saturated fat), 228 mg cholesterol, 644 mg sodium, 20 g carbohydrate, 4 g fiber, 22 g protein.

SKEWERLESS STOVETOP KABOBS

CRAN-APPLE TURKEY SKILLET

GINGERED SPAGHETTI SALAD

Dinner in 30

Busy days don't have to include greasy fast-food fare. Keep your healthy lifestyle on track with these half-hour entrees that are both delicious and good for you...from hearty one-pot meals to juicy burgers and wraps.

Cran-Apple Turkey Skillet F

PREP/TOTAL TIME: 20 min. YIELD: 6 servings

LISA RENSHAW • KANSAS CITY, MISSOURI

This quick and easy skillet meal has such wide appeal that it will become one of your favorite go-to recipes. The end result is a one-dish rendition of a Thanksgiving feast. Best of all, it comes together in just half an hour!

- 2 medium apples, peeled and thinly sliced
- 3/4 cup apple cider *or* unsweetened apple juice
- 3/4 cup reduced-sodium chicken broth
- 1/3 cup dried cranberries
- 1/8 tsp. ground nutmeg
- 3 cups cubed cooked turkey breast
- 1 pkg. (6 oz.) corn bread stuffing mix

1. In a large skillet, combine the apples, apple cider, broth, cranberries and nutmeg. Bring to a boil. Reduce heat; cover and simmer for 4-5 minutes or until apples are tender, stirring occasionally.

2. Stir in turkey and stuffing mix. Cover and cook for 2-3 minutes or until heated through.

Nutrition Facts: 1 cup equals 267 calories, 2 g fat (trace saturated fat), 60 mg cholesterol, 630 mg sodium, 36 g carbohydrate, 2 g fiber, 25 g protein. **Diabetic Exchanges:** 3 lean meat, 1 starch, 1 fruit.

Gingered Spaghetti Salad

PREP/TOTAL TIME: 30 min. YIELD: 8 servings

CINDY HEINBAUGH • AURORA, COLORADO

With a wonderful blend of bright flavors and colors, this cold pasta salad—bursting with yummy vegetables—is ideal for warm summer days. Try it alongside a whole wheat roll for a complete meal!

- 1 pkg. (16 oz.) spaghetti
- 1 cup frozen shelled edamame
- 3 cups cubed cooked chicken breast
- 1 English cucumber, chopped
- 1 medium sweet red pepper, chopped
- 1 small sweet yellow pepper, chopped
- 1 small red onion, chopped
- 1 tsp. minced fresh gingerroot
- 1 cup reduced-fat sesame ginger salad dressing
- 3 green onions, chopped

1. In a Dutch oven, cook spaghetti according to package directions, adding edamame during the last 5 minutes of cooking. Drain and rinse in cold water.

2. Place in a large bowl. Stir in the chicken, cucumber, peppers, red onion and ginger.

3. Drizzle with dressing; toss to coat. Sprinkle with green onions.

Nutrition Facts: 1-3/4 cups equals 364 calories, 5 g fat (1 g saturated fat), 40 mg cholesterol, 431 mg sodium, 53 g carbohydrate, 3 g fiber, 25 g protein.

Skewerless Stovetop Kabobs

PREP/TOTAL TIME: 30 min. YIELD: 4 servings

JENNIFER MITCHELL • ALTOONA, PENNSYLVANIA

My family loves this fast and simple recipe so much, we never have any leftovers. It's also great on the grill. In addition, it's a fine way to use a few items from your garden.

- 1 pork tenderloin (1 lb.), cut into 3/4-in. cubes
- 3/4 cup fat-free Italian salad dressing, *divided*
- 2 large green peppers, cut into 3/4-in. pieces
- 2 small zucchini, cut into 1/2-in. slices
- 1/2 pound medium fresh mushrooms, halved
- 1 large sweet onion, cut into wedges
- 1 cup cherry tomatoes
- 1/4 tsp. pepper
- 1/8 tsp. seasoned salt

1. In a large nonstick skillet, saute pork in 1/4 cup dressing until no longer pink. Remove and keep warm. In the same pan, cook the peppers, zucchini, mushrooms, onion, tomatoes, pepper and seasoned salt in remaining salad dressing until vegetables are tender. Return pork to skillet; heat through.

Nutrition Facts: 2 cups equals 236 calories, 5 g fat (2 g saturated fat), 65 mg cholesterol, 757 mg sodium, 22 g carbohydrate, 4 g fiber, 27 g protein. **Diabetic Exchanges:** 3 lean meat, 2 starch.

Breaded Fish Sandwiches

PREP/TOTAL TIME: 30 min. YIELD: 4 servings

MILDRED CARUSO • BRIGHTON, TENNESSEE

The seasoned breading of this hearty sandwich turns mild-flavored cod or halibut into a taste sensation, and the creamy sauce just keeps it going!

1/2	cup dry bread crumbs
1/2	tsp. garlic powder
1/2	tsp. paprika
1/2	tsp. cayenne pepper
1/4	tsp. lemon-pepper seasoning
4	halibut or cod fillets (6 oz. *each*)
4	whole wheat hamburger buns, split
1	cup shredded lettuce
1/4	cup shredded carrots
1	Tbsp. grated onion, optional

SAUCE:

1/4	cup plain yogurt
1	Tbsp. lemon juice
1/2	tsp. dill weed
1/4	tsp. garlic powder
1/4	tsp. grated lemon peel
1/4	tsp. prepared horseradish

1. In a shallow bowl, combine the first five ingredients. Coat fillets with bread crumb mixture.

2. Using long-handled tongs, moisten a paper towel with cooking oil and lightly coat the grill rack. Grill halibut, covered, over medium heat or broil 4 in. from the heat for 4-5 minutes on each side or until fish flakes easily with a fork.

3. Grill buns, cut side down, over medium heat for 30-60 seconds or until toasted.

4. Meanwhile, in a small bowl, combine the lettuce, carrots and onion if desired; set aside. In another small bowl, combine the sauce ingredients; spread over bun bottoms. Top with halibut and vegetable mixture; replace bun tops.

Nutrition Facts: 1 sandwich equals 337 calories, 7 g fat (1 g saturated fat), 56 mg cholesterol, 356 mg sodium, 28 g carbohydrate, 4 g fiber, 41 g protein. **Diabetic Exchanges:** 5 lean meat, 2 starch.

Easy Greek Pizza

PREP/TOTAL TIME: 30 min. YIELD: 6 servings

JENNIFER BECK • MERIDIAN, IDAHO

Mix up the weeknight doldrums with this change-of-pace dinner. I created this recipe when trying to use up leftovers from a dinner party. If you prefer to go meatless, it's great without the chicken breast, too.

- 1 prebaked 12-in. pizza crust
- 1/2 cup pizza sauce
- 1 tsp. lemon-pepper seasoning, *divided*
- 2 cups shredded cooked chicken breast
- 1-1/2 cups chopped fresh spinach
- 1 small red onion, thinly sliced and separated into rings
- 1/4 cup sliced ripe olives
- 3/4 cup shredded part-skim mozzarella cheese
- 1/2 cup crumbled feta cheese

1. Place crust on an ungreased baking sheet; spread with pizza sauce and sprinkle with 1/2 tsp. lemon-pepper seasoning. Top with chicken, spinach, onion, olives, cheeses and remaining lemon-pepper seasoning.

2. Bake at 450° for 12-15 minutes or until edges are lightly browned and cheese is melted.

Nutrition Facts: 1 slice equals 321 calories, 9 g fat (4 g saturated fat), 49 mg cholesterol, 719 mg sodium, 32 g carbohydrate, 2 g fiber, 26 g protein. **Diabetic Exchanges:** 3 lean meat, 2 starch, 1/2 fat.

Chicken Cutlets With Citrus Cherry Sauce

PREP/TOTAL TIME: 30 min. YIELD: 4 servings

CHARLENE CHAMBERS • ORMOND BEACH, FLORIDA

You'll love the sweet-tart tanginess of this restaurant-quality chicken dish. Served with a salad, this is a meal to remember. It's also good with pork cutlets and dried cranberries instead of chicken and cherries.

- 4 boneless skinless chicken breast halves (6 oz. *each*)
- 1/2 tsp. salt
- 1/4 tsp. pepper
- 1/4 cup all-purpose flour
- 1/2 cup ruby red grapefruit juice
- 1/2 cup orange juice
- 1/3 cup dried cherries
- 2 tsp. Dijon mustard
- 1 Tbsp. butter
- 1 Tbsp. canola oil

1. Flatten chicken breasts to 1/2-in. thickness; sprinkle with salt and pepper. Place flour in a large resealable plastic bag. Add the chicken, a few pieces at a time, and shake to coat; set aside.

2. In a small saucepan, combine the juices, cherries and mustard. Bring to a boil; cook until liquid is reduced to 1/2 cup.

3. In a large skillet over medium heat, cook chicken in butter and oil for 5-7 minutes on each side or until juices run clear. Serve with sauce.

Nutrition Facts: 1 chicken breast half with 2 Tbsp. sauce equals 316 calories, 10 g fat (3 g saturated fat), 102 mg cholesterol, 458 mg sodium, 18 g carbohydrate, trace fiber, 35 g protein. **Diabetic Exchanges:** 5 lean meat, 1 starch, 1 fat.

Place boneless chicken breasts between two pieces of waxed paper or plastic wrap or in a resealable plastic bag. Starting in the center and working out to the edges, pound lightly with the flat side of a meat mallet until the chicken is even in thickness.

CHICKEN CUTLETS WITH CITRUS CHERRY SAUCE

EASY GREEK PIZZA

Pastrami Deli Wraps

PREP/TOTAL TIME: 20 min.   YIELD: 4 servings

NILA GRAHL • GURNEE, ILLINOIS

I sometimes add horseradish when making these wonderful wraps for my husband and me. These work well for larger crowds, too, and the ingredients are easy to multiply.

- 1/4   cup reduced-fat spreadable cream cheese
- 1/4   cup coarsely chopped roasted sweet red pepper
- 4   spinach tortillas (8 in.)
- 4   lettuce leaves
- 4   slices deli pastrami
- 4   slices reduced-fat provolone cheese
- 1/4   cup thinly sliced red onion
- 1   small sweet red pepper, julienned
- 1/2   cup chopped cucumber

1. Place cream cheese and roasted pepper in a small food processor. Cover and process until blended. Spread over tortillas. Layer with remaining ingredients; roll up. Secure with toothpicks.

Nutrition Facts: 1 wrap equals 271 calories, 10 g fat (4 g saturated fat), 29 mg cholesterol, 697 mg sodium, 29 g carbohydrate, 1 g fiber, 15 g protein. **Diabetic Exchanges:** 2 medium-fat meat, 1-1/2 starch, 1 vegetable, 1 fat.

Taco-Stuffed Pepper Cups

PREP/TOTAL TIME: 30 min.   YIELD: 4 servings

PAT HABIGER • SPEARVILLE, KANSAS

When green, red or yellow bell peppers are plentiful, they create a colorful container for this spicy taco mixture that's ready in record time.

- 2   medium green peppers
- 1/2   lb. ground beef *or* lean ground turkey
- 2   Tbsp. chopped onion
- 1   can (16 oz.) kidney beans, rinsed and drained
- 1   can (8 oz.) tomato sauce
- 3   Tbsp. taco seasoning
- 1/4   cup sour cream
- 1/4   cup shredded cheddar cheese
- 1/4   cup chopped tomato

1. Cut tops off peppers and remove seeds. In a large kettle, cook peppers in boiling water for 3-5 minutes. Drain and rinse in cold water; set aside.

2. In a large skillet, cook beef and onion over medium heat until meat is no longer pink; drain. Stir in the beans, tomato sauce and taco seasoning; bring to a boil. Reduce heat; simmer, uncovered, for 5-6 minutes or until heated through.

3. Spoon into peppers. Place in an ungreased 8-in. square baking dish. Bake, uncovered, at 350° for 10-12 minutes or until peppers are tender. Top with sour cream, cheese and tomatoes.

Nutrition Facts: 1 stuffed pepper half (prepared with ground turkey, fat-free sour cream and reduced-fat cheddar cheese) equals 261 calories, 6 g fat (2 g saturated fat), 52 mg cholesterol, 823 mg sodium, 31 g carbohydrate, 7 g fiber, 21 g protein. **Diabetic Exchanges:** 2 lean meat, 2 vegetable, 1-1/2 starch, 1 fat.

Mushroom Bean Burritos Ⓜ

PREP/TOTAL TIME: 30 min.   YIELD: 6 servings

TRISHA KRUSE • EAGLE, IDAHO

The whole family will love this. The filling can be used for tacos, nachos, enchiladas or salads.

- 2   medium sweet red peppers, thinly sliced
- 2   medium onions, sliced
- 1   lb. small fresh mushrooms, quartered
- 1/4   cup water
- 1/4   cup vegetable broth
- 3   garlic cloves, minced
- 1   can (16 oz.) vegetarian refried beans

PASTRAMI DELI WRAPS

MUSHROOM BEAN BURRITOS

3/4 cup salsa

1 Tbsp. chili powder

1 tsp. chipotle hot pepper sauce

6 whole wheat tortilla (8 in.), warmed

3/4 cup shredded reduced-fat cheddar cheese

1. In a large nonstick skillet coated with cooking spray, saute peppers and onions until crisp-tender. Stir in the mushrooms, water, broth and garlic. Bring to a boil. Reduce heat; simmer, uncovered, for 8-10 minutes or until vegetables are tender and liquid has evaporated.

2. Stir in the beans, salsa, chili powder and pepper sauce; heat through.

3. Spoon 1 cup filling off center on each tortilla. Sprinkle with cheese. Fold sides and ends over filling and roll up.

Nutrition Facts: 1 burrito equals 310 calories, 7 g fat (2 g saturated fat), 10 mg cholesterol, 798 mg sodium, 47 g carbohydrate, 9 g fiber, 15 g protein.

Caribbean Chicken Tenderloins

PREP/TOTAL TIME: 20 min. YIELD: 4 servings

LAURA MCALLISTER • MORGANTON, NORTH CAROLINA

This recipe is so fast and tasty. The light and sweet sauce perfectly offsets the bold jerk seasoning.

1 lb. chicken tenderloins

2 tsp. Caribbean jerk seasoning

3 tsp. olive oil, *divided*

2-1/2 cups cut fresh asparagus (2-in. pieces)

1 cup pineapple tidbits, drained

4 green onions, chopped

2 tsp. cornstarch

1 cup unsweetened pineapple juice

1 Tbsp. spicy brown mustard

2 cups hot cooked rice

1. Rub chicken with jerk seasoning. In a large skillet coated with cooking spray, cook chicken in 1 tsp. oil over medium heat for 3-4 minutes on each side or until juices run clear. Remove and keep warm.

2. In the same skillet, saute the asparagus, pineapple and onions in remaining oil for 2-3 minutes or until tender. Combine the cornstarch, pineapple juice and mustard until smooth; gradually stir into the pan. Bring to a boil; cook and stir for 2 minutes or until thickened. Serve with chicken and rice.

Nutrition Facts: 3 oz. cooked chicken with 1/2 cup asparagus mixture and 1/2 cup rice equals 314 calories, 4 g fat (1 g saturated fat), 67 mg cholesterol, 247 mg sodium, 40 g carbohydrate, 2 g fiber, 29 g protein. **Diabetic Exchanges:** 3 lean meat, 2 starch, 1/2 fruit, 1/2 fat.

To prepare **asparagus**, rinse stalks in cold water. Snap the stalk ends as far down as they will easily break when bent, or cut off the tough white portion. Use a veggie peeler to remove the tough skin of larger stalks.

Mediterranean Chicken

PREP/TOTAL TIME: 30 min. **YIELD:** 4 servings

KARA ZILIS • OAK FOREST, ILLINOIS

I've discovered that my friends and family love this flavorful twist on a classic chicken entree. Stewed tomatoes, green beans and brown rice increase the nutritional value, but it tastes just as good as the original.

4	boneless skinless chicken breast halves (4 oz. *each*)
1	Tbsp. olive oil
1	can (14-1/2 oz.) no-salt-added stewed tomatoes
1	can (14-1/2 oz.) cut green beans, drained
1	cup water
1	tsp. dried oregano
1/4	tsp. garlic powder
1-1/2	cups instant brown rice
12	pitted Greek olives, halved
1/2	cup crumbled feta cheese

1. In a large nonstick skillet, brown chicken in oil on each side. Stir in the tomatoes, green beans, water, oregano and garlic powder. Bring to a boil; reduce heat. Cover and simmer for 10 minutes.

2. Stir in rice. Return to a boil. Cover and simmer 8-10 minutes longer or until a meat thermometer reads 170° and rice is tender. Stir in olives; sprinkle with cheese.

Nutrition Facts: 1 chicken breast half with 1 cup rice mixture and 2 Tbsp. cheese equals 394 calories, 12 g fat (3 g saturated fat), 70 mg cholesterol, 724 mg sodium, 37 g carbohydrate, 6 g fiber, 30 g protein. **Diabetic Exchanges:** 3 lean meat, 2 starch, 2 vegetable, 1 fat.

Zesty Hamburger Soup

PREP/TOTAL TIME: 30 min.
YIELD: 10 servings (3-3/4 qt.)

KELLY MILAN • LAKE JACKSON, TEXAS

You won't face early afternoon hunger when this hearty soup is part of your lunch. Freeze leftovers in small batches so a meal for one or two is just moments away.

1	lb. lean ground beef (90% lean)
2	cups sliced celery
1	cup chopped onion
2	tsp. minced garlic
4	cups hot water
2	medium red potatoes, peeled and cubed
2	cups frozen corn
1-1/2	cups uncooked small shell pasta
4	pickled jalapeno slices
4	cups V8 juice
2	cans (10 oz. *each*) diced tomatoes with green chilies
1	to 2 Tbsp. sugar

1. In a Dutch oven, cook the beef, celery and onion over medium heat until meat is no longer pink. Add garlic; cook 1 minute longer. Drain. Stir in the water, potatoes, corn, pasta and jalapeno.

2. Bring to a boil. Reduce heat; cover and simmer for 10-15 minutes or until pasta is tender. Stir in the remaining ingredients. Cook and stir until heated through.

Nutrition Facts: 1-1/2 cups equals 222 calories, 5 g fat (2 g saturated fat), 28 mg cholesterol, 542 mg sodium, 33 g carbohydrate, 4 g fiber, 14 g protein. **Diabetic Exchanges:** 2 vegetable, 1-1/2 starch, 1 lean meat.

Grilled Mixed Green Salad C M

PREP/TOTAL TIME: 25 min. YIELD: 12 servings

JANICE ELDER • CHARLOTTE, NORTH CAROLINA

Grilling the lettuce adds smoky flavor and takes a simple salad to a whole new level. The fruits and nuts offer different dimensions of flavor and texture.

- 2 heads Belgian endive, halved lengthwise
- 2 bunches romaine, halved lengthwise
- 1 head radicchio, quartered lengthwise
- 5 Tbsp. olive oil, *divided*
- 1/2 tsp. salt
- 1/4 tsp. pepper
- 2 Tbsp. balsamic vinegar
- 1 cup fresh blueberries
- 1 medium apple, thinly sliced
- 1/4 cup chopped walnuts, toasted
- 1/4 cup shaved Parmesan cheese

1. Brush the endive, romaine and radicchio with 3 Tbsp. oil. Sprinkle with salt and pepper.

2. Using long-handled tongs, moisten a paper towel with cooking oil and lightly coat the grill rack. Grill the greens, uncovered, over medium heat for 30 seconds on each side or until heated through.

3. Chop the greens and place in a large serving bowl. Whisk vinegar and remaining oil; drizzle over greens and toss to coat. Top with blueberries, apple, walnuts and cheese.

Nutrition Facts: 1 cup equals 117 calories, 8 g fat (1 g saturated fat), 1 mg cholesterol, 157 mg sodium, 10 g carbohydrate, 5 g fiber, 4 g protein. **Diabetic Exchanges:** 1 vegetable, 1 fat, 1/2 starch.

Skillet Ranch Burgers

PREP/TOTAL TIME: 30 min. YIELD: 4 servings

DEBRA JUSTICE • MOODY, TEXAS

Lean ground turkey keeps these burgers light, while jalapenos and ranch dressing mix add great zestiness.

- 1/2 cup soft bread crumbs
- 1 small onion, finely chopped
- 1 small green pepper, finely chopped
- 2 jalapeno peppers, seeded and finely chopped
- 1/4 cup egg substitute
- 1-1/4 tsp. ranch salad dressing mix
- 1 tsp. garlic powder
- 1/2 tsp. hot pepper sauce
- 1 lb. lean ground turkey
- 4 whole wheat hamburger buns, split
- 4 lettuce leaves
- 4 slices tomato
- 4 slices onion

SAUCE:
- 1/2 cup fat-free sour cream
- 1 tsp. ranch salad dressing mix

1. In a large bowl, combine the first eight ingredients. Crumble turkey over mixture and mix well. Shape into four patties.

2. In a large nonstick skillet coated with cooking spray, cook patties over medium heat for 6-8 minutes on each side or until a meat thermometer reads 165° and juices run clear.

3. Serve on buns with lettuce, tomato and onion. Combine sour cream and dressing mix; spoon over burgers.

Editor's Note: When cutting hot peppers, disposable gloves are recommended. Avoid touching your face.

Nutrition Facts: 1 burger equals 373 calories, 12 g fat (3 g saturated fat), 95 mg cholesterol, 772 mg sodium, 39 g carbohydrate, 5 g fiber, 29 g protein. **Diabetic Exchanges:** 3 lean meat, 2 starch, 1 vegetable.

GRILLED MIXED GREEN SALAD

SKILLET RANCH BURGERS

Meat 'n' Potato Kabobs

PREP/TOTAL TIME: 30 min. **YIELD:** 4 servings

HEALTHY COOKING TEST KITCHEN

Even the pickiest eaters at your table won't be able to resist these kabobs, which are as pretty as they are tasty. The surprising secret ingredient? A bit of cola!

1	lb. beef top sirloin steak, cut into 1-in. cubes
1-1/2	tsp. steak seasoning, *divided*
1	tsp. minced garlic
1	cup cola
3	small red potatoes, cubed
1	Tbsp. water
1	cup cherry tomatoes
1	medium sweet orange pepper, cut into 1-in. pieces
1	tsp. canola oil
1	cup pineapple chunks

1. Sprinkle beef cubes with 1 tsp. steak seasoning and garlic; place in a large resealable plastic bag. Add cola. Seal bag and turn to coat; set aside.

2. Place the potatoes and water in a microwave-safe dish; cover and microwave on high for 4 minutes or until tender. Drain. Add the tomatoes, orange pepper, oil and remaining steak seasoning; toss gently to coat.

3. Drain and discard marinade. Alternately thread the beef, vegetables and pineapple onto eight metal or soaked wooden skewers. Grill, covered, over medium-hot heat or broil 4-6 in. from the heat for 4 minutes on each side or until meat reaches desired doneness (for medium-rare, a meat thermometer should read 145°; medium, 160°; well-done, 170°).

Editor's Note: This recipe was tested in a 1,100-watt microwave. This recipe was tested with McCormick's Montreal Steak Seasoning. Look for it in the spice aisle.

Nutrition Facts: 1 kabob (prepared with diet cola) equals 251 calories, 7 g fat (2 g saturated fat), 63 mg cholesterol, 311 mg sodium, 23 g carbohydrate, 3 g fiber, 24 g protein. **Diabetic Exchanges:** 3 lean meat, 1 starch, 1/2 fruit.

Tortellini Primavera

PREP/TOTAL TIME: 30 min. **YIELD:** 5 servings

SUSIE PIETROWSKI • BELTON, TEXAS

This decadent tortellini with spinach, mushrooms and tomatoes always brings compliments. Dressed up with fresh Parmesan cheese, no one even notices it's meatless!

1	pkg. (19 oz.) frozen cheese tortellini
1/2	lb. sliced fresh mushrooms
1	small onion, chopped
2	tsp. butter
2	garlic cloves, minced
2/3	cup fat-free milk
1	pkg. (8 oz.) fat-free cream cheese, cubed
1	pkg. (10 oz.) frozen chopped spinach, thawed and squeezed dry
1	tsp. Italian seasoning
1	large tomato, chopped
1/4	cup shredded Parmesan cheese

1. Cook tortellini according to package directions. Meanwhile, in a large nonstick skillet coated with cooking spray, saute mushrooms and onion in butter until tender. Add garlic; cook 1 minute longer. Stir in milk; heat through. Stir in cream cheese until blended. Add spinach and Italian seasoning; heat through.

2. Drain tortellini; toss with sauce and tomato. Sprinkle with Parmesan cheese.

Nutrition Facts: 1-1/4 cups equals 341 calories, 10 g fat (5 g saturated fat), 28 mg cholesterol, 671 mg sodium, 41 g carbohydrate, 4 g fiber, 23 g protein. **Diabetic Exchanges:** 2-1/2 starch, 2 lean meat, 1 vegetable.

MEAT 'N' POTATO KABOBS

TORTELLINI PRIMAVERA

SPICY SHRIMP WRAPS

Spicy Shrimp Wraps

PREP/TOTAL TIME: 20 min. **YIELD:** 6 servings

FRANKIE ALLEN MANN • WARRIOR, ALABAMA

These hearty grab-and-go wraps are packed with spicy flavor and sweetened with mango. They'll win over family and friends in less time than they take to assemble.

1	cup salsa
1	medium ripe mango, peeled, pitted and diced
1	Tbsp. ketchup
1	envelope reduced-sodium taco seasoning
1	Tbsp. olive oil
1	lb. uncooked medium shrimp, peeled and deveined
6	flour tortillas (10 in.), warmed
1-1/2	cups coleslaw mix
6	Tbsp. reduced-fat sour cream

1. In a small bowl, combine the salsa, mango and ketchup; set aside. In a large resealable plastic bag, combine taco seasoning and oil; add shrimp. Seal bag and shake to coat.

2. In a nonstick skillet or wok, cook shrimp over medium-high heat for 2-3 minutes or until shrimp turn pink. Top tortillas with coleslaw mix, salsa mixture and shrimp. Fold bottom third of tortilla up over filling; fold sides over. Serve with sour cream.

Nutrition Facts: 1 wrap equals 374 calories, 9 g fat (2 g saturated fat), 97 mg cholesterol, 1,010 mg sodium, 46 g carbohydrate, 7 g fiber, 20 g protein. **Diabetic Exchanges:** 3 starch, 2 lean meat, 1 fat.

Tuna Caesar Sandwiches

PREP/TOTAL TIME: 20 min. **YIELD:** 4 servings

GLORIA BRADLEY • NAPERVILLE, ILLINOIS

I've always loved tuna sandwiches because they're such a cinch to make. Plus, they're versatile; you can add so many different ingredients to tuna.

2	cans (5 oz. *each*) white water-packed tuna, drained and flaked
1/4	cup marinated quartered artichoke hearts, drained and chopped
1/4	cup finely chopped onion
1/4	cup reduced-fat mayonnaise
3	Tbsp. grated Parmesan cheese
2	tsp. lemon juice
1	tsp. Dijon mustard
8	slices whole wheat bread, toasted
16	cucumber slices
8	slices tomato
2	cups shredded lettuce

1. In a small bowl, combine the first seven ingredients. Spread over four slices of toast. Top with cucumber, tomato, lettuce and remaining toast.

Nutrition Facts: 1 sandwich equals 338 calories, 12 g fat (3 g saturated fat), 38 mg cholesterol, 797 mg sodium, 30 g carbohydrate, 5 g fiber, 27 g protein. **Diabetic Exchanges:** 3 lean meat, 2 starch, 1 fat.

Sensational Spiced Salmon C

PREP/TOTAL TIME: 25 min. YIELD: 4 servings

MICHELE DOUCETTE
STEPHENVILLE, NEWFOUNDLAND AND LABRADOR

A sweet and spicy rub gives this quick salmon entree fantastic flavor. Paired with a green veggie and rice, it's a delightful weeknight dinner that's special enough for company.

    2 Tbsp. brown sugar
    4 tsp. chili powder
    2 tsp. grated lemon peel
  3/4 tsp. ground cumin
  1/2 tsp. salt
  1/4 tsp. ground cinnamon
    4 salmon fillets (4 oz. *each*)

1. Combine the first six ingredients; rub over salmon. Place in an 11-in. x 7-in. baking dish coated with cooking spray. Bake, uncovered, at 350° for 15-20 minutes or until fish flakes easily with a fork.

Nutrition Facts: 1 fillet equals 244 calories, 13 g fat (3 g saturated fat), 67 mg cholesterol, 392 mg sodium, 9 g carbohydrate, 1 g fiber, 23 g protein. **Diabetic Exchanges:** 3 lean meat, 1/2 starch.

Lasagna Soup

PREP/TOTAL TIME: 30 min. YIELD: 8 servings

SHERYL OLENICK • DEMAREST, NEW JERSEY

All the traditional flavors of lasagna come together in this heartwarming meal-in-a-bowl.

      1 lb. lean ground beef (90% lean)
      1 large green pepper, chopped
      1 medium onion, chopped
      2 garlic cloves, minced
      2 cans (14-1/2 oz. *each*) reduced-sodium beef broth
      2 cans (14-1/2 oz. *each*) diced tomatoes
      1 can (8 oz.) tomato sauce
      1 cup frozen corn
    1/4 cup tomato paste
      2 tsp. Italian seasoning
    1/4 tsp. pepper
  2-1/2 cups uncooked spiral pasta
    1/2 cup shredded Parmesan cheese

1. In a large saucepan, cook the beef, green pepper and onion over medium heat until meat is no longer pink. Add garlic; cook 1 minute longer. Drain.

2. Stir in the broth, tomatoes, tomato sauce, corn, tomato paste, Italian seasoning and pepper. Bring to a boil. Stir in pasta. Return to a boil. Reduce heat; cover and simmer for 10-12 minutes or until pasta is tender. Sprinkle with cheese.

Nutrition Facts: 1-1/3 cups equals 280 calories, 7 g fat (3 g saturated fat), 41 mg cholesterol, 572 mg sodium, 35 g carbohydrate, 4 g fiber, 20 g protein. **Diabetic Exchanges:** 2 lean meat, 2 vegetable, 1-1/2 starch.

Gnocchi with White Beans Ⓜ

PREP/TOTAL TIME: 30 min. YIELD: 6 servings

JULIANNE MEYERS • HINESVILLE, GEORGIA

Warm tummies and hearts on frosty nights with this yummy skillet dish full of spinach, tomatoes, beans, gnocchi, melty cheese and Italian flavors. It makes a fast and easy supper-in-one.

1	medium onion, chopped
1	Tbsp. olive oil
2	garlic cloves, minced
1	pkg. (16 oz.) potato gnocchi
1	pkg. (6 oz.) fresh baby spinach
1	can (15 oz.) white kidney or cannellini beans, rinsed and drained
1	can (14-1/2 oz.) Italian diced tomatoes, undrained
1/4	tsp. pepper
1/2	cup shredded part-skim mozzarella cheese
3	Tbsp. grated Parmesan cheese

1. In a large skillet, saute onion in oil until tender. Add garlic; cook 1 minute longer. Add gnocchi; cook and stir for 5-6 minutes or until golden brown. Stir in spinach; cook until spinach is wilted.

2. Add the beans, tomatoes and pepper; heat through. Sprinkle with cheeses; cover and remove from the heat. Let stand for 3-4 minutes or until cheese is melted.

Editor's Note: Look for potato gnocchi in the pasta or frozen foods section.

Nutrition Facts: 1 cup equals 307 calories, 6 g fat (2 g saturated fat), 13 mg cholesterol, 789 mg sodium, 50 g carbohydrate, 6 g fiber, 13 g protein.

Hearty Pita Tacos

PREP/TOTAL TIME: 30 min. YIELD: 6 servings

JAMIE VALOCCHI • MESA, ARIZONA

You don't need to skimp on flavor when trying to eat healthy. Our 9-year-old daughter enjoys helping us make these tasty tacos and enjoys eating them even more.

1	lb. lean ground beef (90% lean)
1	small sweet red pepper, chopped
2	green onions, chopped
1	can (16 oz.) kidney beans, rinsed and drained
3/4	cup frozen corn
2/3	cup taco sauce
1	can (2-1/4 oz.) sliced ripe olives, drained
1/2	tsp. garlic salt
1/4	tsp. onion powder
1/4	tsp. dried oregano
1/4	tsp. paprika
1/4	tsp. pepper
6	whole wheat pita pocket halves
6	Tbsp. shredded reduced-fat cheddar cheese

Sliced avocado and additional taco sauce, optional

1. In a large skillet, cook the beef, red pepper and onions over medium heat until meat is no longer pink; drain. Stir in the beans, corn, taco sauce, olives and seasonings; heat through.

2. Spoon 3/4 cup beef mixture into each pita half. Sprinkle with cheese. Serve with avocado and additional taco sauce if desired.

Nutrition Facts: 1 filled pita half (calculated without avocado and optional ingredients) equals 339 calories, 10 g fat (4 g saturated fat), 52 mg cholesterol, 787 mg sodium, 38 g carbohydrate, 8 g fiber, 26 g protein. **Diabetic Exchanges:** 3 lean meat, 2-1/2 starch.

HEARTY PITA TACOS

GNOCCHI WITH WHITE BEANS

Beef Stroganoff

PREP/TOTAL TIME: 30 min. YIELD: 5 servings

PATTY RODY • PUYALLUP, WASHINGTON

Creamy and comforting, you'll crave this hearty Beef Stroganoff no matter what the weather.

5	Tbsp. all-purpose flour, *divided*
1/2	tsp. salt
1	lb. beef top sirloin steak, cut into thin strips
4	Tbsp. butter, *divided*
1	cup sliced fresh mushrooms
1/2	cup chopped sweet onion
1	garlic clove, minced
1	Tbsp. tomato paste
1-1/4	cups beef broth
1	cup (8 oz.) sour cream
2	Tbsp. sherry *or* beef broth

Hot cooked egg noodles *or* brown rice

1. In a large resealable plastic bag, combine 2 Tbsp. flour and salt. Add beef, a few pieces at a time, and shake to coat. In a large skillet over medium-high heat, brown beef in 2 Tbsp. butter. Add mushrooms and onion; cook and stir until vegetables are tender. Add garlic; cook 1 minute longer. Remove and keep warm.

2. In the same skillet, melt remaining butter. Stir in tomato paste and remaining flour until smooth. Gradually add broth; bring to a boil. Cook and stir for 2 minutes or until thickened.

3. Carefully return beef mixture to the pan. Add sour cream and sherry; heat through (do not boil). Serve with noodles or rice.

Nutrition Facts: 1 cup (calculated without noodles) equals 338 calories, 21 g fat (13 g saturated fat), 107 mg cholesterol, 581 mg sodium, 11 g carbohydrate, 1 g fiber, 21 g protein.

Hearty Vegetarian Chili ✉

PREP/TOTAL TIME: 30 min. YIELD: 9 servings (2-1/4 qt.)

PAM IVBULS • OMAHA, NEBRASKA

Rich and flavorful, this chili is absolutely packed with fun veggies like mushrooms, beans and sun-dried tomatoes. It's so filling, you'll fool any meat lover.

1-3/4	cups chopped baby portobello mushrooms
1	medium onion, finely chopped
1/2	cup chopped sun-dried tomatoes (not packed in oil)
2	Tbsp. olive oil
2	garlic cloves, minced
1	pkg. (12 oz.) frozen vegetarian meat crumbles
2	cans (16 oz. *each*) chili beans, undrained
2	cans (14-1/2 oz. *each*) no-salt-added diced tomatoes
1/2	cup water
1/2	cup vegetable broth
4-1/2	tsp. chili powder
2	tsp. brown sugar
1/2	tsp. celery salt
1/2	tsp. ground cumin
1	medium ripe avocado, peeled and finely chopped
9	Tbsp. reduced-fat sour cream

1. In a Dutch oven, saute the mushrooms, onion, sun-dried tomatoes in oil until vegetables are tender. Add garlic; cook 1 minute longer. Add meat crumbles; heat through.

2. Stir in the chili beans, tomatoes, water, broth, chili powder, brown sugar, celery salt and cumin. Bring to a boil. Reduce heat; simmer, uncovered, for 10 minutes. Ladle chili into bowls. Top each with avocado and sour cream.

Editor's Note: Vegetarian meat crumbles are a nutritious protein source made from soy. Look for them in the natural foods freezer section.

Nutrition Facts: 1 serving equals 275 calories, 10 g fat (2 g saturated fat), 5 mg cholesterol, 768 mg sodium, 37 g carbohydrate, 12 g fiber, 17 g protein. **Diabetic Exchanges:** 2 lean meat, 2 vegetable, 1-1/2 starch, 1 fat.

BEEF STROGANOFF

HEARTY VEGETARIAN CHILI

Black Bean Chicken with Rice

PREP/TOTAL: 25 min. YIELD: 4 servings

MOLLY NEWMAN • PORTLAND, OREGON

This family favorite only requires a few ingredients I tend to keep on hand, so it's easy to fix on even the busiest weeknight. The corn, black beans and salsa give this complete meal a Southwest-style kick.

    3 tsp. chili powder
    1 tsp. ground cumin
    1 tsp. pepper
  1/4 tsp. salt
    4 boneless skinless chicken breast halves
       (4 oz. *each*)
    2 tsp. canola oil
    1 can (15 oz.) black beans, rinsed and drained
    1 cup frozen corn
    1 cup salsa
    2 cups cooked brown rice

1. Combine the chili powder, cumin, pepper and salt; rub over chicken. In a large nonstick skillet coated with cooking spray, brown chicken in oil on both sides. Stir in the beans, corn and salsa. Cover and cook over medium heat for 10-15 minutes or until a meat thermometer reads 170°.

2. Slice chicken; serve with rice and bean mixture.

Nutrition Facts: 1 chicken breast half with 3/4 cup bean mixture and 1/2 cup rice equals 400 calories, 7 g fat (1 g saturated fat), 63 mg cholesterol, 670 mg sodium, 52 g carbohydrate, 8 g fiber, 32 g protein.

Giant Mushroom Burger

PREP/TOTAL TIME: 30 min. YIELD: 6 servings

JANICE DELAGRANGE • MT. AIRY, MARYLAND

I add mushrooms and onion to well-seasoned lean ground beef before forming it into one giant, crowd-pleasing patty. After grilling it, all I need to do is slice and serve.

1-1/2 lbs. lean ground beef (90% lean)
    1 can (4 oz.) mushroom stems and pieces,
       drained
  1/4 cup egg substitute
  1/2 cup chopped onion
  1/4 cup ketchup
    1 tsp. Italian seasoning
    1 tsp. fennel seed, crushed
  1/4 tsp. pepper
  1/4 tsp. Worcestershire sauce

1. In a large bowl, combine all the ingredients. Pat into a 9-in. circle on a large sheet of waxed paper. Invert onto a greased wire grill basket; peel off waxed paper.

2. Grill, covered, over medium heat or broil 4 in. from the heat for 10-13 minutes on each side or until a meat thermometer reads 160° and meat juices run clear. Cut into six wedges.

Editor's Note: If you do not have a grill basket or wok, use a disposable foil pan. Poke holes in the bottom of the pan with a meat fork to allow liquid to drain.

Nutrition Facts: 1 serving equals 224 calories, 11 g fat (4 g saturated fat), 41 mg cholesterol, 305 mg sodium, 6 g carbohydrate, 1 g fiber, 25 g protein. **Diabetic Exchanges:** 3 lean meat, 1 vegetable.

TERRIFIC TERIYAKI BURGERS

CHIPOTLE SHREDDED BEEF

CHILI TORTILLA BAKE

Beef Entrees

You may notice your mouth watering as you pore over this chapter. It's OK...give in to temptation. These lightened-up classics and tasty new creations are all fair game the next time you're craving steak for dinner.

Chili Tortilla Bake

PREP: 20 min. BAKE: 25 min. YIELD: 6 servings

CELINE WELDY • CAVE CREEK, ARIZONA

Young and old alike enjoy this dish. I'll sometimes assemble it the night before. With only 20 minutes of prep, this quick-to-fix oven entree is ideal for weeknight dining.

- 1 lb. extra-lean ground beef (95% lean)
- 2 cans (8 oz. *each*) no-salt-added tomato sauce
- 1 can (15 oz.) black beans, rinsed and drained
- 1 cup frozen corn
- 1 can (4 oz.) chopped green chilies
- 2 Tbsp. dried minced onion
- 2 Tbsp. chili powder
- 1 tsp. ground cumin
- 1/2 tsp. garlic powder
- 1/2 tsp. dried oregano
- 6 whole wheat tortillas (8 in.)
- 1 cup (4 oz.) shredded reduced-fat cheddar cheese

1. In a large skillet, cook beef over medium heat until no longer pink. Stir in the tomato sauce, beans, corn, green chilies, onion, chili powder, cumin, garlic powder and oregano; heat through.

2. In an 11-in. x 7-in. baking dish coated with cooking spray, layer half of the tortillas, beef mixture and cheese. Repeat layers. Bake, uncovered, at 350° for 25-30 minutes or until bubbly.

Nutrition Facts: 1 piece equals 413 calories, 11 g fat (4 g saturated fat), 56 mg cholesterol, 590 mg sodium, 47 g carbohydrate, 8 g fiber, 28 g protein.

Chipotle Shredded Beef

PREP: 25 min. COOK: 8 hours YIELD: 10 servings

DARCY WILLIAMS • OMAHA, NEBRASKA

This beef is delicious all rolled up in a tortilla, served with corn salsa and eaten as a burrito. You could also serve it over rice or mashed potatoes or in buns.

- 1 small onion, chopped
- 1 tsp. canola oil
- 1 can (28 oz.) diced tomatoes, undrained
- 1/4 cup cider vinegar
- 6 garlic cloves, minced
- 2 chipotle peppers in adobo sauce, chopped
- 2 Tbsp. brown sugar
- 2 bay leaves
- 2 tsp. adobo sauce
- 1/2 tsp. ground cumin
- 1/2 tsp. paprika
- 1/2 tsp. pepper
- 1/4 tsp. ground cinnamon
- 1 boneless beef chuck roast (2-1/2 lbs.)
- 5 cups cooked brown rice

Shredded reduced-fat cheddar cheese and reduced-fat sour cream, optional

1. In a large skillet coated with cooking spray, saute onion in oil until tender. Stir in the tomatoes, vinegar, garlic, peppers, brown sugar, bay leaves, adobo sauce and seasonings. Bring to a boil; reduce heat, simmer, uncovered for 4-6 minutes or until thickened.

2. Place roast in a 5-qt. slow cooker; add tomato mixture. Cover and cook on low heat for 8-9 hours or until meat is tender.

3. Discard bay leaves. Remove meat and shred with two forks. Skim fat from juices; return meat to slow cooker. Using a slotted spoon, serve meat with rice. Top with cheese and sour cream if desired.

Nutrition Facts: 2/3 cup beef mixture with 1/2 cup cooked brown rice (calculated without optional ingredients) equals 345 calories, 13 g fat (4 g saturated fat), 74 mg cholesterol, 194 mg sodium, 31 g carbohydrate, 3 g fiber, 26 g protein.

When **shredding beef** for sandwiches, remove meat from the pan, and reserve the cooking liquid if called for. Place the meat in a shallow pan. With two forks, pull meat in opposite directions to create thin shreds. Return the beef to the pan or use as the recipe directs.

Bean Beef Burgers

PREP/TOTAL TIME: 30 min. YIELD: 6 servings

JENNIFER KUNZ • AUSTIN, TEXAS

When it comes to health, I know how important it is to boost fiber with something as simple as whole grains. So if you want to enjoy a burger without the fat and, as a bonus, sneak in more fiber, give these a try.

- 1 cup water
- 1/2 cup bulgur
- 1 can (15 oz.) black beans, rinsed and drained
- 3 green onions, sliced
- 1 Tbsp. stone-ground mustard
- 1 garlic clove, halved
- 1/4 tsp. salt
- 1/4 tsp. pepper
- 1 egg, lightly beaten
- 1/2 lb. lean ground beef (90% lean)
- 1 Tbsp. canola oil
- 6 whole wheat hamburger buns, split

Spinach leaves, sliced red onion and tomato

1. In a small saucepan, bring water to a boil. Stir in bulgur. Reduce heat; cover and simmer for 15-20 minutes or until tender. In a food processor, combine the beans, onions, mustard and garlic. Cover and pulse until blended. Stir in salt and pepper.

2. In a large bowl, combine the egg, bulgur and bean mixture. Crumble beef over mixture and mix well. Shape into six patties.

3. In a large nonstick skillet, cook patties in oil in batches for 4-5 minutes on each side or until a meat thermometer reads 160° and juices run clear. Serve on buns with spinach, onion and tomato.

Nutrition Facts: 1 burger (calculated without spinach, onion and tomato) equals 307 calories, 8 g fat (2 g saturated fat), 54 mg cholesterol, 517 mg sodium, 42 g carbohydrate, 9 g fiber, 17 g protein. **Diabetic Exchanges:** 2 starch, 2 lean meat, 1 fat.

Round Steak Sauerbraten

PREP: 20 min. COOK: 7 hours YIELD: 10 servings

LINDA BLOOM • MCHENRY, ILLINOIS

It takes only minutes to ready round steak for the slow cooker; then it simmers to a tasty tenderness most of the day. The flavorful beef strips and sauce are nice over hot rice.

- 1 envelope brown gravy mix
- 2 Tbsp. plus 1-1/2 tsp. brown sugar
- 2-1/2 cups cold water, *divided*
- 1 cup chopped onion
- 2 Tbsp. white vinegar
- 2 tsp. Worcestershire sauce
- 4 bay leaves
- 2-1/2 lbs. boneless beef top round steak, cut into 3-in. x 1/2-in. strips
- 2 tsp. salt
- 1 tsp. pepper
- 1/4 cup cornstarch
- 10 cups hot cooked egg noodles

1. In a 5-qt. slow cooker, combine the gravy mix, brown sugar, 2 cups water, onion, vinegar, Worcestershire sauce and bay leaves.

BEAN BEEF BURGERS

ROUND STEAK SAUERBRATEN

2. Sprinkle beef with salt and pepper; stir into gravy mixture. Cover and cook on low for 6-1/2 to 7 hours or until meat is tender.

3. Combine cornstarch and remaining water until smooth; stir into beef mixture. Cover and cook on high for 30 minutes or until thickened. Discard bay leaves. Serve with noodles.

Nutrition Facts: 3/4 cup beef mixture with 1 cup noodles equals 331 calories, 6 g fat (2 g saturated fat), 96 mg cholesterol, 741 mg sodium, 37 g carbohydrate, 2 g fiber, 32 g protein. **Diabetic Exchanges:** 3 lean meat, 2-1/2 starch.

Barley Beef Skillet

10 pts

PREP: 20 min. **COOK:** 1 hour **YIELD:** 4 servings

KIT TUNSTALL • BOISE, IDAHO

Even my 3-year-old loves this family favorite. It's very filling, inexpensive and full of veggies. It's also really good spiced up with chili powder, cayenne or a dash of Tabasco.

  1 lb. lean ground beef (90% lean)
1/4 cup chopped onion
  1 garlic clove, minced
  1 can (14-1/2 oz.) reduced-sodium beef broth
  1 can (8 oz.) tomato sauce
  1 cup water
  2 small carrots, chopped
  1 small tomato, seeded and chopped
  1 small zucchini, chopped
  1 cup medium pearl barley
  2 tsp. Italian seasoning
1/4 tsp. salt
1/8 tsp. pepper

1. In a large skillet, cook beef and onion over medium heat until meat is no longer pink. Add garlic; cook 1 minute longer. Drain. Add the broth, tomato sauce and water; bring to a boil. Stir in the remaining ingredients. Reduce heat; cover and simmer for 45-50 minutes or until barley is tender.

Nutrition Facts: 1-1/2 cups equals 400 calories, 10 g fat (4 g saturated fat), 73 mg cholesterol, 682 mg sodium, 48 g carbohydrate, 10 g fiber, 30 g protein.

Keep in mind that the more fat there is in the meat, the more shrinkage there is during cooking. So if you're making burgers out of regular **ground beef**, shape the patties to be slightly larger than the buns.

Eggplant Zucchini Bolognese

PREP: 30 min. **COOK:** 20 min. **YIELD:** 8 servings

TRISHA KRUSE • EAGLE, IDAHO

I roast the veggies while the pasta cooks, making this a quick dish for weeknights. This meal-in-one blends rustic comfort with fresh flavors.

1	pkg. (16 oz.) penne pasta
1	small eggplant, peeled and cut into 1-in. pieces
1	medium zucchini, cut into 1/4-in. slices
1	medium yellow summer squash, cut into 1/4-in. slices
1	cup chopped onion
2	Tbsp. olive oil
2	tsp. minced garlic
1	tsp. salt
1/2	tsp. pepper
1	lb. lean ground beef (90% lean)
1	can (28 oz.) tomato puree
1	Tbsp. Italian seasoning
1	Tbsp. brown sugar
8	tsp. grated Parmesan cheese

1. Cook pasta according to package directions. In a large bowl, combine the eggplant, zucchini, squash, onion, oil, garlic, salt and pepper. Transfer to two 15-in. x 10-in. x 1-in. baking pans coated with cooking spray. Bake at 425° for 20-25 minutes or until tender.

2. Meanwhile, in a large skillet, cook beef over medium heat until no longer pink; drain. Stir in the tomato puree, Italian seasoning and brown sugar. Drain pasta; stir in tomato mixture and roasted vegetables. Sprinkle with cheese.

Nutrition Facts: 1-1/2 cups equals 395 calories, 10 g fat (3 g saturated fat), 36 mg cholesterol, 378 mg sodium, 56 g carbohydrate, 5 g fiber, 22 g protein.

Homemade Taco Seasoning Mix

PREP/TOTAL TIME: 20 min. **YIELD:** 4 servings per batch

HEALTHY COOKING TEST KITCHEN

This seasoning mix is right on. It tastes like purchased mixes, but is cheaper and has nearly half the sodium. Your heart and wallet will surely thank you!

1/4	cup all-purpose flour
1/4	cup chili powder
3	Tbsp. dried minced onion
1	Tbsp. garlic powder
2-1/2	tsp. salt
2	tsp. dried oregano
2	tsp. ground cumin
1-1/2	tsp. cayenne pepper
1	tsp. ground coriander

ADDITIONAL INGREDIENTS

1	lb. lean ground beef (90% lean)
3/4	cup water
4	whole wheat tortillas (8 in.), warmed

1. Combine the first nine ingredients. Store in an airtight container in a cool dry place for up to 1 year. Yield: 4 batches (about 1 cup total).

2. To prepare tacos: In a large skillet, cook beef over medium heat until no longer pink; drain. Add 1/4 cup taco seasoning mix and water. Bring to a boil; cook and stir for 2 minutes. Fill each tortilla with 1/2 cup beef mixture.

Nutrition Facts: 1 taco equals 338 calories, 13 g fat (4 g saturated fat), 71 mg cholesterol, 619 mg sodium, 26 g carbohydrate, 3 g fiber, 27 g protein.

Lasagna Corn Carne

PREP: 30 min. BAKE: 45 min. + standing
YIELD: 12 servings

MARY LOU WILLS • LA PLATA, MARYLAND

My grandkids always ask me to make this dish, which is sort of like chili in a pan. I came up with the recipe one day using just ingredients I had on hand. It was an instant hit.

- 1 lb. ground beef
- 1 jar (16 oz.) salsa
- 1 can (16 oz.) kidney beans, rinsed and drained
- 1 can (14-3/4 oz.) cream-style corn
- 1 large onion, chopped
- 1 medium green pepper, chopped
- 1 celery rib, chopped
- 3 garlic cloves, minced
- 1 Tbsp. minced fresh basil *or* 1 tsp. dried basil
- 1 tsp. salt
- 1 tsp. chili powder
- 12 lasagna noodles, cooked and drained
- 2 cups (8 oz.) shredded part-skim mozzarella cheese
- 1/2 cup grated Parmesan cheese

1. In a large skillet, cook beef over medium heat until no longer pink; drain. Add the salsa, beans, vegetables, garlic and seasonings. Bring to a boil. Reduce heat; cover and simmer for 15 minutes.

2. Spread a fourth of the meat sauce in a greased 13-in. x 9-in. baking dish; top with four noodles. Repeat layers once. Top with half of the remaining sauce; sprinkle with half of the cheeses. Layer with the remaining noodles, sauce and cheeses.

3. Cover and bake at 350° for 30 minutes. Uncover; bake 15-20 minutes longer or until heated through. Let stand for 15 minutes before cutting.

Nutrition Facts: 1 piece equals 313 calories, 10 g fat (5 g saturated fat), 42 mg cholesterol, 690 mg sodium, 35 g carbohydrate, 5 g fiber, 19 g protein.

Broiled Sirloin Steaks

PREP/TOTAL TIME: 20 min. YIELD: 4 servings

KAROL CHANDLER-EZELL • NACOGDOCHES, TEXAS

A butcher gave me great advice on cooking different types of meat. Broiling after marinating works really well on very lean cuts like this. Let the steaks rest for a couple of minutes before serving to preserve moistness.

- 2 Tbsp. lime juice
- 1 tsp. onion powder
- 1 tsp. garlic powder
- 1/4 tsp. ground mustard
- 1/4 tsp. dried oregano
- 1/4 tsp. dried thyme
- 4 beef top sirloin steaks (5 oz. *each*)
- 1 cup sliced fresh mushrooms

1. In a small bowl, combine the first six ingredients; rub over both sides of steaks.

2. Broil 4 in. from the heat for 7 minutes. Turn steaks; top with mushrooms. Broil 7-8 minutes longer or until meat reaches desired doneness (for medium-rare, a meat thermometer should read 145°; medium, 160°; well-done, 170°) and the mushrooms are tender.

Nutrition Facts: 1 steak with 3 Tbsp. mushrooms equals 187 calories, 7 g fat (3 g saturated fat), 80 mg cholesterol, 60 mg sodium, 3 g carbohydrate, trace fiber, 28 g protein. **Diabetic Exchange:** 4 lean meat.

BROILED SIRLOIN STEAKS

LASAGNA CORN CARNE

Biscuit-Topped Shepherd's Pies

PREP: 30 min. BAKE: 10 min. YIELD: 6 servings

JOSEPHINE PIRO • EASTON, PENNSYLVANIA

Here's a moist, hearty, comforting and cozy meal-in-one to warm your family on chilly fall days. No ramekins? Just spoon into an 8-in. square baking dish. You'll love this.

- 1 lb. lean ground beef (90% lean)
- 1 medium onion, chopped
- 1 celery rib, finely chopped
- 1 pkg. (16 oz.) frozen peas and carrots, thawed and drained
- 1 can (15 oz.) Italian tomato sauce
- 1/4 tsp. pepper
- 1 cup reduced-fat biscuit/baking mix
- 2 Tbsp. grated Parmesan cheese
- 1/4 tsp. dried rosemary, crushed
- 1/2 cup fat-free milk
- 2 Tbsp. butter, melted

1. In a large nonstick skillet, cook the beef, onion and celery over medium heat until meat is no longer pink; drain. Add the vegetables, tomato sauce and pepper; cook and stir for 5-6 minutes or until heated through. Spoon into six 8-oz. ramekins coated with cooking spray; set aside.

2. In a small bowl, combine the biscuit mix, cheese and rosemary. Stir in milk and butter just until moistened. Spoon dough over meat mixture; place ramekins on a baking sheet.

3. Bake at 425° for 10-12 minutes or until biscuits are golden brown.

BISCUIT-TOPPED SHEPHERD'S PIES

Nutrition Facts: 1 serving equals 311 calories, 12 g fat (5 g saturated fat), 59 mg cholesterol, 771 mg sodium, 31 g carbohydrate, 5 g fiber, 22 g protein. **Diabetic Exchanges:** 2 lean meat, 1-1/2 starch, 1 vegetable, 1 fat.

Spicy Goulash

PREP: 25 min. COOK: 5-1/2 hours YIELD: 12 servings

MELISSA POLK • WEST LAFAYETTE, INDIANA

Ground cumin, chili powder and a can of Mexican diced tomatoes jazz up my goulash recipe. Even the elbow macaroni is prepared in the slow cooker.

- 1 lb. lean ground beef (90% lean)
- 4 cans (14-1/2 oz. *each*) Mexican diced tomatoes, undrained
- 2 cans (16 oz. *each*) kidney beans, rinsed and drained
- 2 cups water
- 1 medium onion, chopped
- 1 medium green pepper, chopped
- 1/4 cup red wine vinegar
- 2 Tbsp. chili powder
- 1 Tbsp. Worcestershire sauce
- 2 tsp. beef bouillon granules
- 1 tsp. dried basil
- 1 tsp. dried parsley flakes
- 1 tsp. ground cumin
- 1/4 tsp. pepper
- 2 cups uncooked elbow macaroni

1. In a large skillet, cook beef over medium heat until no longer pink; drain. Transfer to a 5-qt. slow cooker. Stir in the tomatoes, beans, water, onion, green pepper, vinegar, chili powder, Worcestershire sauce, bouillon and seasonings.

2. Cover and cook on low for 5-6 hours or until heated through.

SPICY GOULASH

3. Stir in macaroni; cover and cook 30 minutes longer or until macaroni is tender.

Nutrition Facts: 1 cup equals 223 calories, 4 g fat (2 g saturated fat), 19 mg cholesterol, 741 mg sodium, 34 g carbohydrate, 7 g fiber, 15 g protein.

Pineapple Beef Stir-Fry

iDppt3

PREP: 20 min. + marinating **COOK:** 15 min.
YIELD: 4 servings

JACKIE DRAKE • TROUTMAN, NORTH CAROLINA

Packed with veggies, tender beef and pineapple tidbits, this sweet-and-sour stir-fry is ideal for blustery weeknights or activity-packed weekends.

1	cup unsweetened pineapple juice
1/4	cup white wine *or* reduced-sodium chicken broth
2	Tbsp. brown sugar
2	Tbsp. reduced-sodium soy sauce
1/4	tsp. cayenne pepper
1	beef top sirloin steak (1 lb.), cut into thin strips
2	Tbsp. cornstarch
1-1/2	tsp. olive oil, *divided*
2	large carrots, sliced
1	small onion, halved and sliced
1	medium green pepper, julienned
1/2	cup fresh snow peas
3/4	cup unsweetened pineapple tidbits
2	cups cooked brown rice

1. In a small bowl, combine the first five ingredients. Pour 2/3 cup marinade into a large resealable plastic bag; add the beef. Seal bag and turn to coat; refrigerate for 30 minutes. Cover and refrigerate remaining marinade.

2. In a small bowl, combine cornstarch and reserved marinade until smooth; set aside.

3. Drain and discard marinade. In a large nonstick skillet or wok, stir-fry beef in 1 tsp. oil for 2-3 minutes or until no longer pink. Remove with a slotted spoon and keep warm.

4. Stir-fry carrots and onion in remaining oil for 4 minutes. Add green pepper and snow peas; stir-fry 2-3 minutes longer or until vegetables are crisp-tender.

5. Stir cornstarch mixture and add to the pan. Bring to a boil; cook and stir for 2 minutes or until thickened. Add beef and pineapple; heat through. Serve with rice.

Nutrition Facts: 1 cup stir-fry with 1/2 cup rice equals 388 calories, 7 g fat (2 g saturated fat), 46 mg cholesterol, 324 mg sodium, 51 g carbohydrate, 5 g fiber, 29 g protein.

One-dish meals like stir-fries often call for thin strips of meat, which can be difficult to cut. To make the job easier, **partially freeze** larger cuts before slicing. The meat should be solid enough to slice evenly within 30 minutes.

AFRICAN BEEF CURRY

African Beef Curry

PREP: 15 min. **COOK:** 1-1/2 hours **YIELD:** 4 servings

HEATHER EWALD • BOTHELL, WASHINGTON

This African Beef Curry is a popular dish with my family and friends. It's from my Aunt Linda, who was a missionary in Nigeria for 45 years. The stew is served on a bed of rice and sprinkled with toppings. I put the bowls of toppings on my large turntable, and everyone can take whatever they want. In addition to the coconut, peanuts and raisins, you could also top the stew with chopped cucumbers, pineapple tidbits or mandarin orange slices.

- 1 lb. beef stew meat, cut into 1/2-in. cubes
- 1 can (14-1/2 oz.) diced tomatoes, undrained
- 1 small onion, chopped
- 1 small sweet red pepper, chopped
- 1 small green pepper, chopped
- 1 to 2 Tbsp. curry powder
- 1/2 tsp. salt

Hot cooked rice

Raisins, chopped salted peanuts and flaked coconut, optional

1. In a large saucepan, combine the first seven ingredients. Bring to a boil. Reduce heat; cover and simmer for 1-1/2 to 2 hours or until meat is tender.

2. Serve with rice. Garnish with raisins, peanuts and coconut if desired.

Nutrition Facts: 1 cup (calculated without rice or garnishes) equals 205 calories, 8 g fat (3 g saturated fat), 70 mg cholesterol, 474 mg sodium, 10 g carbohydrate, 3 g fiber, 23 g protein. **Diabetic Exchanges:** 3 lean meat, 2 vegetable.

Beef Cabbage Rolls

PREP: 30 min. **BAKE:** 65 min. **YIELD:** 4 servings

HEALTHY COOKING TEST KITCHEN

A tiny bit of cinnamon adds a unique, slightly sweet taste to these savory stuffed cabbage rolls. Serve them with a side of broccoli for a delectable meal.

- 1/3 cup uncooked brown rice
- 1 medium head cabbage
- 1 medium onion, chopped
- 2 egg whites
- 3 Tbsp. dried currants
- 2 Tbsp. pine nuts
- 2 Tbsp. lemon juice
- 1/2 tsp. dried oregano
- 1/4 tsp. pepper
- 1/8 tsp. salt
- 1/8 tsp. ground cinnamon
- 3/4 lb. lean ground beef (90% lean)
- 2 cans (8 oz. *each*) no-salt-added tomato sauce
- 2 Tbsp. brown sugar
- 1/4 tsp. dried thyme

1. Cook rice according to package directions.

2. Meanwhile, cook cabbage in boiling water just until outer leaves pull away easily from head. Set aside 8 large leaves for rolls. Refrigerate remaining cabbage for another use. Cut out the thick vein from the bottom of each reserved leaf, making a V-shaped cut.

3. In a small nonstick skillet coated with cooking spray, saute onion until tender. In a large bowl, combine the rice, onion, egg whites, currants, pine nuts, lemon juice, oregano, pepper, salt and cinnamon. Crumble beef over mixture and mix well.

4. Place about 1/3 cup beef mixture on each cabbage leaf. Fold in sides, beginning from the cut end. Roll up completely to enclose filling. Place seam side down in a 13-in. x 9-in. baking dish coated with cooking spray. Combine the tomato sauce, brown sugar and thyme; pour over rolls.

5. Cover and bake at 350° for 1 hour or until cabbage is tender and a meat thermometer reads 160°. Uncover; bake 5-10 minutes longer or until sauce reaches desired consistency.

Nutrition Facts: 2 cabbage rolls equals 335 calories, 10 g fat (3 g saturated fat), 53 mg cholesterol, 198 mg sodium, 39 g carbohydrate, 4 g fiber, 22 g protein. **Diabetic Exchanges:** 2-1/2 starch, 2 lean meat, 1/2 fat.

Slowed-Cooked Caribbean Pot Roast

PREP: 30 min. **COOK:** 6 hours **YIELD:** 10 servings

JENN TIDWELL • FAIR OAKS, CALIFORNIA

This hearty dish is a staple in my home during the fall and winter seasons, but considering how simple it is to prepare, anytime is a great time to enjoy it!

2	medium sweet potatoes, cubed
2	large carrots, sliced
1/4	cup chopped celery
1	boneless beef chuck roast (2-1/2 lbs.)
1	Tbsp. canola oil
1	large onion, chopped
2	garlic cloves, minced
1	Tbsp. all-purpose flour
1	Tbsp. sugar
1	Tbsp. brown sugar
1	tsp. ground cumin
3/4	tsp. salt
3/4	tsp. ground coriander
3/4	tsp. chili powder
1/2	tsp. dried oregano
1/8	tsp. ground cinnamon
3/4	tsp. grated orange peel
3/4	tsp. baking cocoa
1	can (15 oz.) tomato sauce

1. Place potatoes, carrots and celery in a 5-qt. slow cooker. In a large skillet, brown meat in oil on all sides. Transfer meat to slow cooker.

2. In the same skillet, saute onion in drippings until tender. Add garlic; cook 1 minute longer. Combine the flour, sugar, brown sugar, seasonings, orange peel and cocoa. Stir in tomato sauce; add to skillet and heat through. Pour over beef.

3. Cover and cook on low for 6-8 hours or until beef and vegetables are tender.

Nutrition Facts: 3 oz. cooked beef with 1/2 cup vegetable mixture equals 278 calories, 12 g fat (4 g saturated fat), 74 mg cholesterol, 453 mg sodium, 16 g carbohydrate, 3 g fiber, 25 g protein. **Diabetic Exchanges:** 3 lean meat, 1 starch, 1 vegetable, 1/2 fat.

Stovetop Meat Loaves

PREP: 20 min. **COOK:** 15 min. **YIELD:** 2 servings

EMILY SUND • GENESEO, ILLINOIS

Who says meat loaf has to bake in the oven for hours? For this convenient recipe, all you need is your stovetop and 35 minutes. Topped with a zesty sauce, it's a fast and easy entree to make for one or two people.

3	Tbsp. 2% milk
2	Tbsp. quick-cooking oats
1	Tbsp. chopped onion
1/4	tsp. salt
1/2	lb. lean ground beef
1/2	tsp. cornstarch
1/2	cup Italian tomato sauce
1/4	cup cold water

1. In a small bowl, combine the milk, oats, onion and salt. Crumble beef over mixture and mix well. Shape into two loaves.

2. In a small nonstick skillet, brown loaves on both sides; drain. Combine the cornstarch, tomato sauce and water until smooth. Pour over meat loaves. Bring to a boil. Reduce heat to medium-low; cover and cook for 15-20 minutes or until meat is no longer pink.

Nutrition Facts: 1 meat loaf equals 259 calories, 10 g fat (4 g saturated fat), 71 mg cholesterol, 922 mg sodium, 16 g carbohydrate, 2 g fiber, 25 g protein. **Diabetic Exchanges:** 3 lean meat, 1 starch.

STOVETOP MEAT LOAVES

Quinoa-Stuffed Peppers

PREP: 35 min. BAKE: 35 min. YIELD: 4 servings

JOYCE MOYNIHAN • LAKEVILLE, MINNESOTA

Quinoa adds crunch, corn lends sweetness and color, and red pepper flakes ratchet up the heat in these tender stuffed peppers. Whole wheat rolls or breadsticks and a pitcher of iced tea make for a standout supper.

- 1 can (14-1/2 oz.) diced tomatoes, undrained
- 1 cup water
- 1/2 cup quinoa, rinsed
- 4 large green peppers
- 3/4 lb. lean ground beef (90% lean)
- 1 large onion, finely chopped
- 3 garlic cloves, minced
- 3 tsp. dried parsley flakes
- 2 tsp. paprika
- 1/2 tsp. salt
- 1/4 to 1/2 tsp. crushed red pepper flakes
- 1/4 tsp. pepper
- 2 cans (8 oz. *each*) no-salt-added tomato sauce, *divided*
- 3/4 cup frozen corn, thawed
- 1/2 cup shredded reduced-fat cheddar cheese

1. Drain tomatoes reserving juice; set aside.

2. In a small saucepan, bring water to a boil. Add quinoa. Reduce heat; simmer, uncovered, for 15-20 minutes or until liquid is absorbed.

3. Meanwhile, cut peppers in half lengthwise and remove seeds. In a Dutch oven, cook peppers in boiling water for 3-5 minutes. Drain and rinse in cold water; invert onto paper towels.

4. In a large skillet, cook the beef, onion, garlic, parsley, paprika, salt, pepper flakes and pepper over medium heat until meat is no longer pink. Stir in one can tomato sauce, corn, quinoa and tomatoes; heat through.

5. Spoon into pepper halves. Place in a 13-in. x 9-in. baking dish coated with cooking spray. Combine the reserved tomato juice and remaining tomato sauce; pour over peppers.

6. Cover and bake at 350° for 30-35 minutes or until peppers are tender. Sprinkle with cheese; bake 5 minutes longer or until cheese is melted.

Editor's Note: Look for quinoa in the cereal, rice or organic food aisle.

Nutrition Facts: 2 stuffed pepper halves equals 386 calories, 11 g fat (5 g saturated fat), 52 mg cholesterol, 622 mg sodium, 47 g carbohydrate, 9 g fiber, 26 g protein.

Hearty Beef Ravioli

PREP/TOTAL TIME: 30 min. YIELD: 6 servings

HEALTHY COOKING TEST KITCHEN

You're only 30 minutes away from a great new pasta dish that's got a Tex-Mex twist. Just add a fresh salad and a slice of crusty bread, and dinner's done in no time!

- 1 pkg. (25 oz.) frozen beef ravioli
- 1/2 lb. extra-lean ground beef (95% lean)
- 1 medium green pepper, chopped
- 1 can (14-1/2 oz.) no-salt-added diced tomatoes
- 1 can (8 oz.) no-salt-added tomato sauce
- 2 Tbsp. reduced-sodium taco seasoning
- 3/4 cup shredded reduced-fat cheddar cheese
- 1 can (2-1/4 oz.) sliced ripe olives, drained

1. Cook ravioli according to package directions.

2. Meanwhile, in a large nonstick skillet, cook beef and green pepper over medium heat until meat is no longer pink. Stir in the tomatoes, tomato sauce and taco seasoning. Bring to a boil. Reduce heat; simmer, uncovered, for 5-7 minutes or until slightly thickened.

3. Drain pasta. Serve with sauce. Sprinkle each serving with 2 Tbsp. cheese and about 1 Tbsp. olives.

Nutrition Facts: 1 serving equals 375 calories, 10 g fat (5 g saturated fat), 44 mg cholesterol, 695 mg sodium, 49 g carbohydrate, 4 g fiber, 21 g protein.

QUINOA-STUFFED PEPPERS

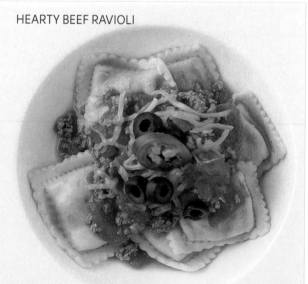

HEARTY BEEF RAVIOLI

TERRIFIC TERIYAKI BURGERS

Terrific Teriyaki Burgers

PREP: 20 min. **GRILL:** 15 min. **YIELD:** 6 servings

MARGARET WILSON • SUN CITY, CALIFORNIA

Golden flecks of pineapple give these burgers a touch of sweetness, while the gingerroot adds some spice. Ground chicken works well in this recipe, too.

1/4	cup ketchup
2	Tbsp. reduced-sodium soy sauce
1	Tbsp. brown sugar
1	Tbsp. unsweetened crushed pineapple
1-1/2	tsp. minced fresh gingerroot
1	garlic clove, minced
1/2	tsp. sesame oil

BURGERS
1	egg white, lightly beaten
1/3	cup dry bread crumbs
3	green onions, chopped
2	Tbsp. unsweetened crushed pineapple
3/4	lb. ground beef
3/4	lb. lean ground turkey
6	slices unsweetened pineapple
6	hamburger buns, split and toasted
6	lettuce leaves
6	slices tomato

1. In a small bowl, combine the ketchup, soy sauce, brown sugar, pineapple, ginger, garlic and sesame oil; set aside.

2. In a large bowl, combine the egg white, bread crumbs, onions, crushed pineapple and 3 Tbsp. reserved ketchup mixture. Crumble beef and turkey over mixture and mix well. Shape into six burgers.

3. Using long-handled tongs, moisten a paper towel with cooking oil and lightly coat the grill rack. Grill burgers, covered, over medium heat or broil 4 in. from the heat for 5-7 minutes on each side or until a meat thermometer reads 165° and juices run clear, brushing occasionally with remaining ketchup mixture.

4. Grill or broil pineapple slices for 2-3 minutes on each side or until heated through. Serve burgers and pineapple on buns with lettuce and tomato.

Nutrition Facts: 1 burger equals 386 calories, 12 g fat (4 g saturated fat), 79 mg cholesterol, 677 mg sodium, 41 g carbohydrate, 2 g fiber, 27 g protein. **Diabetic Exchanges:** 3 lean meat, 2 starch, 1/2 fruit.

Fresh **gingerroot** is available in your grocer's produce section. It should have a smooth skin. If wrinkled and cracked, the root is dry and past its prime.

Slow-Cooked Meat Loaf C

PREP: 15 min. COOK: 3 hours YIELD: 8 servings

SHARON DELANEY-CHRONIS • SOUTH MILWAUKEE, WISCONSIN

What could be easier than this recipe for an Italian-inspired meat loaf made in the slow cooker? No fuss, easy cleanup and great taste; it's all right here!

- 1   cup soft bread crumbs
- 1-1/2 cups spaghetti sauce, *divided*
- 1   egg, lightly beaten
- 2   Tbsp. dried minced onion
- 1   tsp. salt
- 1/2 tsp. garlic powder
- 1/2 tsp. Italian seasoning
- 1/4 tsp. pepper
- 2   lbs. lean ground beef (90% lean)

1. Cut four 20-in. x 3-in. strips of heavy-duty foil; crisscross so they resemble spokes of a wheel. Place strips on the bottom and up the sides of a 3-qt. slow cooker. Coat strips with cooking spray.

2. In a large bowl, combine the bread crumbs, 1 cup spaghetti sauce, egg, onion and seasonings. Crumble beef over mixture and mix well. Shape into a loaf; place in the center of the strips.

3. Spoon remaining spaghetti sauce over meat loaf. Cover and cook on low for 3-4 hours or until a meat thermometer reads 160°. Using foil strips as handles, remove meat loaf to a platter.

Nutrition Facts: 1 slice equals 243 calories, 12 g fat (4 g saturated fat), 98 mg cholesterol, 635 mg sodium, 8 g carbohydrate, 1 g fiber, 24 g protein. **Diabetic Exchanges:** 3 lean meat, 1 fat, 1/2 starch.

Baked Barbecued Brisket

PREP: 20 min. BAKE: 3-1/2 hours YIELD: 16-20 servings

JOAN HALLFORD • NORTH RICHLAND HILLS, TEXAS

This simple brisket recipe never fails me. I always hope there will be a few slices left over for sandwiches the next day.

- 1   Tbsp. all-purpose flour
- 1   fresh beef brisket (5 lbs.)
- 2   to 4 tsp. Liquid Smoke, optional
- 1/2 tsp. celery seed
- 1/4 tsp. pepper
- 1   cup chili sauce
- 1/4 cup barbecue sauce

1. Place flour in a large oven roasting bag; shake to coat bag. Rub brisket with Liquid Smoke if desired, celery seed and pepper; place in bag. Place in a roasting pan. Combine chili sauce and barbecue sauce; pour over brisket. Seal bag.

2. With a knife, cut six 1/2-in. slits in top of bag. Bake at 325° for 3-1/2 to 4 hours or until meat is tender. Let stand for 5 minutes. Carefully remove brisket from bag. Thinly slice meat across the grain.

Editor's Note: This is a fresh beef brisket, not corned beef.

Makeover Beef Stroganoff

PREP/TOTAL TIME: 30 min. **YIELD:** 6 servings

CANDACE CLARK • CONNELL, WASHINGTON

The pros lightened up this classic comfort dish, slashing calories, saturated fat, sodium and cholesterol, without sacrificing one bit of its satisfying flavor.

- 1/2 cup plus 1 Tbsp. all-purpose flour, *divided*
- 1/2 tsp. pepper, *divided*
- 1 beef top round steak (1-1/2 lbs.), cut into thin strips
- 2 Tbsp. canola oil
- 1 cup sliced fresh mushrooms
- 1 small onion, chopped
- 1 garlic clove, minced
- 1 can (14-1/2 oz.) reduced-sodium beef broth
- 1/2 tsp. salt
- 1 cup (8 oz.) reduced-fat sour cream
- 3 cups cooked yolk-free noodles

1. In a large resealable plastic bag, combine 1/2 cup flour and 1/4 tsp. pepper. Add beef, a few pieces at a time, and shake to coat.

2. In a large nonstick skillet over medium-high heat, cook beef in oil in batches until no longer pink. Remove and keep warm. In the same skillet, saute mushrooms and onion in drippings until tender. Add garlic; cook 1 minute longer.

3. Combine remaining flour and broth until smooth; whisk into skillet. Bring to a boil; cook and stir for 2 minutes or until thickened. Add the beef, salt and remaining pepper; heat through. Add sour cream; heat through (do not boil). Serve with noodles.

Nutrition Facts: 1 cup beef Stroganoff with 1/2 cup noodles equals 351 calories, 12 g fat (4 g saturated fat), 78 mg cholesterol, 393 mg sodium, 25 g carbohydrate, 2 g fiber, 33 g protein. **Diabetic Exchanges:** 3 lean meat, 2 fat, 1-1/2 starch.

So-Easy Spaghetti Sauce   F

PREP: 30 min. **COOK:** 5 hours
YIELD: About 2-1/4 qt.

CATHY JOHNSON • SOMERSET, PENNSYLVANIA

Let the slow cooker do all the work for this hearty spaghetti sauce. All you need to do is cook the pasta and bake up some crusty garlic bread.

- 1 lb. lean ground beef (90% lean)
- 1 medium onion, finely chopped
- 1/4 cup finely chopped celery
- 1 can (29 oz.) tomato sauce
- 2-1/2 cups tomato juice
- 1 can (14-1/2 oz.) diced tomatoes, undrained
- 1 can (12 oz.) tomato paste
- 2 tsp. sugar
- 2 tsp. chili powder
- 1 tsp. salt
- 1 tsp. garlic powder
- 1 tsp. dried basil
- 1 tsp. dried oregano
- 1/2 tsp. pepper
- 4 bay leaves

Hot cooked spaghetti

Grated Parmesan cheese, optional

1. In a large skillet, cook the beef, onion and celery over medium heat until meat is no longer pink; drain. In a 4- or 5-qt. slow cooker, combine the tomato sauce, tomato juice, tomatoes, tomato paste, sugar, seasonings and beef mixture.

2. Cover and cook on low for 5-6 hours or until heated through. Discard bay leaves. Serve with spaghetti; sprinkle with cheese if desired.

Nutrition Facts: 3/4 cup (calculated without spaghetti and cheese) equals 125 calories, 3 g fat (1 g saturated fat), 19 mg cholesterol, 744 mg sodium, 16 g carbohydrate, 4 g fiber, 10 g protein. **Diabetic Exchanges:** 1 lean meat, 1 vegetable, 1/2 starch, 1/2 fat.

SO-EASY SPAGHETTI SAUCE

MAKEOVER BEEF STROGANOFF

Hamburger Noodle Casserole

PREP: 30 min. **BAKE:** 35 min. **YIELD:** 10 servings

MARTHA HENSON • WINNSBORO, TEXAS

Whenever I need a hearty dish that serves a crowd, I turn to this casserole. It's a hit with people in any age group.

5	cups uncooked yolk-free noodles
1-1/4	lbs. lean ground beef (90% lean)
2	garlic cloves, minced
3	cans (8 oz. *each*) tomato sauce
1/2	tsp. sugar
1/2	tsp. salt
1/8	tsp. pepper
1	pkg. (8 oz.) reduced-fat cream cheese
1	cup reduced-fat ricotta cheese
1/4	cup fat-free sour cream
3	green onions, thinly sliced, *divided*
2/3	cup shredded reduced-fat cheddar cheese

1. Cook noodles according to package directions. Meanwhile, in a large nonstick skillet over medium heat, cook beef until meat is no longer pink. Add garlic; cook 1 minute longer. Drain. Stir in the tomato sauce, sugar, salt and pepper; heat through. Drain noodles; stir into beef mixture.

2. In a small bowl, beat the cream cheese, ricotta cheese and sour cream until blended. Stir in half of the onions.

3. Spoon half of the noodle mixture into a 13-in. x 9-in. baking dish coated with cooking spray. Top with cheese mixture and remaining noodle mixture.

4. Cover and bake at 350° for 30 minutes. Uncover; sprinkle with cheddar cheese. Bake 5-10 minutes longer or until heated through and cheese is melted. Sprinkle with remaining onions.

Nutrition Facts: 1 cup equals 290 calories, 12 g fat (7 g saturated fat), 56 mg cholesterol, 650 mg sodium, 23 g carbohydrate, 2 g fiber, 22 g protein. **Diabetic Exchanges:** 2 lean meat, 1-1/2 starch, 1 fat.

Whiskey Sirloin Steak C

PREP: 10 min. + marinating **BROIL:** 15 min. **YIELD:** 4 servings

HEALTHY COOKING TEST KITCHEN

Moist, tender and slightly sweet from the marinade, this juicy steak boasts wonderful flavor and oh-so-easy preparation. Serve with potatoes and a green vegetable for a complete meal.

1/4	cup whiskey or apple cider
1/4	cup reduced-sodium soy sauce
1	Tbsp. sugar
1	garlic clove, thinly sliced
1/2	tsp. ground ginger
1	beef top sirloin steak (1 in. thick and 1 lb.)

1. In a large resealable plastic bag, combine the first five ingredients; add the beef. Seal bag and turn to coat; refrigerate for 8 hours or overnight.

2. Drain and discard marinade. Place beef on a broiler pan coated with cooking spray. Broil 4-6 in. from the heat for 7-8 minutes on each side or until meat reaches desired doneness (for medium-rare, a meat thermometer should read 145°; medium, 160°; well-done, 170°).

Nutrition Facts: 3 oz. cooked beef equals 168 calories, 5 g fat (2 g saturated fat), 46 mg cholesterol, 353 mg sodium, 2 g carbohydrate, trace fiber, 25 g protein. **Diabetic Exchange:** 3 lean meat.

HAMBURGER NOODLE CASSEROLE

WHISKEY SIRLOIN STEAK

Flank Steak Pitas

PREP: 15 min. + marinating **GRILL:** 15 min. + standing
YIELD: 4 servings

TAMMY KAMINSKI • STANWOOD, WASHINGTON

This sandwich packs so much flavor, you'll be satisfied without eating a huge serving. The marinade makes the most of tasty ingredients, so you won't even miss the cheese or mayo.

1/4	cup balsamic vinegar
2	Tbsp. water
2	Tbsp. reduced-sodium soy sauce
1	Tbsp. hoisin sauce
2	garlic cloves, minced
1	tsp. Thai chili sauce
3/4	tsp. pepper
1/2	tsp. sesame oil
1	beef flank steak (1 lb.)
4	whole pita breads
4	pieces leaf lettuce, torn
1/4	tsp. sesame seeds

1. In a small bowl, combine the first eight ingredients. Pour 1/4 cup marinade into a large resealable plastic bag; add the beef. Seal bag and turn to coat. Refrigerate for at least 8 hours or overnight. Cover and refrigerate remaining marinade.

2. Drain and discard marinade. Grill, covered, over medium heat for 6-8 minutes on each side or until meat reaches desired doneness (for medium-rare, a meat thermometer should read 145°; medium, 160°; well-done, 170°). Let stand for 10 minutes.

3. Meanwhile, grill pitas, uncovered, over medium heat for 1-2 minutes on each side or until warm. Thinly slice beef across the grain. In a large bowl, toss the beef, lettuce and reserved marinade. Serve in pitas; sprinkle with sesame seeds.

Nutrition Facts: 1 filled pita equals 362 calories, 10 g fat (4 g saturated fat), 54 mg cholesterol, 703 mg sodium, 39 g carbohydrate, 2 g fiber, 28 g protein. **Diabetic Exchanges:** 3 lean meat, 2-1/2 starch.

Beef and Spinach Lasagna

PREP: 10 min. **BAKE:** 40 min. + standing
YIELD: 12 servings

CAROLYN SCHMELING • BROOKFIELD, WISCONSIN

Using no-cook noodles gives you a jump start on assembling this hearty main dish. It cuts nicely after standing a few minutes, revealing tantalizing layers.

1	lb. lean ground beef (90% lean)
1	medium onion, chopped
2	jars (26 oz. *each*) meatless spaghetti sauce
4	garlic cloves, minced
1	tsp. dried basil
1	tsp. dried oregano
1	pkg. (10 oz.) frozen chopped spinach, thawed and squeezed dry
2	cups ricotta cheese
2	cups (8 oz.) shredded part-skim mozzarella cheese, *divided*
9	no-cook lasagna noodles

1. In a large skillet, cook beef and onion over medium heat until meat is no longer pink; drain. Stir in the spaghetti sauce, garlic, basil and oregano. Bring to a boil. Reduce heat; cover and simmer for 10 minutes. In a large bowl, combine the spinach, ricotta and 1 cup mozzarella cheese until combined.

2. Spread 1-1/2 cups meat sauce into a greased 13-in. x 9-in. baking dish. Top with three noodles. Spread 1-1/2 cups sauce to edges of noodles. Top with half of the spinach mixture. Repeat layers. Top with remaining noodles, sauce and remaining mozzarella cheese.

3. Cover and bake at 375° for 30 minutes. Uncover; bake 10-15 minutes longer or until bubbly. Let stand for 10 minutes before cutting.

Nutrition Facts: 1 piece (prepared with lean ground beef) equals 281 calories, 11 g fat (6 g saturated fat), 50 mg cholesterol, 702 mg sodium, 26 g carbohydrate, 3 g fiber, 20 g protein.

Hawaiian Beef Sliders

PREP: 30 min. + marinating **GRILL:** 10 min.
YIELD: 6 servings

MARY RELYEA • CANASTOTA, NEW YORK

Sweet and savory with just a hint of heat, these dynamite burgers are packed with flavor. Pineapple and bacon may sound like an unusual combination, but once you take a bite, you'll discover that they're the perfect match.

1	can (20 oz.) unsweetened crushed pineapple
1	tsp. pepper
1/4	tsp. salt
1-1/2	lbs. lean ground beef (90% lean)
1/4	cup reduced-sodium soy sauce
2	Tbsp. ketchup
1	Tbsp. white vinegar
2	garlic cloves, minced
1/4	tsp. crushed red pepper flakes
18	minature whole wheat buns

Baby spinach leaves

3	center-cut bacon strips, cooked and crumbled

Sliced jalapeno peppers, optional

1. Drain pineapple, reserving juice and 1-1/2 cups pineapple (save remaining pineapple for another use). In a large bowl, combine 3/4 cup reserved crushed pineapple, pepper and salt. Crumble beef over mixture and mix well. Shape into 18 patties; place in two 11-in. x 7-in. dishes.

2. In a small bowl, combine the soy sauce, ketchup, vinegar, garlic, pepper flakes and reserved pineapple juice. Pour half of marinade into each dish; cover and refrigerate for 1 hour, turning once.

3. Drain and discard marinade. Using long-handled tongs, moisten a paper towel with cooking oil and lightly coat the grill rack.

4. Grill patties, covered, over medium heat or broil 4 in. from the heat for 4-5 minutes on each side or until a meat thermometer reads 160° and juices run clear.

5. Grill buns, uncovered, for 1-2 minutes or until toasted. Serve burgers on buns with spinach, remaining pineapple, bacon and jalapeno peppers if desired.

Editor's Note: If miniature whole wheat buns are not available in your area, you can also use whole wheat hot dog buns cut into thirds.

Nutrition Facts: 3 sliders (calculated without peppers) equals 350 calories, 12 g fat (4 g saturated fat), 74 mg cholesterol, 444 mg sodium, 34 g carbohydrate, 4 g fiber, 27 g protein. **Diabetic Exchanges:** 3 lean meat, 1-1/2 starch, 1/2 fruit.

Beef Tenderloin With Roasted Vegetables

PREP: 20 min. + marinating **BAKE:** 1 hour + standing
YIELD: 8-10 servings

JANET SINGLETON • BELLEVUE, OHIO

I appreciate this recipe because it includes a side dish of roasted potatoes, brussels sprouts and carrots. I prepare this entree for celebrations throughout the year.

1	beef tenderloin roast (3 lbs.)
3/4	cup dry white wine *or* beef broth
3/4	cup reduced-sodium soy sauce
4	tsp. minced fresh rosemary
4	tsp. Dijon mustard
1-1/2	tsp. ground mustard
3	garlic cloves, peeled and sliced
1	lb. Yukon Gold potatoes, cut into 1-in. wedges
1	lb. brussels sprouts, halved
1	lb. fresh baby carrots

1. Place tenderloin in a large resealable plastic bag. Combine the wine, soy sauce, rosemary, Dijon mustard, ground mustard and garlic. Pour half of the marinade over tenderloin; seal bag and turn to coat. Refrigerate for 4-12 hours, turning several times. Cover and refrigerate remaining marinade.

2. Place the potatoes, brussels sprouts and carrots in a greased 13-in. x 9-in. baking dish; add reserved marinade and toss to coat. Cover and bake at 425° for 30 minutes; stir.

3. Drain and discard marinade from tenderloin. Place tenderloin over vegetables. Bake, uncovered, for 30-45 minutes or until meat reaches desired doneness (for medium-rare, a meat thermometer should read 145°; medium, 160°; well-done, 170°).

4. Remove beef and let stand for 15 minutes. Check vegetables for doneness. If additional roasting is needed, cover with foil and bake for 10-15 minutes or until tender. Slice beef and serve with vegetables.

Nutrition Facts: 1 serving equals 283 calories, 8 g fat (3 g saturated fat), 60 mg cholesterol, 627 mg sodium, 16 g carbohydrate, 3 g fiber, 33 g protein. **Diabetic Exchanges:** 4 lean meat, 1 vegetable, 1/2 starch.

Makeover Country-Fried Steak

PREP: 20 min. COOK: 15 min. YIELD: 4 servings

HEALTHY COOKING TEST KITCHEN

A healthier country-fried steak? Sounds like an oxymoron, but it's not. This comforting dish keeps its delicious classic flavors while losing over half the fat.

- 1 beef top round steak (1 pound)
- 1/2 tsp. salt
- 1/2 tsp. garlic powder, *divided*
- 1/2 tsp. pepper, *divided*
- 1/4 tsp. onion powder
- 1/2 cup buttermilk
- 3/4 cup plus 4-1/2 tsp. all-purpose flour, *divided*
- 1 Tbsp. canola oil
- 4-1/2 tsp. butter
- 1 cup 2% milk

1. Cut steak into four serving-size pieces; pound to 1/4-in. thickness. Combine the salt, 1/4 tsp. garlic powder, 1/4 tsp. pepper and onion powder; sprinkle over steaks.

2. Place buttermilk and 3/4 cup flour in separate shallow bowls. Dip steaks in buttermilk, then flour.

3. In a large skillet, cook steaks in oil over medium heat for 3-4 minutes on each side or until meat is no longer pink. Remove and keep warm.

4. In a small saucepan, melt butter. Stir in remaining flour until smooth; gradually add milk. Bring to a boil; cook and stir for 1 minute or until thickened. Stir in remaining garlic powder and pepper. Serve with steak.

Nutrition Facts: 1 steak with 1/4 cup gravy equals 318 calories, 13 g fat (5 g saturated fat), 80 mg cholesterol, 410 mg sodium, 19 g carbohydrate, 1 g fiber, 30 g protein.

Portobello Burgundy Beef

PREP: 20 min. COOK: 35 min. YIELD: 4 servings

MELANIE COLEMAN • PITTSBURG, CALIFORNIA

Nothing feels light about this rustic dish! Each bite is filled with mushrooms, beef and carrots wrapped in a savory, Burgundy-flavored sauce. This is comfort food at its finest!

- 1/4 cup plus 1 Tbsp. all-purpose flour, *divided*
- 1 tsp. dried marjoram, *divided*
- 1/2 tsp. salt, *divided*
- 1 beef top round steak (1 lb.), cut into 1/2-in. cubes
- 1 Tbsp. olive oil
- 2 cups sliced baby portobello mushrooms
- 3 garlic cloves, minced
- 3 medium carrots, cut into 1/2-in. pieces
- 1 can (14-1/2 oz.) reduced-sodium beef broth, *divided*
- 1/2 cup Burgundy wine *or* additional reduced-sodium beef broth
- 1 bay leaf
- 4 cups cooked egg noodles

1. Place 1/4 cup flour, 1/2 tsp. marjoram and 1/4 tsp. salt in a large resealable plastic bag. Add beef, a few pieces at a time, and shake to coat. In a large nonstick skillet coated with cooking spray, brown beef in oil.

2. Add mushrooms and garlic; saute until mushrooms are tender. Stir in the carrots, 1-1/2 cups broth, wine, bay leaf, remaining marjoram and salt. Bring to a boil. Reduce heat; cover and simmer for 15-20 minutes or until carrots are tender.

3. Combine remaining flour and broth; stir into pan. Bring to a boil; cook and stir for 2 minutes or until thickened. Discard bay leaf. Serve with noodles.

Nutrition Facts: 1 cup beef mixture with 1 cup noodles equals 384 calories, 9 g fat (2 g saturated fat), 98 mg cholesterol, 484 mg sodium, 39 g carbohydrate, 3 g fiber, 34 g protein. **Diabetic Exchanges:** 3 lean meat, 2 starch, 1 vegetable, 1/2 fat.

PORTOBELLO BURGUNDY BEEF

PAT'S PECAN CHICKEN

HONEY LIME CHICKEN

HOMEMADE CHICKEN
ALFREDO PIZZAS

Chicken Favorites

From hurried weeknight suppers to special Sunday dinners, the perfect
chicken dish is always at your fingertips with this popular chapter. No one
will guess they're eating healthy when these classics are on the menu.

Homemade Chicken Alfredo Pizzas

9 pts

PREP: 30 min. + standing **BAKE:** 15 min.
YIELD: 2 pizzas (6 slices each)

CATHERINE NICKELSON • SCANDIA, MINNESOTA

*Give these mouthwatering Alfredo pizzas a try next time you
need to feed a crowd but want something healthier than
delivery pizza. Even with their from-scratch crust and sauce,
you'll be surprised by how simply they come together.*

- 1 pkg. (1/4 oz.) quick-rise yeast
- 1 cup warm water (120° to 130°)
- 1 tsp. sugar
- 1-1/2 tsp. salt, *divided*
- 2-1/2 to 3 cups all-purpose flour
- 2 Tbsp. cornmeal
- 1 Tbsp. olive oil
- 2 garlic cloves, minced
- 2 Tbsp. butter
- 1 tsp. dried parsley flakes
- 1/4 tsp. pepper
- 4-1/2 tsp. all-purpose flour
- 1-1/2 cups 2% milk
- 3 cups cubed cooked chicken breasts
- 2 large tomatoes, chopped
- 2 cups chopped fresh baby spinach
- 4 cups (16 oz.) shredded part-skim mozzarella cheese
- 1/2 cup shredded Italian cheese blend
- 1 tsp. Italian seasoning

1. In a large bowl, dissolve yeast in warm water. Add
the sugar, 1/2 tsp. salt and 2-1/2 cups flour. Beat until
smooth. Stir in enough remaining flour to form a soft
dough (dough will be sticky).

2. Turn onto a lightly floured surface; knead until
smooth and elastic, about 6-8 minutes. Cover and let
rest for 10 minutes.

3. Sprinkle cornmeal over two 12-in. pizza pans coated
with cooking spray. Divide dough in half. On a floured
surface, roll each portion into a 13-in. circle. Transfer to
prepared pans. Build up edges slightly. Prick dough

thoroughly with a fork; brush with oil. Bake at 425° for
5-8 minutes or until edges are lightly browned.

4. In a small saucepan, saute garlic in butter until
tender. Stir in the parsley, pepper and remaining salt.
Combine flour and milk until smooth. Stir into pan.
Bring to a boil; cook and stir for 2 minutes or until
slightly thickened.

5. Spread over crusts; top with chicken, tomatoes,
spinach, cheeses and Italian seasoning. Bake 10-12
minutes longer or until crusts are lightly browned
and cheeses are melted.

Nutrition Facts: 1 slice equals 328 calories, 13 g fat (7 g
saturated fat), 62 mg cholesterol, 568 mg sodium, 27 g
carbohydrate, 1 g fiber, 26 g protein.

Pat's Pecan Chicken C

PREP: 20 min. **BAKE:** 20 min. **YIELD:** 4 servings

PATRICIA BROWN • BATTLE CREEK, MICHIGAN

*Parmesan, pecans, oregano and basil blend beautifully in this
crunchy, crusted chicken. The recipe couldn't be much easier,
and no one will know it's lower in calories.*

- 1/2 cup fat-free milk
- 1-1/4 cups soft bread crumbs
- 1/2 cup finely chopped pecans
- 1/4 cup grated Parmesan cheese
- 3 tsp. dried oregano
- 3 tsp. dried basil
- 1 tsp. garlic powder
- 4 boneless skinless chicken breast halves (4 oz. *each*)
- 2 tsp. canola oil

1. Place milk in a shallow bowl. In another shallow
bowl, combine the bread crumbs, pecans, cheese and
seasonings. Dip the chicken in milk, then roll it in the
crumb mixture. In a large nonstick skillet, brown
chicken in oil.

2. Transfer to a baking sheet coated with cooking
spray. Bake, uncovered, at 350° for 20-25 minutes or
until a meat thermometer reads 170°.

Nutrition Facts: 1 chicken breast half equals 229 calories, 11 g
fat (2 g saturated fat), 65 mg cholesterol, 143 mg sodium, 6 g
carbohydrate, 1 g fiber, 25 g protein. **Diabetic Exchanges:**
3 lean meat, 2 fat.

Honey Lime Chicken

PREP: 10 min. + marinating **GRILL:** 15 min.
YIELD: 4 servings

ANN NISEWONDER • DALLAS, TEXAS

You'll love this combination! With honey, white wine, lime juice and ginger, it makes a spectacular, slightly sweet grilled entree at any time of year.

- 1 cup white wine *or* chicken broth
- 1/2 cup honey
- 2 Tbsp. lime juice
- 1/4 tsp. ground ginger
- 4 boneless skinless chicken breast halves (4 oz. *each*)
- 1/4 tsp. garlic powder
- 1/4 tsp. salt
- 1/4 tsp. pepper

1. In a large resealable bag, combine the wine, honey, lime juice and ginger; add chicken. Seal bag and turn to coat; refrigerate for 2 hours, turning once.

2. Drain and discard marinade. Combine the garlic powder, salt and pepper; sprinkle over chicken. Using long-handled tongs, moisten a paper towel with cooking oil and lightly coat the grill rack.

3. Grill, uncovered, over medium heat or broil 4 in. from the heat for 6-7 minutes on each side or until a meat thermometer reads 170°.

Nutrition Facts: 1 chicken breast half equals 152 calories, 3 g fat (1 g saturated fat), 63 mg cholesterol, 256 mg sodium, 8 g carbohydrate, trace fiber, 23 g protein. **Diabetic Exchanges:** 3 lean meat, 1/2 starch.

Chicken Casserole Supreme

PREP: 40 min. **BAKE:** 20 min. **YIELD:** 6 servings

JUDY WILSON • SUN CITY WEST, ARIZONA

This casserole is so satisfying on a cold night, and it gets even better the next day. I added apples and raisins on a whim and discovered they really set this apart from other dishes.

HONEY LIME CHICKEN

- 1 cup reduced-sodium chicken broth
- 1 medium apple, peeled and chopped
- 1/2 cup golden raisins
- 1 Tbsp. butter
- 1 pkg. (6 oz.) reduced-sodium stuffing mix
- 1 lb. boneless skinless chicken breasts, cubed
- 1/4 tsp. salt
- 1/4 tsp. pepper
- 1 cup sliced fresh mushrooms
- 1 small onion, chopped
- 1 Tbsp. olive oil
- 3 garlic cloves, minced
- 1-1/2 cups (12 oz.) fat-free sour cream
- 1 can (10-3/4 oz.) reduced-fat reduced-sodium condensed cream of mushroom soup, undiluted
- 4 cups frozen broccoli florets, thawed

1. In a large saucepan, combine the broth, apple and raisins. Bring to a boil. Reduce heat; simmer, uncovered, for 3-4 minutes or until apple is tender. Stir in butter and stuffing mix. Remove from the heat; cover and let stand for 5 minutes.

2. Sprinkle chicken with salt and pepper. In a large skillet, cook the chicken, mushrooms and onion in oil over medium heat until chicken is no longer pink. Add garlic; cook 1 minute longer. Remove from the heat. Stir in sour cream and soup.

3. Transfer to a 13-in. x 9-in. baking dish coated with cooking spray. Layer with broccoli and stuffing mixture. Bake, uncovered, at 350° for 20-25 minutes or until heated through.

Nutrition Facts: 2 cups equals 390 calories, 8 g fat (2 g saturated fat), 59 mg cholesterol, 771 mg sodium, 52 g carbohydrate, 3 g fiber, 26 g protein.

Chicken Kabobs With Peach Glaze F S

PREP: 30 min. **GRILL:** 10 min. **YIELD:** 4 servings

SHARON RICCI • MENDON, NEW YORK

Chicken, peaches and veggies are treated to a delightful glaze. These kabobs pack in flavor. Pair with a dish of couscous or rice, and dinner's served!

- 1 Tbsp. cornstarch
- 1/4 tsp. curry powder
- 1/8 tsp. ground cinnamon
- 1/8 tsp. chili powder
- 2 cans (5-1/2 oz. *each*) peach nectar, *divided*
- 1 lb. boneless skinless chicken breasts, cut into 1-in. cubes
- 2 medium peaches, cut into chunks
- 4 green onions, cut into 1-in. pieces
- 1 small green pepper, cut into 1-in. pieces
- 1 small sweet red pepper, cut into 1-in. pieces

1. In a small saucepan, combine the cornstarch, curry, cinnamon and chili powder. Gradually stir in the peach nectar. Bring to a boil; cook and stir for 2 minutes or until thickened.

2. On eight metal or soaked wooden skewers, alternately thread the chicken, peaches, onions and peppers. Using long-handled tongs, moisten a paper towel with cooking oil and lightly coat the grill rack.

3. Grill kabobs, covered, over medium heat or broil 4 in. from the heat for 10-15 minutes or until juices run clear, turning occasionally and basting with nectar mixture.

Nutrition Facts: 2 kabobs equals 205 calories, 3 g fat (1 g saturated fat), 63 mg cholesterol, 65 mg sodium, 21 g carbohydrate, 2 g fiber, 24 g protein. **Diabetic Exchanges:** 3 lean meat, 1 vegetable, 1 fruit.

Chicken Marinara with Pasta

PREP: 20 min. + marinating COOK: 20 min.
YIELD: 6 servings

JOANIE FUSON • INDIANAPOLIS, INDIANA

My son Logan, 11, and I created this basic but very good dish. It was the first meal he made all by himself (with supervision, of course). Best of all, it was a real hit with the three friends he invited for dinner.

1-1/2	lbs. boneless skinless chicken breasts
1/2	cup reduced-fat Italian salad dressing
1	medium onion, chopped
1	Tbsp. olive oil
2	garlic cloves, minced
1	can (15 oz.) crushed tomatoes
1	can (14-1/2 oz.) diced tomatoes, undrained
1	Tbsp. minced fresh parsley *or* 1 tsp. dried parsley flakes
1	tsp. minced fresh oregano *or* 1/4 tsp. dried oregano
1	tsp. brown sugar
1/4	tsp. salt
1/4	tsp. pepper
9	oz. uncooked whole wheat spaghetti
1/4	cup grated Parmesan cheese
6	Tbsp. shredded part-skim mozzarella cheese

1. Flatten chicken to 1/2-in. thickness; place in a large resealable plastic bag. Add salad dressing. Seal bag and turn to coat; refrigerate for 30 minutes.

2. Meanwhile, in a large nonstick skillet coated with cooking spray, saute onion in oil until tender. Add garlic; cook 1 minute longer. Stir in the tomatoes, parsley, oregano, brown sugar, salt and pepper. Bring to a boil. Reduce heat; simmer, uncovered, for 10-15 minutes or until slightly thickened, stirring occasionally.

3. Drain and discard marinade. Using long-handled tongs, moisten a paper towel with cooking oil and lightly coat the grill rack. Grill the chicken, covered, over medium heat or broil 4 in. from the heat for 4-6 minutes on each side or until it's no longer pink. When chicken is cool enough to handle, cut into 1/4-in. strips.

4. Meanwhile, cook spaghetti according to package directions. Stir Parmesan cheese into sauce. Drain spaghetti. Serve with chicken and sauce; sprinkle with mozzarella cheese.

Nutrition Facts: 1 serving equals 389 calories, 8 g fat (2 g saturated fat), 70 mg cholesterol, 438 mg sodium, 44 g carbohydrate, 8 g fiber, 35 g protein. **Diabetic Exchanges:** 4 lean meat, 2 starch, 2 vegetable.

Sweet 'n' Sour Chicken F

PREP: 15 min. BAKE: 20 min. YIELD: 4 servings

CHRISTINE MCDONALD • RIVERDALE, UTAH

This entree was served at a special dinner hosted by my Sunday school teacher. The ingredients are simple, but the chicken is tender and tasty. I frequently serve it over brown rice, and I'm often asked for the recipe.

4	boneless skinless chicken breast halves (4 oz. *each*)
2/3	cup water
1/3	cup sugar
1/4	cup cider vinegar
1/4	cup reduced-sodium soy sauce
1	medium sweet red pepper, cut into 1-in. pieces
1	medium green pepper, cut into 1-in. pieces
2	Tbsp. cornstarch
3	Tbsp. cold water

Hot cooked brown rice

1. Place chicken in an 11-in. x 7-in. baking dish; set aside. In a small saucepan, bring the water, sugar, vinegar and soy sauce to a boil, stirring constantly. Add peppers; return to a boil. Combine cornstarch and cold water until smooth; gradually stir into pepper mixture. Bring to a boil; cook and stir for 1-2 minutes or until thickened. Pour over chicken.

2. Bake, uncovered, at 350° for 10-13 minutes on each side or until a meat thermometer reaches 170°. Serve with rice.

Nutrition Facts: 1 serving (calculated without rice) equals 231 calories, 2 g fat (trace saturated fat), 66 mg cholesterol, 683 mg sodium, 25 g carbohydrate, 1 g fiber, 28 g protein. **Diabetic Exchanges:** 3 lean meat, 1 starch, 1 vegetable.

Slow Cooker Chicken Stew

PREP: 15 min. COOK: 6 hours YIELD: 6 servings

ANGELA BUCHANAN • LONGMONT, COLORADO

I like to sprinkle this with toasted almonds or cashews and serve with hot couscous. Flavored with cinnamon and a touch of sweetness from the apricots, this stew tastes like you fussed. It's great for potlucks, too!

6	bone-in chicken thighs (about 2-1/4 lbs.), skin removed
1	large onion, chopped
2	medium carrots, sliced
3/4	cup unsweetened apple juice
1	garlic clove, minced
1	tsp. salt
1/2	tsp. ground cinnamon
1/2	tsp. pepper
1	cup chopped dried apricots

Hot cooked couscous

1. Place the chicken, onion and carrots in a 3- or 4-qt. slow cooker coated with cooking spray. In a small bowl, combine the apple juice, garlic, salt, cinnamon and pepper; pour over vegetables.

2. Cover and cook on low for 6-8 hours or until chicken is tender.

3. Remove chicken from slow cooker; shred meat with two forks. Skim fat from cooking juices; stir in apricots. Return shredded chicken to slow cooker; heat though. Serve with couscous.

Nutrition Facts: 1-1/3 cups (calculated without couscous) equals 279 calories, 10 g fat (3 g saturated fat), 87 mg cholesterol, 497 mg sodium, 23 g carbohydrate, 3 g fiber, 25 g protein. **Diabetic Exchanges:** 3 lean meat, 1 vegetable, 1 fruit.

Chicken Enchilada Casserole

PREP: 30 min. BAKE: 30 min. YIELD: 6 servings

AMY JOHNSON • NEW BRAUNFELS, TEXAS

This family-friendly recipe offers a new take on classic enchiladas. If you like yours with a little extra oomph, sprinkle some seeded, fresh chopped jalapenos and cilantro on top.

- 1 large onion, chopped
- 1 medium green pepper, chopped
- 1 tsp. butter
- 3 cups shredded cooked chicken breast
- 2 cans (4 oz. *each*) chopped green chilies
- 1/4 cup all-purpose flour
- 1-1/2 to 2 tsp. ground coriander
- 2-1/2 cups reduced-sodium chicken broth
- 1 cup (8 oz.) reduced-fat sour cream
- 1 cup (4 oz.) reduced-fat Monterey Jack *or* reduced-fat Mexican cheese blend, *divided*
- 12 corn tortillas (6 in.), warmed

1. In a small skillet, saute onion and green pepper in butter until tender. In a large bowl, combine the chicken, green chilies and onion mixture.

2. In a small saucepan, combine flour and coriander. Add broth; stir until smooth. Cook and stir over medium heat until mixture comes to a boil. Cook and stir 1-2 minutes longer or until thickened. Remove from the heat; stir in sour cream and 1/2 cup cheese. Stir 3/4 cup sauce into chicken mixture.

3. Place 1/3 cup chicken mixture down the center of each tortilla. Roll up and place seam side down in a 13-in. x 9-in. baking dish coated with cooking spray. Pour remaining sauce over top; sprinkle with remaining cheese. Bake, uncovered, at 350° for 30-35 minutes or until heated through.

Nutrition Facts: 2 enchiladas equals 383 calories, 12 g fat (6 g saturated fat), 82 mg cholesterol, 710 mg sodium, 37 g carbohydrate, 5 g fiber, 33 g protein. **Diabetic Exchanges:** 4 lean meat, 2 starch, 1 fat.

Buying skinned and boned chicken breasts can cut up to **15 minutes off** your cooking time. Save money by buying larger packages, then rewrap individually or in family-size portions and freeze.

SLOW COOKER CHICKEN STEW

CHICKEN ENCHILADA CASSEROLE

Tropical Chicken Packets

PREP: 15 min. GRILL: 20 min. YIELD: 4 servings

JACQUELINE CORREA • LANDING, NEW JERSEY

Yum! These quick-and-easy chicken packets are destined to become your family's new favorite. The chicken is tender and laced with sweet pineapple and tropical flavors. Cleanup's a breeze—these would be perfect for camping.

- 4 boneless skinless chicken breast halves (6 oz. *each*)
- 1/8 tsp. pepper
- 1 can (20 oz.) unsweetened pineapple chunks, drained
- 1 medium sweet red pepper, julienned
- 1 small onion, sliced and separated into rings
- 1/4 cup packed brown sugar
- 1/4 cup reduced-sodium teriyaki sauce
- 1 tsp. minced fresh gingerroot

1. Sprinkle chicken breasts with pepper; place each on a double thickness of heavy-duty foil (about 18 in. x 12 in.). Top with pineapple, red pepper and onion. Combine the remaining ingredients; spoon over vegetables. Fold foil around mixture and seal tightly.

2. Grill, covered, over medium heat for 20-25 minutes or until chicken juices run clear. Open foil carefully to allow steam to escape.

Nutrition Facts: 1 packet equals 324 calories, 4 g fat (1 g saturated fat), 94 mg cholesterol, 410 mg sodium, 35 g carbohydrate, 2 g fiber, 36 g protein. **Diabetic Exchanges:** 5 lean meat, 1 starch, 1 fruit.

Shredded Barbecue Chicken over Grits

PREP: 20 min. COOK: 25 min. YIELD: 6 servings

ERIN RENOUF MYLROIE • SANTA CLARA, UTAH

There's nothing like juicy meat over steaming grits. And the pumpkin in these grits makes them taste like a spicy, comforting bowl of fall flavors. Your gang will come running to the table for this one.

- 1 lb. boneless skinless chicken breasts
- 1/4 tsp. pepper
- 1 can (14-1/2 oz.) reduced-sodium chicken broth, *divided*
- 1 cup hickory smoke-flavored barbecue sauce
- 1/4 cup molasses
- 1 Tbsp. ground ancho chili pepper
- 1/2 tsp. ground cinnamon
- 2-1/4 cups water
- 1 cup quick-cooking grits
- 1 cup canned pumpkin
- 3/4 cup shredded pepper Jack cheese
- 1 medium tomato, seeded and chopped
- 6 Tbsp. reduced-fat sour cream
- 2 green onions, chopped
- 2 Tbsp. minced fresh cilantro

1. Sprinkle chicken with pepper; place in a large nonstick skillet coated with cooking spray.

2. In a large bowl, combine 1 cup broth, barbecue sauce, molasses, chili pepper and cinnamon; pour over chicken. Bring to a boil. Reduce heat; cover and simmer for 20-25 minutes or until a meat thermometer reads 170°. Shred meat with two forks and return to the skillet.

SHREDDED BARBECUE CHICKEN OVER GRITS

TROPICAL CHICKEN PACKETS

MARVELOUS CHICKEN ENCHILADAS

3. Meanwhile, in a large saucepan, bring water and remaining broth to a boil. Slowly stir in grits and pumpkin. Reduce heat; cook and stir for 5-7 minutes or until thickened. Stir in cheese until melted.

4. Divide grits among six serving bowls; top each with 1/2 cup chicken mixture. Serve with tomato, sour cream, green onions and cilantro.

Nutrition Facts: 1 serving equals 345 calories, 9 g fat (4 g saturated fat), 62 mg cholesterol, 718 mg sodium, 42 g carbohydrate, 4 g fiber, 25 g protein. **Diabetic Exchanges:** 3 lean meat, 2-1/2 starch, 1 fat.

Marvelous Chicken Enchiladas

PREP: 30 min. **BAKE:** 25 min. **YIELD:** 6 enchiladas

REBEKAH SABO • ROCHESTER, NEW YORK

I love Mexican food, and this is one of my favorites. Try using Monterey Jack cheese in place of the cheddar for a slightly milder flavor.

    1   lb. boneless skinless chicken breasts, cut into thin strips
    4   tsp. chili powder
    2   tsp. olive oil
    2   Tbsp. all-purpose flour
1-1/2   tsp. ground coriander
    1   tsp. baking cocoa
    1   cup fat-free milk
    1   cup frozen corn, thawed
    4   green onions, chopped
    1   can (4 oz.) chopped green chilies, drained
  1/2   tsp. salt
  1/2   cup minced fresh cilantro, *divided*
    6   whole wheat tortillas (8 in.)
  1/2   cup salsa
  1/2   cup tomato sauce
  1/2   cup shredded reduced-fat cheddar cheese

1. Sprinkle chicken with chili powder. In a large nonstick skillet coated with cooking spray, cook chicken in oil over medium heat until no longer pink. Sprinkle with flour, coriander and cocoa; stir until blended.

2. Gradually stir in milk. Bring to a boil; cook and stir for 2 minutes or until thickened. Add the corn, onions, chilies and salt; cook and stir 2 minutes longer or until heated through. Remove from the heat. Stir in 1/4 cup cilantro.

3. Spread 2/3 cup filling down the center of each tortilla. Roll up and place seam side down in a 13-in. x 9-in. baking dish coated with cooking spray.

4. In a small bowl, combine the salsa, tomato sauce and remaining cilantro; pour over enchiladas. Sprinkle with cheese. Cover and bake at 375° for 25 minutes or until heated through.

Nutrition Facts: 1 enchilada equals 336 calories, 9 g fat (2 g saturated fat), 49 mg cholesterol, 749 mg sodium, 37 g carbohydrate, 4 g fiber, 25 g protein. **Diabetic Exchanges:** 3 lean meat, 2-1/2 starch, 1/2 fat.

Chicken Florentine Burgers

PREP: 25 min. + cooling **GRILL:** 10 min.
YIELD: 6 servings

MARY CANNATARO • CHICAGO, ILLINOIS

Just try convincing your guests that a recipe this scrumptious is healthier, too. These moist monster burgers are packed with veggies, cheese and loads of great grilled flavor.

1-1/2	cups chopped sweet onions
1-1/2	cups dry white wine *or* reduced-sodium chicken broth
3	garlic cloves, minced
1	pkg. (10 oz.) frozen chopped spinach, thawed and squeezed dry
2/3	cup dry bread crumbs
1/4	cup plus 6 Tbsp. shredded Gruyere *or* Swiss cheese, *divided*
1	Tbsp. Dijon mustard
1/2	tsp. salt
1/2	tsp. pepper
3/4	lb. ground chicken
3/4	lb. extra-lean ground turkey
6	whole wheat hamburger buns, split
6	slices tomato
1	cup fresh baby spinach

1. Place the onion, wine and garlic in a small saucepan. Bring to a boil; cook until wine is reduced to about 1/4 cup. Cool to room temperature.

2. In a large bowl, combine the spinach, bread crumbs, 1/4 cup cheese, mustard, salt, pepper and onion mixture. Crumble meat over mixture and mix well. Shape into six patties.

3. Using long-handled tongs, moisten a paper towel with cooking oil and lightly coat the grill rack. Grill burgers, covered, over medium heat or broil 4 in. from the heat for 5-7 minutes on each side or until a meat thermometer reads 165° and juices run clear. Serve on buns with tomato, spinach and remaining cheese.

Nutrition Facts: 1 burger equals 407 calories, 12 g fat (4 g saturated fat), 72 mg cholesterol, 740 mg sodium, 41 g carbohydrate, 7 g fiber, 36 g protein.

Baked Chicken Cordon Bleu C

PREP: 15 min. **BAKE:** 35 min. **YIELD:** 4 servings

SARAH CHRISTENSON • SAN DIEGO, CALIFORNIA

With only six ingredients, this entree has lots of flavor. This tempting dish is easy enough for a weeknight, but special enough for guests as well.

4	boneless skinless chicken breast halves (6 oz. *each*)
1/4	tsp. salt
1/4	tsp. pepper
4	thin slices prosciutto *or* deli ham
1/2	cup shredded Asiago cheese
1/4	cup seasoned bread crumbs

1. Flatten chicken to 1/4-in. thickness; sprinkle with salt and pepper. Top each with prosciutto and cheese. Roll up and tuck in ends; secure with toothpicks.

2. Transfer to an 11-in. x 7-in. baking dish coated with cooking spray. Sprinkle with bread crumbs. Bake, uncovered, at 350° for 35-45 minutes or until juices run clear.

Nutrition Facts: 1 serving equals 291 calories, 10 g fat (4 g saturated fat), 119 mg cholesterol, 645 mg sodium, 6 g carbohydrate, trace fiber, 43 g protein. **Diabetic Exchanges:** 6 lean meat, 1/2 fat.

Apricot-Almond Chicken Breasts

PREP: 10 min. BAKE: 30 min. YIELD: 4 servings

TRISHA KRUSE • EAGLE, IDAHO

This chicken dish is so delicious, I constantly get asked for the recipe—even my picky eaters clamor for it! It takes only minutes to prepare, so on busy weeknights I can put a healthy supper on the table.

    4 boneless skinless chicken breast halves
       (6 oz. *each*)
  1/2 tsp. salt
  1/4 tsp. pepper
  3/4 cup apricot preserves
  1/4 cup reduced-sodium chicken broth
    1 Tbsp. honey mustard
  1/4 cup sliced almonds

1. Sprinkle chicken with salt and pepper. Place in a 13-in. x 9-in. baking dish coated with cooking spray. Bake, uncovered, at 350° for 15 minutes.

2. In a small bowl, combine the preserves, broth and mustard. Pour over the chicken; sprinkle with almonds. Bake 15-20 minutes longer or until chicken juices run clear.

Nutrition Facts: 1 chicken breast half equals 372 calories, 7 g fat (1 g saturated fat), 94 mg cholesterol, 468 mg sodium, 42 g carbohydrate, 1 g fiber, 36 g protein. **Diabetic Exchanges:** 5 lean meat, 3 starch, 1/2 fat.

Balsamic Roast Chicken [C]

PREP: 20 min. BAKE: 2-1/4 hours + standing
YIELD: 12 servings (1-1/2 cups onion sauce)

TRACY TYLKOWSKI • OMAHA, NEBRASKA

When the aroma from this dish fills your house, your family will think you spent all day cooking. But this elegant, Sunday-special entree, flavored with rosemary, wine and balsamic vinegar, is surprisingly simple to make.

    1 roasting chicken (6 to 7 lbs.)
    2 Tbsp. minced fresh rosemary *or* 2 tsp. dried
       rosemary, crushed
    3 garlic cloves, minced
    1 tsp. salt
    1 tsp. pepper
    2 medium red onions, chopped
  1/2 cup dry red wine *or* reduced-sodium chicken
       broth
  1/2 cup balsamic vinegar

1. Pat chicken dry. In a small bowl, combine the rosemary, garlic, salt and pepper; rub under skin of chicken. Place onions in a shallow roasting pan; top with chicken. Combine wine and balsamic vinegar; pour over chicken.

2. Bake, uncovered, at 350° for 2-1/4 to 2-3/4 hours or until a meat thermometer reads 180°, basting occasionally with pan juices. (Cover loosely with foil if chicken browns too quickly.)

3. Let stand for 15 minutes before carving. Remove and discard skin before serving. Pour onion sauce into a small bowl; skim fat. Serve with chicken.

Nutrition Facts: 3 oz. cooked chicken with 2 Tbsp. onion sauce equals 182 calories, 7 g fat (2 g saturated fat), 77 mg cholesterol, 275 mg sodium, 4 g carbohydrate, trace fiber, 25 g protein. **Diabetic Exchange:** 4 lean meat.

BALSAMIC ROAST CHICKEN

APRICOT-ALMOND CHICKEN BREASTS

Chicken Thighs With Sausage C

PREP: 25 min. **COOK:** 6 hours **YIELD:** 8 servings

JOANNA IOVINO • COMMACK, NEW YORK

Whether you're serving your family or special guests, this comforting entree hits the spot on cold winter nights.

- 2 medium carrots, chopped
- 2 celery ribs, chopped
- 1 large onion, finely chopped
- 8 bone-in chicken thighs (about 3 lbs.), skin removed
- 1 pkg. (14 oz.) smoked turkey sausage, cut into 1/2-in. slices
- 1/4 cup ketchup
- 6 garlic cloves, minced
- 1 Tbsp. Louisiana-style hot sauce
- 1 tsp. dried basil
- 1 tsp. paprika
- 1 tsp. dried thyme
- 1 tsp. browning sauce, optional
- 1/2 tsp. dried oregano
- 1/2 tsp. pepper
- 1/4 tsp. ground allspice

1. In a 4- or 5-qt. slow cooker, combine the carrots, celery and onion. Top with chicken and sausage.

2. In a small bowl, combine the ketchup, garlic, hot sauce, basil, paprika, thyme, browning sauce if desired, oregano, pepper and allspice. Spoon over meats. Cover and cook on low for 6-8 hours or until chicken is tender.

Nutrition Facts: 1 chicken thigh with 1/3 cup sausage mixture equals 280 calories, 12 g fat (4 g saturated fat), 118 mg cholesterol, 675 mg sodium, 8 g carbohydrate, 1 g fiber, 33 g protein. **Diabetic Exchanges:** 5 lean meat, 1/2 starch.

Rich Fettuccine Alfredo

PREP: 20 min. **COOK:** 20 min. **YIELD:** 6 servings

HEALTHY COOKING TEST KITCHEN

Everyone will love this super-creamy, warm and cozy entree on a chilly evening. But no one will ever guess that something this cheesy and delicious could also be lighter! Try it—you'll see what we mean.

- 8 oz. uncooked whole wheat fettuccine
- 2 bacon strips, coarsely chopped
- 1/2 lb. sliced fresh mushrooms
- 1 small onion, chopped
- 1 small sweet red pepper, chopped
- 2 garlic cloves, minced
- 4 oz. fat-free cream cheese, cubed
- 2 Tbsp. cornstarch
- 2 cups whole milk
- 3 cups cubed cooked chicken breast
- 1/3 cup shredded Parmigiano-Reggiano cheese
- 1/2 tsp. salt
- 1/2 cup shredded part-skim mozzarella cheese

1. Cook fettuccine according to package directions. Meanwhile, in a large ovenproof skillet, cook bacon over medium heat until crisp. Using a slotted spoon, remove to paper towels to drain.

2. Saute the mushrooms, onion and pepper in drippings until tender. Add the garlic; cook 1 minute longer. Stir in cream cheese until melted.

3. Combine cornstarch and milk until smooth; stir into skillet. Bring to a boil; cook and stir for 2 minutes or until thickened. Add the chicken, Parmigiano-Reggiano cheese and salt; cook and stir until cheese is melted.

RICH FETTUCCINE ALFREDO

CHICKEN THIGHS WITH SAUSAGE

GRILLED CARIBBEAN LIME CHICKEN

4. Drain fettuccine; add to chicken mixture. Heat through. Sprinkle with mozzarella cheese and reserved bacon. Broil 4-6 in. from the heat for 2-3 minutes or until cheese is melted.

Nutrition Facts: 1-1/3 cups equals 417 calories, 12 g fat (5 g saturated fat), 77 mg cholesterol, 561 mg sodium, 38 g carbohydrate, 5 g fiber, 38 g protein.

Grilled Caribbean Lime Chicken c

PREP: 20 min. + marinating GRILL: 10 min.
YIELD: 8 servings

MARY SHIVERS • ADA, OKLAHOMA

With its amazing tropical salsa, this entree is a showstopper. Add leftover salsa to quesadillas, pork tenderloin or serve it with tortilla chips.

1/2	cup lime juice
1/4	cup olive oil
4	garlic cloves, minced
2	tsp. Greek seasoning
8	boneless skinless chicken breast halves (6 oz. *each*)

SALSA:

2	large tomatoes, seeded and chopped
1	cup diced fresh pineapple
2/3	cup cubed avocado
2	green onions, thinly sliced
1	Tbsp. lime juice
1	Tbsp. cider vinegar
1/2	tsp. salt
1/2	tsp. pepper

1. In a large resealable plastic bag, combine the lime juice, oil, garlic and Greek seasoning; add the chicken. Seal the bag and turn it to coat; refrigerate for 2 hours. In a small bowl, combine the salsa ingredients. Chill until serving.

2. Using long-handled tongs, moisten a paper towel with cooking oil and lightly coat the grill rack. Grill chicken, covered, over medium heat or broil 4 in. from the heat for 5-8 minutes on each side or until a meat thermometer reads 170°. Serve with salsa.

Nutrition Facts: 1 chicken breast half with 1/3 cup salsa equals 260 calories, 10 g fat (2 g saturated fat), 94 mg cholesterol, 371 mg sodium, 7 g carbohydrate, 2 g fiber, 35 g protein.
Diabetic Exchanges: 5 lean meat, 1 fat, 1/2 starch.

Cheese that has been commercially grated or shredded contains **anti-caking agents** that prevent it from blending well into sauces. However, freshly grated or shredded Parmesan cheese has good melting properties.

ASIAN CHICKEN WITH GINGERED VEGETABLES

Asian Chicken with Gingered Vegetables C

PREP: 15 min. + chilling GRILL: 15 min. YIELD: 4 servings

TERESA RALSTON • NEW ALBANY, OHIO

My gang loves this light, colorful and quick meal. Grilled pineapple sprinkled with cinnamon makes a yummy dessert.

1	Tbsp. brown sugar
1	tsp. garlic powder
1/2	tsp. ground ginger
1/2	tsp. Chinese five-spice powder
1/2	tsp. pepper
4	boneless skinless chicken breast halves (6 oz. *each*)
2	cups fresh sugar snap peas, trimmed
1	medium carrot, julienned
2	Tbsp. orange juice
2	Tbsp. reduced-sodium soy sauce
2	tsp. minced fresh gingerroot

1. Combine the first five ingredients; rub over chicken. Cover and refrigerate for 30 minutes.

2. Using long-handled tongs, moisten a paper towel with cooking oil and lightly coat the grill rack. Grill chicken, covered, over medium heat or broil 4 in. from the heat for 6-8 minutes on each side or until a meat thermometer reads 170°.

3. Meanwhile, in a large nonstick skillet coated with cooking spray, combine the remaining ingredients. Cook and stir over medium-high heat for 5-8 minutes or until vegetables are tender. Serve with chicken.

Nutrition Facts: 1 chicken breast half with 1/2 cup vegetables equals 249 calories, 4 g fat (1 g saturated fat), 94 mg cholesterol, 400 mg sodium, 13 g carbohydrate, 3 g fiber, 38 g protein. **Diabetic Exchanges:** 5 lean meat, 1 vegetable.

Crunchy Onion Barbecue Chicken C

PREP: 10 min. BAKE: 25 min. YIELD: 4 servings

JANE HOLEY • CLAYTON, MICHIGAN

I threw this recipe together one night when I had two chicken breasts to use up. After adding french-fried onions and baked-on barbecue sauce, I was thrilled with the moist and tasty result. My husband was, too!

1/2	cup barbecue sauce
1-1/3	cups french-fried onions, crushed
1/4	cup grated Parmesan cheese
1/2	tsp. pepper
4	boneless skinless chicken breast halves (6 oz. *each*)

1. Place barbecue sauce in a shallow bowl. In another shallow bowl, combine the onions, cheese and pepper. Dip both sides of chicken in barbecue sauce, then one side in onion mixture.

2. Place chicken, crumb side up, on a baking sheet coated with cooking spray. Bake at 400° for 22-27 minutes or until a meat thermometer reads 170°.

Nutrition Facts: 1 chicken breast half equals 286 calories, 10 g fat (3 g saturated fat), 97 mg cholesterol, 498 mg sodium, 9 g carbohydrate, trace fiber, 36 g protein. **Diabetic Exchanges:** 5 lean meat, 1 fat, 1/2 starch.

Broccoli Chicken Alfredo

PREP: 20 min. **COOK:** 15 min. **YIELD:** 4 servings

TERRIE FONTENOT • FRESNO, TEXAS

What a fast and simple weeknight supper! This lighter take on Alfredo pasta offers all the comforting flavor families long for—but in a reduced-fat meal. Broccoli and whole wheat pasta boost nutrition.

    2   cups uncooked whole wheat penne pasta
    3   cups frozen chopped broccoli
    1   lb. boneless skinless chicken breasts, cut into 1/2-in. cubes
    2   garlic cloves, minced
    1   cup reduced-fat Alfredo sauce
  1/4   cup grated Parmesan cheese
  1/4   tsp. pepper

1. Cook pasta according to package directions, adding the broccoli during the last 5 minutes of cooking.

2. Meanwhile, in a large nonstick skillet coated with cooking spray, saute chicken until lightly browned. Add garlic; saute 1-2 minutes longer or until chicken is no longer pink and garlic is tender.

3. Drain pasta mixture; add to the pan. Stir in the Alfredo sauce, cheese and pepper; cook and stir until heated through.

Nutrition Facts: 1-1/2 cups equals 470 calories, 11 g fat (6 g saturated fat), 92 mg cholesterol, 599 mg sodium, 51 g carbohydrate, 10 g fiber, 39 g protein.

Simple Sesame Chicken [c]

PREP: 15 min. **COOK:** 10 min./batch **YIELD:** 6 servings

LYNN JONAS • MADISON, WISCONSIN

Returning home after 20 years as a missionary in the Philippines, I tried to make food reminiscent of what we had there and came up with these flavorful strips. This recipe became a family favorite and is often requested at potlucks!

    1/3   cup all-purpose flour
    1/2   tsp. salt
    1/4   tsp. pepper
  1-2/3   cups Caesar salad croutons, crushed
    1/4   cup sesame seeds
      2   eggs, lightly beaten
  1-1/2   lbs. boneless skinless chicken breasts, cut into 1-in. strips
      2   tsp. butter
      2   tsp. canola oil

1. In a shallow bowl, combine the flour, salt and pepper. In another shallow bowl, combine crushed croutons and sesame seeds. Place eggs in a third shallow bowl. Coat chicken with flour mixture, then dip in eggs and coat with crouton mixture.

2. In a large nonstick skillet coated with cooking spray, cook chicken in butter and oil in batches over medium heat for 4-6 minutes on each side or until no longer pink.

Nutrition Facts: 1 serving equals 255 calories, 11 g fat (3 g saturated fat), 120 mg cholesterol, 319 mg sodium, 11 g carbohydrate, 1 g fiber, 27 g protein. **Diabetic Exchanges:** 3 lean meat, 1 starch, 1 fat.

BROCCOLI CHICKEN ALFREDO

SIMPLE SESAME CHICKEN

Makeover Italian Chicken

PREP: 25 min. **BAKE:** 25 min. **YIELD:** 6 servings

SARAH KLIER • GRAND RAPIDS, MICHIGAN

Simple ingredient substitutions add up to a tasty makeover that boasts only about half the fat and a fourth fewer calories than the original. We like math that's that easy!

2-1/2 cups sliced fresh mushrooms
 2 Tbsp. butter
 6 boneless skinless chicken breast halves (6 oz. *each*)
 2 Tbsp. Italian salad dressing mix
 1 can (10-3/4 oz.) reduced-fat reduced-sodium condensed cream of mushroom soup, undiluted
 1 carton (8 oz.) reduced-fat spreadable chive and onion cream cheese
 1/3 cup dry white wine *or* reduced-sodium chicken broth
 1/4 cup fat-free milk
 3 cups uncooked yolk-free whole wheat noodles
 1 Tbsp. minced chives

1. In a large nonstick skillet coated with cooking spray, saute the mushrooms in butter until tender. Remove mushrooms with a slotted spoon and keep warm; set aside.

2. Sprinkle chicken with salad dressing mix. In the same skillet, brown chicken on both sides. Transfer to a 13-in. x 9-in. baking dish coated with cooking spray. Stir the soup, cream cheese, wine, milk and reserved mushrooms into skillet; heat through. Spoon mixture over the chicken.

3. Cover and bake at 350° for 25-30 minutes or until a meat thermometer reads 170°.

4. Meanwhile, cook noodles according to package directions; drain. Serve with chicken and sauce; sprinkle with chives.

MAKEOVER ITALIAN CHICKEN

Nutrition Facts: 1 chicken breast half with 1/2 cup noodles and 1/3 cup sauce equals 417 calories, 16 g fat (8 g saturated fat), 133 mg cholesterol, 860 mg sodium, 26 g carbohydrate, 3 g fiber, 41 g protein.

Orange Barley Chicken

PREP: 30 min. **COOK:** 45 min. **YIELD:** 8 servings

HELEN GLAZIER • SEATTLE, WASHINGTON

My mother used to prepare orange chicken with rice back in the '60s, and it was so good. My version uses pearl barley instead of rice, and I added parsnips for flavor and baby carrots for color.

 1 cup all-purpose flour
 1 tsp. celery salt
 1/2 tsp. pepper
 1 broiler/fryer chicken (3 to 4 lbs.), cut up and skin removed
 2 tsp. olive oil
 1 medium onion, thinly sliced
 1 Tbsp. butter
 3 cups reduced-sodium chicken broth
 3 cups orange juice
 2 medium parsnips, peeled and chopped
1-1/2 cups medium pearl barley
1-1/2 cups sliced fresh mushrooms
1-1/2 cups fresh baby carrots
 2 bay leaves

1. In a large resealable plastic bag, combine the flour, celery salt and pepper. Add chicken, a few pieces at a time, and shake to coat.

2. In a Dutch oven, brown chicken in oil in batches. Remove and keep warm. In the same pan, saute onion in butter until tender. Add the broth, orange juice, parsnips, barley, mushrooms, carrots, bay leaves and chicken. Bring to a boil. Reduce heat; cover and cook for 45-50 minutes or until barley is tender, turning chicken occasionally.

3. Remove from the heat; let stand for 5 minutes. Discard bay leaves.

Nutrition Facts: 1 serving equals 386 calories, 8 g fat (2 g saturated fat), 59 mg cholesterol, 361 mg sodium, 55 g carbohydrate, 8 g fiber, 25 g protein.

Sesame Cilantro Chicken

PREP: 10 min. **BAKE:** 25 min. **YIELD:** 4 servings

BRITTANY BOWEN • FLAGSTAFF, ARIZONA

Slightly sweet, super juicy and drizzled with a wonderfully Asian-inspired sauce, this chicken is definitely delicious enough to serve guests. Wild rice would make an easy side.

 4 boneless skinless chicken breast halves (6 oz. *each*)
 1/2 cup honey
 2 Tbsp. reduced-sodium soy sauce
 1/4 tsp. garlic powder
 1/8 tsp. ground ginger
 1 Tbsp. minced fresh cilantro
 1 Tbsp. sesame seeds, toasted

1. Place chicken in an 11-in. x 7-in. baking dish coated with cooking spray. Combine the honey, soy sauce, garlic powder, ginger and cilantro; spoon 1/4 cup honey mixture over chicken. Set aside the remaining mixture.

2. Cover and bake at 375° for 20 minutes. Uncover; bake 5-10 minutes longer or until a meat thermometer reads 170°. Spoon reserved mixture over chicken; sprinkle with sesame seeds.

Nutrition Facts: 1 serving equals 328 calories, 5 g fat (1 g saturated fat), 94 mg cholesterol, 398 mg sodium, 36 g carbohydrate, trace fiber, 35 g protein. **Diabetic Exchanges:** 5 lean meat, 2 starch.

Mexicali Chicken C

PREP/TOTAL TIME: 30 min. YIELD: 4 servings

AVANELL HEWITT • NORTH RICHLAND HILLS, TEXAS

This recipe has been a family favorite for many years. It's great served with Spanish rice and refried beans. Cilantro may be added to the salsa, if desired.

1	medium tomato, finely chopped
1	small onion, finely chopped
2	jalapeno peppers, seeded and chopped
2	Tbsp. lime juice
1	garlic clove, minced
1/4	tsp. salt
1/8	tsp. pepper

4	boneless skinless chicken breast halves (4 oz. *each*)
1	to 2 tsp. reduced-sodium taco seasoning
4	bacon strips, halved
4	slices reduced-fat provolone cheese
1	medium lime, cut into four wedges

1. In a small bowl, combine the tomato, onion, jalapenos, lime juice, garlic, salt and pepper. Chill until serving.

2. Sprinkle chicken with taco seasoning; set aside. In a large skillet, cook bacon over medium heat until crisp. Remove to paper towels; drain.

3. If grilling the chicken, using long-handled tongs, moisten a paper towel with cooking oil and lightly coat the grill rack. Grill chicken, covered, over medium heat or broil 4 in. from the heat for 4-7 minutes on each side or until a meat thermometer reads 170°.

4. Top with bacon and cheese; cook 1 minute longer or until cheese is melted. Serve with salsa; squeeze lime wedges over top.

Editor's Note: When cutting hot peppers, disposable gloves are recommended. Avoid touching your face.

Nutrition Facts: 1 serving equals 227 calories, 9 g fat (4 g saturated fat), 80 mg cholesterol, 532 mg sodium, 5 g carbohydrate, 1 g fiber, 31 g protein. **Diabetic Exchanges:** 4 lean meat, 1 vegetable, 1/2 fat.

TURKEY AND BLACK BEAN ENCHILADAS

TURKEY DIVAN

FAVORITE SKILLET LASAGNA

Turkey Specialties

Packed with health benefits, this bird's not just for Thanksgiving anymore. From warm-weather roll-ups to comforting casseroles, the dishes that follow are sure to get a thumbs-up rating from everyone at your table.

Favorite Skillet Lasagna

PREP/TOTAL TIME: 30 min. YIELD: 5 servings

LORIE MINER • KAMAS, UTAH

Whole wheat noodles and zucchini pump up nutrition in this delicious, family-friendly dinner. Topped with dollops of ricotta cheese, it has an extra touch of decadence. No one will believe this one's lighter.

- 1/2 lb. Italian turkey sausage links, casings removed
- 1 small onion, chopped
- 1 jar (14 oz.) spaghetti sauce
- 2 cups uncooked whole wheat egg noodles
- 1 cup water
- 1/2 cup chopped zucchini
- 1/2 cup fat-free ricotta cheese
- 2 Tbsp. grated Parmesan cheese
- 1 Tbsp. minced fresh parsley or 1 tsp. dried parsley flakes
- 1/2 cup shredded part-skim mozzarella cheese

1. In a large nonstick skillet, cook sausage and onion over medium heat until no longer pink; drain. Stir in the spaghetti sauce, egg noodles, water and zucchini. Bring to a boil. Reduce heat; cover and simmer for 8-10 minutes or until pasta is tender, stirring occasionally.

2. Combine the ricotta, Parmesan and parsley. Drop by tablespoonfuls over pasta mixture. Sprinkle with mozzarella cheese; cover and cook 3-5 minutes longer or until cheese is melted.

Nutrition Facts: 1 cup equals 250 calories, 10 g fat (3 g saturated fat), 41 mg cholesterol, 783 mg sodium, 24 g carbohydrate, 3 g fiber, 17 g protein. **Diabetic Exchanges:** 2 lean meat, 1-1/2 starch, 1 fat.

Hearty Pasta Casserole

PREP: 45 min. BAKE: 35 min. YIELD: 8 servings

HEALTHY COOKING TEST KITCHEN

Loaded with colorful, flavorful roasted veggies, this recipe became an instant hit with us in the Test Kitchen. This rustic Italian-inspired casserole is also the perfect main dish "to go" because it transports easily and retains heat well. If you and your family are crunched for time during the week, this bake is a great make-ahead, too!

- 2 cups cubed peeled butternut squash
- 1/2 lb. fresh brussels sprouts, halved
- 1 medium onion, cut into wedges
- 2 tsp. olive oil
- 1 pkg. (13-1/4 oz.) whole wheat penne pasta
- 1 lb. Italian turkey sausage links, casings removed
- 2 garlic cloves, minced
- 2 cans (14-1/2 oz. *each*) Italian stewed tomatoes
- 2 Tbsp. tomato paste
- 1-1/2 cups (6 oz.) shredded part-skim mozzarella cheese, *divided*
- 1/3 cup shredded Asiago cheese, *divided*

1. In a large bowl, combine the squash, brussels sprouts and onion; drizzle with oil and toss to coat. Spread vegetables in a single layer in two 15-in. x 10-in. x 1-in. baking pans coated with cooking spray. Bake, uncovered, at 425° for 30-40 minutes or until vegetables are tender.

2. Meanwhile, cook pasta according to package directions. In a large nonstick skillet, cook sausage over medium heat until meat is no longer pink. Add garlic; cook 1 minute longer; drain. Add tomatoes and tomato paste; cook and stir over medium heat until slightly thickened, about 5 minutes.

3. Drain pasta and return to the pan. Add sausage mixture, 1 cup mozzarella, 1/4 cup Asiago and roasted vegetables.

4. Transfer to a 13-in. x 9-in. baking dish coated with cooking spray. Cover and bake at 350° for 30-40 minutes or until heated through. Uncover; sprinkle with remaining cheeses. Bake 5 minutes longer or until cheese is melted.

Nutrition Facts: 1-1/4 cups equals 416 calories, 13 g fat (5 g saturated fat), 47 mg cholesterol, 816 mg sodium, 53 g carbohydrate, 7 g fiber, 24 g protein.

To keep **fresh parsley** in the refrigerator for several weeks, wash the bunch in warm water, shake off excess moisture, wrap in paper towel and seal in a plastic bag.

Turkey Burgers with Sweet Onion Relish

PREP: 25 min. **GRILL:** 10 min. **YIELD:** 6 servings

REBECCA MAGNUSON • SAN DIEGO, CALIFORNIA

People really like this. The sweet onion relish is a little different, which makes this a great meal for entertaining. I often form the turkey mix for these burgers into hot dog shapes for a fun alternative.

1	large sweet onion, chopped
1/4	cup tomato sauce
3	Tbsp. water
2	Tbsp. ketchup
1	Tbsp. sugar
1	garlic clove, minced
1/4	tsp. dried oregano
1/4	tsp. crushed red pepper flakes

BURGERS:

2	egg whites
1-1/2	tsp. poultry seasoning
1/4	tsp. pepper
1-1/2	lbs. lean ground turkey
6	whole wheat hamburger buns, split

1. In a small skillet, combine the first eight ingredients. Cook, uncovered, over medium heat for 10-15 minutes or until onions are tender, stirring occasionally. Set aside.

2. For burgers, in a large bowl, combine the egg whites, poultry seasoning and pepper. Crumble turkey over mixture and mix well. Shape into six patties.

3. Using long-handled tongs, moisten a paper towel with cooking oil and lightly coat the grill rack. Grill burgers, covered, over medium heat or broil 4 in. from the heat for 5-7 minutes on each side or until a meat thermometer reads 165° and juices run clear. Serve on buns with relish.

Nutrition Facts: 1 burger with 4 tsp. relish equals 317 calories, 11 g fat (3 g saturated fat), 90 mg cholesterol, 437 mg sodium, 29 g carbohydrate, 4 g fiber, 25 g protein. **Diabetic Exchanges:** 3 lean meat, 2 starch.

Pizza Pepperoni Pasta

PREP: 25 min. **BAKE:** 25 min. **YIELD:** 8 servings

AMY BIPES • TOPEKA, KANSAS

Turkey pepperoni adds classic Italian flavor to this family-friendly main dish that's done in a flash. It's ideal for busy weeknights or for satisfying a potluck crowd. Serve with a green salad and breadsticks, and dinner's done.

3	cups uncooked whole wheat spiral pasta
1	lb. lean ground turkey
1	medium onion, chopped
2-1/2	cups garden-style spaghetti sauce
1	can (14-1/2 oz.) diced tomatoes, undrained
1/2	tsp. dried basil
1/2	tsp. dried oregano
1/2	tsp. Worcestershire sauce
1/8	tsp. pepper
3	Tbsp. grated Parmesan cheese
4	oz. sliced turkey pepperoni
1/2	cup shredded part-skim mozzarella cheese

1. Cook pasta according to package directions.

2. Meanwhile, in a large nonstick skillet, cook turkey and onion over medium heat until the meat is no longer pink; drain. Stir in the spaghetti sauce, tomatoes, basil, oregano, Worcestershire sauce and pepper; set aside.

3. Drain pasta. Transfer to a 13-in. x 9-in. baking dish coated with cooking spray; sprinkle with Parmesan cheese. Top with spaghetti sauce mixture and pepperoni. Sprinkle with mozzarella cheese.

4. Cover and bake at 350° for 25-30 minutes or until heated through.

Nutrition Facts: 1-1/4 cups equals 299 calories, 10 g fat (3 g saturated fat), 71 mg cholesterol, 752 mg sodium, 30 g carbohydrate, 5 g fiber, 22 g protein. **Diabetic Exchanges:** 3 lean meat, 1-1/2 starch, 1 fat.

Turkey and Black Bean Enchiladas

PREP: 30 min. **BAKE:** 15 min. **YIELD:** 8 servings

SARAH BURLESON • SPRUCE PINE, NORTH CAROLINA

Hearty and satisfying, these slimmed-down enchiladas with whole-wheat tortillas feature a moist and delicious filling you're sure to love.

2	cans (15 oz. *each*) black beans, rinsed and drained, *divided*
1	lb. lean ground turkey
1	medium green pepper, chopped

TURKEY BURGERS WITH SWEET ONION RELISH

1 small onion, chopped

1 can (15 oz.) enchilada sauce, *divided*

1 cup (4 oz.) shredded reduced-fat Mexican cheese blend, *divided*

8 whole wheat tortillas (8 in.), warmed

1. In a small bowl, mash 1 can black beans; set aside. In a large nonstick skillet, cook the turkey, pepper and onion over medium heat until meat is no longer pink; drain. Add the mashed beans, remaining beans, half of the enchilada sauce and 1/2 cup cheese; heat through.

2. Place 2/3 cupfuls of bean mixture down the center of each tortilla. Roll up and place seam side down in two 11-in. x 7-in. baking dishes coated with cooking spray. Pour remaining enchilada sauce over the top; sprinkle with remaining cheese. Bake, uncovered, at 425° for 15-20 minutes or until heated through.

Nutrition Facts: 1 enchilada equals 363 calories, 11 g fat (3 g saturated fat), 55 mg cholesterol, 808 mg sodium, 42 g carbohydrate, 7 g fiber, 24 g protein.

Baked Mostaccioli

PREP: 35 min. **BAKE:** 30 min. **YIELD:** 6 servings

DONNA EBERT • RICHFIELD, WISCONSIN

I often serve this for dinner parties and always get tons of compliments. It's easier than it seems!

8 oz. uncooked mostaccioli

1/2 lb. lean ground turkey

1 small onion, chopped

1 can (14-1/2 oz.) diced tomatoes, undrained

1 can (6 oz.) tomato paste

1/3 cup water

1 tsp. dried oregano

1/2 tsp. salt

1/8 tsp. pepper

2 cups (16 oz.) fat-free cottage cheese

1 tsp. dried marjoram

1-1/2 cups (6 oz.) shredded part-skim mozzarella cheese

1/4 cup grated Parmesan cheese

1. Cook mostaccioli according to package directions. Meanwhile, in a large saucepan, cook turkey and onion over medium heat until meat is no longer pink; drain if necessary.

2. Stir in the tomatoes, tomato paste, water, oregano, salt and pepper. Bring to a boil. Reduce heat; cover and simmer for 15 minutes.

3. In a small bowl, combine cottage cheese and marjoram; set aside. Drain mostaccioli.

4. Spread 1/2 cup meat sauce into an 11-in. x 7-in. baking dish coated with cooking spray. Layer with half of the mostaccioli, meat sauce and mozzarella cheese. Top with the cottage cheese mixture. Layer with the remaining mostaccioli, meat sauce and mozzarella cheese. Sprinkle with grated Parmesan cheese (dish will be full).

5. Bake, uncovered, at 350° for 30-40 minutes or until bubbly and heated through.

Nutrition Facts: 1-1/3 cups equals 278 calories, 7 g fat (3 g saturated fat), 39 mg cholesterol, 607 mg sodium, 32 g carbohydrate, 3 g fiber, 23 g protein. **Diabetic Exchanges:** 3 medium-fat meat, 2 vegetable, 1-1/2 starch.

Coconut-Crusted Turkey Strips

PREP/TOTAL TIME: 30 min. **YIELD:** 6 servings

AGNES WARD • STRATFORD, ONTARIO

These Coconut-Crusted Turkey Strips with a plum dipping sauce are just the thing to serve for a light supper or extra-special appetizer. My granddaughter made them last year, and they were a big hit with everyone.

- 2 egg whites
- 2 tsp. sesame oil
- 1/2 cup flaked coconut, toasted
- 1/2 cup dry bread crumbs
- 2 Tbsp. sesame seeds, toasted
- 1/2 tsp. salt
- 1-1/2 lbs. turkey breast tenderloins, cut into 1/2-in. strips

Cooking spray

DIPPING SAUCE:
- 1/2 cup plum sauce
- 1/3 cup unsweetened pineapple juice
- 1-1/2 tsp. prepared mustard
- 1 tsp. cornstarch

1. In a shallow bowl, whisk egg whites and oil. In another shallow bowl, combine the coconut, bread crumbs, sesame seeds and salt. Dip turkey in egg mixture, then coat with coconut mixture.

2. Place on baking sheets coated with cooking spray; spritz turkey with cooking spray. Bake at 425° for 4-6 minutes on each side or until golden brown and juices run clear.

3. Meanwhile, in a small saucepan, combine the sauce ingredients. Bring to a boil; cook and stir for 2 minutes or until thickened. Serve with turkey strips.

Nutrition Facts: 3 oz. cooked turkey with 2 Tbsp. sauce equals 278 calories, 8 g fat (3 g saturated fat), 56 mg cholesterol, 519 mg sodium, 22 g carbohydrate, 1 g fiber, 30 g protein. **Diabetic Exchanges:** 3 lean meat, 1 starch, 1/2 fat.

Moist & Tender Turkey Breast

PREP: 10 min. **COOK:** 4 hours **YIELD:** 12 servings

HEIDI VAWDREY • RIVERTON, UTAH

This easy dish will be very popular in your home. Your family will love the taste, and you will love how quickly it comes together. Everyone will look forward to the leftovers.

- 1 bone-in turkey breast (6 to 7 lbs.)
- 4 fresh rosemary sprigs
- 4 garlic cloves, peeled

1 Tbsp. brown sugar

1/2 tsp. coarsely ground pepper

1/4 tsp. salt

1. Place turkey breast in a 6-qt. slow cooker. Place rosemary and garlic around the turkey. Combine the brown sugar, pepper and salt; sprinkle over turkey. Cover and cook on low for 4-6 hours or until the turkey is tender.

Nutrition Facts: 7 oz. cooked turkey equals 318 calories, 12 g fat (3 g saturated fat), 122 mg cholesterol, 154 mg sodium, 2 g carbohydrate, trace fiber, 47 g protein.

Curry Turkey Stir-Fry

PREP/TOTAL TIME: 25 min. **YIELD:** 4 servings

LAUREEN RUSH • ELK RIVER, MINNESOTA

Chicken also works well in this satisfying meal-in-one. If you're in a hurry, use instant brown rice.

1/2 tsp. cornstarch

2 Tbsp. reduced-sodium soy sauce

1 Tbsp. minced fresh cilantro

1 Tbsp. honey

1 tsp. curry powder

1 tsp. sesame or canola oil

1 garlic clove, minced

1/8 tsp. crushed red pepper flakes, optional

1 large sweet red pepper, julienned

1 Tbsp. canola oil

3 green onions, cut into 3-in. pieces

2 cups cubed cooked turkey breast

2 cups cooked brown rice

1. In a small bowl, combine the cornstarch, soy sauce, cilantro, honey, curry, sesame oil, garlic and pepper flakes if desired until blended; set aside.

2. In a large skillet or wok, stir-fry the red pepper in oil for 2 minutes or until crisp-tender. Add green onions; stir-fry 1-2 minutes longer or until the vegetables are tender.

3. Stir cornstarch mixture and add to the pan. Bring to a boil; cook and stir for 2 minutes or until thickened. Add turkey; heat through. Serve with rice.

Nutrition Facts: 3/4 cup stir-fry with 1/2 cup rice equals 287 calories, 7 g fat (1 g saturated fat), 60 mg cholesterol, 351 mg sodium, 31 g carbohydrate, 3 g fiber, 25 g protein. **Diabetic Exchanges:** 3 lean meat, 1-1/2 starch, 1 fat.

Sausage Spinach Pizza

PREP: 35 min. + rising **BAKE:** 10 min.
YIELD: 2 pizzas (8 slices each)

ELENA FALK • VERSAILLES, OHIO

My husband loves this pizza, and it's the best way for him to get his fix while staying in his carb range. Putting cheese and seasonings in the crust lets you get by with less on top.

1 pkg. (1/4 oz.) active dry yeast

1 cup warm water (110° to 115°)

2-1/4 cups all-purpose flour

2 Tbsp. olive oil

1 Tbsp. sugar

2 tsp. Italian seasoning

1/2 tsp. salt

1/2 cup shredded Asiago cheese

3/4 lb. Italian turkey sausage links, thinly sliced

1 can (14-1/2 oz.) Italian diced tomatoes, undrained

2 cups fresh baby spinach

6 slices reduced-fat provolone cheese, halved

1. In a large bowl, dissolve yeast in water. Add the flour, oil, sugar, Italian seasoning and salt; beat on medium speed for 3 minutes or until smooth. Stir in Asiago cheese.

2. Turn onto a lightly floured surface; knead until smooth and elastic, about 5-6 minutes. Place in a bowl coated with cooking spray, turning once to coat the top. Cover and let rise in a warm place until doubled, about 1 hour.

3. Punch dough down; divide in half. On a floured surface, roll each portion into a 13-in. circle. Transfer to two 12-in. pizza pans coated with cooking spray. Build up edges slightly. Prick dough thoroughly with a fork. Bake at 425° for 5-8 minutes or until edges are lightly browned.

4. Meanwhile, in a large nonstick skillet, cook sausage over medium heat until no longer pink; drain. Place tomatoes in a food processor; cover and pulse until finely chopped.

5. Spread the tomatoes over crusts; layer with spinach, sausage and provolone cheese. Bake at 425° for 8-12 minutes or until the crusts and cheese are lightly browned.

Nutrition Facts: 2 slices equals 314 calories, 12 g fat (4 g saturated fat), 39 mg cholesterol, 729 mg sodium, 34 g carbohydrate, 2 g fiber, 17 g protein. **Diabetic Exchanges:** 2 starch, 2 lean meat, 1 vegetable, 1/2 fat.

SAUSAGE SPINACH PIZZA

Spicy Turkey Tacos

PREP/TOTAL TIME: 25 min.   YIELD: 4 servings

KENDRA DOSS • KANSAS CITY, MISSOURI

So easy, so healthy and so good—I love these whenever I'm in the mood for a little Mexican food. With a hint of cinnamon, these tacos have an unusual blend of seasonings that's exotic and mouthwatering.

8	taco shells
1	lb. extra-lean ground turkey
1	small red onion, finely chopped
1	cup salsa
1/2	tsp. dried oregano
1/2	tsp. paprika
1/2	tsp. ground cinnamon
1/2	tsp. ground cumin
2	cups shredded lettuce
1/2	cup shredded pepper Jack cheese
1/4	cup fat-free sour cream

Cubed avocado and additional salsa, optional

1. Heat taco shells according to package directions.

2. Meanwhile, in a large nonstick skillet, cook turkey and onion over medium heat until meat is no longer pink. Stir in salsa and spices; heat through.

3. Fill each taco shell with 1/3 cup turkey mixture. Serve with lettuce, cheese, sour cream and optional ingredients if desired.

Nutrition Facts: 2 tacos (calculated without optional ingredients) equals 324 calories, 11 g fat (4 g saturated fat), 63 mg cholesterol, 502 mg sodium, 23 g carbohydrate, 2 g fiber, 35 g protein. **Diabetic Exchanges:** 4 lean meat, 1 starch, 1 vegetable, 1 fat.

Turkey Spiral Skillet

PREP: 15 min.   COOK: 25 min.   YIELD: 8 servings

MANDY PHELPS • GRESHAM, OREGON

Family-friendly and everyday delicious, this dish is a little healthier and lighter twist on classic beef and pasta dishes. It's fast and full of flavor.

1	pkg. (16 oz.) whole wheat spiral pasta
1	lb. extra-lean ground turkey
1	medium sweet orange pepper, finely chopped
1	cup sliced fresh mushrooms
1	small onion, finely chopped
3	garlic cloves, minced
1	can (14-1/2 oz.) Italian stewed tomatoes, undrained
1	jar (14 oz.) spaghetti sauce
1/4	tsp. pepper
1	can (2-1/4 oz.) sliced ripe olives, drained
2	Tbsp. grated Parmesan cheese

1. Cook pasta according to package directions.

2. Meanwhile, in a large nonstick skillet, cook the turkey, orange pepper, mushrooms, onion and garlic until turkey is no longer pink; drain. Add the tomatoes, spaghetti sauce and pepper. Bring to a boil. Reduce heat; simmer, uncovered, for 10-15 minutes or until slightly thickened, stirring occasionally.

3. Drain pasta; add to skillet. Stir in olives; heat through. Sprinkle with cheese just before serving.

Nutrition Facts: 1-1/2 cups equals 351 calories, 5 g fat (1 g saturated fat), 25 mg cholesterol, 542 mg sodium, 53 g carbohydrate, 9 g fiber, 26 g protein.

Sausage Spinach Pasta Bake

PREP: 35 min.   BAKE: 25 min.   YIELD: 10 servings

KIM FORNI • CLAREMONT, NEW HAMPSHIRE

I've fixed this many times and like to make it differently on occasion. I've swapped in other meats, such as chicken sausage, veal or ground pork, and added summer squash, zucchini, green beans and mushrooms, depending on what's in season. Also, fresh herbs really perk up the flavors.

SPICY TURKEY TACOS

TURKEY SPIRAL SKILLET

TURKEY DIVAN

1 pkg. (16 oz.) whole wheat spiral pasta
1 lb. Italian turkey sausage links, casings removed
1 medium onion, chopped
5 garlic cloves, minced
1 can (28 oz.) crushed tomatoes
1 can (14-1/2 oz.) diced tomatoes, undrained
1 tsp. dried oregano
1 tsp. dried basil
1/4 tsp. pepper
1 pkg. (10 oz.) frozen chopped spinach, thawed and squeezed dry
1/2 cup half-and-half cream
2 cups (8 oz.) shredded part-skim mozzarella cheese
1/2 cup grated Parmesan cheese

1. Cook pasta according to package directions.

2. Meanwhile, in a large skillet, cook turkey and onion over medium heat until meat is no longer pink. Add garlic. Cook 1 minute longer; drain. Stir in the tomatoes, oregano, basil and pepper. Bring to a boil. Reduce heat; simmer, uncovered, for 10 minutes.

3. Drain pasta; stir into turkey mixture. Add spinach and cream; heat through. Transfer to a 13-in. x 9-in. baking dish coated with cooking spray. Sprinkle with cheeses. Bake, uncovered, at 350° for 25-30 minutes or until golden brown.

Nutrition Facts: 1-1/3 cups equals 377 calories, 11 g fat (5 g saturated fat), 50 mg cholesterol, 622 mg sodium, 45 g carbohydrate, 8 g fiber, 25 g protein. **Diabetic Exchanges:** 3 lean meat, 2 starch, 2 vegetable, 1/2 fat.

Turkey Divan

PREP/TOTAL TIME: 30 min. YIELD: 8 servings

HEALTHY COOKING TEST KITCHEN

It looks and tastes decadent, but at just 291 calories per serving, this classic entree isn't much of a splurge. Pair it with a side salad and slice of whole grain bread for a complete meal.

1-1/2 cups water
16 fresh asparagus spears, trimmed
2 egg whites
1 egg
2 Tbsp. fat-free milk
1-1/4 cups seasoned bread crumbs
1 pkg. (17.6 oz.) turkey breast cutlets
1/4 cup butter, cubed
8 slices deli ham
8 slices reduced-fat Swiss cheese

1. In a large skillet, bring water to a boil. Add asparagus; cover and boil for 3 minutes. Drain and pat dry.

2. In a shallow bowl, beat the egg whites, egg and milk. Place bread crumbs in another shallow bowl. Dip turkey in egg mixture, then coat with crumbs.

3. In a large skillet, cook turkey in butter in batches for 2-3 minutes on each side or until meat is no longer pink. Layer with a ham slice, two asparagus spears and cheese. Cover and cook for 1 minute or until cheese is melted. Transfer to a platter; keep warm.

Nutrition Facts: 1 serving equals 291 calories, 12 g fat (6 g saturated fat), 100 mg cholesterol, 595 mg sodium, 16 g carbohydrate, 1 g fiber, 31 g protein. **Diabetic Exchanges:** 3 lean meat, 2 fat, 1 starch.

Italian Turkey Roll-Ups

PREP/TOTAL TIME: 20 min. **YIELD:** 6 servings

KAY HEDRICK • GIBSONVILLE, NORTH CAROLINA

These quick-and-easy wraps, with a fresh combination of creamy Havarti, turkey and veggies, have it all. They taste light, healthful and delectable, but they will definitely fill you up, too. Serve with a salad, fruit or a bowl of soup.

    1   pkg. (8 oz.) fat-free cream cheese
    1   Tbsp. Italian seasoning
  1/2   tsp. onion powder
  1/4   tsp. garlic powder
    6   whole wheat tortillas (8 in.), room temperature
    6   slices deli turkey
    3   oz. Havarti cheese, cut into six slices
1-1/2   cups shredded lettuce
    3   plum tomatoes, thinly sliced
    1   medium carrot, shredded
    1   small cucumber, thinly sliced
    3   thin slices red onion, separated into rings

1. In a small bowl, beat the cream cheese, Italian seasoning, onion powder and garlic powder until smooth. Spread 1 heaping Tbsp. over each tortilla. Layer each with a slice of turkey and cheese. Top with remaining ingredients. Roll up tightly and secure with toothpicks.

Nutrition Facts: 1 roll-up equals 271 calories, 8 g fat (3 g saturated fat), 24 mg cholesterol, 662 mg sodium, 29 g carbohydrate, 3 g fiber, 18 g protein. **Diabetic Exchanges:** 2 medium-fat meat, 1 starch, 1 vegetable.

Sausage and Pumpkin Pasta

PREP: 20 min. **COOK:** 15 min. **YIELD:** 4 servings

KATIE WOLLGAST • FLORISSANT, MISSOURI

Flavored with pumpkin and white wine, this delightful pasta with Italian turkey sausage makes a stress-free weekday meal that's special enough to serve to company.

    2   cups uncooked multigrain bow tie pasta
  1/2   lb. Italian turkey sausage links, casings removed
  1/2   lb. sliced fresh mushrooms
    1   medium onion, chopped
    4   garlic cloves, minced
    1   cup reduced-sodium chicken broth
    1   cup canned pumpkin
  1/2   cup white wine *or* additional reduced-sodium chicken broth
  1/2   tsp. rubbed sage
  1/4   tsp. salt
  1/4   tsp. garlic powder
  1/4   tsp. pepper
  1/4   cup grated Parmesan cheese
    1   Tbsp. dried parsley flakes

1. Cook pasta according to package directions.

2. Meanwhile, in a large nonstick skillet coated with cooking spray, cook the sausage, mushrooms and onion over medium heat until meat is no longer pink. Add garlic; cook 1 minute longer. Drain. Stir in the broth, pumpkin, wine, sage, salt, garlic powder and pepper. Bring to a boil. Reduce heat; simmer, uncovered, for 5-6 minutes or until slightly thickened.

3. Drain pasta; add to the skillet and heat through. Just before serving, sprinkle with cheese and parsley.

Nutrition Facts: 1-3/4 cups equals 348 calories, 9 g fat (2 g saturated fat), 38 mg cholesterol, 733 mg sodium, 42 g carbohydrate, 7 g fiber, 23 g protein. **Diabetic Exchanges:** 2-1/2 starch, 2 lean meat, 1 vegetable, 1/2 fat.

Makeover Sweet Potato Sausage Skillet

PREP: 20 min. **COOK:** 15 min. **YIELD:** 8 servings

NATALIE SIMONS • AKRON, OHIO

This skillet supper is a real flavor sensation. The Healthy Cooking Test Kitchen transformed it into a much-better-for-you version that you can be proud to serve.

3	cups uncooked whole wheat spiral pasta
2	medium sweet potatoes, peeled and cut into 1/2-in. cubes
1	Tbsp. water
8	oz. smoked turkey sausage, cut into 1/4-in. slices
1	medium green pepper, chopped
1	small onion, chopped
1	Tbsp. olive oil
1	garlic clove, minced
1	can (14-1/2 oz.) diced tomatoes, undrained
1	cup half-and-half cream
1/4	tsp. salt
1/4	tsp. pepper
3/4	cup shredded cheddar cheese

1. Cook pasta according to package directions. Meanwhile, place potatoes and water in a microwave-safe bowl. Cover and microwave on high for 4-5 minutes or until potatoes are almost tender.

2. In a large nonstick skillet, cook the sausage, green pepper and onion in oil over medium heat for 5 minutes or until vegetables are tender. Add garlic; cook 1 minute longer.

3. Stir in the tomatoes, cream, salt, pepper and potatoes; heat through. Drain pasta; stir into skillet.

Sprinkle with cheese. Cover and let stand for 5 minutes or until cheese is melted.

Nutrition Facts: 1-1/4 cups equals 253 calories, 10 g fat (5 g saturated fat), 44 mg cholesterol, 500 mg sodium, 28 g carbohydrate, 4 g fiber, 12 g protein. **Diabetic Exchanges:** 1-1/2 starch, 1 medium-fat meat, 1 vegetable, 1 fat.

Family-Favorite Taco Salad

PREP/TOTAL TIME: 20 min. **YIELD:** 6 servings

LYNNE GRAVES • PALISADE, MINNESOTA

This lighter, healthier version of classic Southwestern fare is a tradition with my family. I love the fact that it's delicious and such a fast-to-fix meal on busy weeknights.

1-1/2	lbs. lean ground turkey
1	can (14-1/2 oz.) diced tomatoes, undrained
2	tsp. dried minced onion
2	tsp. chili powder
1	tsp. garlic powder
1	tsp. seasoned salt
1/2	tsp. ground cumin
1/4	tsp. pepper
6	cups shredded lettuce
1/2	cup shredded reduced-fat Mexican cheese blend
6	Tbsp. fat-free sour cream, optional

1. In a large nonstick skillet, cook turkey over medium heat until meat is no longer pink; drain. Stir in tomatoes and seasonings; heat through.

2. Divide lettuce among six plates; top each with 2/3 cup turkey mixture, 4 tsp. cheese and 1 Tbsp. sour cream if desired.

Nutrition Facts: 1 serving (calculated without sour cream) equals 239 calories, 12 g fat (4 g saturated fat), 99 mg cholesterol, 551 mg sodium, 9 g carbohydrate, 2 g fiber, 25 g protein. **Diabetic Exchanges:** 3 lean meat, 1 vegetable, 1 fat.

MAKEOVER SWEET POTATO SAUSAGE SKILLET

FAMILY-FAVORITE TACO SALAD

Turkey Mole with Rice

PREP: 20 min. COOK: 15 min. YIELD: 4 servings

TRISHA KRUSE • EAGLE, IDAHO

This is a wonderful Tex-Mex dish. A smoky chipotle pepper makes the sauce extra special!

1-1/2	cups chunky salsa
1/4	cup plus 2 Tbsp. unsalted peanuts, *divided*
1	chipotle pepper in adobo sauce
1	Tbsp. lime juice
1/4	tsp. baking cocoa
1	pkg. (20 oz.) turkey breast tenderloins, cut into 1-in. pieces
2	tsp. olive oil
1/3	cup reduced-sodium chicken broth
2	cups cooked brown rice
2	Tbsp. minced fresh cilantro

1. In a food processor, combine the salsa, 1/4 cup peanuts, chipotle pepper, lime juice and cocoa; cover and process until blended.

2. In a large skillet, cook turkey in oil over medium heat for 6-8 minutes or until no longer pink. Add broth and salsa mixture. Bring to a boil. Reduce heat; simmer, uncovered for 10 minutes. Serve with rice; sprinkle with cilantro and remaining nuts.

Nutrition Facts: 1 cup chicken mixture with 1/2 cup rice and 1-1/2 tsp. peanuts equals 393 calories, 12 g fat (2 g saturated fat), 69 mg cholesterol, 514 mg sodium, 32 g carbohydrate, 3 g fiber, 39 g protein. **Diabetic Exchanges:** 5 lean meat, 2 fat, 1-1/2 starch, 1 vegetable.

TURKEY MOLE WITH RICE

Healthy Turkey Burgers

PREP/TOTAL TIME: 20 min. YIELD: 4 servings

CATHERINE VANSTEENKISTE • RAY, MICHIGAN

Even though they're new to his palate, my 81-year-old dad loves these! Savory and sweet, these easy, fun burgers will lure you away from your pub favorite with just one bite.

1/4	cup egg substitute
1/4	cup seasoned bread crumbs
1/4	cup dried cranberries or cherries
3	Tbsp. crumbled feta cheese
1	lb. lean ground turkey
4	whole wheat hamburger buns, split

1. In a large bowl, combine the egg substitute, bread crumbs, cranberries and feta cheese. Crumble turkey over mixture and mix well. Shape into four patties.

2. Using long-handled tongs, moisten a paper towel with cooking oil and lightly coat the grill rack. Grill the patties, covered, over medium heat or broil 4 in. from the heat for 5-7 minutes on each side or until a meat thermometer reads 165° and juices run clear. Serve on buns.

Nutrition Facts: 1 burger equals 354 calories, 13 g fat (3 g saturated fat), 92 mg cholesterol, 502 mg sodium, 34 g carbohydrate, 4 g fiber, 27 g protein.

Zippy Turkey and Rice

PREP: 45 min. BAKE: 35 min. YIELD: 8 servings

THOMAS LINDGREN • HACKENSACK, MINNESOTA

Hearty and healthful, this yummy casserole is chock-full of rice, beans, tomatoes and cheese. Serve it with fresh fruit or a side salad for a comforting, satisfying meal.

1	cup uncooked brown rice
1	lb. lean ground turkey
1	large onion, chopped
1	can (14-1/2 oz.) diced tomatoes with mild green chilies, undrained
2/3	cup picante sauce
2	tsp. chili powder
2	tsp. ground cumin
1	can (16 oz.) kidney beans, rinsed and drained
1	cup (4 oz.) shredded reduced-fat cheddar cheese, *divided*

1. Cook rice according to package directions.

2. Meanwhile, in a large nonstick skillet, cook turkey and onion over medium heat until meat is no longer pink; drain. Stir in the tomatoes, picante sauce, chili powder and cumin; heat though. Remove from the heat, stir in kidney beans, 1/2 cup cheese and cooked rice. Transfer to a 13-in. x 9-in. baking dish coated with cooking spray.

3. Cover and bake at 350° for 30 minutes. Uncover; sprinkle with remaining cheese. Bake 5-10 minutes longer or until cheese is melted.

Nutrition Facts: 1-1/4 cups equals 294 calories, 9 g fat (3 g saturated fat), 55 mg cholesterol, 593 mg sodium, 35 g carbohydrate, 5 g fiber, 20 g protein. **Diabetic Exchanges:** 3 lean meat, 1-1/2 starch, 1 vegetable.

HERBED TURKEY TETRAZZINI

Herbed Turkey Tetrazzini

PREP: 30 min. **BAKE:** 25 min. **YIELD:** 12 servings

BRIGITTE GARRINGER • COPPER CANYON, TEXAS

There are many versions of this old-fashioned casserole. Mine offers a little more zip due to the thyme and lemon peel. It's a nice way to use up those turkey leftovers.

    6   cups uncooked egg noodles
  1/3   cup sliced green onions
    2   Tbsp. olive oil
    1   lb. sliced fresh mushrooms
    3   Tbsp. minced fresh parsley
    1   Tbsp. minced fresh thyme *or* 1 tsp. dried thyme
    2   bay leaves
    1   garlic clove, minced
    2   tsp. grated lemon peel
  1/4   cup butter
  1/4   cup all-purpose flour
    2   cups chicken broth
    1   egg yolk, lightly beaten
    1   cup milk
    4   cups cubed cooked turkey
Salt and pepper to taste

  1/3   cup dry bread crumbs
  1/3   cup grated Parmesan cheese
  1/2   cup sliced almonds, toasted

1. Cook noodles according to package directions. Meanwhile, in a Dutch oven, saute onions in oil for 3 minutes. Add the mushrooms, parsley, thyme and bay leaves. Cook until mushrooms are lightly browned. Add garlic; cook 1 minute longer. Discard bay leaves.

2. Transfer mushroom mixture to a small bowl; stir in lemon peel and set aside. Drain noodles; set aside.

3. In the Dutch oven, melt butter over medium heat. Stir in flour until smooth. Whisk in broth. Bring to a boil; cook and stir for 2 minutes or until thickened. Combine egg yolk and milk; stir into white sauce. Cook and stir 2 minutes longer.

4. Stir in mushroom mixture and turkey; heat through. Fold in noodles. Season with salt and pepper.

5. Spoon into a greased 13-in. x 9-in. baking dish. Toss bread crumbs and cheese; sprinkle over the top. Bake, uncovered, at 350° for 25-30 minutes or until lightly browned. Sprinkle with almonds.

Nutrition Facts: 1-1/3 cups equals 326 calories, 14 g fat (5 g saturated fat), 91 mg cholesterol, 296 mg sodium, 28 g carbohydrate, 2 g fiber, 22 g protein.

PORK CHOPS WITH HERB PESTO

HAM TETRAZZINI

BAJA PORK TACOS

Pork, Ham & More

Today's health-conscious cooks know the value of setting a hearty, homemade meal on the table. They also know that pork can be a great way to satisfy a hungry crew while keeping fat and calories at bay!

Baja Pork Tacos

PREP: 10 min. COOK: 8 hours YIELD: 12 servings

ARIELLA WINN • MESQUITE, TEXAS

This delicious recipe is my copy-cat version of the most excellent Mexican food we ever had in Flagstaff, Arizona. The original recipe used beef instead of pork, but this comes mighty close to the same flavor.

    1   boneless pork sirloin roast (3 lbs.)
    5   cans (4 oz. *each*) chopped green chilies
    2   Tbsp. reduced-sodium taco seasoning
    1   Tbsp. ground cumin
   24   corn tortillas (6 in.), warmed
    3   cups shredded lettuce
 1-1/2   cups (6 oz.) shredded part-skim mozzarella
         cheese

1. Cut roast in half; place in a 3- or 4-qt. slow cooker. In a small bowl, combine the chilies, taco seasoning and cumin; pour over pork. Cover and cook on low for 8-9 hours or until meat is tender.

2. Remove pork; cool slightly. Skim fat from cooking juices. Shred meat with two forks; return to the slow cooker and heat through. Spoon 1/4 cup onto each tortilla; top each with 2 tablespoons lettuce and 1 tablespoon cheese.

Nutrition Facts: 2 tacos equals 326 calories, 10 g fat (4 g saturated fat), 76 mg cholesterol, 469 mg sodium, 28 g carbohydrate, 4 g fiber, 30 g protein. **Diabetic Exchanges:** 3 lean meat, 2 starch, 1 fat.

Teriyaki Pork

PREP: 10 min. + marinating COOK: 20 min.
YIELD: 4 servings

MOLLY GEE • PLAINWELL, MICHIGAN

I like to season tender pork loin and an assortment of crisp-tender vegetables with a garlicky soy sauce marinade for this savory, no-fuss stir-fry.

   3/4   cup reduced-sodium chicken broth, *divided*
   1/3   cup reduced-sodium soy sauce
    2   Tbsp. red wine vinegar
    2   tsp. honey
    2   tsp. garlic powder

    1   lb. boneless pork loin chops, cut into thin
         strips
    1   Tbsp. canola oil
    2   cups fresh broccoli florets
    3   medium carrots, sliced
    3   celery ribs, sliced
    4   cups shredded cabbage
    6   green onions, sliced
    1   Tbsp. cornstarch
Hot cooked brown rice, optional

1. In a small bowl, combine 1/4 cup broth, soy sauce, vinegar, honey and garlic powder. Pour 1/3 cup marinade into a large resealable plastic bag; add the pork. Seal bag and turn to coat; refrigerate for 1 hour. Cover and refrigerate remaining marinade.

2. Drain and discard marinade. In large nonstick skillet or wok, stir-fry pork in oil for 2-3 minutes or until no longer pink. Remove and keep warm.

3. In the same pan, stir-fry the broccoli and carrots in reserved marinade for 2 minutes. Add the celery; stir-fry for 2 minutes. Add the cabbage and the green onions; stir-fry 2-3 minutes longer or until the vegetables are crisp-tender.

4. Combine cornstarch and remaining broth until smooth; stir into vegetable mixture. Bring to a boil; cook and stir until thickened. Return pork to the pan; heat through. Serve with rice if desired.

Nutrition Facts: 1-1/2 cups (calculated without rice) equals 302 calories, 11 g fat (3 g saturated fat), 63 mg cholesterol, 802 mg sodium, 20 g carbohydrate, 5 g fiber, 30 g protein. **Diabetic Exchanges:** 3 lean meat, 1 starch, 1/2 fat.

Pork products are naturally salty, so keep the sodium down in your final dishes by using seasonings such as garlic and onion powders. These seasonings tend to **absorb moisture** from the air, especially during warm weather months. Store them in airtight spice jars to keep them as free from moisture and humidity as possible.

Honey-Glazed Ham C

PREP: 10 min. **COOK:** 4-1/2 hours **YIELD:** 14 servings

JACQUIE STOLZ • LITTLE SIOUX, IOWA

Here's an easy solution for feeding a large group. The simple ham is perfect for family dinners where time in the kitchen is as valuable as space in the oven.

1	boneless fully cooked ham (4 lbs.)
1-1/2	cups ginger ale
1/4	cup honey
1/2	tsp. ground mustard
1/2	tsp. ground cloves
1/4	tsp. ground cinnamon

Sour cream, optional

1. Cut ham in half; place in a 5-qt. slow cooker. Pour ginger ale over ham. Cover and cook on low for 4-5 hours or until heated through.

2. Combine honey, mustard, cloves and cinnamon; stir until smooth. Spread over ham; cook 30 minutes longer. Garnish with the sour cream if desired.

Nutrition Facts: 4 oz. ham equals 166 calories, 5 g fat (2 g saturated fat), 66 mg cholesterol, 1,347 mg sodium, 8 g carbohydrate, trace fiber, 24 g protein.

Pork Chops with Scalloped Potatoes

PREP: 30 min. **COOK:** 8 hours **YIELD:** 6 servings

ELIZABETH JOHNSTON • GLENDALE, ARIZONA

This is a wonderful dish. My sister gave me the recipe as a casserole baked in the oven, but I've also fixed it in the slow cooker and on the stovetop. Everyone who has tasted it loves it. It's a homey meal that feels Sunday-special.

4	medium potatoes, peeled and thinly sliced
6	bone-in pork loin chops (7 oz. *each*)
1	Tbsp. canola oil
2	large onions, sliced and separated into rings
2	tsp. butter
3	Tbsp. all-purpose flour
1/4	tsp. salt
1/4	tsp. pepper
1	can (14-1/2 oz.) reduced-sodium chicken broth
1	cup fat-free milk

1. Place potatoes in a 5- or 6-qt. slow cooker coated with cooking spray. In a large nonstick skillet, brown pork chops in oil in batches.

2. Place chops over potatoes. Saute onions in drippings until tender; place over chops. Melt butter in skillet. Combine the flour, salt, pepper and broth until smooth. Stir into pan. Add milk. Bring to a boil; cook and stir for 2 minutes or until thickened.

3. Pour sauce over onions. Cover and cook on low for 8-10 hours or until pork is tender. Skim fat and thicken cooking juices if desired.

Nutrition Facts: 1 pork chop with 3/4 cup potatoes equals 372 calories, 12 g fat (4 g saturated fat), 90 mg cholesterol, 389 mg sodium, 29 g carbohydrate, 2 g fiber, 35 g protein. **Diabetic Exchanges:** 4 lean meat, 2 starch, 1 fat.

HONEY-GLAZED HAM

PORK CHOPS WITH SCALLOPED POTATOES

GLAZED PORK WITH STRAWBERRY COUSCOUS

Glazed Pork with Strawberry Couscous

PREP: 15 min. **BAKE:** 1 hour 20 min. + standing
YIELD: 10 servings

BERNICE JANOWSKI • STEVENS POINT, WISCONSIN

This is a delicious dish I often serve guests. I typically save it for when mint and strawberries are plentiful in my garden.

2	tsp. dried marjoram
1	tsp. salt
1	tsp. seasoned pepper
1	bone-in pork loin roast (5 lbs.)
1/2	cup seedless strawberry jam
1/2	cup orange juice, divided
1	can (14-1/2 oz.) chicken broth
1	pkg. (10 oz.) plain couscous
1	cup fresh strawberries, quartered
1/4	cup minced fresh mint
2	tsp. grated orange peel

1. Line the bottom of a large shallow roasting pan with foil; set aside. Combine the marjoram, salt and pepper; rub over roast. Place in pan. Bake, uncovered, at 350° for 1 hour.

2. Combine jam and 1/4 cup orange juice; brush half over pork. Bake 20-30 minutes longer or until a meat thermometer reads 160°, basting with remaining jam mixture every 10 minutes. Let stand for 10 minutes before slicing.

3. Meanwhile, in a small saucepan, bring broth to a boil. Stir in couscous. Cover and remove from the heat; let stand for 5 minutes or until liquid is absorbed. Fluff with a fork; stir in the strawberries, mint, orange peel and remaining orange juice. Serve with pork.

Nutrition Facts: 4 oz. cooked meat with 1/2 cup couscous mixture equals 383 calories, 11 g fat (4 g saturated fat), 92 mg cholesterol, 493 mg sodium, 35 g carbohydrate, 2 g fiber, 36 g protein. **Diabetic Exchanges:** 4 lean meat, 2 starch, 1 fat.

Have leftover pork? Freeze it in a resealable storage bag. Each time you have **extra pork,** add it to the bag. When the bag is full, set the contents in a slow cooker and cover with your favorite barbecue sauce. Set to low and cook until heated through. Shred the pork for sandwiches.

APPLE PORK ROAST

Apple Pork Roast C

PREP: 35 min. **BAKE:** 1-1/4 hours + standing
YIELD: 10 servings

FLORENCE LAPOINTE • DRYDEN, ONTARIO

This is a delicious way to make a pork roast, and it's my husband's favorite. The gravy is very tasty without all of the fat. The flavors of apple and apricot lend a delightful touch.

1	boneless pork loin roast (3 lbs.)
2	garlic cloves, sliced
2	Tbsp. Dijon mustard
1	tsp. red wine vinegar
3/4	tsp. dried thyme
1/2	tsp. rubbed sage
3/4	cup reduced-sodium beef broth
3/4	cup unsweetened apple juice
1/4	cup apricot jam
1-1/2	cups chopped peeled apples
1	Tbsp. cornstarch
1	Tbsp. reduced-fat sour cream

1. Cut eight to ten 1-in. slits in top of roast; insert garlic slices. In a large nonstick skillet coated with cooking spray, brown roast on all sides. Transfer to a roasting pan.

2. In a small bowl, combine the mustard, vinegar, thyme and sage; brush over roast. In a small saucepan, combine the broth, apple juice and jam. Cook and stir over medium heat until jam is melted; pour over roast. Arrange apples around roast.

3. Cover and bake at 350° for 1-1/4 to 1-1/2 hours or until a meat thermometer reads 160°, basting occasionally. Remove roast to a warm serving platter; let stand for 10 minutes before slicing.

4. Meanwhile, skim fat from pan juices. Set aside 1/2 cup juices; pour remaining juices and apples into a large saucepan. Combine cornstarch and sour cream until smooth; stir into reserved pan juices. Stir into saucepan. Bring to a boil over medium heat; cook and stir for 2 minutes or until slightly thickened. Serve with roast.

Nutrition Facts: 4 oz. cooked pork with 1/4 cup gravy equals 278 calories, 10 g fat (4 g saturated fat), 84 mg cholesterol, 158 mg sodium, 11 g carbohydrate, 1 g fiber, 33 g protein. **Diabetic Exchanges:** 4 lean meat, 1 starch.

Simple Sweet Pork Chops

PREP: 10 min. **BAKE:** 40 min. **YIELD:** 6 servings

SHERRI MELOTIK • OAK CREEK, WISCONSIN

Simple enough to whip up for busy weeknights, these tender pork chops are all juiced up with sweet pineapple and just the right touch of jalapeno. They're perfect for the whole family.

ated product(s) at any participating retailer.

will reimburse the face value of this coupon plus our specified
has redeemed this original coupon with the purchase of the item(s)
stitutes fraud. Failure to provide invoices showing sufficient purchase
oupons. Coupons submitted become our property. Reimbursement will
eemed coupon. For redemption mail to: **PepsiCo Canada ULC, P.O. Box
R 0E7.**

included in the face value where applicable.

ANADA. No Cash Value.

OTHER COUPON. Unauthorized reproduction is unlawful.

30, 2018.

ULC, 2018

15108744

6 boneless pork loin chops (6 oz. *each*)

1 can (20 oz.) unsweetened pineapple chunks, undrained

3 Tbsp. brown sugar

1 jalapeno pepper, seeded and finely chppped

1 Tbsp. reduced-sodium soy sauce

1/2 tsp. chili powder

1/4 tsp. garlic powder

1. Place pork chops in a 13-in. x 9-in. baking dish coated with cooking spray. Combine remaining ingredients; pour over chops. Cover and bake at 350° for 30 minutes. Bake, uncovered, 10-15 minutes longer or until a meat thermometer reads 160°.

Editor's Note: When cutting hot peppers, disposable gloves are recommended. Avoid touching your face.

Nutrition Facts: 1 pork chop with about 1/3 cup sauce equals 303 calories, 10 g fat (4 g saturated fat), 82 mg cholesterol, 161 mg sodium, 19 g carbohydrate, 1 g fiber, 33 g protein. **Diabetic Exchanges:** 5 lean meat, 1 fruit.

Jambalaya

PREP: 20 min. COOK: 6-1/4 hours YIELD: 12 servings

SHERRY HUNTWORK • GRETNA, NEBRASKA

Sausage, chicken and shrimp keep this dish hearty and satisfying. Made easy with canned items and other kitchen staples, it's ideal for casual get-togethers.

1 lb. smoked Polish sausage, cut into 1/2-in. slices

1/2 lb. boneless skinless chicken breasts, cut into 1-in. cubes

1 can (14-1/2 oz.) beef broth

1 can (14-1/2 oz.) diced tomatoes, undrained

2 celery ribs, chopped

1/3 cup tomato paste

4 garlic cloves, minced

1 Tbsp. dried parsley flakes

1-1/2 tsp. dried basil

1 tsp. cayenne pepper

1/2 tsp. salt

1/2 tsp. dried oregano

1 lb. cooked medium shrimp, peeled and deveined

2 cups cooked rice

1. In a 5-qt. slow cooker, combine the first 12 ingredients. Cover and cook on low for 6-7 hours or until chicken is no longer pink.

2. Stir in shrimp and rice. Cover and cook 15 minutes longer or until heated through.

Nutrition Facts: 1 cup equals 228 calories, 11 g fat (4 g saturated fat), 95 mg cholesterol, 693 mg sodium, 12 g carbohydrate, 1 g fiber, 18 g protein.

Ham Tetrazzini

PREP: 15 min. COOK: 4 hours YIELD: 5 servings

SUSAN BLAIR • STERLING, MICHIGAN

I modified a recipe that came with my slow cooker to reduce the fat without sacrificing taste. I've served this at parties, family dinners and potlucks. Everyone is pleasantly surprised to find they're eating healthy.

1 can (10-3/4 oz.) reduced-sodium condensed cream of mushroom soup, undiluted

1 cup sliced fresh mushrooms

1 cup cubed fully cooked ham

1/2 cup fat-free evaporated milk

2 Tbsp. white wine *or* water

1 tsp. prepared horseradish

1 pkg. (7 oz.) spaghetti

1/2 cup shredded Parmesan cheese

1. In a 3-qt. slow cooker, combine the soup, mushrooms, ham, milk, wine and horseradish. Cover and cook on low for 4 hours.

2. Cook spaghetti according to package directions; drain. Add the spaghetti and cheese to slow cooker; toss to coat.

Nutrition Facts: 1 cup equals 290 calories, 6 g fat (3 g saturated fat), 24 mg cholesterol, 759 mg sodium, 39 g carbohydrate, 2 g fiber, 16 g protein. **Diabetic Exchanges:** 2-1/2 starch, 1 lean meat, 1/2 fat.

HAM TETRAZZINI

JAMBALAYA

Pork Chop Cacciatore

PREP: 30 min. COOK: 8 hours YIELD: 6 servings

TRACY HIATT GRICE • SOMERSET, WISCONSIN

It's hard to believe the wonderful flavor of these tender chops could come from such an easy recipe! Pair it with noodles and a simple green salad, and dinner's served.

6	bone-in pork loin chops (7 oz. *each*)
3/4	tsp. salt, *divided*
1/4	tsp. pepper
1	Tbsp. olive oil
1	cup sliced fresh mushrooms
1	small onion, chopped
1	celery rib, chopped
1	small green pepper, chopped
2	garlic cloves, minced
1	can (14-1/2 oz.) diced tomatoes
1/2	cup water, *divided*
1/2	tsp. dried basil
2	Tbsp. cornstarch
4-1/2	cups cooked egg noodles

1. Sprinkle chops with 1/2 tsp. salt and pepper. In a large skillet, brown chops in oil in batches. Transfer to a 4-or 5-qt. slow cooker coated with cooking spray. Saute the mushrooms, onion, celery and green pepper in drippings until tender. Add the garlic; cook 1 minute longer. Stir in the tomatoes, 1/4 cup water, basil and remaining salt; pour over chops.

2. Cover and cook on low for 8-9 hours or until pork is tender. Remove meat to a serving platter; keep warm. Skim fat from cooking juices if necessary; transfer to a small saucepan. Bring liquid to a boil. Combine cornstarch and remaining water until smooth. Gradually stir into the pan. Bring to a boil; cook and stir for 2 minutes or until thickened. Serve with meat and noodles.

Nutrition Facts: 1 pork chop with 3/4 cup noodles and 1/2 cup sauce equals 371 calories, 12 g fat (4 g saturated fat), 110 mg cholesterol, 458 mg sodium, 29 g carbohydrate, 3 g fiber, 35 g protein. **Diabetic Exchanges:** 4 lean meat, 1-1/2 starch, 1 vegetable, 1/2 fat.

Pizza Lover's Pie

PREP: 20 min. BAKE: 20 min. YIELD: 8 servings

CAROL GILLESPIE • CHAMBERSBURG, PENNSYLVANIA

Love pizza? Then you'll adore the tasty spin this recipe puts on it. Plus, it's virtually effortless to tailor for picky eaters.

1/4	lb. bulk pork sausage
1/2	cup chopped green pepper
1/4	cup chopped onion
1	loaf (1 lb.) frozen bread dough, thawed and halved
2	cups (8 oz.) shredded part-skim mozzarella cheese
1/2	cup grated Parmesan cheese
1	can (8 oz.) pizza sauce
8	slices pepperoni
1	can (4 oz.) mushroom stems and pieces, drained
1/4	tsp. dried oregano

1. In a large skillet, cook the sausage, pepper and onion over medium heat until meat is no longer pink; drain. Set aside.

2. Roll half of dough into a 12-in. circle. Transfer to a greased 9-in. deep-dish pie plate. Layer with half of the mozzarella cheese, Parmesan cheese and pizza sauce. Top with the sausage mixture, pepperoni, mushrooms and 1/8 teaspoon oregano.

PORK CHOP CACCIATORE

PIZZA LOVER'S PIE

PORK CHOPS WITH HERB PESTO

3. Roll out remaining dough to fit top of pie. Place over filling; seal edges. Layer with remaining pizza sauce, cheeses and oregano.

4. Bake at 400° for 18-22 minutes or until crust is golden brown.

Nutrition Facts: 1 piece equals 305 calories, 12 g fat (5 g saturated fat), 27 mg cholesterol, 743 mg sodium, 32 g carbohydrate, 3 g fiber, 17 g protein. **Diabetic Exchanges:** 2 starch, 2 medium-fat meat.

Pork Chops With Herb Pesto C

PREP: 15 min. + marinating **GRILL:** 10 min.
YIELD: 4 servings

LISA BYNUM • BRANDON, MISSISSIPPI

You won't believe how much a handful of fresh garden herbs can pump up the flavor of ordinary pork chops when you try this easy entree. These juicy chops would be fantastic alongside garlic mashed potatoes.

> 4 bone-in pork loin chops (3/4 in. thick and 7 oz. *each*)
> 1/4 tsp. salt
> 1/8 tsp. pepper
> 2 Tbsp. water
> 1 Tbsp. *each* minced fresh rosemary, sage, thyme, parsley and basil
> 1 Tbsp. olive oil
> 3 garlic cloves, minced

1. Sprinkle pork with salt and pepper. In a small bowl, combine the water, herbs, oil and garlic; brush over both sides of chops. Cover and refrigerate for at least 1 hour.

2. Using long-handled tongs, moisten a paper towel with cooking oil and lightly coat the grill rack. Grill chops, covered, over medium heat or broil 4 in. from the heat for 4-5 minutes on each side or until a meat thermometer reads 160°.

Nutrition Facts: 1 pork chop equals 241 calories, 12 g fat (4 g saturated fat), 86 mg cholesterol, 212 mg sodium, 1 g carbohydrate, trace fiber, 30 g protein. **Diabetic Exchanges:** 4 lean meat, 1 fat.

Slow-Cooked Pork and Beans

PREP: 15 min. **COOK:** 6 hours **YIELD:** 12 servings

PATRICIA HAGER • NICHOLASVILLE, KENTUCKY

I like to get this dish started before leaving for work in the morning. When I get home, my supper's ready! It's a hearty slow cooker meal that is also good for a potluck. A generous helping of tender pork and beans is perfect alongside a slice of warm corn bread.

> 1 boneless whole pork loin roast (3 lbs.)
> 1 medium onion, sliced
> 3 cans (15 oz. *each*) pork and beans
> 1-1/2 cups barbecue sauce
> 1/4 cup packed brown sugar
> 1 tsp. garlic powder

1. Cut roast in half; place in a 5-qt. slow cooker. Top with onion. In a large bowl, combine the beans, barbecue sauce, brown sugar and garlic powder; pour over meat. Cover and cook on low for 6 hours or until meat is tender.

2. Remove roast; shred with two forks. Return meat to slow cooker; heat through.

Nutrition Facts: 1 cup equals 217 calories, 6 g fat (2 g saturated fat), 56 mg cholesterol, 404 mg sodium, 16 g carbohydrate, 2 g fiber, 24 g protein.

Tangy Barbecued Pork Chops ⓒ

PREP: 35 min. BAKE: 25 min. YIELD: 6 servings

NELLA PARKER • HERSEY, MICHIGAN

This tasty pork dish makes a great entree and has become a family tradition over the years. It's lower in carbs, and the sweet, tangy sauce is fantastic spooned over chicken, too. I make extra sauce when I'm serving mashed potatoes.

1	medium onion, sliced
1/2	cup water
3	Tbsp. cider vinegar
2	Tbsp. sugar
1	Tbsp. prepared mustard
1	lemon slice
1/4	tsp. salt
1/4	tsp. pepper
1/8	tsp. crushed red pepper flakes
1/2	cup ketchup
2	Tbsp. Worcestershire sauce
1	tsp. Liquid Smoke, optional
6	bone-in pork loin chops (7 oz. *each*)
1	Tbsp. canola oil

1. In a small saucepan, combine the first nine ingredients. Bring to a boil. Reduce heat: simmer, uncovered, for 20 minutes. Stir in the ketchup, Worcestershire sauce and Liquid Smoke if desired; heat through. Discard lemon.

2. Meanwhile, in a large skillet, brown pork chops in oil in batches. Transfer to a 13-in. x 9-in. baking dish coated with cooking spray; pour sauce over chops.

3. Cover and bake at 350° for 25-30 minutes or until a meat thermometer reads 160°.

Nutrition Facts: 1 chop equals 279 calories, 11 g fat (3 g saturated fat), 86 mg cholesterol, 500 mg sodium, 13 g carbohydrate, 1 g fiber, 31 g protein. **Diabetic Exchanges:** 4 lean meat, 1 starch.

Creamy Pepperoni Ziti

PREP: 15 min. BAKE: 25 min. YIELD: 9 servings

CHARLANE GATHY • LEXINGTON, KENTUCKY

You can easily feed a crowd with this simple dish that's ready in about 40 minutes. Its comforting flair will make it a fast favorite at your next potluck or weeknight dinner.

1	pkg. (16 oz.) ziti *or* small tube pasta
1	can (10-3/4 oz.) condensed cream of mushroom soup, undiluted
3/4	cup shredded part-skim mozzarella cheese
3/4	cup chopped pepperoni
1/2	cup *each* chopped onion, mushrooms, green pepper and tomato
1/2	cup half-and-half cream
1/4	cup chicken broth
1/4	tsp. salt
1/4	tsp. garlic powder
1/4	tsp. pepper
1/2	cup grated Parmesan cheese

1. Cook pasta according to package directions; drain. In a large bowl, combine the pasta, soup, mozzarella cheese, pepperoni, onion, mushrooms, green pepper, tomato, cream, broth and seasonings.

2. Transfer to a greased 13-in. x 9-in. baking dish. Sprinkle with Parmesan cheese. Cover and bake at 350° for 20 minutes. Uncover; bake 5-10 minutes longer or until bubbly.

Nutrition Facts: 1 cup equals 340 calories, 12 g fat (6 g saturated fat), 27 mg cholesterol, 696 mg sodium, 43 g carbohydrate, 2 g fiber, 15 g protein. **Diabetic Exchanges:** 3 starch, 1 high-fat meat, 1/2 fat.

Old-Fashioned Lamb Stew

PREP: 20 min. **COOK:** 3 hours **YIELD:** 10-12 servings

MICHELLE WISE • SPRING MILLS, PENNSYLVANIA

This hearty stew is chock-full of tender lamb chunks and lots of vegetables. Sometimes, I prepare this recipe in my slow cooker for added ease.

- 1/4 cup all-purpose flour
- 1 tsp. salt
- 1/2 tsp. pepper
- 3 lbs. boneless lamb, cut into 3-in. pieces
- 2 Tbsp. canola oil
- 1 can (28 oz.) diced tomatoes, undrained
- 1 medium onion, cut into eighths
- 1 Tbsp. dried parsley flakes
- 2 tsp. dried rosemary, crushed
- 1/4 tsp. garlic powder
- 4 large carrots, cut into 1/2-in. pieces
- 4 medium potatoes, peeled and cut into 1-in. pieces
- 1 pkg. (10 oz.) frozen peas
- 1 can (4 oz.) mushroom stems and pieces, drained

1. In a large resealable plastic bag, combine flour, salt and pepper; add lamb and toss to coat. In a Dutch oven, brown the lamb in oil; drain. Add tomatoes, onion, parsley, rosemary and garlic powder. Cover and simmer for 2 hours.

2. Add carrots and potatoes; cover and cook 1 hour longer or until the meat is tender. Add peas and mushrooms; heat through. Thicken if desired.

Nutrition Facts: 1 cup equals 273 calories, 8 g fat (2 g saturated fat), 74 mg cholesterol, 426 mg sodium, 22 g carbohydrate, 4 g fiber, 27 g protein.

Sausage Pizza

PREP: 20 min. **BAKE:** 15 min. **YIELD:** 8 slices

HEALTHY COOKING TEST KITCHEN

Spicy sausage, onions, mushrooms and plenty of cheese make this pizza from our home economists a real keeper. It beats the delivery variety every time—and there's no wait! Bake up two or more and keep one on hand for busy nights.

- 1 loaf (1 lb.) frozen bread dough, thawed
- 3/4 lb. bulk hot Italian sausage
- 1/2 cup sliced onion
- 1/2 cup sliced fresh mushrooms
- 1/2 cup chopped green pepper
- 1/2 cup pizza sauce
- 2 cups (8 oz.) shredded part-skim mozzarella cheese

1. With greased fingers, pat dough onto an ungreased 12-in. pizza pan. Prick dough thoroughly with a fork. Bake at 400° for 10-12 minutes or until lightly browned. Meanwhile, in a large skillet, cook the sausage, onion, mushrooms and green pepper over medium heat until sausage is no longer pink; drain.

2. Spread pizza sauce over crust. Top with sausage mixture; sprinkle with cheese. Bake at 400° for 12-15 minutes or until golden brown. Or wrap pizza and freeze for up to 2 months.

3. To use frozen pizza: Unwrap and place on a pizza pan; thaw in the refrigerator. Bake at 400° for 18-22 minutes or until golden brown.

Nutrition Facts: 1 slice (prepared with turkey sausage and reduced-fat cheese) equals 311 calories, 11 g fat (4 g saturated fat), 39 mg cholesterol, 754 mg sodium, 33 g carbohydrate, 2 g fiber, 20 g protein. **Diabetic Exchanges:** 2 starch, 1-1/2 lean meat, 1-1/2 fat.

To quickly use a huge supply of **garden tomatoes**, wash and core them, then puree them in the blender with lemon juice, onion and celery for a delicious vegetable juice. You can even simmer several batches until slightly thickened for a healthy spaghetti sauce or until very thick for pizza sauce. Freeze the extras.

SAUSAGE PIZZA

Applesauce-Glazed Pork Chops

7 pt.

PREP/TOTAL TIME: 30 min. YIELD: 4 servings

BRENDA CAMPBELL • OLYMPIA, WASHINGTON

Perfect for hectic weeknights, this half-hour entree easily satisfies. The tender chops get special treatment from an effortless sauce.

4	bone-in pork loin chops (7 oz. *each*)
1	cup unsweetened applesauce
1/4	cup packed brown sugar
1	Tbsp. barbecue sauce
1	Tbsp. Worcestershire sauce
1	garlic clove, minced
1/2	tsp. salt
1/2	tsp. pepper

1. Place pork chops in a 13-in. x 9-in. baking dish coated with cooking spray. In a small bowl, combine the remaining ingredients; spoon over chops.

2. Bake, uncovered, at 350° for 20-25 minutes or until a meat thermometer reads 160°.

Nutrition Facts: 1 pork chop with 1/3 cup sauce equals 291 calories, 9 g fat (3 g saturated fat), 86 mg cholesterol, 442 mg sodium, 22 g carbohydrate, 1 g fiber, 30 g protein. **Diabetic Exchanges:** 4 lean meat, 1 starch, 1/2 fruit.

Makeover Rigatoni With Bacon and Asparagus

PREP: 25 min. COOK: 20 min. YIELD: 8 servings

JOANIE FUSON • INDIANAPOLIS, INDIANA

Wouldn't it be great to find a company-worthy dish that not only impresses with its taste, but with its nutrition numbers, too? That's just what I got when I asked the "Healthy Cooking" team to lighten up my rigatoni dish.

1	pkg. (16 oz.) spiral pasta
1	lb. fresh asparagus, trimmed and coarsely chopped
8	bacon strips
1	garlic clove, minced
2	Tbsp. butter
1	Tbsp. olive oil
2/3	cup half-and-half cream
1/2	cup shredded part-skim mozzarella cheese
1/2	tsp. salt
1/4	cup minced fresh parsley
1/8	tsp. coarsely ground pepper
1/4	cup grated Parmigiano-Reggiano cheese

1. Cook pasta according to package directions.

2. Meanwhile, in a Dutch oven, bring 2 cups water to a boil. Add asparagus; cover and boil for 3 minutes. Drain and immediately place asparagus in ice water. Drain and pat dry.

3. In the same pan, cook bacon over medium heat until crisp. Remove to paper towels to drain. Crumble bacon and set aside.

4. Saute garlic in butter and oil until tender. Stir in cream. Bring to a boil. Reduce heat; simmer, uncovered, for 3-4 minutes or until slightly thickened.

5. Stir in mozzarella cheese until melted. Drain pasta; add to pan. Stir in the salt, asparagus, parsley and reserved bacon. Sprinkle with pepper and Parmigiano-Reggiano cheese.

MAKEOVER RIGATONI WITH BACON AND ASPARAGUS

APPLESAUCE-GLAZED PORK CHOPS

ASIAN PORK TENDERLOIN

Nutrition Facts: 1-1/4 cups equals 345 calories, 13 g fat (6 g saturated fat), 32 mg cholesterol, 428 mg sodium, 44 g carbohydrate, 2 g fiber, 15 g protein.

Asian Pork Tenderloin C

PREP: 10 min. + marinating **BAKE:** 20 min.
YIELD: 6 servings

APRIL LANE • GREENEVILLE, TENNESSEE

This quick-to-prepare entree bursts with flavor. Throw together the marinade before work, so it's ready to toss together when you walk through the door at night.

1/3	cup packed brown sugar
1/3	cup reduced-sodium soy sauce
2	Tbsp. lemon juice
2	Tbsp. sesame oil
2	Tbsp. Worcestershire sauce
4	garlic cloves, minced
1	Tbsp. ground mustard
1	tsp. pepper
2	pork tenderloins (3/4 lb. *each*)

1. In a small bowl, combine the first eight ingredients. Pour 1/2 cup marinade into a large resealable plastic bag. Add the pork; seal bag and turn to coat. Refrigerate for 8 hours or overnight. Cover and refrigerate remaining marinade.

2. Drain and discard marinade. Place pork on a rack in a shallow roasting pan. Bake at 450° for 20-25 minutes or until a meat thermometer reads 160°, basting occasionally with reserved marinade. Let stand for 5 minutes before slicing.

Nutrition Facts: 3 oz. cooked pork equals 218 calories, 8 g fat (2 g saturated fat), 63 mg cholesterol, 510 mg sodium, 12 g carbohydrate, trace fiber, 24 g protein. **Diabetic Exchanges:** 3 lean meat, 1 starch.

Mustard Bourbon Kabobs C

PREP: 10 min. + marinating **GRILL:** 10 min.
YIELD: 4 servings

BARBARA WHITE • KATY, TEXAS

You'll love the tangy and subtly sweet blend of mustard and bourbon in these tasty, no-fuss kabobs. Make a little extra marinade and serve them with a side of brown rice.

6	Tbsp. brown sugar
6	Tbsp. Dijon mustard
3	Tbsp. bourbon or apple cider
3	Tbsp. reduced-sodium soy sauce
1	pork tenderloin (1 lb.), cut into 3/4-in. cubes

1. In a small bowl, combine the brown sugar, mustard, bourbon and soy sauce. Pour 3/4 cup marinade into a large resealable plastic bag; add pork. Seal bag and turn to coat; refrigerate for 8 hours or overnight. Cover and refrigerate remaining marinade.

2. Drain and discard marinade. Thread pork onto four metal or soaked wooden skewers. Using long-handled tongs, moisten a paper towel with cooking oil and lightly coat the grill rack.

3. Grill kabobs, covered, over medium heat or broil 4 in. from the heat for 8-10 minutes or until juices run clear, turning and basting occasionally with the reserved marinade.

Nutrition Facts: 1 kabob equals 172 calories, 4 g fat (1 g saturated fat), 63 mg cholesterol, 355 mg sodium, 8 g carbohydrate, 0 fiber, 23 g protein. **Diabetic Exchanges:** lean meat, 1/2 starch.

Grilled Spicy Pork Tenderloin Ⓒ

PREP: 15 min. + marinating **GRILL:** 25 min.
YIELD: 4 servings

MARY ANN LEE • CLIFTON PARK, NEW YORK

Tender and full of flavor, this juicy tenderloin couldn't be much more convenient on busy work nights. Make ahead the night before, marinate during the day, then simply grill when you get home.

2	Tbsp. brown sugar
3/4	tsp. salt
3/4	tsp. dried thyme
1/4	tsp. onion powder
1/4	tsp. garlic powder
1/4	tsp. ground mustard
1/4	tsp. ground cumin
1/4	tsp. dried oregano
1/4	tsp. ground allspice
1/4	tsp. pepper
1	pork tenderloin (1 lb.)

SAUCE:

1/2	cup cola
1	Tbsp. brown sugar
1/4	tsp. ground cinnamon
1/4	tsp. chili powder

1. In a small bowl, combine the first 10 ingredients; rub over pork. Cover and refrigerate for 8 hours or overnight.

2. In a small bowl, combine sauce ingredients. Using long-handled tongs, moisten a paper towel with cooking oil and lightly coat the grill rack. Prepare sauce ingredients; set aside.

3. Prepare grill for indirect heat using a drip pan. Place pork over drip pan and grill, covered, over indirect medium-hot heat for 25-30 minutes or until a meat thermometer reads 160°, basting occasionally with reserved sauce. Let roast stand for 5 minutes before slicing.

Nutrition Facts: 3 oz. cooked pork equals 188 calories, 4 g fat (1 g saturated fat), 63 mg cholesterol, 495 mg sodium, 14 g carbohydrate, 1 g fiber, 23 g protein. **Diabetic Exchanges:** 3 lean meat, 1 starch.

Pork Chops with Parmesan Sauce Ⓒ

PREP/TOTAL TIME: 20 min. **YIELD:** 4 servings

HEALTHY COOKING TEST KITCHEN

Moist and tender chops make a speedy and comforting weeknight meal. These are dressed with a smooth, creamy sauce seasoned with Parmesan, onion and a hint of nutmeg, parsley and thyme. Here's a new family favorite!

4	boneless pork loin chops (4 oz. *each*)
1/2	tsp. salt
1/4	tsp. pepper
1	Tbsp. butter
2	Tbsp. all-purpose flour
1	cup fat-free milk
1/3	cup grated Parmesan cheese

2 Tbsp. grated onion
3 tsp. minced fresh parsley
1/4 tsp. dried thyme
1/4 tsp. ground nutmeg

1. Sprinkle pork chops with salt and pepper. In a large nonstick skillet coated with cooking spray, cook chops in butter over medium heat until meat juices run clear; remove and keep warm.

2. Combine flour and milk until smooth; stir into pan. Bring to a boil; cook and stir for 2 minutes or until thickened. Stir in remaining ingredients; heat through. Serve with chops.

Nutrition Facts: 1 pork chop with 3 Tbsp. sauce equals 244 calories, 11 g fat (5 g saturated fat), 69 mg cholesterol, 475 mg sodium, 7 g carbohydrate, trace fiber, 27 g protein. **Diabetic Exchanges:** 4 lean meat, 1/2 starch, 1/2 fat.

Honey Lemon Schnitzel   8 pp

PREP/TOTAL TIME: 25 min. **YIELD:** 4 servings

CAROLE FRASER • NORTH YORK, ONTARIO

These pork cutlets are coated in a sweet sauce with honey, lemon juice and butter. They're certainly good enough for company, but perfect for a quick, weeknight meal, too. Very seldom are there any leftovers.

2 Tbsp. all-purpose flour
1/2 tsp. salt
1/2 tsp. pepper   OMIT SAUCE*
4 pork sirloin cutlets (4 oz. *each*)
2 Tbsp. butter
1/4 cup lemon juice *
1/4 cup honey *

1. In a large resealable plastic bag, combine the flour, salt and pepper. Add pork, two pieces at a time, and shake to coat. In a large skillet, cook pork in butter over medium heat for 3-4 minutes on each side or until juices run clear. Remove and keep warm.

2. Add lemon juice and honey to the skillet; cook and stir for 3 minutes or until thickened. Return pork to pan; cook 2-3 minutes longer or until heated through.

Nutrition Facts: 1 cutlet equals 298 calories, 13 g fat (6 g saturated fat), 88 mg cholesterol, 393 mg sodium, 22 g carbohydrate, trace fiber, 24 g protein.

Pork Chops with Orange Sauce [C]

PREP: 15 min. + marinating **BROIL:** 15 min.
YIELD: 4 servings

MARY CHANDLER • GRAND TOWER, ILLINOIS

Tangy orange and pineapple juices flavor the marinade that dresses up these tender and juicy chops. Add mashed potatoes or rice and a simple side salad for a fuss-free supper.

1 cup orange juice
1/2 cup unsweetened pineapple juice
1/4 cup reduced-sodium soy sauce
2 Tbsp. honey
2 garlic cloves, minced
1/2 tsp. grated orange peel
1/4 tsp. pepper
4 bone-in pork loin chops (7 oz. *each*)
1 Tbsp. cornstarch

1. In a small bowl, combine the first seven ingredients. Pour a scant 1 cup into a large resealable plastic bag; add pork chops. Seal bag and turn to coat; refrigerate for 8 hours or overnight. Cover and refrigerate remaining marinade for sauce.

2. Drain and discard marinade. Using long-handled tongs, moisten a paper towel with cooking oil and lightly coat the grill rack.

3. Grill chops, covered, over medium heat or broil 4 in. from the heat for 4-5 minutes on each side or until a meat thermometer reads 160°.

4. Meanwhile, in a small saucepan, combine cornstarch and reserved marinade. Bring to a boil; cook and stir for 2 minutes or until thickened. Serve with chops.

Nutrition Facts: 1 pork chop with 3 Tbsp. sauce equals 269 calories, 8 g fat (3 g saturated fat), 86 mg cholesterol, 451 mg sodium, 15 g carbohydrate, trace fiber, 31 g protein. **Diabetic Exchanges:** 4 lean meat, 1 starch.

HONEY LEMON SCHNITZEL

PORK CHOPS WITH ORANGE SAUCE

Caraway Pork Chops And Red Cabbage

8 pts

PREP: 20 min. **COOK:** 20 min. **YIELD:** 4 servings

JUDY REBMAN • FREDERICK, ILLINOIS

My husband loves cooked red cabbage. This is my healthy spin on a savory one-skillet supper that my 18-year-old son also enjoys. I serve it with mashed potatoes.

- 4 boneless pork loin chops (5 oz. *each*)
- 1-1/4 tsp. caraway seeds, *divided*
- 1 tsp. rotisserie chicken seasoning
- 1 tsp. brown sugar
- 1 Tbsp. canola oil
- 4 cups shredded red cabbage
- 1 medium apple, peeled and thinly sliced
- 1/2 small onion, sliced
- 1 Tbsp. water
- 1 Tbsp. red wine vinegar
- 1/2 tsp. salt
- 1/2 tsp. reduced-sodium chicken bouillon granules
- 4 Tbsp. apple jelly

1. Season pork chops with 1 tsp. caraway seeds, chicken seasoning and brown sugar. In a large nonstick skillet coated with cooking spray, brown chops in oil. Remove and keep warm.

2. Add the cabbage, apple, onion, water, vinegar, salt, bouillon granules and remaining caraway seeds to the skillet. Cover and cook over medium heat for 10 minutes, stirring occasionally.

3. Place chops over cabbage mixture; top each with 1 Tbsp. apple jelly. Cover and cook 10-12 minutes longer or until meat is tender.

Nutrition Facts: 1 pork chop with 3/4 cup cabbage mixture equals 319 calories, 12 g fat (3 g saturated fat), 68 mg cholesterol, 523 mg sodium, 25 g carbohydrate, 2 g fiber, 29 g protein. **Diabetic Exchanges:** 4 lean meat, 1 starch, 1 vegetable, 1 fat.

Zesty Herbed Lamb Chops C

PREP/TOTAL TIME: 30 min. **YIELD:** 4 servings

CORA ANDERSON • SEATTLE, WASHINGTON

I often serve this sauce with seared scallops or grilled salmon or halibut. It's really good either way. I also modify the recipe when there are fresh herbs in season. I've made a version with basil instead of mint, and I sometimes swap thyme for oregano for a more subtle flavor.

- 1/2 cup fresh mint leaves
- 1/4 cup minced fresh oregano
- 1/4 cup packed fresh parsley sprigs, stems removed
- 1/4 cup lemon juice
- 3 Tbsp. water
- 6 garlic cloves
- 1 Tbsp. olive oil
- 1/4 tsp. salt

Dash pepper

LAMB CHOPS:
- 8 lamb loin chops (3 oz. *each*)
- 1/2 tsp. salt
- 1/2 tsp. pepper
- 1 Tbsp. olive oil

CARAWAY PORK CHOPS AND RED CABBAGE

ZESTY HERBED LAMB CHOPS

JEWELED BUFFET HAM

1. In a food processor, combine the first nine ingredients; cover and pulse until blended. Set aside half of the sauce. Brush remaining sauce over chops; sprinkle with salt and pepper.

2. In a large skillet coated with cooking spray, cook chops in oil over medium heat for 7-10 minutes on each side or until meat reaches desired doneness (for medium-rare, a meat thermometer should read 145°; medium, 160°; well-done, 170°). Serve with reserved mint sauce.

Nutrition Facts: 2 lamb chops with 4 tsp. sauce equals 236 calories, 14 g fat (3 g saturated fat), 68 mg cholesterol, 509 mg sodium, 5 g carbohydrate, 1 g fiber, 22 g protein.

Jeweled Buffet Ham

8pp

PREP: 10 min. BAKE: 2-1/2 hours YIELD: 15 servings

AGNES WARD • STRATFORD, ONTARIO

Cranberry sauce and mandarin oranges make a beautiful, aromatic glaze for this spiral-sliced cooked ham. This recipe will be a crowd-pleaser any time of the year, but it's wonderful during the holidays due to the lovely cranberry-and-orange flavor that it offers. Best of all, it only takes a few moments of prep work before popping it in the oven!

  1 bone-in fully cooked spiral-sliced ham (7 lbs.)
  1 can (14 oz.) whole-berry cranberry sauce
  1 can (11 oz.) mandarin oranges, drained
  1 can (8 oz.) jellied cranberry sauce
1/2 cup orange juice
1/2 tsp. garlic powder
1/8 tsp. hot pepper sauce

1. Place ham on a rack in a shallow roasting pan. Bake, uncovered, at 325° for 2 hours.

2. In a large saucepan, combine the remaining ingredients. Cook and stir over medium heat until heated through.

3. Brush ham with some of the glaze; bake 30-60 minutes longer or until a meat thermometer reads 140°, brushing occasionally with remaining glaze.

Nutrition Facts: 6 oz. ham equals 329 calories, 5 g fat (1 g saturated fat), 47 mg cholesterol, 1,915 mg sodium, 34 g carbohydrate, 1 g fiber, 38 g protein.

Ham that is **cooked and smoked** and/or cured can be eaten without heating but is generally heated to 140° for optimal flavor.

TILAPIA WITH GRAPEFRUIT SALSA

APRICOT-PINEAPPLE GLAZED SHRIMP

INDIVIDUAL TUNA CASSEROLES

Fish & Seafood

Did you know some nutritionists recommend eating two seafood meals each week? Well, we've got dozens of tempting choices featuring fish, shrimp and more. Now you just have to decide which entree to make first.

Individual Tuna Casseroles

PREP: 30 min. **BAKE:** 25 min. **YIELD:** 6 servings

CHERYL WOODSON • LIBERTY, MISSOURI

Tuna casserole gets updated with this unique and flavorful recipe. Friends and family will love the appeal, not to mention that it's lower in saturated fat and calories.

1-1/2	cups uncooked whole wheat penne pasta
1	can (12 oz.) white water-packed tuna, drained
1	can (10-3/4 oz.) reduced-fat reduced-sodium condensed cream of mushroom soup, undiluted
1-1/4	cups water-packed artichoke hearts, rinsed, drained and chopped
1/2	cup reduced-fat sour cream
1/4	cup roasted sweet red peppers, drained and chopped
3	Tbsp. chopped onion
3	Tbsp. sun-dried tomatoes (not packed in oil), chopped
2	Tbsp. Greek olives, chopped
1	Tbsp. snipped fresh dill *or* 1 tsp. dill weed
1	Tbsp. capers, drained
2	garlic cloves, minced
1	tsp. grated lemon peel
1/2	tsp. crushed red pepper flakes
1/2	cup dry bread crumbs
1/4	cup grated Parmesan cheese
1/2	tsp. Italian seasoning

1. Cook pasta according to package directions.

2. Meanwhile, in a large bowl, combine the tuna, soup, artichokes, sour cream, peppers, onion, sun-dried tomatoes, olives, dill, capers, garlic, lemon peel and pepper flakes. Drain the pasta; stir into the tuna mixture. Divide among six 10-oz. ramekins or custard cups.

3. In a small bowl, combine the bread crumbs, cheese and Italian seasoning. Sprinkle over tuna mixture. Place ramekins on a baking sheet. Bake, uncovered at 350° for 25-30 minutes or until golden brown.

Nutrition Facts: 1 serving equals 321 calories, 7 g fat (3 g saturated fat), 35 mg cholesterol, 801 mg sodium, 38 g carbohydrate, 4 g fiber, 24 g protein.

Tilapia with Grapefruit Salsa

PREP: 25 min. + marinating **COOK:** 10 min.
YIELD: 2 servings

EMILY SEEFELDT • RED WING, MINNESOTA

Not only is tilapia a tender and attractive fish, but it's a snap to find these fillets in single serving sizes. Ideal for two, this favorite is draped in a spicy grapefruit salsa.

1/3	cup unsweetened grapefruit juice
1/2	tsp. ground cumin
1	garlic clove, minced
1/4	tsp. grated grapefruit peel
1/8	tsp. salt
1/8	tsp. pepper
Dash to 1/8 tsp. cayenne pepper	
2	tilapia fillets (6 oz. *each*)
1/2	cup canned black beans, rinsed and drained
1/3	cup chopped pink grapefruit sections
1/4	cup chopped red onion
1	Tbsp. minced fresh cilantro
1	to 2 tsp. chopped jalapeno pepper
2	tsp. butter

1. For marinade, in a small bowl, combine the first seven ingredients. Set aside 1 Tbsp. Place tilapia in a large resealable plastic bag; add remaining marinade. Seal bag and turn to coat. Refrigerate for 1 hour.

2. In a small bowl, combine the beans, grapefruit sections, onion, cilantro, jalapeno and reserved marinade. Cover and refrigerate until serving.

3. Drain and discard marinade. In a small skillet over medium heat, cook tilapia in butter for 4-5 minutes on each side or until fish flakes easily with a fork. Serve with salsa.

Editor's Note: When cutting hot peppers, disposable gloves are recommended. Avoid touching your face.

Nutrition Facts: 1 fillet with 1/2 cup salsa equals 264 calories, 6 g fat (3 g saturated fat), 93 mg cholesterol, 369 mg sodium, 18 g carbohydrate, 4 g fiber, 36 g protein. **Diabetic Exchanges:** 5 lean meat, 1 starch, 1 fat.

Grilled Shrimp with Cilantro Dipping Sauce [c]

PREP: 25 min. + marinating **GRILL:** 5 min.
YIELD: 4 servings

ELIZABETH LUBIN • HUNTINGTON BEACH, CALIFORNIA

I came up with this recipe when my daughter grew a beautiful jalapeno plant last summer. I already had cilantro in the garden, so it seemed like a great combination for a tasty sauce.

- 2 Tbsp. minced fresh cilantro
- 2 Tbsp. olive oil
- 1 Tbsp. minced fresh chives
- 1 garlic clove, minced
- 1 pound uncooked medium shrimp, peeled and deveined

DIPPING SAUCE:
- 1 cup fresh cilantro leaves
- 1 cup fat-free mayonnaise
- 1 jalapeno pepper, seeded
- 1 garlic clove, peeled
- 1 Tbsp. white vinegar
- 1 tsp. sugar

Dash cayenne pepper

1. In a large resealable plastic bag, combine the cilantro, oil, chives and garlic. Add the shrimp; seal bag and turn to coat. Cover and refrigerate for 1 hour.

2. In a blender, combine the sauce ingredients; cover and process until blended. Chill until serving.

3. Thread shrimp onto four metal or soaked wooden skewers. Grill, covered, over medium heat for 2-3 minutes on each side or until shrimp turn pink. Serve with sauce.

Editor's Note: When cutting hot peppers, disposable gloves are recommended. Avoid touching your face.

Nutrition Facts: 1 skewer with 1/4 cup sauce equals 208 calories, 10 g fat (2 g saturated fat), 144 mg cholesterol, 615 mg sodium, 11 g carbohydrate, 1 g fiber, 19 g protein.

Salmon Spirals With Cucumber Sauce [c]

PREP: 20 min. + marinating **GRILL:** 10 min.
YIELD: 4 skewers (1-1/3 cups sauce)

ROSALIND POPE • GREENSBORO, NORTH CAROLINA

When you serve up this dish, it'll be hard to tell which impresses your guests more: the delicious taste or the classy presentation.

- 1 salmon fillet (1 lb.)
- 8 fresh dill sprigs
- 1/4 cup lime juice
- 1 Tbsp. olive oil
- 2 tsp. Dijon mustard

SAUCE:
- 1 cup (8 oz.) fat-free plain yogurt
- 1/4 cup fat-free mayonnaise
- 2 Tbsp. finely chopped seeded peeled cucumber
- 2 Tbsp. snipped fresh dill
- 1 Tbsp. lemon juice

1. Remove skin from fillet and discard. Cut fillet lengthwise into four strips. Place two dill sprigs on each strip; roll up. Thread salmon onto four metal or soaked wooden skewers.

2. In a large resealable plastic bag, combine the lime juice, oil and mustard; add the salmon. Seal bag and turn to coat; refrigerate salmon for 30 minutes, turning occasionally.

3. Drain and discard marinade. Using long-handled tongs, moisten a paper towel with cooking oil and

GRILLED SHRIMP WITH CILANTRO DIPPING SAUCE

SALMON SPIRALS WITH CUCUMBER SAUCE

CRAB MACARONI CASSEROLE

lightly coat the grill rack. Grill the salmon, covered, over high heat or broil 3-4 in. from the heat for 4-5 minutes on each side or until the fish flakes easily with a fork.

4. Meanwhile, in a small bowl, combine the sauce ingredients. Serve with salmon.

Nutrition Facts: 1 skewer with 1/3 cup sauce equals 253 calories, 13 g fat (3 g saturated fat), 70 mg cholesterol, 233 mg sodium, 8 g carbohydrate, trace fiber, 25 g protein.

Open-Faced Crab Melts

PREP/TOTAL TIME: 10 min. **YIELD:** 4 servings

FLORENCE MCCLELLAND • FREDONIA, NEW YORK

Not only do these versatile sandwiches make a change-of-pace lunch, but you can serve them at everything from fancy teas to last-minute suppers. Add some chili sauce and a little prepared horseradish to the crab mixture to mix things up a bit.

4	English muffins, split
1/3	cup mayonnaise
1	Tbsp. lemon juice
1/2	tsp. pepper
1/4	tsp. dried tarragon
1	can (6 oz.) crabmeat, drained, flaked and cartilage removed
1	cup (4 oz.) shredded cheddar cheese

1. Broil English muffins 4-6 in. from the heat for 2-3 minutes or until golden brown.

2. In a large bowl, combine the mayonnaise, lemon juice, pepper and tarragon; stir in crab. Spread over each muffin half; sprinkle with cheddar cheese. Broil for 2-3 minutes or until cheese is melted.

Nutrition Facts: 1 serving (1 each) equals 411 calories, 24 g fat (8 g saturated fat), 75 mg cholesterol, 676 mg sodium, 28 g carbohydrate, 2 g fiber, 19 g protein.

Crab Macaroni Casserole

PREP: 25 min. **BAKE:** 20 min. **YIELD:** 6 servings

JASON EGNER • EDGERTON, WISCONSIN

Cold winter evenings are much more tolerable with this comforting casserole. Whole wheat macaroni boosts nutrition, while the melted cheese topping makes it rich and so satisfying. We like it best with a veggie side.

2	cups uncooked whole wheat elbow macaroni
3	Tbsp. chopped onion
2	Tbsp. butter
3	Tbsp. all-purpose flour
1-1/2	cups fat-free milk
2	cans (6 oz. *each*) lump crabmeat, drained
1	cup (8 oz.) reduced-fat sour cream
1/2	cup shredded Swiss cheese
1/2	tsp. salt
1/2	tsp. ground mustard
1	cup (4 oz.) shredded fat-free cheddar cheese, *divided*

1. Cook macaroni according to package directions.

2. Meanwhile, in a large skillet, saute onion in butter until tender. Combine flour and milk until smooth; stir into pan. Bring to a boil; cook and stir for 1-2 minutes or until thickened. Remove from the heat. Drain macaroni. Add the crabmeat, sour cream, Swiss cheese, salt, mustard, macaroni and 1/4 cup cheddar cheese to the skillet.

3. Transfer to an 11-in. x 7-in. baking dish coated with cooking spray. Sprinkle with remaining cheddar cheese. Bake, uncovered, at 350° for 20-25 minutes or until heated through.

Nutrition Facts: 1 cup equals 380 calories, 11 g fat (6 g saturated fat), 86 mg cholesterol, 619 mg sodium, 38 g carbohydrate, 4 g fiber, 31 g protein. **Diabetic Exchanges:** 3 lean meat, 2 starch, 1-1/2 fat.

Spicy Shrimp Fettuccine

PREP: 20 min. **COOK:** 15 min. **YIELD:** 6 servings

TRISHA KRUSE • EAGLE, IDAHO

Pasta gets a kick from red pepper flakes in this change-of-pace dish featuring shrimp, garlic and basil served in a tomato sauce.

- 9 oz. uncooked whole wheat fettuccine
- 4 garlic cloves, minced
- 3 Tbsp. olive oil
- 1-1/2 lbs. uncooked medium shrimp, peeled and deveined
- 2 cups reduced-sodium tomato juice
- 1/2 cup tomato sauce
- 1/2 to 1 tsp. crushed red pepper flakes
- 1/4 tsp. salt
- 1/4 tsp. pepper
- 4 tsp. cornstarch
- 1/4 cup white wine *or* reduced-sodium chicken broth
- 2 Tbsp. minced fresh basil

1. Cook fettuccine according to package directions.

2. Meanwhile, in a large nonstick skillet, saute garlic in oil until tender. Stir in the shrimp, tomato juice, tomato sauce, pepper flakes, salt and pepper. In a small bowl, combine cornstarch and wine until smooth; stir into skillet. Bring to a boil. Reduce heat; simmer, uncovered, for 5-6 minutes or until shrimp turn pink and sauce is thickened.

3. Drain fettuccine; stir into skillet. Sprinkle with basil just before serving.

Nutrition Facts: 1-1/3 cups equals 348 calories, 9 g fat (1 g saturated fat), 138 mg cholesterol, 374 mg sodium, 38 g carbohydrate, 5 g fiber, 26 g protein. **Diabetic Exchanges:** 3 lean meat, 2 starch, 1 vegetable, 1 fat.

Veggie Tuna Burgers

PREP/TOTAL TIME: 30 min. **YIELD:** 6 servings

LAURA DAVIS • RUSTON, LOUISIANA

You don't have to be a health nut to enjoy the flavor of these moist and nutritious burgers. They're an easy way to get my children to eat their vegetables.

- 1/4 cup finely chopped onion
- 1 garlic clove, minced
- 1 cup *each* shredded zucchini, yellow summer squash and carrots
- 1 egg, lightly beaten
- 2 cups soft whole wheat bread crumbs
- 1 can (6 oz.) light water-packed tuna, drained and flaked
- 1/4 tsp. salt
- 1/4 tsp. pepper
- 1 tsp. butter
- 6 hamburger buns, split
- 6 slices reduced-fat cheddar cheese
- 6 lettuce leaves
- 6 slices tomato

1. In a large nonstick skillet coated with cooking spray, saute onion and garlic for 1 minute. Add the zucchini, yellow squash and carrots; saute until tender. Drain and cool to room temperature.

2. In a large bowl, combine the egg, bread crumbs, tuna, salt and pepper. Add vegetable mixture. Shape into six 3-1/2-in. patties.

3. Coat the same skillet again with cooking spray; cook patties in butter for 3-5 minutes on each side or until lightly browned. Serve on buns with cheese, lettuce and tomato.

Nutrition Facts: 1 burger equals 275 calories, 8 g fat (4 g saturated fat), 58 mg cholesterol, 643 mg sodium, 32 g carbohydrate, 3 g fiber, 20 g protein. **Diabetic Exchanges:** 2 starch, 2 lean meat, 1 vegetable.

Shrimp and Pineapple Fried Rice

PREP/TOTAL TIME: 30 min. **YIELD:** 6 servings

LYNNE VAN WAGENEN • SALT LAKE CITY, UTAH

Pineapple chunks give fried rice a tropical twist, while shrimp and cashews turn this simple favorite into a restaurant-quality meal everyone will love.

    2   eggs
    1   small onion, chopped
    1   tsp. canola oil
    3   garlic cloves, minced
    3   cups cooked instant brown rice
    1   can (20 oz.) unsweetened pineapple chunks, drained
  1/2   lb. cooked medium shrimp, peeled and deveined
  1/2   cup chopped cashews
  1/2   cup frozen peas, thawed
    2   green onions, sliced
    3   Tbsp. reduced-sodium soy sauce
    1   Tbsp. hoisin sauce
    1   tsp. sugar
    1   tsp. sesame oil
  1/4   tsp. pepper

1. In a small bowl, whisk eggs. Heat a large nonstick skillet coated with cooking spray over medium heat. Add eggs; cook and stir until set; remove from the skillet and keep warm.

2. In the same skillet, saute onion in oil until tender. Add garlic; cook 1 minute longer. Stir in the rice, pineapple, shrimp, cashews, peas and green onions; heat through. Combine the soy sauce, hoisin sauce, sugar, sesame oil and pepper; stir into rice mixture. Stir in eggs.

Nutrition Facts: 1-1/3 cups equals 342 calories, 10 g fat (2 g saturated fat), 128 mg cholesterol, 521 mg sodium, 46 g carbohydrate, 4 g fiber, 16 g protein.

Scrumptious California Salmon

PREP: 35 min. **BAKE:** 10 min. **YIELD:** 4 servings

DUSTIN ANDERSON • FILLMORE, CALIFORNIA

California cuisine is all about balancing flavors. This recipe brings out the sweetness in citrus and honey and balances it with a pop of ancho chili pepper and balsamic vinegar.

    3   garlic cloves, minced
    1   tsp. minced shallot
    1   cup orange juice
    1   Tbsp. balsamic vinegar
    3   Tbsp. honey
    1   Tbsp. ground ancho chili pepper
  1/4   tsp. salt
  1/8   tsp. pepper
    1   salmon fillet (1 lb.)
    2   tsp. canola oil
    2   Tbsp. minced fresh cilantro

1. In a small saucepan coated with cooking spray, saute garlic and shallot until tender. Add orange juice and vinegar. Bring to a boil. Reduce heat; simmer, uncovered, for 20-25 minutes or until reduced to 1/4 cup. Stir in the honey, chili pepper, salt and pepper.

2. In a large ovenproof skillet, brown salmon in oil on both sides. Brush with 1/4 cup sauce. Bake, uncovered, at 400° for 8-10 minutes or until fish flakes easily with a fork.

3. Brush with remaining sauce and sprinkle with fresh cilantro.

Nutrition Facts: 3 oz. cooked salmon equals 317 calories, 15 g fat (3 g saturated fat), 67 mg cholesterol, 217 mg sodium, 21 g carbohydrate, trace fiber, 23 g protein.

SCRUMPTIOUS CALIFORNIA SALMON

SHRIMP AND PINEAPPLE FRIED RICE

Salmon with Tomato Shallot Sauce C

PREP: 20 min. **COOK:** 15 min. **YIELD:** 4 servings

KIMBERLY CUTLER • FLORENCE, ARIZONA

Light and refreshing, this is a great treatment for salmon that perfectly suits any occasion. Capers add a delightful burst of tangy saltiness.

4	salmon fillets (4 oz. *each*)
1	Tbsp. grated lemon peel
1/2	tsp. white pepper
1/8	tsp. salt
3/4	cup chopped shallots
2	tsp. olive oil
1	garlic clove, minced
1	tsp. capers, drained
3/4	cup dry white wine *or* reduced-sodium chicken broth
2	medium tomatoes, seeded and chopped
1/2	tsp. dried basil

1. Sprinkle fillets with lemon peel, white pepper and salt; set aside.

2. In a large nonstick skillet, saute the shallots in oil until tender. Add garlic and capers; cook 1 minute longer. Stir in wine; add reserved salmon.

3. Reduce heat; cover and cook for 8-10 minutes or until fish flakes easily with a fork. Add tomatoes and basil; heat through.

Nutrition Facts: 1 fillet with 1/3 cup sauce equals 297 calories, 15 g fat (3 g saturated fat), 67 mg cholesterol, 171 mg sodium, 10 g carbohydrate, 1 g fiber, 24 g protein.

SALMON WITH TOMATO SHALLOT SAUCE

Spicy Shrimp & Peppers with Pasta

PREP: 20 min. **COOK:** 25 min. **YIELD:** 4 servings

AMY MILLS • SEBRING, FLORIDA

Spice up any weeknight with this filling and tasty family dish. It goes together in no time and features tender shrimp, veggies, whole wheat pasta and just the right amount of heat.

1	cup sliced baby portobello mushrooms
1	medium sweet yellow pepper, cut into 1/2-in. pieces
1	medium green pepper, cut into 1/2-in. pieces
1	shallot, minced
2	Tbsp. olive oil
1	garlic clove, minced
1/2	tsp. crushed red pepper flakes
1	can (28 oz.) crushed tomatoes
1	tsp. Italian seasoning
1/2	tsp. salt
6	oz. uncooked multigrain linguine
1	pound uncooked medium shrimp, peeled and deveined
3	Tbsp. minced fresh parsley *or* 1 Tbsp. dried parsley flakes

1. In a large nonstick skillet coated with cooking spray, saute the mushrooms, peppers and shallot in oil until tender. Add garlic and pepper flakes; cook 1 minute longer.

2. Stir in the tomatoes, Italian seasoning and salt. Bring to a boil. Reduce heat; simmer, uncovered, for 12-15 minutes or until vegetables are tender.

3. Meanwhile, cook linguine according to package directions. Add shrimp to sauce; cook and stir for 5-7 minutes or until shrimp turn pink.

4. Drain linguine; stir into sauce. Heat through. Sprinkle with parsley.

Nutrition Facts: 2 cups equals 385 calories, 10 g fat (1 g saturated fat), 138 mg cholesterol, 697 mg sodium, 53 g carbohydrate, 10 g fiber, 28 g protein.

SPICY SHRIMP & PEPPERS WITH PASTA

Snapper with Zucchini & Mushrooms C

PREP: 25 min. **COOK:** 10 min. **YIELD:** 4 servings

LISA GLOGOW • ALISO VIEJO, CALIFORNIA

Looking for a way to keep your family's meals light and high in veggie content? This recipe is it. Colorful tomatoes, mushrooms and zucchini make a surprisingly filling topping for this fish. It's yummy with pork, too.

- 3 cups diced zucchini
- 2 cups halved fresh mushrooms
- 3/4 cup chopped sweet onion
- 2 Tbsp. olive oil, *divided*
- 3 garlic cloves, minced
- 1 can (14-1/2 oz.) diced tomatoes, undrained
- 2 tsp. minced fresh basil *or* 1/2 tsp. dried basil
- 2 tsp. minced fresh oregano *or* 1/2 tsp. dried oregano
- 1/4 tsp. salt
- 1/4 tsp. pepper
- 1/4 tsp. crushed red pepper flakes, optional
- 4 red snapper *or* orange roughy fillets (6 oz. *each*)

1. In a large nonstick skillet coated with cooking spray, saute the zucchini, mushrooms and onion in 1 Tbsp. oil until crisp-tender. Add garlic; cook 1 minute longer. Stir in the tomatoes, basil, oregano, salt, pepper and pepper flakes if desired. Bring to a boil. Reduce heat; cover and simmer for 12-15 minutes or until vegetables are tender.

2. Meanwhile, in another large nonstick skillet coated with cooking spray, cook the fillets in remaining oil over medium heat for 4-6 minutes on each side or until fish flakes easily with a fork. Serve with the vegetable mixture.

Nutrition Facts: 1 fillet with 1 cup vegetables equals 253 calories, 8 g fat (1 g saturated fat), 102 mg cholesterol, 414 mg sodium, 14 g carbohydrate, 4 g fiber, 32 g protein. **Diabetic Exchanges:** 4 lean meat, 2 vegetable, 1-1/2 fat.

To choose the freshest zucchini, look for a firm, heavy squash with a moist stem end and a shiny, unblemished skin. Smaller zucchini are generally sweeter and more tender than their larger counterparts.

APRICOT-PINEAPPLE GLAZED SHRIMP

Apricot-Pineapple Glazed Shrimp

PREP: 30 min. **GRILL:** 10 min. **YIELD:** 14 appetizers

TRISHA KRUSE • EAGLE, IDAHO

This is one of my favorite grill recipes. The glaze is sweet, tangy and addictive, and the shrimp tastes fantastic over rice, on salad or as an appetizer.

1	cup apricot preserves
1/4	cup finely chopped dried apricots
2	Tbsp. finely chopped onion
1	Tbsp. rice vinegar
1	Tbsp. Dijon mustard
1	garlic clove, halved
1/4	tsp. salt
28	uncooked jumbo shrimp, peeled and deveined
2	cups cubed fresh pineapple (about 14 pieces)
1	medium sweet red pepper, cut into 14 pieces

1. Place first seven ingredients in a food processor. Cover and process until blended; set aside half of sauce for serving.

2. On each of 14 metal or soaked wooden appetizer skewers, thread shrimp, pineapple and red pepper. Grill, covered, over medium heat for 3-4 minutes on each side or until shrimp turn pink, basting frequently with remaining sauce. Serve with reserved sauce.

Nutrition Facts: 1 kabob with about 2-1/2 tsp. sauce equals 120 calories, 1 g fat (trace saturated fat), 62 mg cholesterol, 139 mg sodium, 21 g carbohydrate, 1 g fiber, 9 g protein.
Diabetic Exchanges: 1-1/2 starch, 1 lean meat.

Baked Salmon Cakes

PREP/TOTAL TIME: 30 min. **YIELD:** 4 servings

NIKKI HADDAD • GERMANTOWN, MARYLAND

Baked in muffin pans and served with sauce on the side, these cute cakes make a fantastic light meal. You can also bake a double batch and freeze some for a quick, healthful supper later in the month.

1	can (14-3/4 oz.) salmon, drained, bones and skin removed
1-1/2	cups soft whole wheat bread crumbs
1/2	cup finely chopped sweet red pepper
1/2	cup egg substitute
3	green onions, thinly sliced
1/4	cup finely chopped celery
1/4	cup minced fresh cilantro
3	Tbsp. fat-free mayonnaise
1	Tbsp. lemon juice
1	garlic clove, minced
1/8	to 1/4 tsp. hot pepper sauce —OMIT

6 PPV = 2 CAKES

SAUCE:

2	Tbsp. fat-free mayonnaise
1/4	tsp. capers, drained
1/4	tsp. dill weed

Dash lemon juice

1. In a large bowl, combine the first 11 ingredients. Place 1/3 cup salmon mixture into eight muffin cups coated with cooking spray. Bake at 425° for 10-15 minutes or until a meat thermometer reads 160°.

2. Meanwhile, combine the sauce ingredients. Serve with salmon.

Nutrition Facts: 2 salmon cakes with 1-1/2 tsp. sauce equals 266 calories, 9 g fat (2 g saturated fat), 48 mg cholesterol, 914 mg sodium, 17 g carbohydrate, 3 g fiber, 28 g protein.

Salmon & Slaw Sliders

PREP/TOTAL TIME: 30 min. **YIELD:** 4 servings

EDRIE O'BRIEN • DENVER, COLORADO

This recipe first came about using leftover salmon and slaw. Now we plan to make it all the time. It's a nice alternative to burgers and always well-received at parties. The salmon can also be broiled.

1/2	cup chopped cabbage
1/2	cup chopped fennel bulb
1	green onion, chopped
1/4	cup fat-free mayonnaise, *divided*
1	Tbsp. fat-free plain yogurt
1-3/4	tsp. salt-free seasoning blend, *divided*
4	salmon fillets (4 oz. *each*)

Cooking spray
4 whole wheat dinner rolls, split

1. In a small bowl, combine the cabbage, fennel and onion. Combine 2 Tbsp. mayonnaise, yogurt and 1/4 tsp. seasoning blend; pour over cabbage mixture and toss to coat. Chill until serving.

2. Spritz salmon with cooking spray; sprinkle with remaining seasoning blend.

3. Using long-handled tongs, moisten a paper towel with cooking oil and lightly coat the grill rack. Grill fillets, covered, over medium heat or broil 4 in. from the heat for 10-12 minutes or until fish flakes easily with a fork. Remove and keep warm.

4. Grill rolls, cut side down, over medium heat for 30-60 seconds or broil 4 in. from the heat until toasted. Spread with remaining mayonnaise; top each with a fillet and 1/4 cup coleslaw. Replace roll tops.

Nutrition Facts: 1 sandwich equals 335 calories, 15 g fat (3 g saturated fat), 86 mg cholesterol, 388 mg sodium, 22 g carbohydrate, 2 g fiber, 26 g protein.

Grilled Tuna Steaks C

PREP: 10 min. + marinating **GRILL:** 10 min.
YIELD: 4 servings

JAN HUNTINGTON • PAINESVILLE, OHIO

After enjoying yellowfin tuna at a restaurant in southwest Florida, I came up with this recipe so I could enjoy the flavor of my favorite fish at home.

2	Tbsp. lemon juice
1	Tbsp. olive oil
2	garlic cloves, minced
2	tsp. minced fresh thyme *or* 1/2 tsp. dried thyme
4	tuna steaks (6 oz. *each*)
1/4	tsp. salt
1/4	tsp. pepper

1. In a large resealable plastic bag, combine the lemon juice, oil, garlic and thyme. Add the tuna; seal bag and turn to coat. Refrigerate for up to 30 minutes, turning occasionally.

2. Remove tuna from bag; sprinkle with salt and pepper. Drain and discard marinade. Using long-handled tongs, moisten a paper towel with cooking oil and lightly coat the grill rack.

3. Grill tuna, covered, over medium-hot heat or broil 4 in. from the heat for 3-4 minutes on each side for medium-rare or until slightly pink in the center.

Nutrition Facts: 1 tuna steak equals 218 calories, 5 g fat (1 g saturated fat), 77 mg cholesterol, 211 mg sodium, 1 g carbohydrate, trace fiber, 40 g protein. **Diabetic Exchanges:** 5 lean meat, 1/2 fat.

GRILLED TUNA STEAKS

SALMON & SLAW SLIDERS

Shrimp Lo Mein

PREP: 25 min. **COOK:** 15 min. **YIELD:** 4 servings

SHERRI STARKIN • LYLE, WASHINGTON

This recipe is simple, fast, healthy and very adaptable. You can change the seafood or vegetables to your taste.

- 1 pound uncooked medium shrimp, peeled and deveined
- 2 garlic cloves, sliced

Dash blackened seasoning

- 6 oz. uncooked multigrain linguine
- 4 tsp. cornstarch
- 1/3 cup water
- 1/4 cup ketchup
- 2 Tbsp. reduced-sodium soy sauce
- 2 Tbsp. sherry *or* reduced-sodium chicken broth
- 2 tsp. honey
- 1/4 tsp. ground ginger
- 1/4 tsp. crushed red pepper flakes
- 2 Tbsp. olive oil, *divided*
- 1 celery rib, sliced
- 1 medium carrot, chopped
- 1/2 cup sliced fresh mushrooms
- 1/4 cup fresh broccoli florets
- 2 Tbsp. chopped cashews
- 1 can (8 oz.) unsweetened pineapple chunks, drained

1. In a small bowl, combine the shrimp, garlic and blackened seasoning; set aside. Cook linguine according to package directions.

2. Meanwhile, in a small bowl, combine the cornstarch, water, ketchup, soy sauce, sherry, honey, ginger and pepper flakes until blended; set aside.

3. In a large nonstick skillet or wok, stir-fry shrimp in 1 Tbsp. oil for 2-3 minutes or until no longer pink. Remove with a slotted spoon and keep warm.

4. Stir-fry celery and carrot in remaining oil for 5 minutes. Add the mushrooms, broccoli and cashews; stir-fry 4-6 minutes longer or until vegetables are crisp-tender.

5. Stir cornstarch mixture and add to the pan. Bring to a boil; cook and stir for 2 minutes or until thickened. Drain linguine; stir into skillet. Add shrimp and pineapple; heat through.

Nutrition Facts: 1 cup equals 401 calories, 11 g fat (2 g saturated fat), 138 mg cholesterol, 678 mg sodium, 53 g carbohydrate, 6 g fiber, 25 g protein.

Orange Tilapia In Parchment F C

PREP/TOTAL TIME: 30 min. **YIELD:** 4 servings

TIFFANY DIEBOLD • NASHVILLE, TENNESSEE

Sweet orange juice and spicy cayenne pepper give this no-fuss dish fabulous flavor. A bonus? Cleanup is a breeze!

- 1/4 cup orange juice
- 4 tsp. grated orange peel
- 1/4 tsp. salt
- 1/4 tsp. cayenne pepper
- 1/4 tsp. pepper
- 4 tilapia fillets (6 oz. *each*)
- 1/2 cup julienned carrot
- 1/2 cup julienned zucchini

combine

1. In a small bowl, combine the first five ingredients; set aside. Cut parchment paper or heavy-duty foil into four 18-in. x 12-in. lengths; place a fish fillet on each. Top with carrot and zucchini; drizzle with reserved orange juice mixture.

2. Fold parchment paper over fish. Working from the bottom inside corner, fold up about 3/4 in. of the paper and crimp both layers to seal. Repeat, folding edges up and crimping, until a half-moon-shaped packet is formed. Repeat for remaining packets. Place on baking sheets.

3. Bake at 450° for 12-15 minutes or until fish flakes easily with a fork. Open packets carefully to allow steam to escape.

Nutrition Facts: 1 packet equals 158 calories, 2 g fat (1 g saturated fat), 83 mg cholesterol, 220 mg sodium, 4 g carbohydrate, 1 g fiber, 32 g protein. **Diabetic Exchange:** 5 lean meat.

Rosemary Shrimp With Spaghetti

PREP/TOTAL TIME: 30 min. **YIELD:** 4 servings

CANDACE HAVELY • STERLING, COLORADO

I came up with this recipe on a busy weeknight when I was pressed for time. Now it's my go-to dish whenever I need a quick, nutritious meal. Serve this with garlic bread so you can scoop every last bit of goodness off your plate.

- 8 oz. uncooked whole wheat spaghetti
- 1 pound uncooked medium shrimp, peeled and deveined
- 2 garlic cloves, minced
- 1-1/2 tsp. minced fresh rosemary *or* 1/2 tsp. dried rosemary, crushed
- 1 Tbsp. olive oil
- 2 cups fresh baby spinach
- 2 Tbsp. lemon juice

SHRIMP LO MEIN

CRISPY COD WITH VEGGIES

1/4 tsp. salt

1/4 tsp. pepper

1/4 cup crumbled feta cheese

1. Cook spaghetti according to package directions.

2. Meanwhile, in a large nonstick skillet, cook the shrimp, garlic and rosemary in oil over medium heat for 4-5 minutes or until shrimp turn pink. Add spinach; cook and stir until spinach is wilted.

3. Drain spaghetti; add to the pan. Stir in the lemon juice, salt and pepper; heat through. Sprinkle with feta cheese; remove from the heat. Cover and let stand for 3-5 minutes or until cheese is melted.

Nutrition Facts: 1-1/2 cups equals 349 calories, 7 g fat (2 g saturated fat), 142 mg cholesterol, 366 mg sodium, 46 g carbohydrate, 8 g fiber, 29 g protein.

Crispy Cod with Veggies

PREP: 15 min. **BAKE:** 25 min. **YIELD:** 2 servings

HEALTHY COOKING TEST KITCHEN

Take the chill off brisk evenings and warm the body and soul with this light but nourishing entree from our Test Kitchen pros. Round out the meal with a loaf of crusty bread.

2 cups broccoli coleslaw mix

1/2 cup chopped fresh tomato

4 tsp. chopped green onion

2 garlic cloves, minced

2 cod fillets (6 oz. *each*)

Pepper to taste

1/4 cup crushed potato sticks

3 Tbsp. seasoned bread crumbs

2 Tbsp. grated Parmesan cheese

4 tsp. butter, melted

1. In a large bowl, combine the coleslaw mix, tomato, onion and garlic; spread into an 11-in. x 7-in. baking pan coated with cooking spray. Top with cod fillets; sprinkle with pepper.

2. Combine the potato sticks, bread crumbs, cheese and butter; sprinkle over fillets. Bake, uncovered, at 450° for 25-30 minutes or until the fish flakes easily with a fork.

Nutrition Facts: 1 fillet with 1 cup vegetables equals 316 calories, 12 g fat (6 g saturated fat), 89 mg cholesterol, 445 mg sodium, 18 g carbohydrate, 3 g fiber, 34 g protein. **Diabetic Exchanges:** 5 very lean meat, 2 fat, 1 vegetable, 1/2 starch.

Hoisin Salmon Fillets [c]

PREP: 10 min. + marinating **GRILL:** 10 min.
YIELD: 6 servings

JERI FAROUGH • PERRYVILLE, MISSOURI

Fabulous Asian flavor in no time flat—this moist salmon is special enough for guests, easy enough for weekdays. I usually serve this entree with steamed brown rice, broccoli and a fresh fruit salad.

- 3 green onions, chopped
- 1/3 cup reduced-sodium soy sauce
- 1/4 cup hoisin sauce
- 3 Tbsp. lemon juice
- 1 Tbsp. grated lemon peel
- 1/2 tsp. pepper
- 6 salmon fillets (4 oz. *each*)

1. In a large resealable plastic bag, combine the first six ingredients. Add the salmon; seal bag and turn to coat. Refrigerate for 30 minutes, turning occasionally.

2. Drain and discard marinade. Using long-handled tongs, moisten a paper towel with cooking oil and lightly coat the grill rack. Place salmon skin side down on grill rack.

3. Grill, covered, over medium heat or broil 4 in. from the heat for 10-12 minutes or until fish flakes easily with a fork.

Nutrition Facts: 1 salmon fillet equals 224 calories, 12 g fat (3 g saturated fat), 67 mg cholesterol, 401 mg sodium, 3 g carbohydrate, trace fiber, 23 g protein. **Diabetic Exchanges:** 3 lean meat, 2 fat.

Lime-Marinated Orange Roughy [F][S][C]

PREP: 10 min. + marinating **BROIL:** 10 min.
YIELD: 4 servings

PAM CORDER • MONROE, LOUISIANA

This dish is simple, flavorful and not fattening at all. And since it's so quick, you can have company over and spend all your time visiting.

- 4 orange roughy fillets (6 oz. *each*)
- 1/3 cup water
- 1/3 cup lime juice
- 2 Tbsp. honey
- 1 Tbsp. canola oil
- 1/2 tsp. dill weed

1. Place fillets in a 13-in. x 9-in. baking dish. In a small bowl, combine the remaining ingredients; set aside 3 Tbsp. marinade. Pour remaining marinade over fillets; turn to coat. Cover and refrigerate for 1 hour.

2. Drain and discard marinade. Transfer fillets to a broiler pan coated with cooking spray. Broil 4-6 in. from the heat for 4-6 minutes on each side or until fish flakes easily with a fork, basting frequently with reserved marinade.

Nutrition Facts: 1 fillet equals 169 calories, 3 g fat (trace saturated fat), 102 mg cholesterol, 123 mg sodium, 6 g carbohydrate, trace fiber, 28 g protein. **Diabetic Exchanges:** 4 lean meat, 1/2 starch, 1/2 fat.

Grilled Tilapia with Lemon Basil Vinaigrette [c]

PREP/TOTAL TIME: 25 min. YIELD: 4 servings

BETH COOPER • COLUMBUS, OHIO

We aren't big fish eaters, but a friend made this for us, and we couldn't believe how wonderful it was! Now we eat it regularly.

- 3 Tbsp. lemon juice
- 3 Tbsp. minced fresh basil, *divided*
- 2 Tbsp. olive oil
- 2 garlic cloves, minced
- 2 tsp. capers, drained
- 1/2 tsp. grated lemon peel
- 4 tilapia fillets (6 oz. *each*)
- 1/2 tsp. salt
- 1/4 tsp. pepper

1. For vinaigrette, in a small bowl, whisk the lemon juice, 2 Tbsp. basil, olive oil, garlic, capers and lemon peel; set aside 2 Tbsp. for sauce. Sprinkle fillets with salt and pepper. Brush both sides of fillets with remaining vinaigrette.

2. Using long-handled tongs, moisten a paper towel with cooking oil and lightly coat the grill rack. Grill, covered, over medium heat or broil 4 in. from the heat for 3-4 minutes on each side or until fish flakes easily with a fork. Brush with reserved vinaigrette and sprinkle with remaining basil.

Nutrition Facts: 1 fillet equals 206 calories, 8 g fat (2 g saturated fat), 83 mg cholesterol, 398 mg sodium, 2 g carbohydrate, trace fiber, 32 g protein. **Diabetic Exchanges:** 5 lean meat, 1-1/2 fat.

Feta Shrimp Skillet

PREP: 20 min. COOK: 20 min. YIELD: 4 servings

SONALI RUDER • NEW YORK, NEW YORK

A Mediterranean-style blend of feta, wine, garlic and oregano seasons this bold, beautiful dish. Serve it with crusty bread to soak up the delightful sauce.

- 1 medium onion, finely chopped
- 1 Tbsp. olive oil
- 3 garlic cloves, minced
- 2 cans (14-1/2 oz. *each*) diced tomatoes, undrained
- 1/4 cup white wine, optional
- 1 tsp. dried oregano
- 1/2 tsp. pepper
- 1/4 tsp. salt
- 1 pound uncooked medium shrimp, peeled and deveined
- 2 Tbsp. minced fresh parsley
- 3/4 cup crumbled feta cheese

1. In a large nonstick skillet, saute onion in oil until tender. Add garlic; cook 1 minute longer. Stir in the tomatoes, wine if desired, oregano, pepper and salt. Bring to a boil. Reduce heat; simmer, uncovered, for 5-7 minutes or until sauce is slightly thickened.

2. Stir in shrimp and parsley. Cook and stir over medium heat for 5-6 minutes or until shrimp turn pink. Remove from the heat; sprinkle with cheese. Cover and let stand for 5-10 minutes or until cheese is softened.

Nutrition Facts: 1-1/4 cups (calculated without wine) equals 240 calories, 8 g fat (3 g saturated fat), 149 mg cholesterol, 748 mg sodium, 16 g carbohydrate, 5 g fiber, 25 g protein. **Diabetic Exchanges:** 3 lean meat, 1 starch, 1 fat.

GRILLED TILAPIA WITH LEMON BASIL VINAIGRETTE

FETA SHRIMP SKILLET

SOUTHWEST SPINACH STRATA

CRISPY SEASONED POLENTA SQUARES

ENCHILADA PIE

Meatless Mains

These entrees are so flavorful and filling, you won't miss the meat. In fact, we bet these healthful selections, loaded with fresh produce and inspired by international cuisines, will become new family favorites in your home.

Enchilada Pie M

PREP: 40 min. COOK: 4 hours YIELD: 8 servings

JACQUELINE CORREA • LANDING, NEW JERSEY

This impressive, hearty dish is the perfect choice for vegetarians and meat eaters alike.

- 1 pkg. (12 oz.) frozen vegetarian meat crumbles
- 1 cup chopped onion
- 1/2 cup chopped green pepper
- 2 tsp. canola oil
- 1 can (16 oz.) kidney beans, rinsed and drained
- 1 can (15 oz.) black beans, rinsed and drained
- 1 can (10 oz.) diced tomatoes and green chilies, undrained
- 1/2 cup water
- 1-1/2 tsp. chili powder
- 1/2 tsp. ground cumin
- 1/4 tsp. pepper
- 6 whole wheat tortillas (8 in.)
- 2 cups (8 oz.) shredded reduced-fat cheddar cheese

1. Cut three 25-in. x 3-in. strips of heavy-duty foil; crisscross so they resemble spokes of a wheel. Place strips on the bottom and up the sides of a 5-qt. slow cooker. Coat strips with cooking spray.

2. In a large saucepan, cook the meat crumbles, onion and green pepper in oil until vegetables are tender. Stir in both cans of beans, tomatoes, water, chili powder, cumin and pepper. Bring to a boil. Reduce heat; simmer, uncovered, for 10 minutes.

3. In prepared slow cooker, layer about 3/4 cup bean mixture, one tortilla and 1/3 cup cheese. Repeat layers five times. Cover and cook on low for 4-5 hours or until heated through and cheese is melted.

4. Using foil strips as handles, remove the pie to a serving platter.

Editor's Note: Vegetarian meat crumbles are a nutritious protein source made from soy. Look for them in the natural foods freezer section.

Nutrition Facts: 1 piece equals 367 calories, 11 g fat (4 g saturated fat), 20 mg cholesterol, 818 mg sodium, 41 g carbohydrate, 9 g fiber, 25 g protein. **Diabetic Exchanges:** 3 starch, 2 lean meat, 1 fat.

Southwest Spinach Strata M

PREP: 20 min. BAKE: 45 min. + standing
YIELD: 6 servings

DEBORAH BIGGS • OMAHA, NEBRASKA

With a mix of whole wheat and white bread, spinach and black beans, this main-dish strata has an amazing savory flavor the whole family will love. Pinto or cannellini beans may be substituted for black beans with fantastic success.

- 2-1/2 cups cubed day-old white bread
- 2-1/2 cups cubed day-old whole wheat bread
- 2/3 cup black beans, rinsed and drained
- 1 pkg. (10 oz.) frozen chopped spinach, thawed and squeezed dry
- 1-1/2 cups (6 oz.) shredded reduced-fat cheddar cheese
- 1 cup Southwestern-style egg substitute
- 2 cups fat-free milk
- 1/4 cup minced fresh cilantro
- 1/4 tsp. salt
- 6 Tbsp. reduced-fat sour cream
- 6 Tbsp. salsa

1. Place half of the bread cubes in an 8-in. square baking dish coated with cooking spray. Layer with beans, spinach and half of the cheese. Top with remaining bread cubes.

2. In a large bowl, whisk the egg substitute, milk, cilantro and salt. Pour over top. Let stand for 5 minutes.

3. Bake, uncovered, at 350° for 40 minutes. Sprinkle with remaining cheese. Bake 5 minutes longer or until cheese is melted and a knife inserted near the center comes out clean. Let stand for 10 minutes before cutting. Serve with sour cream and salsa.

Nutrition Facts: 1 piece with 1 Tbsp. sour cream and 1 Tbsp. salsa equals 264 calories, 9 g fat (5 g saturated fat), 27 mg cholesterol, 736 mg sodium, 28 g carbohydrate, 4 g fiber, 20 g protein. **Diabetic Exchanges:** 2 starch, 2 lean meat, 1/2 fat.

Spring Frittata C M

4 pts

PREP: 35 min. BAKE: 30 min. YIELD: 6 servings

DIANE HIGGINS • TAMPA, FLORIDA

With roasted veggies, Asiago cheese and plenty of dill, this frittata is packed with spring flavors. It looks impressive, but it's really a snap to make.

- 1/2 cup chopped leek (white portion only)
- 1/2 cup cut fresh asparagus (1-in. pieces)
- 2 tsp. olive oil
- 1/4 tsp. salt
- 1/4 tsp. pepper
- 1 cup sliced fresh mushrooms
- 1 cup shredded Asiago cheese
- 4 eggs
- 1 cup egg substitute
- 1/4 cup fat-free milk
- 1 Tbsp. snipped fresh dill *or* 1 tsp. dill weed
- 1 Tbsp. minced fresh parsley *or* 1 tsp. dried parsley flakes

1. In small bowl, combine leek and asparagus. Drizzle with oil and sprinkle with salt and pepper; toss to coat. Transfer to a baking sheet coated with cooking spray. Bake at 400° for 20-25 minutes or until tender, stirring occasionally. Reduce heat to 350°.

2. Place mushrooms on the bottom of a 9-in. deep-dish pie plate coated with cooking spray. Top with roasted vegetables and cheese. In a large bowl, whisk the remaining ingredients; pour over cheese.

3. Bake for 30-35 minutes or until a knife inserted near the center comes out clean. Let stand for 5 minutes. Cut into wedges.

Nutrition Facts: 1 wedge equals 163 calories, 10 g fat (4 g saturated fat), 158 mg cholesterol, 282 mg sodium, 4 g carbohydrate, 1 g fiber, 14 g protein.

Vegetable-Stuffed Portobellos M

PREP: 20 min. BROIL: 15 min. YIELD: 4 servings

ELIZABETH DOSS • CALIFORNIA CITY, CALIFORNIA

I often substitute portobellos for hamburger patties, but in this open-faced recipe, they take the place of buns. My family loves this tasty, healthful dinner, and it's ready in no time.

- 1 can (15 oz.) white kidney *or* cannellini beans, rinsed and drained
- 2 Tbsp. olive oil, *divided*
- 1 Tbsp. water
- 1 tsp. dried rosemary, crushed
- 1 garlic clove, peeled and halved
- 1/4 tsp. salt
- 1/4 tsp. pepper
- 4 large portobello mushrooms (4 to 4-1/2 in.), stems removed
- 1 medium sweet red pepper, finely chopped
- 1 medium red onion, finely chopped
- 1 medium zucchini, finely chopped
- 1/2 cup shredded pepper Jack cheese

1. In a food processor, combine the beans, 1 Tbsp. oil, water, rosemary, garlic, salt and pepper. Cover and process until pureed; set aside.

2. Place mushrooms on a broiler pan coated with cooking spray. Broil 4 in. from the heat for 6-8 minutes on each side or until mushrooms are tender.

3. Meanwhile, in a small nonstick skillet coated with cooking spray, saute the red pepper, red onion and zucchini in remaining oil until tender.

4. Spread about 1/3 cup reserved bean mixture over each mushroom; top with 1/2 cup vegetable mixture. Sprinkle with cheese. Broil 2-3 minutes longer or until cheese is melted.

Nutrition Facts: 1 stuffed mushroom equals 252 calories, 12 g fat (4 g saturated fat), 15 mg cholesterol, 378 mg sodium, 26 g carbohydrate, 7 g fiber, 11 g protein. **Diabetic Exchanges:** 2 lean meat, 2 vegetable, 1 starch, 1 fat.

SPRING FRITTATA

VEGETABLE-STUFFED PORTOBELLOS

Black Bean Veggie Burritos Ⓜ

PREP: 30 min. **BAKE:** 25 min. **YIELD:** 8 servings

CARISSA SUMNER • ALEXANDRIA, VIRGINIA

Sweet potatoes give these baked burritos a unique twist. Packed with tender veggies, cheese and spices, they'll make a mouthwatering dinner any night.

- 1 large sweet potato, peeled and cut into 1/2-in. cubes
- 1 medium onion, finely chopped
- 1 Tbsp. water
- 1 can (15 oz.) black beans, rinsed and drained
- 1 cup frozen corn
- 1 medium green pepper, chopped
- 2 Tbsp. lemon juice
- 3 garlic cloves, minced
- 1 Tbsp. chili powder
- 2 tsp. dried oregano
- 1 tsp. ground cumin
- 8 whole wheat tortillas (8 in.), warmed
- 2 cups (8 oz.) shredded Monterey Jack cheese
- 1/2 cup fat-free plain yogurt
- 1/2 cup salsa

1. In a large microwave-safe bowl, combine the sweet potato, onion and water. Cover and microwave on high for 4-5 minutes or until potato is almost tender. Stir in the beans, corn, green pepper, lemon juice, garlic and seasonings.

2. Spoon a heaping 1/2 cup filling off center on each tortilla. Sprinkle with 1/4 cup cheese. Fold sides and ends over filling and roll up.

3. Place seam side down in a 13-in. x 9-in. baking dish coated with cooking spray. Cover and bake at 350° for 25-30 minutes or until heated through. Serve with yogurt and salsa.

Nutrition Facts: 1 burrito with 1 Tbsp. yogurt and 1 Tbsp. salsa equals 362 calories, 12 g fat (5 g saturated fat), 25 mg cholesterol, 505 mg sodium, 47 g carbohydrate, 7 g fiber, 16 g protein.

Makeover Macaroni And Cheese Ⓜ

PREP/TOTAL TIME: 30 min. **YIELD:** 8 servings

NANCY LANGROCK • SOUTHBURY, CONNECTICUT

Creamy and cheesy with comfort in every bite, this lightened-up classic is sure to become a family favorite at your house, too!

- 1 pkg. (16 oz.) elbow macaroni
- 2 Tbsp. all-purpose flour
- 2 cups fat-free milk
- 1 pkg. (16 oz.) reduced-fat process cheese (Velveeta), cubed
- 1 cup (4 oz.) shredded sharp cheddar cheese, *divided*

1. Cook macaroni according to package directions. Meanwhile, in a large saucepan, combine flour and milk until smooth. Bring to a boil; cook and stir for 2 minutes or until thickened. Stir in process cheese and 1/2 cup cheddar cheese until smooth. Drain macaroni; stir into cheese sauce.

2. Remove from the heat; sprinkle with remaining cheese. Cover and let stand for 5 minutes or until cheese is melted.

Nutrition Facts: 1 cup equals 403 calories, 11 g fat (6 g saturated fat), 36 mg cholesterol, 944 mg sodium, 54 g carbohydrate, 2 g fiber, 23 g protein.

HASH BROWN SUPREME

Hash Brown Supreme

PREP: 20 min. **COOK:** 15 min. **YIELD:** 4 servings

JENNIFER BISTLINE • CONFLUENCE, PENNSYLVANIA

This is a great way to use up leftover fresh vegetables. In addition to the potatoes, use whatever you have on hand to brighten up the recipe. My family likes this meal best when it's garnished with sour cream. If you are not big on spicy foods, simply leave out the jalapeno pepper.

1	small onion, finely chopped
1/2	cup sliced fresh mushrooms
1/2	cup chopped green pepper
1	Tbsp. canola oil
3	cups frozen shredded hash brown potatoes
1	medium tomato, finely chopped
1/2	cup shredded reduced-fat cheddar cheese
2	Tbsp. sliced ripe olives
1	jalapeno pepper, seeded and sliced
1/4	tsp. seasoned salt
1/8	tsp. pepper
1	Tbsp. minced chives

1. In a large nonstick skillet, saute the onion, mushrooms and pepper in oil until tender. Add hash browns; cook over medium heat for 8-10 minutes or until potatoes are browned, stirring occasionally.

2. Stir in the tomato, cheese, olives, jalapeno, seasoned salt and pepper. Cover and cook for 2 minutes or until cheese is melted. Sprinkle with chives; cut into wedges.

Editor's Note: When cutting hot peppers, disposable gloves are recommended. Avoid touching your face.

Nutrition Facts: 1 wedge equals 142 calories, 7 g fat (2 g saturated fat), 10 mg cholesterol, 233 mg sodium, 15 g carbohydrate, 2 g fiber, 6 g protein. **Diabetic Exchanges:** 1 medium-fat meat, 1 vegetable, 1/2 starch.

Fettuccine with Mushrooms and Tomatoes M

PREP/TOTAL TIME: 30 min. **YIELD:** 6 servings

PHYLLIS SCHMALZ • KANSAS CITY, KANSAS

I can toss this dish together in just 30 minutes on a busy weeknight. And it's elegant enough to serve as a meatless entree for guests.

1	pkg. (12 oz.) fettuccine
1	lb. fresh mushrooms, halved
1	large onion, chopped
1	large green pepper, chopped
1	tsp. olive oil
4	garlic cloves, minced
3	Tbsp. all-purpose flour

3	cups 1% milk
1	tsp. salt
1/4	tsp. pepper
1/2	cup sun-dried tomatoes (not packed in oil), thinly sliced
1	cup (4 oz.) shredded reduced-fat Swiss cheese
1/4	cup grated Parmesan cheese

1. Cook fettuccine according to package directions. Meanwhile, in a large nonstick skillet, saute the mushrooms, onion and green pepper in oil for 4-6 minutes or until vegetables are tender. Add garlic; cook 1 minute longer.

2. In a small bowl, combine the flour, milk, salt and pepper until smooth; gradually stir into mushroom mixture. Add tomatoes. Bring to a boil; cook and stir for 2 minutes or until thickened. Stir in cheeses. Drain fettuccine; toss with sauce.

Nutrition Facts: 1-1/3 cups equals 387 calories, 8 g fat (4 g saturated fat), 17 mg cholesterol, 662 mg sodium, 60 g carbohydrate, 5 g fiber, 23 g protein.

Grilled Veggie Pizza

PREP: 30 min. BAKE: 10 min. YIELD: 6 servings

SUSAN MARSHALL • COLORADO SPRINGS, COLORADO

Excess summer bounty is perfect for this delightfully simple pizza. Grilling the veggies first brings out rich, caramelized flavors. Also try it with a sprinkling of olives or pine nuts before adding the cheese.

8	small fresh mushrooms, halved
1	small zucchini, cut into 1/4-in. slices
1	small sweet yellow pepper, sliced
1	small sweet red pepper, sliced
1	small onion, sliced
1	Tbsp. white wine vinegar
1	Tbsp. water
4	tsp. olive oil, *divided*
2	tsp. minced fresh basil *or* 1/2 tsp. dried basil
1/4	tsp. salt

1/4	tsp. pepper
1	prebaked 12-in. thin whole wheat pizza crust
1	can (8 oz.) pizza sauce
2	small tomatoes, chopped
2	cups (8 oz.) shredded part-skim mozzarella cheese

1. In a large bowl, combine the mushrooms, zucchini, peppers, onion, vinegar, water, 3 tsp. oil and seasonings. Transfer to a grill wok or basket. Grill, covered, over medium heat for 8-10 minutes or until tender, stirring once.

2. Prepare grill for indirect heat. Brush crust with remaining oil; spread with pizza sauce. Top with grilled vegetables, tomatoes and cheese. Grill, covered, over indirect medium heat for 10-12 minutes or until edges are lightly browned and cheese is melted. Rotate pizza halfway through cooking to ensure evenly browned crust.

Editor's Note: If you do not have a grill wok or basket, use a disposable foil pan. Poke holes in the bottom of the pan with a meat fork to allow liquid to drain.

Nutrition Facts: 1 slice equals 274 calories, 11 g fat (5 g saturated fat), 22 mg cholesterol, 634 mg sodium, 30 g carbohydrate, 5 g fiber, 17 g protein. **Diabetic Exchanges:** 2 starch, 2 medium-fat meat, 1 vegetable.

Olive oil can be stored at room temperature or in the refrigerator for 1 year. When chilled, the oil turns cloudy and thick. **Chilled olive oil** will return to its original consistency when left at room temperature for a short period of time.

FETTUCCINE WITH MUSHROOMS AND TOMATOES

GRILLED VEGGIE PIZZA

Southwestern Bean Chowder M

PREP: 20 min. **COOK:** 35 min. **YIELD:** 8 servings (2 qt.)

JULIANNE MEYERS • HINESVILLE, GEORGIA

I'm really fortunate that my children are great eaters. They and my husband love this soup. My favorite beans for this are white kidney beans—they have a terrific texture.

2	cans (15 oz. *each*) white kidney *or* cannellini beans, rinsed and drained, *divided*
1	medium onion, chopped
1/4	cup chopped celery
1/4	cup chopped green pepper
1	Tbsp. olive oil
2	garlic cloves, minced
3	cups vegetable broth
1-1/2	cups frozen corn, thawed
1	medium carrot, shredded
1	can (4 oz.) chopped green chilies
1	Tbsp. ground cumin
1/2	tsp. chili powder
4-1/2	tsp. cornstarch
2	cups 2% milk
1	cup (4 oz.) shredded cheddar cheese

Minced fresh cilantro and additional shredded cheddar cheese, optional

1. In a small bowl, mash one can beans with a fork; set aside.

2. In a Dutch oven, saute the onion, celery and pepper in oil until tender. Add garlic; cook 1 minute longer. Stir in the mashed beans, broth, corn, carrot, chilies, cumin, chili powder and remaining beans. Bring to a boil. Reduce heat; simmer, uncovered, for 20 minutes.

3. Combine cornstarch and milk until smooth. Stir into bean mixture. Bring to a boil; cook and stir for 2 minutes or until thickened. Stir in cheese until melted. Serve with cilantro and additional cheese if desired.

Nutrition Facts: 1 cup (calculated without additional cheese) equals 236 calories, 8 g fat (4 g saturated fat), 20 mg cholesterol, 670 mg sodium, 31 g carbohydrate, 6 g fiber, 11 g protein. **Diabetic Exchanges:** 2 starch, 1 lean meat, 1/2 fat.

Crispy Seasoned Polenta Squares M

PREP: 30 min. + cooling **COOK:** 10 min.
YIELD: 9 servings

SHELLY BEVINGTON-FISHER • HERMISTON, OREGON

Crisp polenta squares make a delightful side for a variety of main dishes. Sun-dried tomatoes and just the right amount of seasoning make them seem special...a dollop of sour cream adds the finishing touch!

4	cups water
1/2	cup chopped sun-dried tomatoes (not packed in oil)
1	tsp. salt
1	tsp. dried minced onion
1	tsp. dried minced garlic
1	cup cornmeal
1/2	cup grated Parmesan cheese
1/2	tsp. dried oregano
1	egg
1/4	cup fat-free milk
1/2	cup seasoned bread crumbs
2	tsp. dried cilantro flakes
1	Tbsp. olive oil
9	Tbsp. reduced-fat sour cream

1. In a large heavy saucepan, bring the water, tomatoes, salt, onion and garlic to a boil. Reduce heat to a gentle boil; slowly whisk in cornmeal. Cook and stir with a wooden spoon for 15-20 minutes or until polenta is thickened and pulls away cleanly from the

SOUTHWESTERN BEAN CHOWDER

CRISPY SEASONED POLENTA SQUARES

sides of the pan. Stir in cheese and oregano. Spread into a 9-in. square baking pan coated with cooking spray. Cool to room temperature, about 30 minutes.

2. Cut polenta into nine squares. In a shallow bowl, whisk egg and milk. In another shallow bowl, combine bread crumbs and cilantro. Dip polenta in the egg mixture, then bread crumb mixture.

3. In a large nonstick skillet coated with cooking spray, cook the polenta in oil in batches for 1-2 minutes on each side or until golden brown. Serve with sour cream.

Nutrition Facts: 1 square with 1 Tbsp. reduced-fat sour cream equals 134 calories, 5 g fat (2 g saturated fat), 18 mg cholesterol, 456 mg sodium, 18 g carbohydrate, 2 g fiber, 5 g protein. **Diabetic Exchanges:** 1 starch, 1 fat.

Vegetable Pad Thai M

PREP: 25 min. **COOK:** 15 min. **YIELD:** 6 servings

SARA LANDRY • BROOKLINE, MASSACHUSETTS

Classic flavors of Thailand abound in this fragrant and easy dish featuring peanuts, tofu and noodles. New to tofu? It beefs up protein in this satisfying entree—a delicious way to introduce it to your diet.

  1 pkg. (12 oz.) whole wheat fettuccine
1/4 cup rice vinegar
  3 Tbsp. reduced-sodium soy sauce
  2 Tbsp. brown sugar
  2 Tbsp. fish sauce or additional reduced-sodium soy sauce
  1 Tbsp. lime juice

    Dash Louisiana-style hot sauce
  1 pkg. (12 oz.) extra-firm tofu, drained and cut into 1/2-in. cubes
  3 tsp. canola oil, *divided*
  2 medium carrots, grated
  2 cups fresh snow peas, halved
  3 garlic cloves, minced
  2 eggs, lightly beaten
  2 cups bean sprouts
  3 green onions, chopped
1/2 cup minced fresh cilantro
1/4 cup unsalted peanuts, chopped

1. Cook fettuccine according to package directions. Meanwhile, in a small bowl, combine the vinegar, soy sauce, brown sugar, fish sauce, lime juice and hot sauce until smooth; set aside.

2. In a large skillet or wok, stir-fry tofu in 2 tsp. oil until golden brown. Remove and keep warm. Stir-fry the carrots and snow peas in remaining oil for 1-2 minutes. Add the garlic, cook 1 minute longer or until the vegetables are crisp-tender. Add eggs; cook and stir until set.

3. Drain pasta; add to the vegetable mixture. Stir vinegar mixture and add to the skillet. Bring to a boil. Add the tofu, bean sprouts and onions; heat through. Sprinkle with cilantro and peanuts.

Nutrition Facts: 1-1/3 cups equals 383 calories, 11 g fat (2 g saturated fat), 71 mg cholesterol, 806 mg sodium, 61 g carbohydrate, 10 g fiber, 18 g protein.

Asian Quinoa F M

PREP: 20 min. **COOK:** 20 min. + standing
YIELD: 4 servings

SONYA LABBE • SANTA MONICA, CALIFORNIA

I love to cook and come up with new recipes. I serve this dish at least once a month and sometimes more. For a different twist, I'll occasionally add a scrambled egg or use soy sauce instead of the rice vinegar.

1	cup water
2	Tbsp. rice vinegar
2	Tbsp. plum sauce
2	garlic cloves, minced
1	tsp. minced fresh gingerroot
1	tsp. sesame oil
1/4	tsp. salt
1/4	tsp. crushed red pepper flakes
1/2	cup quinoa, rinsed
1	medium sweet red pepper, chopped
1/2	cup sliced water chestnuts, chopped
1/2	cup fresh sugar snap peas, trimmed and halved
2	green onions, thinly sliced

1. In a large saucepan, combine the first eight ingredients; bring to a boil. Add quinoa. Reduce heat; cover and simmer for 12-15 minutes or until water is absorbed.

2. Remove from the heat. Add the red pepper, water chestnuts, peas and onions; fluff with a fork. Cover and let stand for 10 minutes.

Editor's Note: Look for quinoa in the cereal, rice or organic food aisle.

Nutrition Facts: 2/3 cup equals 138 calories, 3 g fat (trace saturated fat), 0 cholesterol, 205 mg sodium, 25 g carbohydrate, 3 g fiber, 4 g protein.

Mexican Lentils and Rice M

PREP: 15 min. **COOK:** 40 min. **YIELD:** 4 servings

SHANNON KOENE • BLACKSBURG, VIRGINIA

You'll love this simple, quick-cooking, throw-in-the-pan-and-simmer meal!

1	medium onion, chopped
1	Tbsp. olive oil
2	garlic cloves, minced
1-1/2	cups vegetable broth
1/2	cup dried lentils, rinsed
3	tsp. chili powder
1-1/2	tsp. ground cumin
1	cup frozen corn
1	cup salsa
1/4	cup tomato paste
1	tsp. dried oregano
1	tsp. white vinegar
2	cups hot cooked brown rice
3/4	cup shredded reduced-fat sharp cheddar cheese

1. In a large saucepan, saute onion in oil until tender. Add garlic; cook 1 minute longer. Add the broth, lentils, chili powder and cumin. Bring to a boil. Reduce heat; cover and simmer for 20-25 minutes or until lentils are almost tender.

2. Stir in the corn, salsa, tomato paste, oregano and vinegar. Bring to a boil. Reduce heat; cover and simmer 10 minutes longer or until lentils are tender. Serve with rice; sprinkle with cheese.

Nutrition Facts: 1 cup lentil mixture with 1/2 cup brown rice and 3 Tbsp. cheese equals 387 calories, 10 g fat (4 g saturated fat), 15 mg cholesterol, 770 mg sodium, 60 g carbohydrate, 13 g fiber, 17 g protein.

Makeover Penne with Vodka Cream Sauce M

PREP: 15 min. **COOK:** 40 min. **YIELD:** 8 servings

DEBRA TORRES • CLARION, PENNSYLVANIA

This version of my original recipe is still creamy, rich and restaurant-quality special, but it now has less than half the original recipe's fat and cholesterol. It's tough to tell it apart from my full-fat version.

- 1 large onion, chopped
- 1 Tbsp. olive oil
- 4 garlic cloves, minced
- 2 cans (one 28 oz., one 14.5 oz.) diced tomatoes
- 1/4 cup vodka
- 1 pkg. (12 oz.) whole wheat penne pasta
- 2 tsp. prepared pesto
- 1/4 tsp. salt
- 1/4 tsp. crushed red pepper flakes
- 2 Tbsp. all-purpose flour
- 1/2 cup heavy whipping cream
- 1 cup whole milk
- 1/2 cup shredded Parmesan cheese

1. In a large saucepan, saute onion in oil until tender. Add garlic; cook 1 minute longer. Stir in tomatoes and vodka. Bring to a boil. Reduce heat; simmer, uncovered, for 30-35 minutes or until slightly thickened, stirring occasionally.

2. Meanwhile, cook the penne according to the package directions.

3. Stir the pesto, salt and pepper flakes into tomato mixture. In a small bowl, combine flour and cream

until smooth; stir into pan. Add milk. Bring to a boil; cook and stir for 2 minutes or until slightly thickened. Drain penne; serve with sauce. Sprinkle with cheese.

Nutrition Facts: 2/3 cup pasta with 2/3 cups sauce and 1 Tbsp. cheese equals 324 calories, 11 g fat (5 g saturated fat), 27 mg cholesterol, 379 mg sodium, 44 g carbohydrate, 7 g fiber, 12 g protein. **Diabetic Exchanges:** 2 starch, 2 fat, 1 lean meat, 1 vegetable.

Beans & Spinach M

PREP/TOTAL TIME: 25 min. **YIELD:** 6 servings

PATRICK AND HELEN REDDY • WILMINGTON, NORTH CAROLINA

One of our favorite appetizers at a local restaurant is made with white beans and escarole. It's nearly impossible to find escarole where we live, so we subbed in baby spinach and were pleasantly surprised by the result. Enjoy!

- 4 garlic cloves, sliced
- 2 Tbsp. olive oil
- 2 large onions, chopped
- 1 lb. fresh baby spinach
- 1 can (15 oz.) white kidney *or* cannellini beans, rinsed and drained
- 1/2 cup white wine *or* reduced-sodium chicken broth
- 3/4 tsp. salt
- 1/4 tsp. pepper

1. In a large nonstick skillet, saute garlic in oil until tender. Remove garlic and discard. Add onions to pan; saute until crisp-tender.

2. Stir in the remaining ingredients. Cook and stir over medium heat for 10-12 minutes or until spinach is wilted. Serve with a slotted spoon.

Nutrition Facts: 3/4 cup equals 138 calories, 5 g fat (1 g saturated fat), 0 cholesterol, 446 mg sodium, 17 g carbohydrate, 5 g fiber, 5 g protein. **Diabetic Exchanges:** 2 vegetable, 1 fat, 1/2 starch.

MAKEOVER PENNE WITH VODKA CREAM SAUCE

BEANS & SPINACH

Lactose-Free Spinach Lasagna Ⓜ

PREP: 45 min. **BAKE:** 35 min. + standing
YIELD: 12 servings

PEGGY KERN • RIVERSIDE, CALIFORNIA

Think you don't like tofu? It tastes just like ricotta cheese in this fabulous dish.

1-3/4 cups sliced fresh mushrooms
1/4 cup chopped onion
1 Tbsp. olive oil
1 pkg. (10 oz.) frozen chopped spinach, thawed and squeezed dry
2 garlic cloves, minced
2 cans (14-1/2 oz. *each*) diced tomatoes, undrained
1 can (8 oz.) tomato sauce
1 can (6 oz.) tomato paste
2 Tbsp. minced fresh basil *or* 2 tsp. dried basil
1 tsp. dried marjoram
9 uncooked lasagna noodles
1 pkg. (14 oz.) firm tofu, drained and cubed
2 eggs, lightly beaten
2 Tbsp. dried parsley flakes
1/2 tsp. salt
1/4 tsp. pepper
1-1/2 cups (6 oz.) shredded mozzarella-flavored soy cheese
1 cup (4 oz.) shredded cheddar-flavored soy cheese

1. In a large nonstick skillet coated with cooking spray, saute mushrooms and onion in oil until tender. Add spinach and garlic; cook 2 minutes longer. Stir in the tomatoes, tomato sauce, tomato paste, basil and marjoram. Bring to a boil. Reduce heat; cover and simmer for 15 minutes, stirring occasionally.

2. Meanwhile, cook lasagna noodles according to package directions; drain.

3. In a small bowl, combine the tofu, eggs, parsley, salt and pepper. Place three noodles in the bottom of a 13-in. x 9-in. baking dish coated with cooking spray. Layer with half of the tofu mixture, 1-1/2 cups spinach mixture, 1/2 cup mozzarella-flavored soy cheese and 1/3 cup cheddar-flavored soy cheese. Repeat layers. Top with remaining noodles and spinach mixture; sprinkle with remaining cheeses.

4. Cover and bake at 375° for 35-40 minutes or until heated through. Let the lasagna stand for 10 minutes before cutting.

Nutrition Facts: 1 piece equals 216 calories, 7 g fat (1 g saturated fat), 35 mg cholesterol, 531 mg sodium, 24 g carbohydrate, 3 g fiber, 14 g protein. **Diabetic Exchanges:** 2 vegetable, 1 medium-fat meat, 1 starch.

Two-Bean Veggie Pizza Ⓜ

PREP: 30 min. **BAKE:** 10 min. **YIELD:** 8 slices

LAURA LETNES • FARGO, NORTH DAKOTA

This is my much healthier version of a black bean pizza I had in Guatemala. It's so delicious!

1 medium onion, sliced
2 tsp. canola oil
3/4 cup canned kidney beans, rinsed and drained
3/4 cup canned black beans, rinsed and drained
1/2 cup salsa
1 Tbsp. hickory smoke-flavored barbecue sauce
1 sprig fresh parsley, stems removed
1 small garlic clove, peeled and halved
3/4 tsp. ground cumin
1/4 tsp. pepper
Dash hot pepper sauce

LACTOSE-FREE SPINACH LASAGNA

TWO-BEAN VEGGIE PIZZA

VEGGIE-CHEESE STUFFED SHELLS

1 prebaked 12-in. thin pizza crust
1 cup frozen corn, thawed
1 can (14-1/2 oz.) diced tomatoes, drained
3/4 cup shredded sharp cheddar cheese
3/4 cup shredded pepper Jack cheese

1. In a small nonstick skillet, cook onion in oil over low heat for 15-20 minutes or until onion is golden brown, stirring occasionally.

2. Meanwhile, in a food processor, combine the beans, salsa, barbecue sauce, fresh parsley, garlic, cumin, pepper and pepper sauce; cover and process until pureed.

3. Place crust on a baking sheet; spread with bean mixture. Top with caramelized onions, corn, tomatoes and cheeses. Bake at 450° for 8-10 minutes or until edges are lightly browned and cheese is melted.

Nutrition Facts: 1 slice equals 278 calories, 10 g fat (5 g saturated fat), 23 mg cholesterol, 561 mg sodium, 35 g carbohydrate, 4 g fiber, 13 g protein. **Diabetic Exchanges:** 2 starch, 1 lean meat, 1 vegetable, 1/2 fat.

Veggie-Cheese Stuffed Shells M

PREP: 20 min. **BAKE:** 35 min. **YIELD:** 2 servings

SHARON DELANEY-CHRONIS • SOUTH MILWAUKEE, WISCONSIN

Need a great-tasting meatless dish you can count on? These pleasing pasta shells are packed with veggies, three kinds of cheese and comforting flavor.

6 uncooked jumbo pasta shells
2/3 cup reduced-fat ricotta cheese
1/2 cup shredded part-skim mozzarella cheese, *divided*
1/4 cup shredded carrot
1/4 cup shredded zucchini
2 Tbsp. grated Parmesan cheese
1/2 tsp. dried parsley flakes
1/2 tsp. dried oregano
1/8 tsp. garlic powder
1/8 tsp. pepper
3/4 cup meatless spaghetti sauce, *divided*

1. Cook the pasta according to package directions. Meanwhile, in a small bowl, combine the ricotta cheese, 1/4 cup mozzarella cheese, carrot, zucchini, Parmesan cheese, parsley, oregano, garlic powder and pepper.

2. Spread 1/4 cup spaghetti sauce in a 3-cup baking dish coated with cooking spray. Drain shells; stuff with cheese mixture. Place in prepared baking dish. Top with remaining spaghetti sauce.

3. Cover and bake at 350° for 25 minutes. Uncover; sprinkle with remaining mozzarella. Bake 10-15 minutes longer or until bubbly.

Nutrition Facts: 3 stuffed shells equals 326 calories, 10 g fat (6 g saturated fat), 40 mg cholesterol, 721 mg sodium, 37 g carbohydrate, 3 g fiber, 21 g protein. **Diabetic Exchanges:** 2 medium-fat meat, 2 vegetable, 1-1/2 starch.

Linguine with Edamame And Tomatoes M

PREP/TOTAL TIME: 25 min. **YIELD:** 4 servings

DIANA RIOS • LYTLE, TEXAS

Featuring garden-fresh basil, cherry tomatoes and edamame, this bright and hearty pasta makes for a marvelous meatless meal on any busy weeknight.

8	oz. uncooked multigrain linguine
1-1/2	cups frozen shelled edamame
4	green onions, thinly sliced
1	Tbsp. olive oil
2	cups cherry tomatoes, halved
3	garlic cloves, minced
1	tsp. dried oregano
1/2	tsp. salt
1/4	cup white wine or reduced-sodium chicken broth
3/4	cup crumbled feta cheese
2	Tbsp. minced fresh basil

1. Cook linguine according to package directions, adding edamame during the last 5 minutes; drain, reserving 1/2 cup cooking liquid.

2. In a large nonstick skillet, saute onions in oil until tender. Add the tomatoes, garlic, oregano and salt. Add wine and reserved cooking liquid; cook and stir for 2 minutes.

3. Add linguine and edamame; cook and stir 2-3 minutes longer. Remove from the heat. Sprinkle with cheese and basil; toss to coat.

Nutrition Facts: 1-1/2 cups equals 370 calories, 11 g fat (3 g saturated fat), 11 mg cholesterol, 514 mg sodium, 54 g carbohydrate, 10 g fiber, 17 g protein.

Scrumptious Vegetable Lasagna M

PREP: 30 min. **BAKE:** 40 min. + standing
YIELD: 12 servings

COLLEEN CASSADY • LANCASTER, NEW HAMPSHIRE

My sister insists that I make this every year for one of our holiday family get-togethers.

9	whole wheat lasagna noodles
2	medium yellow summer squash, cut into 1/4-in. slices
2	medium zucchini, cut into 1/4-in. slices
1	large green pepper, chopped
1/2	lb. sliced fresh mushrooms
1	large sweet onion, chopped
1	Tbsp. olive oil
1	jar (25 oz.) marinara sauce
1	carton (15 oz.) fat-free ricotta cheese
9	slices reduced-fat provolone cheese, halved
2	cups (8 oz.) shredded part-skim mozzarella cheese
1	cup grated Parmesan cheese

1. Cook noodles according to package directions.

2. Meanwhile, in a large nonstick skillet coated with cooking spray, saute the squash, zucchini, green pepper, mushrooms and onion in oil until tender.

3. Drain noodles. Rinse in cold water and drain again. Spread 1/4 cup marinara sauce in a 13-in. x 9-in. baking dish coated with cooking spray. Top with three noodles, a scant 1 cup marinara sauce, 2 cups vegetable mixture, 1/2 cup ricotta cheese, six halved slices of provolone cheese, 2/3 cup mozzarella cheese and 1/3 cup Parmesan cheese. Repeat layers twice.

4. Cover and bake at 375° for 30 minutes. Uncover; bake 10-15 minutes longer or until bubbly. Let stand for 10 minutes before cutting.

Nutrition Facts: 1 piece equals 269 calories, 9 g fat (5 g saturated fat), 30 mg cholesterol, 441 mg sodium, 27 g carbohydrate, 4 g fiber, 19 g protein. **Diabetic Exchanges:** 2 lean meat, 2 vegetable, 1 starch, 1 fat.

Black Bean Pasta F M

PREP/TOTAL TIME: 25 min. **YIELD:** 6 servings

ASHLYNN AZAR • ALBUQUERQUE, NEW MEXICO

This filling vegetarian dish is loaded with flavor. I use fresh rosemary when I have it on hand.

- 9   oz. uncooked whole wheat fettuccine
- 1-3/4 cups sliced baby portobello mushrooms
- 1   Tbsp. olive oil
- 1   garlic clove, minced
- 1   can (15 oz.) black beans, rinsed and drained
- 1   can (14-1/2 oz.) diced tomatoes
- 1   tsp. dried rosemary, crushed
- 1/2 tsp. dried oregano
- 2   cups fresh baby spinach

1. Cook fettuccine according to package directions. Meanwhile, in a large skillet, saute mushrooms in oil until tender; add garlic, cook 2 minutes longer.

2. Stir in the black beans, tomatoes, rosemary and oregano. Cook and stir until heated through. Stir in the spinach until wilted. Drain fettuccine. Serve with bean mixture.

Nutrition Facts: 2/3 cup bean mixture with 2/3 cup pasta equals 255 calories, 3 g fat (trace saturated fat), 0 cholesterol, 230 mg sodium, 45 g carbohydrate, 9 g fiber, 12 g protein. **Diabetic Exchanges:** 3 starch, 1 lean meat, 1/2 fat.

Zucchini Tomato Frittata C M

PREP: 20 min. **COOK:** 15 min. **YIELD:** 4 servings

KIM SOSEBEE • CLEVELAND, GEORGIA

"Frittata" is Italian for omelet, and this dinner entree is packed full of veggies. Egg substitute and low-fat cheese lighten it up, making for a healthy meal. It's great for a quick late-night bite.

- 1/3   cup sun-dried tomatoes (not packed in oil)
- 1   cup boiling water
- 1-1/2 cups egg substitute
- 1/2   cup 2% cottage cheese
- 2   green onions, chopped
- 1/4   cup minced fresh basil or 1 Tbsp. dried basil
- 1/8   tsp. crushed red pepper flakes
- 1   cup sliced zucchini
- 1   cup fresh broccoli florets
- 1   medium sweet red pepper, chopped
- 2   tsp. canola oil
- 2   Tbsp. grated Parmesan cheese

1. Place tomatoes in a small bowl. Cover with boiling water; let stand for 5 minutes. Drain and set aside.

2. In a large bowl, whisk the egg substitute, cottage cheese, onions, basil, pepper flakes and reserved tomatoes; set aside. In a 10-in. ovenproof skillet, saute the zucchini, broccoli and red pepper in oil until tender. Reduce heat; top with reserved egg mixture. Cover and cook for 4-6 minutes or until nearly set.

3. Uncover skillet. Sprinkle with Parmesan cheese. Broil 3-4 in. from the heat for 2-3 minutes or until eggs are completely set. Let stand for 5 minutes. Cut into wedges.

Nutrition Facts: 1 wedge equals 138 calories, 4 g fat (1 g saturated fat), 6 mg cholesterol, 484 mg sodium, 11 g carbohydrate, 3 g fiber, 15 g protein. **Diabetic Exchanges:** 2 lean meat, 2 vegetable.

BLACK BEAN PASTA

ZUCCHINI TOMATO FRITTATA

Risotto-Stuffed Portobellos

PREP: 45 min. **BAKE:** 20 min. **YIELD:** 4 servings

RIAN MACDONALD • POWDER SPRINGS, GEORGIA

I invented this dish one night when I was having last-minute guests. I ran to a local farm stand for some amazing produce and created this using fresh portobellos and leftover risotto. My friends still ask for the recipe!

1	can (14-1/2 oz.) reduced-sodium chicken or vegetable broth
1	cup water
2	celery ribs, finely chopped
2	medium carrots, finely chopped
1	large onion, finely chopped
1	Tbsp. olive oil
1	cup uncooked arborio rice
1/2	cup chopped shallots
1	garlic clove, minced
1	cup dry white wine or additional broth
1/2	cup grated Parmesan cheese
4	green onions, finely chopped
4	large portobello mushrooms (4 to 4-1/2 in.), stems removed

Cooking spray

1/4	tsp. salt
1/8	tsp. pepper
1/4	cup shredded part-skim mozzarella cheese

1. In a small saucepan, heat broth and water and keep warm. In a large nonstick skillet coated with cooking spray, saute the celery, carrots and onion in oil until crisp-tender. Add the rice, shallots and garlic; cook and stir for 2-3 minutes. Reduce heat; stir in wine. Cook and stir until all of the liquid is absorbed.

2. Add heated broth mixture, 1/2 cup at a time, stirring constantly. Allow the liquid to absorb between additions. Cook just until risotto is creamy and rice is almost tender. (Cooking time is about 20 minutes.) Remove from the heat; add Parmesan cheese and green onions. Stir until cheese is melted.

3. Spritz mushrooms with cooking spray; sprinkle with salt and pepper. Fill each with 1 cup risotto mixture and sprinkle with mozzarella cheese. Place in a 13-in. x 9-in. baking dish coated with cooking spray.

4. Bake, uncovered, at 350° for 20-25 minutes or until mushrooms are tender and cheese is melted.

Nutrition Facts: 1 stuffed mushroom equals 380 calories, 9 g fat (3 g saturated fat), 13 mg cholesterol, 680 mg sodium, 57 g carbohydrate, 4 g fiber, 14 g protein.

Instant Potato Gnocchi F S M

PREP/TOTAL TIME: 30 min. **YIELD:** 4 servings

SARAH OTT • BLANCHARDVILLE, WISCONSIN

This tasty gnocchi is much easier than it looks and contains almost no saturated fat. Just serve with your favorite jarred pasta sauce, and you're set!

1	cup mashed potato flakes
1	cup boiling water
1	egg, lightly beaten
1-1/2	cups all-purpose flour
1/2	tsp. dried basil
1/4	tsp. garlic powder
1/8	tsp. salt
1/8	tsp. pepper
6	cups water

Pasta sauce of your choice

Grated Parmesan cheese, optional

1. Place potato flakes in a large bowl. Stir in boiling water; add egg. Stir in flour and seasonings. On a lightly floured surface, knead 10-12 times, forming a soft dough.

2. Divide dough into four portions. On a floured surface, roll each portion into 1/2-in.-thick ropes; cut into 3/4-in. pieces. Press and roll each piece with a lightly floured fork.

3. In a large saucepan, bring water to a boil. Cook gnocchi in batches for 30-60 seconds or until they float. Remove with a slotted spoon. Serve with sauce; sprinkle with cheese if desired.

RISOTTO-STUFFED PORTOBELLOS

INSTANT POTATO GNOCCHI

Nutrition Facts: 1-1/2 cups (calculated without sauce and cheese) equals 250 calories, 2 g fat (trace saturated fat), 53 mg cholesterol, 126 mg sodium, 50 g carbohydrate, 2 g fiber, 8 g protein.

Mediterranean Chickpeas

8 pts

PREP/TOTAL TIME: 25 min. **YIELD:** 4 servings

ELAINE OBER • BROOKLINE, MASSACHUSETTS

Olives, oregano and artichoke hearts boost flavor in this colorful and hearty meatless main dish. It goes together in minutes with convenient pantry items. Try a little feta cheese on top for something extra special.

1	cup water
3/4	cup uncooked whole wheat couscous
1	medium onion, chopped
1	Tbsp. olive oil
2	garlic cloves, minced
1	can (15 oz.) garbanzo beans *or* chickpeas, rinsed and drained
1	can (14-1/2 oz.) no-salt-added stewed tomatoes, cut up
1	can (14 oz.) water-packed artichoke hearts, rinsed, drained and chopped
1/2	cup Greek olives, coarsely chopped
1	Tbsp. lemon juice
1/2	tsp. dried oregano

Dash pepper

Dash cayenne pepper

1. In a small saucepan, bring water to a boil. Stir in the couscous. Remove from the heat; cover and let stand for 5-10 minutes or until water is absorbed. Fluff with a fork.

2. Meanwhile, in a large nonstick skillet, saute onion in oil until tender. Add garlic; cook 1 minute longer. Sir in the garbanzo beans, tomatoes, artichokes, olives, lemon juice, oregano and peppers. Cook and stir until heated through. Serve with couscous.

Nutrition Facts: 1 cup garbanzo bean mixture with 2/3 cup couscous equals 340 calories, 10 g fat (1 g saturated fat), 0 cholesterol, 677 mg sodium, 51 g carbohydrate, 9 g fiber, 11 g protein.

Black Beans with Brown Rice

8 pts

PREP: 15 min. **COOK:** 20 min. **YIELD:** 5 servings

SHEILA MEYER • NORTH CANTON, OHIO

Your family will never miss the meat in this robust, vibrant and fresh-tasting main dish. Served over brown rice, it makes a healthy, stick-to-the-ribs dinner.

1	small green pepper, chopped
1/2	cup chopped sweet red pepper
1/2	cup chopped sweet yellow pepper
1/2	cup chopped red onion
2	Tbsp. canola oil
2	cans (15 oz. *each*) black beans, rinsed and drained
1	can (14-1/2 oz.) diced tomatoes, undrained
2	Tbsp. cider vinegar
1/2	tsp. garlic salt
1/8	tsp. pepper
1/8	tsp. cayenne pepper
2-1/2	cups hot cooked brown rice

1. In a large saucepan, saute peppers and onion in oil until tender. Stir in the beans, tomatoes, vinegar, garlic salt, pepper and cayenne. Bring to a boil. Reduce heat; simmer, uncovered, for 12-15 minutes or until it reaches the desired consistency, stirring occasionally. Serve with rice.

Nutrition Facts: 3/4 cup bean mixture with 1/2 cup rice equals 327 calories, 7 g fat (1 g saturated fat), 0 cholesterol, 614 mg sodium, 55 g carbohydrate, 11 g fiber, 12 g protein.

MAKEOVER ROSEMARY MUFFINS

ROSEMARY-GARLIC FOCCACIA BREAD

IRISH SODA BREAD

The Bread Basket

Golden loaves of bread, sweet muffins, delicate scones perfect alongside warm tea...you can enjoy these aromatic delights and still keep your healthy-eating goals in check. Just consider the delightful recipes here.

Makeover Rosemary Muffins M

PREP: 20 min. BAKE: 20 min. YIELD: 1 dozen

MARLEA RICE WARREN • ST. LOUIS PARK, MINNESOTA

The experts created light, full-flavored muffins that accompany any meal beautifully. While they knocked off a hefty amount of saturated fat, calories, sodium and cholesterol from the original, these tasty makeover muffins never let on that they're healthier than my original.

- 1-1/2 cups all-purpose flour
- 1-1/2 cups whole wheat flour
-     2 tsp. sugar
-     1 tsp. baking powder
-   3/4 tsp. baking soda
-   1/2 tsp. salt
-     2 eggs
- 1-1/2 cups (12 oz.) reduced-fat plain yogurt
-   1/2 cup fat-free milk
-   1/4 cup canola oil
-     1 Tbsp. Dijon mustard
-   1/2 cup crumbled goat cheese
-   1/2 cup chopped Greek olives
-     1 Tbsp. minced fresh rosemary *or* 1 tsp. dried rosemary, crushed

1. In a large bowl, combine the first six ingredients. In another bowl, combine the eggs, yogurt, milk, oil and mustard. Stir into dry ingredients just until moistened. Fold in the cheese, olives and rosemary.

2. Coat muffin cups with cooking spray; fill three-fourths full with batter. Bake at 375° for 20-25 minutes or until a toothpick inserted in muffin comes out clean. Cool for 5 minutes before removing from pan to a wire rack. Serve warm.

Nutrition Facts: 1 muffin equals 217 calories, 9 g fat (2 g saturated fat), 43 mg cholesterol, 394 mg sodium, 27 g carbohydrate, 2 g fiber, 8 g protein. **Diabetic Exchanges:** 2 starch, 1 fat.

Irish Soda Bread

PREP: 20 min. BAKE: 50 min. + cooling
YIELD: 1 loaf (16 slices)

PADMINI ROY-DIXON • COLUMBUS, OHIO

My husband's family is Irish. Wanting to impress my future mother-in-law, I baked this bread and took it along with me when I met her the first time. Needless to say, it worked!

-   3/4 cup raisins
-     1 cup boiling water
-     2 cups all-purpose flour
-     1 cup whole wheat flour
-   1/3 cup sugar
-     3 tsp. baking powder
-     1 tsp. baking soda
-     1 tsp. salt
-     1 egg
-     2 cups buttermilk
-   1/4 cup butter, melted

1. Place raisins in a small bowl. Cover with boiling water; let stand for 5 minutes. Drain and pat dry.

2. In a large bowl, combine the flours, sugar, baking powder, baking soda and salt. In a small bowl, whisk the egg, buttermilk and butter. Stir into dry ingredients just until moistened. Fold in raisins.

3. Transfer to a 9-in. x 5-in. loaf pan coated with cooking spray. Bake at 350° for 50-60 minutes or until a toothpick inserted near the center comes out clean. Cool for 10 minutes before removing from pan to a wire rack.

Nutrition Facts: 1 slice equals 161 calories, 4 g fat (2 g saturated fat), 22 mg cholesterol, 359 mg sodium, 28 g carbohydrate, 2 g fiber, 4 g protein. **Diabetic Exchanges:** 2 starch, 1 fat.

To test baking powder for **freshness**, place 1 teaspoon baking powder in a cup and add 1/3 cup hot tap water. If active bubbling occurs, the products are fine. If not, you should discard the powder and replace it.

ROSEMARY-GARLIC FOCACCIA BREAD

Rosemary-Garlic Focaccia Bread Ⓜ

PREP: 30 min. + rising **BAKE:** 15 min.
YIELD: 1 loaf (12 wedges)

TAMMY BOLLMAN • MINATARE, NEBRASKA

This bread smells wonderful when it's baking in the oven. I make it mostly during the summer when rosemary is abundant in the garden, but also around the holidays when rosemary plants are available in the stores.

3/4	cup warm fat-free milk (70° to 80°)
1/4	cup water (70° to 80°)
1/4	cup butter, softened
1	egg
2-3/4	cups bread flour
2	Tbsp. sugar
2	tsp. kosher salt, *divided*
2	tsp. active dry yeast
4	tsp. olive oil
4	garlic cloves, minced
1	Tbsp. minced fresh rosemary

1. In bread machine pan, place the milk, water, butter, egg, flour, sugar, 1 tsp. salt and yeast in order suggested by manufacturer. Select dough setting (check dough after 5 minutes of mixing; add 1 to 2 Tbsp. of water or flour if needed).

2. When cycle is completed, turn dough onto a lightly floured surface. Punch dough down. Cover and let rest for 10 minutes. Shape into an 11-in. circle; place on a baking sheet coated with cooking spray. Cover and let rise until doubled, about 30 minutes.

Using the end of a wooden spoon handle, make several 1/4-in. indentations in dough.

3. Brush with oil. Sprinkle with garlic, rosemary and remaining salt. Bake at 400° for 15-20 minutes or until golden brown. Cut into wedges.

Editor's Note: We recommend you do not use a bread machine's time-delay feature for this recipe.

Nutrition Facts: 1 wedge equals 162 calories, 6 g fat (3 g saturated fat), 28 mg cholesterol, 353 mg sodium, 24 g carbohydrate, 1 g fiber, 5 g protein. **Diabetic Exchanges:** 1-1/2 starch, 1 fat.

Fruited Bran Muffins

PREP: 20 min. **BAKE:** 20 min. **YIELD:** 9 muffins

BETSY KING • DULUTH, MINNESOTA

Juicy blueberries and an apple make a nice addition to these hearty muffins. Bran cereal helps pump up fiber to 5 grams.

1-1/2	cups All-Bran
3/4	cup whole wheat flour
3	Tbsp. sugar
1/2	tsp. baking powder
1/2	tsp. baking soda
1/2	tsp. ground cinnamon
1	egg
3/4	cup buttermilk
1/4	cup mashed ripe banana
1/4	cup molasses
2	Tbsp. canola oil
1/2	cup chopped peeled tart apple
1/2	cup fresh *or* frozen blueberries

1. In a small bowl, combine the first six ingredients. In another bowl, combine the egg, buttermilk, banana, molasses and oil. Stir into dry ingredients just until moistened. Fold in apple and blueberries.

2. Coat muffin cups with cooking spray or use paper liners; fill three-fourths full with batter. Bake at 350° for 20-25 minutes or until a toothpick inserted near the center comes out clean. Cool for 5 minutes before removing from pan to a wire rack. Serve warm.

Editor's Note: If using frozen blueberries, use without thawing to avoid discoloring the batter.

Nutrition Facts: 1 muffin equals 160 calories, 5 g fat (1 g saturated fat), 24 mg cholesterol, 150 mg sodium, 30 g carbohydrate, 5 g fiber, 4 g protein. **Diabetic Exchanges:** 2 starch, 1/2 fat.

Old-Fashioned Biscuits M

PREP: 20 min. **BAKE:** 15 min. **YIELD:** 4 biscuits

HEALTHY COOKING TEST KITCHEN

Fresh-from-the-oven biscuits can be yours in no time. Best of all, they don't have to break your commitment to eating right. Serve them with breakfast or with a steaming mug of coffee or tea. Either way, you'll love every bite!

- 1/2 cup all-purpose flour
- 1/2 cup cake flour
- 1 tsp. baking powder
- 1 tsp. sugar
- 1/4 tsp. salt
- 1/8 tsp. baking soda
- 3/4 oz. cold reduced-fat cream cheese
- 1 Tbsp. cold butter
- 1/4 cup plus 1/2 tsp. buttermilk, *divided*

1. In a small bowl, combine the flours, baking powder, sugar, salt and baking soda. Cut in cream cheese and butter until mixture resembles coarse crumbs. Stir in 1/4 cup buttermilk just until moistened. Turn onto a lightly floured surface; knead 5-6 times.

2. Pat or roll out to 1/2-in. thickness; cut with a floured 2-in. biscuit cutter.

3. Place 2 in. apart on a baking sheet coated with cooking spray. Brush with remaining buttermilk. Bake at 400° for 12-15 minutes or until golden brown. Serve warm.

Nutrition Facts: 1 biscuit equals 167 calories, 4 g fat (3 g saturated fat), 12 mg cholesterol, 355 mg sodium, 27 g carbohydrate, 1 g fiber, 4 g protein. **Diabetic Exchanges:** 2 starch, 1 fat.

Pumpkin Spice Bagels F

PREP: 30 min. + standing **BAKE:** 15 min.
YIELD: 9 servings

KRISTY REEVES • LEROY, KANSAS

Enjoy pumpkin pie flavor with these classic bagels. For a change, adjust the spices to suit your taste buds.

- 2/3 cup plus 2 Tbsp. water (70° to 80°), *divided*
- 1/2 cup canned pumpkin
- 1/3 cup packed brown sugar
- 1 tsp. salt
- 1-1/2 tsp. ground cinnamon
- 3/4 tsp. ground nutmeg
- 1/2 tsp. ground allspice
- 1/2 tsp. ground cloves
- 3 cups bread flour
- 1 pkg. (1/4 oz.) active dry yeast
- 1 egg white
- 1 Tbsp. cornmeal

1. In bread machine pan, place 2/3 cup water, pumpkin, brown sugar, salt, spices, flour and yeast in order suggested by manufacturer. Select dough setting (check dough after 5 minutes of mixing; add 1 to 2 Tbsp. of water or flour if needed).

2. When cycle is completed, turn dough onto a lightly floured surface. Shape into nine balls. Push thumb through centers to form a 1-in. hole. Stretch and shape dough to form an even ring. Cover and let rest for 10 minutes; flatten rings slightly.

3. Fill a Dutch oven two-thirds full with water; bring to a boil. Drop bagels, two at a time, into boiling water. Cook for 45 seconds; turn and cook 45 seconds longer. Remove with a slotted spoon; drain on paper towels.

4. Whisk egg white and remaining water; brush over bagels. Coat a baking sheet with cooking spray and sprinkle with cornmeal. Place bagels 2 in. apart on prepared pan. Bake at 400° for 15-20 minutes or until golden brown. Remove to wire racks to cool.

Nutrition Facts: 1 bagel equals 180 calories, trace fat (trace saturated fat), 0 cholesterol, 273 mg sodium, 40 g carbohydrate, 2 g fiber, 6 g protein.

PUMPKIN SPICE BAGELS

Italian Spinach Braid

PREP: 20 min. + rising **BAKE:** 20 min. **YIELD:** 6 servings

PAT JASPER • NORTHLAKE, ILLINOIS

I've been making this recipe for over 25 years. It's how I got my kids to eat spinach when they were little. This is the dish I'm asked to make the most.

1	loaf (1 lb.) frozen whole wheat bread dough, thawed
1	lb. lean ground beef (90% lean)
1	pkg. (10 oz.) frozen chopped spinach, thawed and squeezed dry
2/3	cup shredded part-skim mozzarella cheese
2	Tbsp. grated Romano cheese
3/4	tsp. dried minced garlic
3/4	tsp. fennel seed
3/4	tsp. dried oregano
1/2	tsp. salt
1	egg white, beaten

Pizza sauce, optional

1. Roll dough into a 12-in. x 9-in. rectangle. Transfer to a 15-in. x 10-in. x 1-in. baking pan coated with cooking spray. Cover and let rise in a warm place until doubled, about 1 hour.

2. Meanwhile, in a large skillet, cook beef over medium heat until no longer pink; drain. Transfer to a large bowl; add the spinach, cheeses, garlic, fennel seed, oregano and salt.

3. Spread beef mixture lengthwise down the center of dough. On each long side, cut 1-in.-wide strips 3 in. into center.

4. Starting at one end, fold alternating strips at an angle across filling. Pinch ends to seal. Brush with egg white. Bake at 350° for 20-25 minutes or until golden brown. Serve with pizza sauce if desired.

Nutrition Facts: 1 piece (calculated without pizza sauce) equals 366 calories, 12 g fat (4 g saturated fat), 57 mg cholesterol, 709 mg sodium, 38 g carbohydrate, 6 g fiber, 30 g protein. **Diabetic Exchanges:** 3 lean meat, 2-1/2 starch.

Makeover Zucchini Bread

PREP: 20 min. **BAKE:** 45 min. + cooling
YIELD: 2 loaves (12 slices each)

MARJORIE CURTIS • HADDAM, CONNECTICUT

This makeover bread has a golden top, lots of sweet cinnamon flavor and a slimmed-down nutritional profile. It's perfect for your next afternoon snack.

1-1/2	cups sugar
1/2	cup unsweetened applesauce
2	eggs
1/3	cup canola oil
3	tsp. vanilla extract
3	cups all-purpose flour
2-1/2	tsp. ground cinnamon
2	tsp. baking powder
1	tsp. salt
1/2	tsp. baking soda
2	cups shredded zucchini
3/4	cup chopped walnuts

1. In a large bowl, beat the sugar, applesauce, eggs, oil and vanilla until well blended. Combine the flour, cinnamon, baking powder, salt and baking soda; gradually beat into sugar mixture until blended. Stir in zucchini and walnuts.

2. Transfer to two 8-in. x 4-in. loaf pans coated with cooking spray. Bake at 350° for 45-55 minutes or until a toothpick inserted near the center comes out clean. Cool for 10 minutes before removing from pans to wire racks.

Nutrition Facts: 1 slice equals 168 calories, 6 g fat (1 g saturated fat), 18 mg cholesterol, 165 mg sodium, 26 g carbohydrate, 1 g fiber, 3 g protein. **Diabetic Exchanges:** 2 starch, 1 fat.

ITALIAN SPINACH BREAD

MAKEOVER ZUCCHINI BREAD

BLUEBERRY-CITRUS MINI LOAVES

Blueberry-Citrus Mini Loaves

PREP: 15 min. **BAKE:** 40 min. + cooling
YIELD: 2 loaves (6 slices each)

HEIDI LINDSEY • PRAIRIE DU SAC, WISCONSIN

Moist and packed with flavor, these healthful treats hit the spot. With subtle orange peel, blueberries and hearty whole wheat flour, they offer a delectable way to get your family going in the morning!

1	cup all-purpose flour
1	cup whole wheat pastry flour
3/4	cup sugar
1/2	tsp. salt
1/2	tsp. baking soda
1	egg
3/4	cup orange juice
1/4	cup canola oil
1	Tbsp. grated orange peel
1/2	cup fresh *or* frozen blueberries
1/4	cup chopped pecans

1. In a large bowl, combine the flours, sugar, salt and baking soda. In a small bowl, whisk the egg, orange juice, oil and orange peel. Stir into dry ingredients just until moistened. Fold in blueberries and pecans.

2. Transfer to two 5-3/4-in. x 3-in. x 2-in. loaf pans coated with cooking spray. Bake at 350° for 40-45 minutes or until a toothpick inserted near the center comes out clean. Cool for 10 minutes before removing from pans to wire racks.

Editor's Note: If using frozen blueberries, use without thawing to avoid discoloring the batter.

Nutrition Facts: 1 slice equals 189 calories, 7 g fat (1 g saturated fat), 18 mg cholesterol, 157 mg sodium, 29 g carbohydrate, 2 g fiber, 3 g protein.

Sweet Potato Biscuits

PREP/TOTAL TIME: 30 min. **YIELD:** 17 biscuits

DELYNNE RUTLEDGE • LOVELADY, TEXAS

Flaky and bursting with flavor from honey and sweet potatoes, these biscuits are wonderful any time, but they're best right from the oven.

2	cups all-purpose flour
1/3	cup yellow cornmeal
2-1/2	tsp. baking powder
1/2	tsp. salt
1/3	cup cold butter
1	cup mashed sweet potato
1/2	cup fat-free milk
2	Tbsp. honey

1. In a large bowl, combine the flour, cornmeal, baking powder and salt. Cut in butter until mixture resembles coarse crumbs. Stir in the sweet potato, milk and honey just until moistened. Turn onto a lightly floured surface; knead 5-8 times. Pat out to 1/2-in. thickness; cut with a floured 2-in. biscuit cutter.

2. Place 2 in. apart on an ungreased baking sheet. Bake at 400° for 14-18 minutes or until lightly browned. Serve warm.

Nutrition Facts: 1 biscuit equals 120 calories, 4 g fat (2 g saturated fat), 10 mg cholesterol, 162 mg sodium, 19 g carbohydrate, 1 g fiber, 2 g protein. **Diabetic Exchanges:** 1 starch, 1 fat.

CRANBERRY ORANGE BAGELS

Cranberry Orange Bagels F

PREP: 30 min. + standing BAKE: 20 min. YIELD: 9 bagels

KRISTY REEVES • LEROY, KANSAS

Dried cranberries and grated orange peel add bright flavor to these scrumptious morning treats. Switch up the taste, if you'd like, by using raisins and cinnamon.

1	cup plus 4 Tbsp. water (70° to 80°), *divided*
1/2	cup dried cranberries
1/3	cup packed brown sugar
4-1/2	tsp. grated orange peel
1	tsp. salt
1/4	tsp. ground cloves
3	cups bread flour
1	pkg. (1/4 oz.) active dry yeast
1	Tbsp. sugar
1	egg white
1	Tbsp. cornmeal

1. In bread machine pan, place 1 cup plus 2 Tbsp. water, cranberries, brown sugar, orange peel, salt, cloves, flour and yeast in order suggested by manufacturer. Select dough setting (check dough after 5 minutes of mixing; add 1 to 2 Tbsp. of water or flour if needed).

2. When cycle is completed, turn dough onto a lightly floured surface. Shape into nine balls. Push thumb through centers to form a 1-in. hole. Stretch and shape dough to form an even ring. Cover and let rest for 10 minutes; flatten rings slightly.

3. Fill a Dutch oven two-thirds full with water; add sugar and bring to a boil. Drop bagels, two at a time, into boiling water. Cook for 45 seconds; turn and cook 45 seconds longer. Remove with a slotted spoon; drain on paper towels.

4. Whisk egg white and remaining water; brush over bagels. Coat a baking sheet with cooking spray and sprinkle with cornmeal. Place bagels 2 in. apart on prepared pan. Bake at 400° for 18-22 minutes or until golden brown. Remove to wire racks to cool.

Nutrition Facts: 1 bagel equals 197 calories, trace fat (trace saturated fat), 0 cholesterol, 272 mg sodium, 45 g carbohydrate, 2 g fiber, 6 g protein.

Bountiful Loaves

PREP: 30 min. + rising **BAKE:** 25 min. + cooling
YIELD: 2 loaves (16 slices each)

JENNIFER FERRO • DRUMHELLER, ALBERTA

This healthy, rustic bread fills you up. It's delicious as is or with dried cranberries instead of raisins.

2	pkg. (1/4 oz. *each*) active dry yeast
3	tsp. sugar, *divided*
2-1/2	cups warm water (110° to 115°)
3	cups whole wheat flour
1	cup old-fashioned oats
1/2	cup oat bran
1/2	cup toasted wheat germ
1/2	cup ground flaxseed
1	egg
2	Tbsp. olive oil
2	tsp. salt
2-1/2	cups all-purpose flour
1/2	cup sunflower kernels
1/2	cup raisins

1. In a large bowl, dissolve yeast and 1 tsp. sugar in warm water; let stand for 5 minutes. Add the whole wheat flour, oats, oat bran, wheat germ, flaxseed, egg, oil, salt, 1 cup all-purpose flour and remaining sugar. Beat until smooth. Stir in the sunflower kernels, raisins and enough remaining flour to form a firm dough (dough will be sticky).

2. Turn onto a lightly floured surface; knead until smooth and elastic, about 6-8 minutes. Place in a bowl coated with cooking spray, turning once to coat the top. Cover and let rise in a warm place until doubled, about 1 hour.

3. Punch dough down. Turn onto a lightly floured surface; divide in half. Shape into two round loaves. Place on a baking sheet coated with cooking spray. Cover and let rise until nearly doubled, about 30 minutes.

4. Bake at 375° for 25-30 minutes or until golden brown. Remove from baking sheet to wire rack to cool.

Nutrition Facts: 1 slice equals 133 calories, 4 g fat (trace saturated fat), 7 mg cholesterol, 161 mg sodium, 23 g carbohydrate, 3 g fiber, 5 g protein. **Diabetic Exchanges:** 1-1/2 starch, 1/2 fat.

Basil Marmalade Scones

PREP: 20 min. **BAKE:** 15 min. **YIELD:** 8 scones

HANNAH WALLACE • WENATCHEE, WASHINGTON

Orange marmalade and fragrant basil give these delightful scones a slightly sweet, garden-fresh flavor. They're tender and moist and perfect with morning or afternoon tea.

2	cups all-purpose flour
3	Tbsp. sugar
2	tsp. baking powder
1/2	tsp. salt
3	Tbsp. cold butter
3	Tbsp. minced fresh basil *or* 1 Tbsp. dried basil
2	eggs
1/3	cup fat-free milk
1/3	cup orange marmalade

1. In a small bowl, combine the flour, sugar, baking powder and salt. Cut in butter until mixture resembles coarse crumbs. Stir in basil. Whisk eggs and milk; stir into crumb mixture just until moistened. Turn onto a floured surface; knead 5 times.

2. Divide dough in half. Transfer one portion to a baking sheet coated with cooking spray. Pat into a 7-in. circle. Spread marmalade to within 1/2 in. of edge. Pat remaining dough into a 7-in. circle. Place over marmalade; seal edges. Cut into eight wedges, but do not separate. Bake at 400° for 15-20 minutes or until golden brown. Serve warm.

Nutrition Facts: 1 scone equals 224 calories, 6 g fat (3 g saturated fat), 64 mg cholesterol, 308 mg sodium, 38 g carbohydrate, 1 g fiber, 5 g protein.

BOUNTIFUL LOAVES

BASIL MARMALADE SCONES

Double Corn Corn Bread

PREP: 15 min. **BAKE:** 40 min. + cooling
YIELD: 1 loaf (6 slices)

SILVANA NARDONE • BROOKLYN, NEW YORK

Looking for a delightful bread to dunk in a bowl of chowder or chili? Try this tasty recipe. It's one of my son's all-time favorites. He could eat it for breakfast, lunch and dinner.

1	cup gluten-free all-purpose baking flour
1	cup cornmeal
1/4	cup sugar
1	Tbsp. baking powder
1	tsp. baking soda
1	tsp. salt
2	eggs, lightly beaten
1	cup rice milk
1/4	cup canola oil
1	Tbsp. cider vinegar
1	cup frozen corn, thawed

1. In a large bowl, combine the flour, cornmeal, sugar, baking powder, baking soda and salt. In a small bowl, whisk the eggs, rice milk, oil and vinegar. Stir into dry ingredients just until moistened; stir in corn.

2. Transfer to an 8-in. x 4-in. loaf pan coated with cooking spray. Bake at 350° for 40-45 minutes or until top is lightly browned and a toothpick inserted near the center comes out clean. Cool on a wire rack.

Editor's Note: Read all ingredient labels for possible gluten content prior to use. Ingredient formulas can change, and production facilities vary among brands. If you're concerned that your brand may contain gluten, contact the company.

Nutrition Facts: 1 slice equals 334 calories, 13 g fat (1 g saturated fat), 71 mg cholesterol, 842 mg sodium, 51 g carbohydrate, 4 g fiber, 7 g protein.

DOUBLE CORN CORN BREAD

Peanut Butter-Banana Muffins **F S C**

2 ℓℓ

PREP: 25 min. **BAKE:** 10 min./batch **YIELD:** 4 dozen

PATTY PUTTER • MARION, KANSAS

These bite-size muffins make a great treat. Banana and peanut butter are ideal partners and taste terrific with chocolate.

1	cup old-fashioned oats
1	cup whole wheat flour
1/2	cup all-purpose flour
1/2	cup sugar
1	tsp. baking powder
1/2	tsp. baking soda
1/2	tsp. salt
1	egg
3/4	cup fat-free milk
3/4	cup mashed ripe bananas
1/2	cup creamy peanut butter
1/3	cup unsweetened applesauce
1/2	tsp. vanilla extract
3/4	cup miniature semisweet chocolate chips

TOPPING

1/3	cup packed brown sugar
1/3	cup dry roasted peanuts, coarsely chopped
1/3	cup miniature semisweet chocolate chips

1. In a large bowl, combine the first seven ingredients. In a small bowl, combine the egg, milk, bananas, peanut butter, applesauce and vanilla. Stir into dry ingredients just until moistened. Fold in chocolate chips.

2. Fill greased or paper-lined miniature muffin cups three-fourths full. For topping, in a small bowl, combine the brown sugar, peanuts and chocolate chips. Sprinkle over muffins. Bake at 350° for 10-13 minutes or until a toothpick inserted near the center comes out clean.

3. Cool for 5 minutes before removing from pans to wire racks. Serve warm.

Nutrition Facts: 1 muffin equals 80 calories, 3 g fat (1 g saturated fat), 4 mg cholesterol, 71 mg sodium, 12 g carbohydrate, 1 g fiber, 2 g protein. **Diabetic Exchange:** 1 starch.

Honey Lemon Muffins

PREP/TOTAL TIME: 30 min. **YIELD:** 10 muffins

RACHEL HART • WILDOMAR, CALIFORNIA

Honey's subtle essence comes through in every bite of these succulent little muffins, providing the perfect counterpoint to the bright taste of lemon.

1	cup all-purpose flour
1/2	cup whole wheat flour
1	tsp. baking powder
1/4	tsp. baking soda
1/4	tsp. salt
1	egg
1/2	cup honey
1/4	cup lemon juice

GLUTEN-FREE AUTUMN BREAD

1/4 cup butter, melted
1/2 tsp. grated lemon peel
DRIZZLE:
1/4 cup confectioners' sugar
1 tsp. lemon juice
Additional grated lemon peel

1. In a large bowl, combine the flours, baking powder, baking soda and salt. In another bowl, combine the egg, honey, lemon juice, butter and lemon peel. Stir into dry ingredients just until moistened.

2. Coat muffin cups with cooking spray or use paper liners; fill one-half full with batter.

3. Bake at 375° for 15-18 minutes or until a toothpick inserted near the center comes out clean. Cool for 5 minutes before removing from pan to a wire rack.

4. In a small bowl, combine confectioners' sugar and lemon juice; drizzle over warm muffins. Sprinkle with additional lemon peel.

Nutrition Facts: 1 muffin equals 178 calories, 5 g fat (3 g saturated fat), 33 mg cholesterol, 171 mg sodium, 31 g carbohydrate, 1 g fiber, 3 g protein. **Diabetic Exchanges:** 2 starch, 1 fat.

Gluten-Free Autumn Bread

PREP: 20 min. **BAKE:** 50 min. + cooling
YIELD: 1 loaf (16 slices)

CHRISTINE LEVINE • WALDORF, MARYLAND

This moist, yummy loaf has a golden-brown crust and added sweetness from bananas, raisins and carrots.

1 cup mashed ripe bananas (2 to 3 medium)
1 cup packed brown sugar
1/4 cup unsweetened applesauce
1/4 cup canola oil
2 eggs
1 cup sorghum flour
1 cup brown rice flour
1-1/2 tsp. baking powder
1 tsp. baking soda
1 tsp. xanthan gum
1/2 tsp. salt
1/2 tsp. ground cinnamon
1 cup shredded carrots
1/2 cup raisins
1/3 cup chopped walnuts

1. In a large bowl, beat the bananas, brown sugar, applesauce, oil and eggs until well blended. Combine the flours, baking powder, baking soda, xanthan gum, salt and cinnamon; gradually beat into banana mixture until blended. Stir in the carrots, raisins and walnuts.

2. Transfer to a 9-in. x 5-in. loaf pan coated with cooking spray. Bake at 350° for 50-60 minutes or until a toothpick inserted near the center comes out clean. Cool for 10 minutes before removing from pan to a wire rack.

Editor's Note: Read all ingredient labels for possible gluten content prior to use. Ingredient formulas can change, and production facilities vary among brands. If you're concerned that your brand may contain gluten, contact the company.

Nutrition Facts: 1 slice equals 199 calories, 6 g fat (1 g saturated fat), 26 mg cholesterol, 212 mg sodium, 35 g carbohydrate, 2 g fiber, 3 g protein. **Diabetic Exchanges:** 2 starch, 1 fat, 1/2 fruit.

No-Knead Whole Wheat Rolls [F]

PREP: 15 min. + rising BAKE: 10 min. YIELD: 1 dozen

DEBORAH PATRAUCHUK • SICAMOUS, BRITISH COLUMBIA

Tender and moist, these easy whole wheat rolls boast a great herb flavor!

1	pkg. (1/4 oz.) active dry yeast
1-1/4	cups warm water (110° to 115°)
2	cups all-purpose flour
1	cup whole wheat flour
2	Tbsp. butter, softened
1	Tbsp. honey
1	Tbsp. molasses
1	tsp. salt
1	tsp. Italian seasoning

1. In a large bowl, dissolve yeast in warm water. Add the remaining ingredients. Beat on medium speed for 3 minutes (dough will be sticky). Do not knead. Cover and let rise in a warm place until doubled, about 30 minutes.

2. Stir dough down. Set aside 1/4 cup batter. Fill muffin cups coated with cooking spray half full. Top each with 1 tsp. reserved batter. Cover and let rise until doubled, about 8-12 minutes.

3. Bake at 375° for 10-15 minutes or until golden brown. Cool for 1 minute before removing from pan to a wire rack.

Nutrition Facts: 1 roll equals 139 calories, 2 g fat (1 g saturated fat), 5 mg cholesterol, 212 mg sodium, 26 g carbohydrate, 2 g fiber, 4 g protein. **Diabetic Exchange:** 1-1/2 starch.

Swiss Cheese Muffins [M]

PREP/TOTAL TIME: 30 min. YIELD: 1 dozen

MARY RELYEA • CANASTOTA, NEW YORK

Ideal as a snack, a quick breakfast or alongside a bowl of chili or stew, these tasty muffins hit the spot. Their savory yet mild flavors make them a hit with all ages. Best of all, I can whip them up and have them on the table in just half an hour!

2	cups all-purpose flour
1	Tbsp. sugar
3/4	tsp. salt

1/2 tsp. baking soda
  2 eggs
  1 cup (8 oz.) reduced-fat sour cream
  2 Tbsp. canola oil
1/2 cup shredded Swiss cheese
  2 green onions, chopped

1. In a small bowl, combine the flour, sugar, salt and baking soda. In another bowl, combine the eggs, sour cream and oil. Stir into dry ingredients just until moistened. Fold in cheese and onions.

2. Coat muffin cups with cooking spray or use paper liners; fill three-fourths full with batter. Bake at 375° for 15-18 minutes or until a toothpick inserted in muffin comes out clean. Cool for 5 minutes before removing from pan to a wire rack. Serve warm.

Nutrition Facts: 1 muffin equals 157 calories, 6 g fat (2 g saturated fat), 46 mg cholesterol, 237 mg sodium, 19 g carbohydrate, 1 g fiber, 6 g protein. **Diabetic Exchanges:** 1 starch, 1 fat.

Gluten-Free Banana Nut Muffins **S**

PREP: 20 min. BAKE: 20 min. YIELD: 1 dozen

GINGERLEMONGIRL • TASTEOFHOME.COM COMMUNITY

You don't have to be gluten-intolerant to appreciate the sweet essence of grains and bananas in these delectable muffins.

1-1/2 cups mashed ripe bananas (2 to 3 medium)
  2/3 cup sugar
    2 eggs
  1/4 cup fat-free plain yogurt
    2 Tbsp. plus 1-1/2 tsp. canola oil
    1 tsp. vanilla extract
  1/2 cup millet flour
  1/2 cup sorghum flour
  1/2 cup tapioca flour
    1 Tbsp. ground flaxseed
    2 tsp. baking powder
  1/2 tsp. baking soda
  1/4 tsp. xanthan gum
  1/3 cup chopped walnuts

1. In a large bowl, beat the first six ingredients until well blended. In a large bowl, combine the flours, flax, baking powder, baking soda and xanthan gum; gradually beat into banana mixture until blended. Stir in walnuts.

2. Coat muffin cups with cooking spray or use paper liners; fill three-fourths full with batter. Bake at 350° for 18-22 minutes or until a toothpick inserted near the center comes out clean.

3. Cool for 5 minutes before removing from pan to a wire rack.

Editor's Note: Read all ingredient labels for possible gluten content prior to use. Ingredient formulas can change, and production facilities vary among brands. If you're concerned that your brand may contain gluten, contact the company.

Nutrition Facts: 1 muffin equals 191 calories, 6 g fat (1 g saturated fat), 35 mg cholesterol, 135 mg sodium, 32 g carbohydrate, 2 g fiber, 4 g protein. **Diabetic Exchanges:** 2 starch, 1 fat.

Rustic Rye Bread **F**

PREP: 20 min. + rising BAKE: 30 min. + cooling
YIELD: 2 loaves (12 slices each)

HOLLY WADE • HARRISONBURG, VIRGINIA

This gorgeous rye bread has just a touch of sweetness and the perfect amount of caraway seeds. With a crusty top and firm texture, it holds up well to sandwiches...but a pat of butter will do the job, too.

      1 pkg. (1/4 oz.) active dry yeast
  1-3/4 cups warm water (110° to 115°), *divided*
    1/4 cup packed brown sugar
    1/4 cup light molasses
      3 Tbsp. caraway seeds
      2 Tbsp. canola oil
      3 tsp. salt
  1-3/4 cups rye flour
    3/4 cup whole wheat flour
  1-3/4 to 2-1/4 cups all-purpose flour

1. In a large bowl, dissolve yeast in 1/4 cup warm water. Add the brown sugar, molasses, caraway seeds, oil, salt and remaining water; mix well. Add the rye flour, whole wheat flour and 1-3/4 cups all-purpose flour. Beat until smooth. Stir in enough remaining flour to form a firm dough.

2. Turn onto a lightly floured surface; knead until smooth and elastic, about 6-8 minutes. Place in a bowl coated with cooking spray, turning once to coat the top. Cover and let rise in a warm place until doubled, about 1 hour.

3. Punch dough down; shape into two round loaves. Place on a baking sheet coated with cooking spray. Cover and let rise until doubled, about 1 hour.

4. Bake at 350° for 30-35 minutes or until golden brown. Remove from pan to wire rack to cool.

Nutrition Facts: 1 slice equals 104 calories, 2 g fat (trace saturated fat), 0 cholesterol, 298 mg sodium, 21 g carbohydrate, 2 g fiber, 2 g protein. **Diabetic Exchange:** 1 starch.

RUSTIC RYE BREAD

SESAME BEEF STIR-FRY

FRESH VEGETABLE OMELET

TOASTED CLUBS WITH DILL MAYO

Table for Two

When you cook for a duo, you want the right size recipe. This chapter is full of good-for-you breakfasts, lunches and suppers perfect for a pair. Or whip up one of these entrees for yourself and save the rest for tomorrow.

Toasted Clubs with Dill Mayo

PREP/TOTAL TIME: 20 min. YIELD: 2 servings

JENNY FLAKE • NEWPORT BEACH, CALIFORNIA

Simple to prepare, appealing to the eyes and loaded with flavor, this bistro-style sandwich couldn't be better! Swap in whatever lean deli meats and cheeses you have on hand—turkey and Swiss make a great combo, too.

    2   Tbsp. fat-free mayonnaise
  1/4   tsp. dill weed
  3/4   tsp. lemon juice, *divided*
  1/8   tsp. pepper
    4   slices whole wheat bread, toasted
    4   thin slices deli roast beef
    4   thin slices deli ham
    2   slices reduced-fat provolone cheese
    2   Bibb lettuce leaves
    2   slices tomato
    2   center-cut bacon strips, cooked and crumbled
  1/4   cup alfalfa sprouts
  1/4   medium ripe avocado, peeled and sliced

1. In a small bowl, combine the mayonnaise, dill, 1/4 tsp. lemon juice and pepper; spread over toast. Layer two slices with beef, ham, cheese, lettuce, tomato, bacon and alfalfa sprouts.

2. Drizzle avocado with remaining lemon juice; place over alfalfa sprouts. Top with remaining toast. Secure with toothpicks.

Nutrition Facts: 1 sandwich equals 328 calories, 13 g fat (4 g saturated fat), 47 mg cholesterol, 1,056 mg sodium, 29 g carbohydrate, 6 g fiber, 26 g protein.

Fresh Vegetable Omelet C M

PREP: 30 min. BAKE: 10 min. YIELD: 2 servings

EDIE DESPAIN • LOGAN, UTAH

Breakfast feels extra-special when you wake up to a lovely, satisfying and good-for-you omelet. Chock-full of fresh vegetables and great flavor, it's a filling main dish you'll be proud to serve.

    4   egg whites
  1/4   cup water
  1/4   tsp. cream of tartar
    2   eggs
  1/4   tsp. salt
    1   tsp. butter
    1   medium tomato, chopped
    1   small zucchini, chopped
    1   small onion, chopped
  1/4   cup chopped green pepper
  1/2   tsp. Italian seasoning
  1/3   cup shredded reduced-fat cheddar cheese

1. In a small bowl, beat the egg whites, water and cream of tartar until stiff peaks form. In a large bowl, beat eggs and salt until thick and lemon-colored, about 5 minutes. Fold in the whites.

2. In a 10-in. ovenproof skillet coated with cooking spray, melt butter. Pour egg mixture into skillet. Cook for 5 minutes over medium heat or until puffed and lightly browned on the bottom. Bake, uncovered, at 350° for 10-12 minutes or until a knife inserted 2 in. from edge comes out clean.

3. Meanwhile, in a large skillet, saute the tomato, zucchini, onion, green pepper and Italian seasoning until tender. Carefully run a knife around edge of ovenproof skillet to loosen. With a knife, score center of omelet. Place vegetables on one side and sprinkle with cheese; fold other side over filling. Slide onto a serving plate; cut in half.

Nutrition Facts: 1/2 omelet equals 222 calories, 11 g fat (5 g saturated fat), 231 mg cholesterol, 617 mg sodium, 12 g carbohydrate, 3 g fiber, 20 g protein. **Diabetic Exchanges:** 3 lean meat, 2 vegetable, 1/2 fat.

Italian seasoning can be found in the spice aisle of most grocery stores. Basic blends often contain marjoram, thyme, rosemary, savory, sage, oregano and basil. If your grocery store does not carry Italian seasoning, ask the manager if it can be ordered.

Grilled Jerk Shrimp Orzo Salad

PREP: 25 min. GRILL: 25 min. YIELD: 2 servings

EILEEN BUDNYK • PALM BEACH GARDENS, FLORIDA

You'll go crazy over the heat, seasonings and appearance of this colorful main-dish salad. Try it!

- 1 large ear sweet corn in husk
- 1 tsp. olive oil
- 1/3 cup uncooked whole wheat orzo pasta
- 6 fresh asparagus spears, trimmed
- 1/2 lb. uncooked medium shrimp, peeled and deveined
- 1 Tbsp. Caribbean jerk seasoning
- 1 small sweet red pepper, chopped

DRESSING:
- 2 Tbsp. white vinegar
- 1 Tbsp. water
- 1 Tbsp. lime juice
- 1 Tbsp. olive oil
- 1/8 tsp. salt
- 1/8 tsp. pepper

1. Carefully peel back corn husk to within 1 in. of bottom; remove silk. Brush corn with oil. Rewrap corn in husk and secure with kitchen string. Grill corn, covered, over medium heat for 25-30 minutes or until tender, turning often.

2. Meanwhile, cook orzo according to package directions. Drain and rinse in cold water; set aside.

3. Thread asparagus spears onto two parallel metal or soaked wooden skewers. Rub shrimp with jerk seasoning; thread onto two skewers. Grill asparagus and shrimp, covered, over medium heat for 5-8

minutes or until asparagus is crisp-tender and shrimp turn pink, turning once.

4. Cut corn from cob; place in a large bowl. Cut asparagus into 1-in. pieces; add to bowl. Add the shrimp, orzo and pepper. In a small bowl, whisk the dressing ingredients. Pour over salad; toss to coat.

Nutrition Facts: 2 cups equals 352 calories, 12 g fat (2 g saturated fat), 138 mg cholesterol, 719 mg sodium, 38 g carbohydrate, 8 g fiber, 26 g protein. **Diabetic Exchanges:** 3 lean meat, 2 starch, 1 vegetable, 1 fat.

Stuffed Ranch Chicken C

PREP: 15 min. BAKE: 25 min. YIELD: 2 servings

LADONNA REED • PONCA CITY, OKLAHOMA

My husband and I are trying to eat healthier, so I keep on the lookout for light, flavorful foods that serve two. Stuffed with red pepper, green onion and creamy ranch dressing, this supper is a definite winner.

- 1 bacon strip, cut in half lengthwise
- 2 boneless skinless chicken breast halves (4 oz. *each*)
- 2 Tbsp. fat-free ranch salad dressing
- 3 Tbsp. finely chopped fresh mushrooms
- 3 Tbsp. finely chopped sweet red pepper
- 3 Tbsp. finely chopped green onions
- 2 tsp. cornstarch
- 6 Tbsp. fat-free evaporated milk

1. In a small nonstick skillet, cook bacon over medium heat until cooked but not crisp. Drain on paper towel. Flatten chicken to 1/4-in. thickness; spread with ranch dressing. Top with mushrooms, red pepper and onions. Roll up and wrap a piece of bacon around each; secure with a toothpick if needed.

2. Place in a shallow 1-qt. baking dish coated with cooking spray. Bake, uncovered, at 350° for 25-30

GRILLED JERK SHRIMP ORZO SALAD

STUFFED RANCH CHICKEN

CRAB-STUFFED MANICOTTI

minutes or until chicken juices run clear. Remove and keep warm. Remove toothpicks.

3. Strain pan juices. In a small saucepan, combine cornstarch and milk until smooth; stir in pan juices. Bring to a boil; cook and stir for 1 minute or until thickened. Serve with chicken.

Nutrition Facts: 1 chicken breast half with 2 Tbsp. sauce equals 220 calories, 5 g fat (1 g saturated fat), 67 mg cholesterol, 339 mg sodium, 15 g carbohydrate, 1 g fiber, 28 g protein. Diabetic Exchanges: 3 very lean meat, 1 starch, 1 fat.

Crab-Stuffed Manicotti

10PPV

PREP: 25 min. BAKE: 25 min. YIELD: 2 servings

SONYA POLFLIET • ANZA, CALIFORNIA

I love pasta, and my husband loves seafood. I combined them to create this dish, and he raved that this is the best meal ever.

- 4 uncooked manicotti shells
- 1 Tbsp. butter
- 4 tsp. all-purpose flour
- 1 cup fat-free milk
- 1 Tbsp. grated Parmesan cheese
- 2 pouches (3.53 oz. *each*) premium crabmeat, drained
- 1/3 cup reduced-fat ricotta cheese
- 1/4 cup shredded part-skim mozzarella cheese
- 1/4 tsp. lemon-pepper seasoning
- 1/4 tsp. pepper
- 1/8 tsp. garlic powder

Minced fresh parsley

1. Cook manicotti according to package directions. In a small saucepan, melt butter. Stir in flour until smooth; gradually add milk. Bring to a boil; cook and stir for 2 minutes or until thickened. Remove from the heat; stir in Parmesan cheese.

2. In a small bowl, combine crab, ricotta cheese, mozzarella cheese, lemon-pepper, pepper and garlic powder. Drain manicotti; stuff with crab mixture. Spread 1/4 cup sauce in an 8-in. square baking dish coated with cooking spray. Top with stuffed manicotti. Pour remaining sauce over top.

3. Cover and bake at 350° for 25-30 minutes or until heated through. Sprinkle with parsley before serving.

Nutrition Facts: 2 stuffed manicotti equals 359 calories, 12 g fat (7 g saturated fat), 98 mg cholesterol, 793 mg sodium, 38 g carbohydrate, 1 g fiber, 26 g protein. Diabetic Exchanges: 2 starch, 2 lean meat, 1 fat, 1/2 fat-free milk.

If grated Parmesan is called for, use finely grated cheese sold in containers with shaker tops. If grating your own, use the finest section on your **grating tool**. You can also use a food processor. Cut cheese into 1-inch cubes and process 1 cup of cubes at a time until finely grated.

Cranberry Chicken Wraps

9 pts

PREP/TOTAL TIME: 20 min. YIELD: 2 servings

SARAH WHITE • SALT LAKE CITY, UTAH

Loaded with cranberries, chicken, apples and spinach, these nutritious wraps are fast, tender and flavorful.

1	cup shredded cooked chicken breast
1	cup chopped apple
1/4	cup plus 2 tsp. fat-free Miracle Whip, *divided*
1/4	cup dried cranberries
3	Tbsp. crumbled feta cheese
1/4	tsp. minced fresh rosemary *or* 1/8 tsp. dried rosemary, crushed
1/8	tsp. pepper
2	whole wheat tortillas (8 in.), room temperature
1/2	cup fresh baby spinach

1. In a small bowl, combine the chicken, apple, 1/4 cup Miracle Whip, cranberries, feta cheese, rosemary and pepper. Spread remaining Miracle Whip over tortillas. Top with chicken mixture and spinach. Roll up and secure with toothpicks.

Nutrition Facts: 1 wrap equals 387 calories, 7 g fat (2 g saturated fat), 60 mg cholesterol, 614 mg sodium, 49 g carbohydrate, 5 g fiber, 27 g protein.

Chuck Wagon Chow

7 pts

PREP/TOTAL TIME: 20 min. YIELD: 2 servings

DOROTHY COWAN • FERNDALE, CALIFORNIA

Try serving this mild chili-like dish with tortilla chips or flour tortillas. It cooks up in a single pot; it's great for camping, too.

1/3	lb. lean ground beef
1	small onion, chopped
1/4	cup chopped green pepper
1	garlic clove, minced
1	can (7 oz.) whole kernel corn, drained
3/4	cup kidney beans, rinsed and drained
1/2	cup tomato sauce
1	Tbsp. chili powder
1/8	tsp. pepper

1. In a large saucepan, cook the beef, onion and green pepper over medium heat until meat is no longer pink. Add garlic; cook 1 minute longer. Drain. Add the corn, beans, tomato sauce and seasonings; cover and cook 5-10 minutes longer or until heated through.

Nutrition Facts: 1-1/2 cups equals 300 calories, 7 g fat (3 g saturated fat), 46 mg cholesterol, 509 mg sodium, 38 g carbohydrate, 9 g fiber, 24 g protein. **Diabetic Exchanges:** 2-1/2 lean meat, 2 starch, 1 vegetable.

Creamy Pork Chop Dinner

PREP: 10 min. **BAKE:** 1 hour **YIELD:** 2 servings

JOYCE VALENTINE • SANFORD, COLORADO

Hearty and comforting, this meat-and-potatoes meal is rich with homemade goodness—and it's easy to prepare. Sometimes I use chicken thighs instead of pork chops.

- 2 medium potatoes, peeled and cut into 1/4-in. slices
- 2 medium carrots, sliced
- 2 boneless pork loin chops (3/4 in. thick and 4 oz. *each*)
- 1 Tbsp. onion soup mix
- 1-1/2 tsp. cornstarch
- 1 can (10-3/4 oz.) ready-to-serve creamy chicken soup *(1 CAN CREAMY CHICKEN) (+ 1/2 CAN WATER)*

1. Place the potatoes and carrots in a 1-qt. baking dish coated with cooking spray. In a large skillet coated with cooking spray, brown pork chops on both sides. Place over vegetables.

2. In a small bowl, combine the soup mix, cornstarch and soup until blended. Pour over pork chops. Cover and bake at 350° for 1 hour or until meat and potatoes are tender.

Nutrition Facts: 1 serving equals 360 calories, 11 g fat (3 g saturated fat), 57 mg cholesterol, 807 mg sodium, 40 g carbohydrate, 6 g fiber, 27 g protein.

Turkey with Apple Slices

PREP/TOTAL TIME: 15 min. **YIELD:** 2 servings

MARY LOU WAYMAN • SALT LAKE CITY, UTAH

Any day can be "Turkey Day" when you make this smaller-scale main course. The moist tenderloins and tangy apple glaze offer the goodness of turkey without a refrigerator full of leftovers.

- 2 turkey breast tenderloins (about 4 oz. *each*)
- 1 Tbsp. butter
- 2 Tbsp. maple syrup
- 1 Tbsp. cider vinegar
- 1 tsp. Dijon mustard
- 1/2 tsp. chicken bouillon granules
- 1 medium tart apple, sliced

1. In a large skillet, cook turkey in butter over medium heat for 4-5 minutes on each side or until the juices run clear. Remove from the skillet; cover and keep warm.

2. In the same skillet, combine the syrup, vinegar, mustard and bouillon. Add the apple; cook and stir over medium heat for 2-3 minutes or until apple is tender. Serve with turkey.

Nutrition Facts: 1 serving equals 263 calories, 7 g fat (4 g saturated fat), 71 mg cholesterol, 374 mg sodium, 24 g carbohydrate, 2 g fiber, 27 g protein. **Diabetic Exchanges:** 3 lean meat, 1-1/2 fat, 1 starch, 1/2 fruit.

Asian Pork Supper

PREP: 10 min. + marinating **BAKE:** 20 min.
YIELD: 2 servings

ANNEMARIE HARRIS • HADDONFIELD, NEW JERSEY

Here's a light, delicious dish that will soon be a favorite. Serve it with jasmine rice and broccoli.

- 1/2 cup reduced-sodium soy sauce
- 1 Tbsp. minced fresh gingerroot
- 1-1/2 tsp. sesame oil
- 2 whole cloves
- 1 pork tenderloin (3/4 lb.)
- 1/4 cup sesame seeds
- 1 Tbsp. honey
- 1 Tbsp. brown sugar

1. In a large resealable plastic bag, combine the soy sauce, ginger, sesame oil and cloves. Add the pork; seal bag and turn to coat. Refrigerate for 8 hours or overnight.

2. Drain and discard marinade. Place sesame seeds in a shallow dish. Roll pork in sesame seeds and place in a 13-in. x 9-in. baking dish coated with cooking spray. Drizzle with honey; sprinkle with brown sugar.

3. Bake, uncovered, at 425° for 20-30 minutes or until a meat thermometer reads 160°.

Nutrition Facts: 5 oz. cooked pork equals 324 calories, 12 g fat (2 g saturated fat), 95 mg cholesterol, 437 mg sodium, 19 g carbohydrate, trace fiber, 37 g protein. **Diabetic Exchanges:** 5 lean meat, 1 starch, 1 fat.

ASIAN PORK SUPPER

Mushroom Cheese Ravioli M

PREP/TOTAL TIME: 25 min. **YIELD:** 2 servings

CATHY HALL • PHOENIX, ARIZONA

You'd never guess this creamy, rich and colorful dish is light. Add a frosty glass of iced tea, spinach salad and fruit for an easy meal.

- 2 cups refrigerated cheese ravioli
- 1/2 cup sliced fresh mushrooms
- 1 Tbsp. chopped onion
- 1 Tbsp. pine nuts
- 1 Tbsp. chopped sweet yellow pepper
- 1 Tbsp. chopped sweet red pepper
- 1 tsp. olive oil
- 2 tsp. cornstarch
- 1/2 cup reduced-sodium chicken *or* vegetable broth
- 1/4 cup fat-free half-and-half
- 1/8 tsp. salt
- 1/8 tsp. pepper

Grated Parmesan cheese, optional

1. Cook ravioli according to package directions.

2. Meanwhile, in a small nonstick saucepan coated with cooking spray, saute the mushrooms, onion, nuts and peppers in oil until tender.

3. Combine the cornstarch, broth, half-and-half, salt and pepper until smooth. Gradually stir into the pan. Bring to a boil; cook and stir for 2 minutes or until mixture is thickened.

4. Drain ravioli. Stir into sauce; heat through. Sprinkle with cheese if desired.

Nutrition Facts: 1-1/2 cups (calculated without cheese) equals 367 calories, 11 g fat (5 g saturated fat), 40 mg cholesterol, 717 mg sodium, 48 g carbohydrate, 3 g fiber, 18 g protein.

MUSHROOM CHEESE RAVIOLI

Spiced French Toast

PREP: 15 min. + chilling **COOK:** 5 min. **YIELD:** 2 servings

BEVERLY HAUGEN • HENDERSON, NEVADA

I make this recipe for my family and friends, and it's a hit every time. It fills them up, but not out!

- 2 eggs
- 2 egg whites
- 3/4 cup fat-free milk
- 1 Tbsp. sugar
- 1 Tbsp. molasses
- 1/4 tsp. ground ginger
- 1/4 tsp. ground allspice
- 1/8 tsp. salt
- 6 slices French bread (3/4 in. thick)
- 2 tsp. butter

1. In a large bowl, combine the first eight ingredients. Place the bread slices in an ungreased 13-in. x 9-in. baking dish; pour egg mixture over top. Cover and refrigerate overnight.

2. Heat butter on a griddle; cook bread for 2-3 minutes on each side or until golden brown.

Nutrition Facts: 3 slices equals 352 calories, 10 g fat (4 g saturated fat), 223 mg cholesterol, 662 mg sodium, 47 g carbohydrate, 2 g fiber, 18 g protein.

Bacon-Broccoli Quiche Cups

PREP: 10 min. **BAKE:** 25 min. **YIELD:** 2 servings

IRENE STEINMEYER • DENVER, COLORADO

Chock-full of veggies and melted cheese, this comforting and colorful egg bake has become a holiday brunch classic at my home. For a tasty variation, try substituting asparagus for broccoli and Swiss for cheddar cheese.

- 4 bacon strips, diced
- 1/4 cup fresh broccoli florets
- 1/4 cup chopped onion
- 1 garlic clove, minced
- 3 eggs
- 1 Tbsp. dried parsley flakes
- 1/8 tsp. seasoned salt, optional

Dash pepper

- 1/4 cup shredded cheddar cheese
- 2 Tbsp. chopped tomato

1. In a large skillet, cook bacon over medium heat until crisp. Using a slotted spoon, remove to paper towels; drain, reserving 1 Tbsp. drippings. In the drippings, cook broccoli and onion over medium heat for 2-3 minutes or until vegetables are tender. Add garlic; cook 1 minute longer.

2. In a small bowl, beat the eggs, parsley, seasoned salt if desired and pepper. Stir in bacon and broccoli mixture; add cheese and tomato.

3. Pour into two 10-oz. ramekins or custard cups coated with cooking spray. Bake at 400° for 22-25 minutes or until a knife inserted near the center comes out clean.

Nutrition Facts: 1 serving (prepared with egg substitute and reduced-fat cheese; calculated without seasoned salt) equals 173 calories, 9 g fat (4 g saturated fat), 21 mg cholesterol, 486 mg sodium, 5 g carbohydrate, 1 g fiber, 17 g protein.

Sesame Beef Stir-Fry

PREP/TOTAL TIME: 30 min. **YIELD:** 2 servings

CHARLENE CHAMBERS • ORMOND BEACH, FLORIDA

Soy sauce and gingerroot add great flavor to this quick beef stir-fry. It couldn't be simpler to make, but it's definitely elegant enough to serve someone special.

    2 tsp. cornstarch
  1/2 cup reduced-sodium beef broth
    4 tsp. reduced-sodium soy sauce
    1 Tbsp. minced fresh gingerroot
    1 garlic clove, minced
  1/2 lb. beef top sirloin steak, thinly sliced
    2 tsp. sesame seeds, toasted, *divided*
    2 tsp. peanut *or* canola oil, *divided*
    2 cups fresh broccoli florets
    1 small sweet yellow pepper, julienned
    1 cup hot cooked brown rice

1. In a small bowl, combine the first five ingredients until blended; set aside.

2. In a large nonstick skillet or wok, stir-fry beef and 1 tsp. sesame seeds in 1 tsp. oil until no longer pink. Remove and keep warm.

3. Stir-fry broccoli in remaining oil for 2 minutes. Add pepper; stir-fry 4-6 minutes longer or until vegetables are crisp-tender.

4. Stir cornstarch mixture and add to the pan. Bring to a boil; cook and stir for 2 minutes or until thickened. Add beef; heat through. Serve with rice. Sprinkle with remaining sesame seeds.

Nutrition Facts: 2 cups stir-fry with 1/2 cup rice equals 363 calories, 12 g fat (3 g saturated fat), 47 mg cholesterol, 606 mg sodium, 33 g carbohydrate, 5 g fiber, 31 g protein. **Diabetic Exchanges:** 3 lean meat, 2 starch, 1 vegetable, 1 fat.

Cajun Shrimp Stir-Fry

PREP/TOTAL TIME: 25 min. **YIELD:** 2 servings

GINNY KOCHIS • SPRINGFIELD, VIRGINIA

Squash and red onion add color to this tasty one-dish meal with just the right amount of Cajun kick.

1	small zucchini, sliced
1/2	medium yellow summer squash, sliced
1/2	medium red onion, chopped
1	Tbsp. canola oil
1/2	lb. uncooked medium shrimp, peeled and deveined
1	tsp. Cajun seasoning
1/2	tsp. garlic powder
1/8	tsp. pepper

Dash crushed red pepper flakes

1	cup hot cooked brown rice

1. In a large skillet or wok, stir-fry the zucchini, yellow squash and onion in oil for 2-3 minutes or until crisp-tender. Add shrimp and seasonings; stir-fry 3 minutes longer or until shrimp turn pink. Serve with rice.

Nutrition Facts: 1 cup shrimp mixture with 1/2 cup rice equals 297 calories, 10 g fat (1 g saturated fat), 138 mg cholesterol, 417 mg sodium, 30 g carbohydrate, 4 g fiber, 23 g protein. **Diabetic Exchanges:** 3 lean meat, 1-1/2 fat, 1 starch, 1 vegetable.

Scrambled Eggs With Cream Cheese F C

PREP/TOTAL TIME: 15 min. **YIELD:** 2 servings

DEBBIE CLAY • ALOHA, OREGON

What a tasty, protein-packed meal! We love to add a little hot sauce to these eggs.

1	cup egg substitute
1	green onion, thinly sliced
1/8	tsp. pepper
1	tsp. butter
1/4	cup fat-free cream cheese, cubed

1. In a small bowl, whisk the egg substitute, onion and pepper. In a small nonstick skillet, heat butter over medium heat. Add egg mixture; cook and stir until almost set. Stir in cream cheese. Cook and stir until completely set.

Nutrition Facts: 1 cup equals 107 calories, 2 g fat (1 g saturated fat), 7 mg cholesterol, 423 mg sodium, 4 g carbohydrate, trace fiber, 16 g protein. **Diabetic Exchange:** 2 lean meat.

Zucchini Tomato Soup

PREP/TOTAL TIME: 20 min. **YIELD:** 2 servings

NANCY JOHNSON • LAVERNE, OKLAHOMA

There's garden-fresh flavor in every spoonful of this easy-to-make soup. I like it for a low-calorie lunch, along with a roll and fruit for dessert. It serves just two, so you don't end up with leftovers.

2 small zucchini, coarsely chopped
1/4 cup chopped red onion
1-1/2 tsp. olive oil
1/8 tsp. salt
1 cup Spicy Hot V8 juice
1 small tomato, cut into thin wedges
Dash *each* pepper and dried basil
2 Tbsp. shredded cheddar cheese, optional
1 to 2 Tbsp. crumbled cooked bacon, optional

1. In a large skillet, saute zucchini and onion in oil until crisp-tender. Sprinkle with salt. Add the V8 juice, tomato, pepper and basil; cook until heated through. Sprinkle with cheese and bacon if desired.

Nutrition Facts: 1 serving (calculated without cheese and bacon) equals 89 calories, 4 g fat (1 g saturated fat), 0 cholesterol, 545 mg sodium, 12 g carbohydrate, 3 g fiber, 3 g protein. **Diabetic Exchanges:** 2 vegetable, 1/2 fat.

Chicken Spaghetti Salad

PREP/TOTAL TIME: 20 min. **YIELD:** 2 servings

HOLLY SIPHAVONG • EUREKA, CALIFORNIA

I make this quick dish when I'm in a hurry and am not hungry enough to eat a huge meal.

3 oz. uncooked spaghetti
1/2 cup shredded cooked chicken breast
1/2 cup julienned cucumber
1/3 cup julienned carrot
1 Tbsp. white vinegar
1 Tbsp. reduced-sodium soy sauce
2 tsp. canola oil
1 tsp. minced fresh gingerroot
3/4 tsp. sugar
1/4 tsp. minced garlic

1. Cook spaghetti according to package directions; drain and rinse in cold water. Combine the spaghetti, chicken, cucumber and carrot. In a small saucepan, combine the vinegar, soy sauce, oil, ginger, sugar and

garlic. Bring to a boil; remove from the heat. Drizzle over spaghetti mixture and toss to coat.

Nutrition Facts: 1-1/2 cups equals 282 calories, 7 g fat (1 g saturated fat), 36 mg cholesterol, 343 mg sodium, 34 g carbohydrate, 3 g fiber, 19 g protein. **Diabetic Exchanges:** 2 starch, 2 lean meat, 1 vegetable.

Makeover Deluxe Grilled Cheese Ⓜ

PREP/TOTAL TIME: 15 min. **YIELD:** 2 servings

HEALTHY COOKING TEST KITCHEN

With a few simple tricks, our Test Kitchen actually boosted the fantastic toasty taste of these mouthwatering sandwiches, but slashed fat, calories and cholesterol to less than half!

1 small onion, halved and thinly sliced
4 slices French bread (1/2 in. thick)
Butter-flavored cooking spray
1 oz. herbed fresh goat cheese
1/2 small tart apple, thinly sliced
1/2 cup shredded reduced-fat cheddar cheese

1. In a small skillet coated with cooking spray, saute onion until tender; set aside.

2. Place bread slices on a baking sheet; spritz with butter-flavored cooking spray. Broil 4 in. from the heat for 2-3 minutes or until golden-brown.

3. Spread goat cheese over two untoasted sides of bread slices. Top with the apple slices and reserved onion; sprinkle with cheddar cheese. Broil 2-3 minutes longer or until cheese is melted. Top with the remaining slices.

Nutrition Facts: 1 sandwich equals 225 calories, 12 g fat (6 g saturated fat), 30 mg cholesterol, 400 mg sodium, 18 g carbohydrate, 2 g fiber, 12 g protein. **Diabetic Exchanges:** 2 medium-fat meat, 1 starch.

CHICKEN SPAGHETTI SALAD

MAKEOVER DELUXE GRILLED CHEESE

Thyme Chicken Marsala

6 pts

PREP/TOTAL TIME: 30 min. YIELD: 2 servings

DOROTHY SMITH • EL DORADO, ARKANSAS

Here's a quick little recipe with restaurant presentation and flavor, perfect for impromptu entertaining. The simple wine sauce comes together in minutes.

2	boneless skinless chicken breast halves (4 oz. *each*)
1	Tbsp. all-purpose flour
1/8	tsp. plus 1/4 tsp. salt, *divided*
1/8	tsp. plus 1/4 tsp. pepper, *divided*
1	medium carrot, julienned
1	small sweet yellow *or* red pepper, julienned
3	tsp. olive oil, *divided*
2	garlic cloves, minced
1/3	cup marsala wine *or* reduced-sodium chicken broth
1	Tbsp. minced fresh thyme *or* 1 tsp. dried thyme

1. Place chicken in a large resealable plastic bag; flatten to 1/4-in. thickness. Add flour and 1/8 tsp. each salt and pepper; shake to coat. Set aside.

2. In a large skillet, saute the carrot and yellow pepper in 1-1/2 tsp. oil for 3 minutes or until vegetables are tender. Add garlic and remaining salt and pepper; cook 1 minute longer. Transfer to two serving plates; keep warm.

3. In the same skillet, heat remaining oil over medium heat. Cook the chicken for 3-4 minutes on each side or until meat is no longer pink; place over vegetables. Add the wine and thyme to the pan; cook for 1 minute, stirring to loosen browned bits. Serve with chicken.

Nutrition Facts: 1 chicken breast half equals 285 calories, 10 g fat (2 g saturated fat), 63 mg cholesterol, 365 mg sodium, 15 g carbohydrate, 2 g fiber, 24 g protein. **Diabetic Exchanges:** 3 lean meat, 1 starch, 1 fat.

THYME CHICKEN MARSALA

Oven Fish 'n' Chips

9 pts

PREP: 20 min. BAKE: 25 min. YIELD: 2 servings

JANICE MITCHELL • AURORA, COLORADO

Crunchy fillets with a kick of cayenne and crispy potatoes make a quick and tasty light meal for two.

1	Tbsp. olive oil
1/4	tsp. pepper, *divided*
2	medium potatoes, peeled
3	Tbsp. all-purpose flour
1	egg
1	Tbsp. water
1/3	cup crushed cornflakes
1-1/2	tsp. grated Parmesan cheese
Dash cayenne pepper	
1/2	lb. haddock fillets
Tartar sauce, optional	

1. In a large bowl, combine oil and 1/8 tsp. pepper. Cut potatoes lengthwise into 1/2-in. strips. Add to oil mixture and toss to coat. Place on a baking sheet coated with cooking spray. Bake at 425° for 25-30 minutes or until golden-brown and crisp.

2. Meanwhile, in a shallow bowl, combine flour and remaining pepper. In another shallow bowl, beat egg and water. In a third bowl, combine the cornflakes, cheese and cayenne. Dredge fillets in flour, then dip in egg mixture and coat with crumbs.

3. Place on a baking sheet coated with cooking spray. Bake at 425° for 10-15 minutes or until the haddock flakes easily with a fork. Serve with chips and tartar sauce if desired.

Nutrition Facts: 1 serving (calculated without tartar sauce) equals 358 calories, 10 g fat (2 g saturated fat), 131 mg cholesterol, 204 mg sodium, 39 g carbohydrate, 2 g fiber, 28 g protein. **Diabetic Exchanges:** 3 very lean meat, 2-1/2 starch, 2 fat.

Mushroom & Swiss Turkey Burgers

10 pts

PREP/TOTAL TIME: 30 min. YIELD: 2 servings

MELEYNA NOMURA • SCOTTSDALE, ARIZONA

This recipe also works great on the grill. I use the leftover spinach in pesto or omelets or to make another batch of burgers.

1-3/4	cups sliced baby portobello mushrooms
1	tsp. olive oil
1	garlic clove, minced
1/4	tsp. salt, *divided*
1/8	tsp. pepper, *divided*
1/4	cup frozen chopped spinach, thawed and squeezed dry
2	Tbsp. chopped sweet onion
1/2	lb. lean ground turkey
1	slice reduced-fat Swiss cheese, cut in half
2	whole wheat hamburger buns, split and toasted
2	lettuce leaves
2	slices sweet onion
2	slices tomato

HAMBURGER SHEPHERD'S PIE

1. In a small skillet, cook mushrooms in oil until tender. Add garlic; cook 1 minute longer. Stir in 1/8 tsp. salt and a dash of pepper. Remove from the heat; set aside.

2. In a small bowl, combine the spinach, chopped onion and remaining salt and pepper. Crumble turkey over mixture and mix well. Shape into two patties.

3. In a large nonstick skillet coated with cooking spray, cook patties over medium heat for 4 minutes. Turn and cook 3 minutes longer. Top burgers with cheese; cover and cook 3-6 minutes longer or until a meat thermometer reads 165° and cheese is melted. Serve on buns with lettuce, onion, tomato and reserved mushroom mixture.

Nutrition Facts: 1 burger equals 371 calories, 16 g fat (4 g saturated fat), 95 mg cholesterol, 645 mg sodium, 30 g carbohydrate, 5 g fiber, 30 g protein.

Hamburger Shepherd's Pie

PREP: 20 min. BAKE: 30 min. YIELD: 2 servings

ELAINE WILLIAMS • SURREY, BRITISH COLUMBIA

Transform leftovers into a light but filling one-dish meal sized for two. This is a simple and scrumptious recipe.

- 1/2 lb. lean ground beef (90% lean)
- 2 Tbsp. chopped onion
- 1 cup frozen cut green beans, thawed
- 2/3 cup condensed tomato soup, undiluted
- 1/4 tsp. Italian seasoning
- 1/8 tsp. pepper
- 1 cup mashed potatoes (prepared with milk)

Dash paprika

1. In a small skillet, cook beef and onion over medium heat until meat is no longer pink; drain. Add the beans, soup, Italian seasoning and pepper. Transfer to a 7-in. pie plate coated with cooking spray.

2. Spread mashed potatoes over the top; sprinkle with paprika. Bake, uncovered, at 350° for 30-35 minutes or until heated through.

Nutrition Facts: 1/2 pie equals 330 calories, 10 g fat (4 g saturated fat), 71 mg cholesterol, 927 mg sodium, 35 g carbohydrate, 5 g fiber, 26 g protein.

A pinch is thought to be the amount of a dry ingredient that can be held between your thumb and forefinger. A dash **is a very small amount** of seasoning added with a quick downward stroke of the hand. A pinch or a dash of an ingredient is between 1/16 and a scant 1/8 teaspoon.

My Healthy Life

Five *Healthy Cooking* readers created healthful, life-changing plans for themselves and their families. Here, they share their stories as well as some of the recipes that received thumbs-up ratings from their gang!

Daily Jump Start

A healthy, balanced breakfast will give you the fuel your body needs to power through the morning. Jump-start your day with one of these quick and delicious choices, sure to be a big hit with your whole family.

For Judy Parker and her family, the decision to eat right and get healthy was brought on by a life-altering event. "I was diagnosed with cancer at 33," she says. "Fortunately, it was non-aggressive, and the tumor was removed, but it was a wake-up call. We realized life is short, and we only get one body, so we'd better take care of it."

Judy, her husband, Ladd, and their four children, ages 7 to 14, decided to change their eating habits and make activity a priority. "We exercise regularly—we even trained for a triathlon. Our two youngest competed in a kids' version, with our then 5-year-old daughter racing on a tricycle! I took third place once—not bad for a 40-year-old competing against 20-year-olds!"

Judy carries her healthy approach into the kitchen as well. "Ladd and I model good eating habits, because the kids are more likely to follow suit. To make it easy, I keep veggies and fruit on hand, and they know if they want dessert, they must eat their vegetables." Judy's family starts their days right with flavorful breakfast items such as these.

Wholesome Whole Grain Waffles M

PREP: 15 min. **COOK:** 5 min./batch **YIELD:** 12 waffles

JUDY PARKER • MOORE, OKLAHOMA

I created this recipe by tweaking one I had. I added flaxseed, substituted some whole wheat flour for the all-purpose variety, applesauce for some oil and fat-free milk for whole. My family loved the changes, and now this is a favorite.

- 1 cup all-purpose flour
- 1 cup whole wheat flour
- 3 Tbsp. ground flaxseed
- 3 tsp. baking powder
- 1/2 tsp. salt
- 2 eggs, *separated*
- 2 cups fat-free milk
- 3 Tbsp. canola oil
- 3 Tbsp. unsweetened applesauce

Mixed fresh berries and confectioners' sugar, optional

1. In a large bowl, combine the flours, flaxseed, baking powder and salt. Combine the egg yolks, milk, oil and applesauce; stir into the dry ingredients until the mixture is just moistened.

2. In a small bowl, beat egg whites until stiff peaks form; fold into the batter.

BERRY NUTRITIOUS SMOOTHIES

WHOLESOME WHOLE GRAIN WAFFLES

3. Bake in a preheated waffle iron according to manufacturer's directions until golden brown. Serve with berries and confectioners' sugar if desired.

Nutrition Facts: 2 waffles (calculated without berries and confectioners' sugar) equals 278 calories, 11 g fat (1 g saturated fat), 70 mg cholesterol, 456 mg sodium, 37 g carbohydrate, 4 g fiber, 11 g protein. **Diabetic Exchanges:** 2-1/2 starch, 1-1/2 fat.

Berry Nutritious Smoothies F S

PREP/TOTAL TIME: 5 min. YIELD: 3 servings

JUDY PARKER • MOORE, OKLAHOMA

This recipe came from experimenting with a different combination of fruit, yogurt and juice. I generally use whatever fresh or frozen fruit I have on hand, but I always include a frozen banana. We often substitute grape or pineapple juice for the orange juice.

1	cup orange juice
1/2	cup fat-free plain yogurt
1/2	cup silken firm tofu
1	medium ripe banana, sliced and frozen
1/2	cup frozen unsweetened strawberries
1/2	cup frozen unsweetened raspberries
2	Tbsp. toasted wheat germ

1. In a blender, combine all ingredients; cover and process for 30 seconds or until smooth. Pour into chilled glasses; serve immediately.

Nutrition Facts: 1 cup equals 141 calories, 1 g fat (trace saturated fat), 1 mg cholesterol, 35 mg sodium, 28 g carbohydrate, 3 g fiber, 6 g protein.

Easy Breakfast Quesadillas

PREP/TOTAL TIME: 20 min. YIELD: 6 servings

JUDY PARKER • MOORE, OKLAHOMA

We love Mexican food, and this was my attempt to have it for breakfast. If my kids will eat it, then I know it's a winner, and they all love this dish!

4	eggs
1	cup egg substitute
6	whole wheat tortillas (8 in.)
1	cup (4 oz.) shredded reduced-fat cheddar cheese
3	turkey bacon strips, diced and cooked
6	Tbsp. salsa
6	Tbsp. fat-free sour cream

1. In a small bowl, whisk the eggs and egg substitute. Coat a large skillet with cooking spray. Add the egg mixture; cook and stir over medium heat until eggs are completely set.

2. Heat another large nonstick skillet coated with cooking spray; add one tortilla. Top with 1/3 cup cheese, scant 2 tablespoons bacon, 1 cup egg mixture and one tortilla. Cook over medium heat for 2-3 minutes on each side or until lightly browned.

3. Repeat with remaining tortillas, cheese, bacon and eggs, spraying pan as needed. Cut each quesadilla into six wedges. Serve with salsa and sour cream.

Nutrition Facts: 3 wedges with 1 tablespoon salsa and 1 tablespoon sour cream equals 299 calories, 12 g fat (4 g saturated fat), 164 mg cholesterol, 588 mg sodium, 27 g carbohydrate, 2 g fiber, 19 g protein.

Gluten-Free Favorites

Sensitivities to wheat, barley and rye can really make menu planning tough.
With gluten-free ingredients becoming readily available, it's a snap to
create meals that let everyone at your table enjoy the dinner.

Eating right can seem daunting, but imagine doing it with major dietary restrictions. "I tested positive for celiac disease after I'd been living with it for years," says Melissa McCrady, a news anchor and reporter from Wauwatosa, Wisconsin.

"I'd been having stomach trouble for a long time, and was originally diagnosed with irritable bowel syndrome. But in 2009, I went weeks with daily headaches, nausea and dizziness—I even blacked out. My doctor told me that it was stomach related, and after many tests, I was correctly diagnosed."

Melissa gave up gluten, a protein found in breads and other foods that contain wheat, barley or rye. "I'm so sensitive to it," she explains, "I even had to replace cosmetics with gluten-free versions."

Although she's always been fitness minded, Melissa says her diagnosis encourages her to be even healthier. "The reason I've lost weight and feel healthier is partly because I've eliminated most processed foods from my diet." Here, she shares a favorite meal made from fresh ingredients.

GLUTEN-FREE KAHLUA DESSERT

Gluten-Free Mashed Potatoes F M

PREP/TOTAL TIME: 30 min. **YIELD:** 8 servings

MELISSA MCCRADY • WAUWATOSA, WISCONSIN

This simple recipe creates a big batch of fluffy mashed potatoes. You'll be happy for it, as these taste just as good as they look!

4	large potatoes (about 3 lbs.), peeled and quartered
1	medium onion, chopped
1	pkg. (8 oz.) fat-free cream cheese, cubed
1	cup fat-free milk
1-1/4	tsp. salt
1/4	tsp. pepper

1. Place potatoes and onion in a large saucepan and cover with water. Bring to a boil. Reduce heat; cover and simmer for 15-20 minutes or until tender. Drain; transfer to a large bowl.

2. Add the cream cheese, milk, salt and pepper; beat until the potato mixture is fluffy.

Editor's Note: Read all ingredient labels for possible gluten content prior to use. Ingredient formulas can change, and production facilities vary among brands. If you're concerned that your brand may contain gluten, contact the company.

Nutrition Facts: 3/4 cup equals 191 calories, 1 g fat (trace saturated fat), 3 mg cholesterol, 548 mg sodium, 38 g carbohydrate, 3 g fiber, 9 g protein.

Gluten-Free Kahlua Dessert

PREP: 30 min. + chilling **YIELD:** 12 servings

MELISSA MCCRADY • WAUWATOSA, WISCONSIN

Whether you eat a gluten-free diet or not, you'll delight in every bite of this creamy treat that's accented with subtle notes of Kahlua liqueur.

1	cup gluten-free cornflakes, crushed
2	Tbsp. butter, melted
2	tsp. unflavored gelatin
1/4	cup cold water
12	oz. reduced-fat cream cheese
2	Tbsp. sugar
2/3	cup fat-free sweetened condensed milk
1/4	cup Kahlua (coffee liqueur)
2	cups fat-free whipped topping
2	oz. dark chocolate candy bar, melted

Fresh raspberries and mint leaves, optional

GLUTEN-FREE GRILLED FLANK STEAK

1. Combine cornflake crumbs and butter; press onto the bottom of a 9-in. square pan coated with cooking spray. Refrigerate for 10 minutes.

2. Meanwhile, in a small saucepan, sprinkle gelatin over cold water; let stand for 1 minute. Heat over low heat, stirring until gelatin is completely dissolved. Remove from the heat; set aside.

3. In a large bowl, beat cream cheese and sugar until smooth. Beat in the milk, Kahlua and gelatin mixture until blended. Gently fold in whipped topping; pour over crust. Cover and refrigerate for at least 4 hours or until firm.

4. Drizzle with melted chocolate; garnish with raspberries and mint leaves if desired.

Editor's Note: Read all ingredient labels for possible gluten content prior to use. Ingredient formulas can change, and production facilities vary among brands. If you're concerned that your brand may contain gluten, contact the company.

Nutrition Facts: 1 piece (calculated without raspberries) equals 217 calories, 9 g fat (6 g saturated fat), 28 mg cholesterol, 176 mg sodium, 25 g carbohydrate, 1 g fiber, 5 g protein. **Diabetic Exchanges:** 2 fat, 1-1/2 starch.

Gluten-Free Grilled Flank Steak C

PREP: 25 min. + marinating **GRILL:** 15 min.
YIELD: 8 servings

MELISSA MCCRADY • WAUWATOSA, WISCONSIN

Red wine and thyme are the perfect ingredients to turn tender steak into mouthwatering fare. While it offers the added bonus of being gluten-free, any guest at your table will love it.

3/4   cup gluten-free reduced-sodium tamari soy sauce
   2   Tbsp. dried thyme
   1   beef flank steak (2 lbs.)
   3   bunches green onions, chopped
1/3   cup reduced-fat butter
1-1/2   cups dry red wine *or* reduced-sodium beef broth

1. In a large resealable plastic bag, combine soy sauce and thyme. Add the beef; seal bag and turn to coat. Refrigerate for at least 8 hours or overnight.

2. Drain and discard marinade. Grill steak, covered, over medium heat or broil 4 in. from the heat for 6-8 minutes on each side or until meat reaches desired doneness (for medium-rare, a meat thermometer should read 145°; medium, 160°; well-done, 170°). Let stand for 5 minutes.

3. Meanwhile, in a small saucepan, saute onions in butter until tender. Add wine; bring to a boil. Reduce heat; simmer, uncovered, for 10-15 minutes or until sauce is slightly thickened.

4. To serve, thinly slice the steak across the grain; serve with sauce.

Editor's Note: Read all ingredient labels for possible gluten content prior to use. Ingredient formulas can change, and production facilities vary among brands. If you're concerned that your brand may contain gluten, contact the company.

Nutrition Facts: 3 ounces cooked beef with 2 tablespoons sauce equals 234 calories, 12 g fat (6 g saturated fat), 64 mg cholesterol, 486 mg sodium, 4 g carbohydrate, 1 g fiber, 24 g protein. **Diabetic Exchanges:** 3 lean meat, 1 fat.

Fast & From Scratch

A busy schedule can make healthy eating a big challenge, and so can the convenience foods that often go along with a hectic day. These no-fuss recipes keep you from missing a beat–on your calendar and your diet.

Some might say Sarah Klier of Grand Rapids, Michigan, has a tougher time feeding her family healthy meals than some moms. "Both my husband, Ryan, and toddler son, Joseph, have food sensitivities," she explains. "Nearly everything I make needs to come from scratch...and Joseph's been picky."

But this stay-at-home mom (Sarah also has a newborn) uses her family's special diets as another way to make nutritious choices. "We read labels on everything—not just for allergies—but to avoid high fructose corn syrup, partially hydrogenated oils and MSG."

The family has fully embraced their gradual move to a healthier way of life. "We're sometimes looked at as a little extreme by our extended family because of our diet, but we don't mind eating lots of vegetables and staying away from packaged foods—and we're healthier." The menu she shares on these pages features fantastic flavor and an assortment of fruits and veggies, so it's a great choice for Sarah's family and yours as well.

SATURDAY NIGHT PIZZA

Saturday Night Pizza

PREP: 20 min. + rising **BAKE:** 15 min. **YIELD:** 8 servings

SARAH KLIER • GRAND RAPIDS, MICHIGAN

Pizza gets a good-for-you treatment with this tasty idea. Four different vegetables and white whole wheat flour deliver 6 grams of fiber in every serving.

2	to 2-1/2 cups white whole wheat flour
1	pkg. (1/4 oz.) quick-rise yeast
1	Tbsp. dried oregano
1	tsp. salt
1	tsp. garlic powder
1	cup warm water (120° to 130°)
2	Tbsp. olive oil
1/2	lb. Italian turkey sausage links, casings removed
1	cup spaghetti sauce
1	cup fresh baby spinach
1	cup sliced fresh mushrooms
1	medium green pepper, sliced
1	medium onion, sliced
2	cups (8 oz.) shredded part-skim mozzarella cheese

1. In a small bowl, combine 2 cups flour, yeast, oregano, salt and garlic powder. Add water and oil; beat just until moistened. Stir in enough remaining flour to form a soft dough (dough will be sticky).

2. Turn onto a lightly floured surface; knead until smooth and elastic, about 6-8 minutes. Place in a bowl coated with cooking spray, turning once to coat the top. Cover and let rise for 30 minutes.

3. Meanwhile, in a large nonstick skillet, cook sausage until no longer pink; drain and set aside.

4. On a floured surface, roll dough into a 15-in. circle. Transfer to a 14-in. pizza pan coated with cooking spray. Build up edges slightly. Prick dough thoroughly with a fork. Bake at 450° for 5-8 minutes or until lightly browned.

5. Spread crust with spaghetti sauce. Top with spinach, mushrooms, pepper, onion and sausage. Sprinkle with cheese. Bake 15-20 minutes longer or until cheese is melted.

Nutrition Facts: 1 slice equals 298 calories, 12 g fat (4 g saturated fat), 34 mg cholesterol, 756 mg sodium, 32 g carbohydrate, 6 g fiber, 17 g protein. **Diabetic Exchanges:** 2 starch, 2 medium-fat meat.

White Bean Dip C M

PREP/TOTAL TIME: 15 min. **YIELD:** 1-1/2 cups

SARAH KLIER • GRAND RAPIDS, MICHIGAN

Great accompanying fresh veggies or as a sandwich spread, this dip brings a touch of sophistication and loads of flavor and nutrients to any meal.

1/4	cup soft bread crumbs
2	Tbsp. dry white wine or water
2	Tbsp. olive oil
2	Tbsp. lemon juice
1	can (15 oz.) white kidney *or* cannellini beans, rinsed and drained
4-1/2	tsp. minced fresh parsley
3	garlic cloves, peeled and halved
1/2	tsp. salt
1/2	tsp. snipped fresh dill *or* 1/4 tsp. dill weed
1/8	tsp. cayenne pepper

Assorted fresh vegetables

1. In a small bowl, combine bread crumbs and wine. In a food processor, combine the oil, lemon juice, beans, parsley, garlic, salt, dill and cayenne; cover and process until smooth. Add bread crumb mixture; process until blended. Serve with vegetables.

Nutrition Facts: 1/4 cup (calculated without vegetables) equals 107 calories, 5 g fat (1 g saturated fat), 0 cholesterol, 299 mg sodium, 12 g carbohydrate, 3 g fiber, 3 g protein. **Diabetic Exchanges:** 1 starch, 1 fat.

Swedish Apple Pie

PREP: 15 min. **BAKE:** 25 min. **YIELD:** 8 servings

SARAH KLIER • GRAND RAPIDS, MICHIGAN

This hearty and decadent apple pie serves up homemade flavor in every bite. The blend of whole wheat and all-purpose flours offers more fiber and less fat than a traditional pie crust.

1/2	cup sugar
1/4	cup whole wheat flour
1/4	cup all-purpose flour
1	tsp. baking powder
1/2	tsp. salt
1/2	tsp. ground cinnamon
1	egg
1/4	tsp. vanilla extract
2	medium tart apples, chopped
3/4	cup chopped walnuts or pecans, toasted

Confectioners' sugar, optional

1. In a large bowl, combine the sugar, flours, baking powder, salt and cinnamon. In a small bowl, whisk egg and vanilla. Stir into dry ingredients just until moistened. Fold in apples and walnuts.

2. Transfer to a 9-in. pie plate coated with cooking spray. Bake at 350° for 25-30 minutes or until a toothpick inserted near the center comes out clean. Sprinkle with confectioners' sugar if desired. Serve warm.

Nutrition Facts: 1 piece equals 174 calories, 7 g fat (1 g saturated fat), 26 mg cholesterol, 207 mg sodium, 25 g carbohydrate, 2 g fiber, 5 g protein. **Diabetic Exchanges:** 1-1/2 starch, 1 fat.

Naturally Delicious

When it comes to eating right, nothing fits the bill like graden-fresh produce! Whether harvested from your backyard or purchased from a farmers market, fresh ingredients turn everyday meals into healthy opportunities.

Ask *Healthy Cooking* Field Editor Nancy Brown of Dahinda, Illinois, about eating right, and she'll talk more about quality ingredients than calories. "I mostly eat natural, whole foods to get the best nutritional value," she says.

And with good reason. When Nancy was 18, her mom died of a heart attack. "I was a budding cook and just getting into the health craze," she says. "After that, I decided to take care of myself for the people I love. That was 30 years ago."

Today, Nancy, who owns a log home-building business and writes a recipe column for her local paper, is an avid organic gardener who also buys produce from the farmers market. "We grow some of our own produce, but I also want to support farmers' efforts to find alternatives to chemicals."

Nancy also stays energized by exercising. "Besides chasing after my kids, I do yoga and aerobics."

To keep things easy, Nancy relies on planning. "When I know what's for dinner, we can have healthy, quick meals and no excuses," she says.

LEMON FLUFF DESSERT

Weeknight Chicken and Pasta

10pts

PREP/TOTAL TIME: 25 min. **YIELD:** 4 servings

NANCY BROWN • DAHINDA, ILLINOIS

I came up with this dish to use up leftover chicken one night when I had unexpected guests. It was such a success that I make a variation of it almost weekly.

- 2 cups uncooked whole wheat bow tie pasta
- 1 small onion, chopped
- 1 small sweet red pepper, chopped
- 1 Tbsp. olive oil
- 1 garlic clove, minced
- 1-1/2 cups cubed cooked chicken breast
- 1/2 cup reduced-fat sour cream
- 1/4 cup fat-free milk
- 1/2 tsp. salt
- 1/2 tsp. pepper
- 1/2 tsp. dried tarragon
- 1/2 tsp. dried thyme
- 2 Tbsp. shredded Parmesan cheese
- 2 tsp. minced chives

1. Cook pasta according to package directions.

2. Meanwhile, in a large nonstick skillet, saute onion and red pepper in oil until tender. Add garlic; cook 1 minute longer. Stir in the chicken, sour cream, milk and seasonings; heat through. Drain pasta; stir into skillet. Sprinkle with cheese and chives.

Nutrition Facts: 1-1/4 cups equals 394 calories, 9 g fat (3 g saturated fat), 53 mg cholesterol, 399 mg sodium, 48 g carbohydrate, 7 g fiber, 28 g protein.

Whole Wheat Bread **F S M**

PREP: 20 min. + rising **BAKE:** 25 min. + cooling
YIELD: 1 loaf (16 slices)

NANCY BROWN • DAHINDA, ILLINOIS

I make this bread so often I have the recipe memorized. My kids love it for an after-school snack, but it's also great with soup, stew and more.

- 1-1/8 tsp. active dry yeast
- 1-1/4 cups warm water (110° to 115°)
- 1/4 cup packed brown sugar
- 2 Tbsp. reduced-fat butter, melted
- 3/4 tsp. salt
- 1-1/2 cups whole wheat flour
- 2 to 2-1/2 cups all-purpose flour

1. In a large bowl, dissolve yeast in warm water. Add the brown sugar, butter, salt, whole wheat flour and 1 cup all-purpose flour. Beat until smooth. Stir in enough remaining flour to form a firm dough (dough will be sticky).

2. Turn onto a lightly floured surface; knead until smooth and elastic, about 6-8 minutes. Place in a bowl coated with cooking spray, turning once to coat the top. Cover and let rise for 1 hour.

3. Punch dough down and turn onto a floured surface; shape into a loaf. Place in a 9-in. x 5-in. loaf pan coated with cooking spay. Cover and let rise until doubled, about 1 hour.

4. Bake at 375° for 25-30 minutes or until golden brown. Remove from pan to a wire rack to cool.

Nutrition Facts: 1 slice equals 129 calories, 1 g fat (1 g saturated fat), 2 mg cholesterol, 125 mg sodium, 27 g carbohydrate, 2 g fiber, 4 g protein. **Diabetic Exchange:** 1-1/2 starch.

Lemon Fluff Dessert S C

PREP: 15 min. + chilling **YIELD:** 20 servings

NANCY BROWN • DAHINDA, ILLINOIS

This came from my grandmother, who owned a bakery. Her recipe was a full-fat version. I wanted to lighten it up, but I also didn't want to mess with it too much, so I only made a few healthy substitutions. The final outcome was sweet, lemony and light. We sometimes serve it with sliced strawberries over the top of individual pieces.

1	can (12 oz.) evaporated milk
1-1/2	cups graham cracker crumbs
1/3	cup butter, melted
1	pkg. (.3 oz.) sugar-free lemon gelatin
1	cup boiling water
3	Tbsp. lemon juice
1	pkg. (8 oz.) reduced-fat cream cheese
3/4	cup sugar
1	tsp. vanilla extract

1. Pour milk into a large metal bowl; place mixer beaters in the bowl. Cover and refrigerate for at least 2 hours.

2. In a small bowl, combine graham cracker crumbs and butter; set aside 1 tablespoon for topping. Press remaining crumb mixture into a 13-in. x 9-in. baking dish. Chill until set.

3. Meanwhile, in a small bowl, dissolve gelatin in boiling water. Stir in lemon juice; cool.

4. In another bowl, beat the cream cheese, sugar and vanilla until smooth. Add gelatin mixture and mix well. Beat evaporated milk until soft peaks form; fold into cream cheese mixture. Pour over crust. Sprinkle with reserved crumbs. Refrigerate for at least 2 hours before serving. Refrigerate leftovers.

Nutrition Facts: 1 piece equals 135 calories, 7 g fat (4 g saturated fat), 21 mg cholesterol, 136 mg sodium, 15 g carbohydrate, trace fiber, 3 g protein. **Diabetic Exchanges:** 1 starch, 1 fat.

Healthy for Life

We all know crash-dieting does more harm than good, but finding an eating plan that works for the long haul takes a lot of discipline. Need a little inspiration? The recipes on these pages provide a nudge in the right direction.

When it comes to healthy habits, sticking to them can be the hardest part. We found a *Healthy Cooking* Field Editor with impressive tenacity, and she's ready to share her secrets...and recipes.

"For me, it comes down to determination and patience," says Pat Swart, a retired interior designer and architect turned syndicated columnist from Bridgeton, New Jersey. "And the thought of what I'd become if I did not exercise.

"I lift hand weights and walk 5 days a week," says Pat, who has kept up her fitness routine for 30 years. She also cut back on salt 4 decades ago and has been eating healthfully for the past 10 years. "I realized the effect fattening recipes can have and knew mine needed to be lightened."

Pat's menu spotlights her commitment to eating right and offers simple flavors that taste great. "My friends are hooked on these," she says. With their everyday ingredients, fresh taste and minimal prep work, these recipes have a taste we're sure you'll love now...and 10 years from now, too!

ASPARAGUS WITH TARRAGON LEMON SAUCE

Asparagus with Tarragon Lemon Sauce

PREP/TOTAL TIME: 15 min. YIELD: 6 servings

PATRICIA SWART • BRIDGETON, NEW JERSEY

With its effortless prep and delightful flavor, this is a side dish you're sure to love.

2	lbs. fresh asparagus, trimmed
3	Tbsp. olive oil
1	tsp. all-purpose flour
3	Tbsp. fat-free milk
1	Tbsp. lemon juice
2	tsp. minced fresh tarragon

Dash salt

1. Place the asparagus in a steamer basket; place in a large saucepan over 1 in. of water. Bring to a boil; cover and steam for 3-5 minutes or until stems are crisp-tender. Drain.

2. Meanwhile, in a small saucepan, combine olive oil and flour. Gradually stir in milk until smooth. Bring to a boil; cook and stir for 1 minute or until thickened. Remove from the heat. Stir in the lemon juice, tarragon and salt. Serve with asparagus.

Nutrition Facts: 1 serving equals 83 calories, 7 g fat (1 g saturated fat), trace cholesterol, 36 mg sodium, 4 g carbohydrate, 1 g fiber, 2 g protein. **Diabetic Exchanges:** 1 vegetable, 1 fat.

Pork Chops with Apricot Sauce C

PREP/TOTAL TIME: 30 min. YIELD: 6 servings

PATRICIA SWART • BRIDGETON, NEW JERSEY

Apricot preserves bring a very special flavor to the pork. I serve it with corn bread, which can be made in advance and tastes great with any meat.

6	boneless pork loin chops (6 oz. *each*)
1/2	tsp. garlic pepper blend
1	Tbsp. olive oil
1	cup sugar-free apricot preserves
1	Tbsp. minced chives
1/4	tsp. salt

1. Sprinkle pork with garlic pepper blend.

2. In a large nonstick skillet coated with cooking spray, brown chops in oil on each side. Combine the preserves, chives and salt; spoon over chops. Reduce

heat; cover and cook for 8-10 minutes or until a meat thermometer reads 160°. Serve with sauce.

Nutrition Facts: 1 chop with 2 tablespoons sauce equals 273 calories, 12 g fat (4 g saturated fat), 82 mg cholesterol, 169 mg sodium, 13 g carbohydrate, trace fiber, 33 g protein. **Diabetic Exchanges:** 5 lean meat, 1 starch, 1/2 fat.

Buttermilk Corn Bread M

PREP/TOTAL: 30 min. **YIELD:** 8 servings

PATRICIA SWART • BRIDGETON, NEW JERSEY

This tender corn bread couldn't be easier to make, and it's a delicious addition to any menu.

1	cup all-purpose flour
1	cup yellow cornmeal
1	Tbsp. sugar
2	tsp. baking powder
1	tsp. baking soda
1/4	tsp. salt
2	eggs
1	cup buttermilk
3	Tbsp. butter, melted

1. In a large bowl, combine the flour, cornmeal, sugar, baking powder, baking soda and salt. In a small bowl, whisk the eggs, buttermilk and butter. Stir into dry ingredients just until moistened.

2. Transfer to a 9-in. square baking pan coated with cooking spray. Bake at 400° for 15-20 minutes or until top is lightly browned and a toothpick inserted near the center comes out clean. Serve warm.

Nutrition Facts: 1 piece equals 194 calories, 6 g fat (3 g saturated fat), 65 mg cholesterol, 412 mg sodium, 28 g carbohydrate, 2 g fiber, 6 g protein. **Diabetic Exchanges:** 2 starch, 1 fat.

For the best results when making **corn bread**, avoid overmixing the batter. Stir it by hand just until moistened. (Lumps in the batter are a good thing.) In addition, don't let the mixed batter stand before baking. Have the oven preheated and the skillet or pan ready to go.

CHOCOLATE CHIP COOKIES

SWEDISH TEA RING

GLUTEN-FREE ANGEL FOOD CAKE

Cakes, Pies & More

A demanding sweet tooth can make it hard to stick to a healthy lifestyle. No need to skip dessert: Our rich cheesecakes, chocolaty bars and chewy cookies will do the trick. You'll cure your craving *and* stay on track!

Gluten-Free Angel Food Cake F

PREP: 15 min. BAKE: 45 min. + cooling
YIELD: 16 servings

ANNE WIEBE • GLADSTONE, MANITOBA

My daughter can't have gluten, and my husband is diabetic, so there are a lot of special recipes at our house. This cake is always on our family gathering table.

1-1/2 cups egg whites (about 10)
3/4 cup plus 1/2 cup sugar, *divided*
1/4 cup cornstarch
1/4 cup white rice flour
1/4 cup tapioca flour
1/4 cup potato starch
1-1/2 tsp. cream of tartar
3/4 tsp. salt
3/4 tsp. vanilla extract
Assorted fresh fruit, optional

1. Place egg whites in a large bowl; let stand at room temperature for 30 minutes. Sift 3/4 cup sugar, cornstarch, flours and potato starch together twice; set aside.

2. Add cream of tartar, salt and vanilla to egg whites; beat on medium speed until soft peaks form. Gradually add remaining sugar, about 2 Tbsp. at a time, beating on high until stiff peaks form. Gradually fold in flour mixture, about 1/2 cup at a time.

3. Gently spoon into an ungreased 10-in. tube pan. Cut through the batter with a knife to remove air pockets. Bake on the lowest oven rack at 350° for 45-50 minutes or until lightly browned and entire top appears dry. Immediately invert pan; cool completely, about 1 hour.

4. Run a knife around side and center tube of pan. Remove cake to a plate. Top with fruit if desired.

Editor's Note: Read all ingredient labels for possible gluten content prior to use. Ingredient formulas can change, and production facilities vary among brands. If you're concerned that your brand may contain gluten, contact the company.

Nutrition Facts: 1 slice (calculated without fruit) equals 101 calories, trace fat (0 saturated fat), 0 cholesterol, 149 mg sodium, 23 g carbohydrate, trace fiber, 3 g protein. **Diabetic Exchange:** 1-1/2 starch.

Chocolate Chip Cookies

PREP: 15 min. BAKE: 10 min./batch + cooling
YIELD: 4 dozen

BETHANY THAYER • TROUTVILLE, VIRGINIA

Chocolate chip cookies are almost anyone's favorites, and these are sure to please!

1/2 cup reduced-fat margarine
3/4 cup sugar
3/4 cup packed brown sugar
2 eggs
1/4 cup (2 oz.) reduced-fat plain yogurt
2 tsp. vanilla extract
2-1/2 cups all-purpose flour
1 tsp. baking soda
1 tsp. salt
1-1/2 cups miniature semisweet chocolate chips
1/2 cup chopped walnuts, toasted

1. In a large bowl, lightly cream the margarine and sugars. Add eggs, one at a time, beating well after each addition. Beat in the yogurt and vanilla. Combine the flour, baking soda and salt; gradually add to the creamed mixture. Stir in the chocolate chips and walnuts.

2. Drop by heaping tablespoonfuls 2 in. apart onto baking sheets coated with cooking spray. Bake at 375° for 8-10 minutes or until cookies are golden brown. Remove to wire racks.

Nutrition Facts: 1 cookie equals 94 calories, 4 g fat (1 g saturated fat), 9 mg cholesterol, 93 mg sodium, 15 g carbohydrate, 1 g fiber, 1 g protein. **Diabetic Exchanges:** 1 starch, 1/2 fat.

When you're baking an **angel food cake,** use an oven thermometer to make sure the oven is not baking at a different temperature than you set it. Remember to place the pan on the lowest rack to allow sufficient air circulation over the top of such a tall cake.

Cocoa-Almond Meringue Cookies F S C

PREP: 20 min. BAKE: 50 min. + standing YIELD: 3 dozen

HEALTHY COOKING TEST KITCHEN

Here's a simple recipe that makes a great hostess gift. It also comes in handy around the holidays.

4	egg whites
1/2	tsp. coconut extract
1/4	tsp. almond extract
1/4	tsp. vanilla extract
1/4	tsp. cream of tartar
1/8	tsp. salt
1	cup sugar
1/4	cup plus 1 Tbsp. baking cocoa, *divided*

1. Place egg whites in a large bowl; let stand at room temperature for 30 minutes. Add the extracts, cream of tartar and salt; beat on medium speed until soft peaks form. Gradually beat in sugar, 1 Tbsp. at a time, on high until stiff peaks form and sugar is dissolved.

2. Fold in 1/4 cup cocoa. Place mixture in a pastry or heavy-duty resealable plastic bag; cut a small hole in the corner of bag. Pipe meringue in 2-in. circles onto parchment paper-lined baking sheets. Bake at 250° for 50-60 minutes or until set and dry. Turn off oven; leave cookies in oven for 1-1/2 hours.

3. Dust the cookies with the remaining cocoa. Carefully remove from the parchment paper. Store in an airtight container.

Nutrition Facts: 1 cookie equals 26 calories, trace fat (0 saturated fat), 0 cholesterol, 14 mg sodium, 6 g carbohydrate, trace fiber, 1 g protein. **Diabetic Exchange:** 1/2 starch.

COCOA-ALMOND MERINGUE COOKIES

Low-Fat Carrot Cake F S

PREP: 30 min. BAKE: 30 min. + cooling
YIELD: 16 servings

REBECCA BAIRD • SALT LAKE CITY, UTAH

Loaded with spice and carrot flavor, this moist and luscious cake is guaranteed to impress.

2	cups packed brown sugar
1/2	cup buttermilk
2	egg whites
1	egg
2	Tbsp. canola oil
1	tsp. vanilla extract
2-1/2	cups cake flour
1	tsp. baking soda
1	tsp. ground cinnamon
1/2	tsp. ground allspice
1/4	tsp. ground nutmeg
1/4	tsp. ground cloves
1/8	tsp. salt
3	cups grated carrots
1	can (8 oz.) unsweetened crushed pineapple, drained
2	oz. reduced-fat cream cheese
1	cup confectioners' sugar
1/2	tsp. lemon juice
1/8	tsp. vanilla extract

1. In a large bowl, beat the brown sugar, buttermilk, egg whites, egg, oil and vanilla until well blended. Combine the flour, baking soda, spices and salt; gradually beat into sugar mixture until blended. Fold in carrots and pineapple. Pour into a 13-in. x 9-in. baking dish coated with cooking spray.

2. Bake at 350° for 30-35 minutes or until a toothpick inserted near the center comes out clean. Cool completely on a wire rack.

3. In a small bowl, beat cream cheese until fluffy. Add the confectioners' sugar, lemon juice and vanilla; beat until smooth. Drizzle over cake.

Nutrition Facts: 1 piece equals 263 calories, 3 g fat (1 g saturated fat), 16 mg cholesterol, 98 mg sodium, 56 g carbohydrate, 1 g fiber, 3 g protein.

Swedish Tea Ring

PREP: 30 min. + rising BAKE: 20 min. + cooling
YIELD: 1 ring (24 slices)

ELSIE EPP • NEWTON, KANSAS

This showstopper will add a special touch to any dessert buffet. It's a lovely confection for coffee gatherings, too.

1	Tbsp. active dry yeast
1-1/2	cups warm water (110° to 115°)
1/4	cup sugar
1/4	cup canola oil
2	egg whites, lightly beaten
1-1/4	tsp. salt
5-1/2	to 6 cups all-purpose flour
1/2	cup chopped walnuts

SWEDISH TEA RING

1/2 cup chopped maraschino cherries, patted dry
1/4 cup packed brown sugar
1 tsp. ground cinnamon
2 Tbsp. butter, melted

ICING:
1 cup confectioners' sugar
1 to 2 Tbsp. fat-free milk

1. In a large bowl, dissolve yeast in warm water. Add the sugar, oil, egg whites, salt and 1 cup flour; beat until smooth. Stir in enough remaining flour to form a soft dough.

2. Turn onto a lightly floured surface; knead until smooth, about 6-8 minutes. Place in a bowl coated with cooking spray, turning once to coat the top. Cover and let rise until doubled, about 1 hour.

3. Combine the walnuts, cherries, brown sugar and cinnamon; set aside. Punch dough down; roll into an 18-in. x 12-in. rectangle. Brush with butter; sprinkle with nut mixture to within 1/2 in. of edges. Roll up jelly-roll style, starting with a long side; pinch seam to seal.

4. Place seam side down on a 14-in. pizza pan coated with cooking spray; pinch ends together to form a ring. With scissors, cut from outside edge two-thirds of the way toward center of ring at scant 1-in. intervals. Separate the strips slightly; twist them to allow filling to show. Cover and let rise until doubled, about 40 minutes.

5. Bake at 400° for 20-25 minutes or until golden brown. Remove from pan to a wire rack to cool. Combine icing ingredients; drizzle over tea ring.

Nutrition Facts: 1 slice equals 196 calories, 5 g fat (1 g saturated fat), 3 mg cholesterol, 142 mg sodium, 34 g carbohydrate, 1 g fiber, 4 g protein. **Diabetic Exchanges:** 2 starch, 1 fat.

Refrigerate **cinnamon roll dough** between kneading and rising, or after shaping it. Store it in a tightly covered bowl or a resealable plastic bag and, if needed, punch it down after 1 to 2 hours and each subsequent day.

MAKEOVER CHERRY PIE DELIGHT

Makeover Cherry Pie Delight F S

PREP: 30 min. BAKE: 10 min. YIELD: 8 servings

HEALTHY COOKING TEST KITCHEN

Chock-full of cherries, this little gem is packed with all the flavors that make cherry pie a classic, in a far lighter form.

- 1   sheet refrigerated pie pastry
- 1   egg white
- 1   Tbsp. water
- 2   tsp. coarse sugar
- 1/2 cup sugar
- 1/4 cup cornstarch
- 1   cup cherry juice blend
- 2   cans (14-1/2 oz. *each*) pitted tart cherries, drained
- 1   cup reduced-fat vanilla ice cream

1. Roll out pastry onto a lightly floured surface. Cut into 1/2-in.-wide strips; make a lattice crust. Beat egg white and water; brush over top. Sprinkle with coarse sugar. Using a floured 2-in. round cookie cutter, cut out eight circles. Place 2 in. apart on ungreased baking sheets. Bake at 450° for 10-12 minutes or until lightly browned. Remove to a wire rack.

2. Meanwhile, in a small saucepan, combine sugar and cornstarch. Stir in cherry juice until smooth. Bring to a boil; cook and stir for 2 minutes or until thickened. Remove from the heat; add cherries.

3. Spoon about 1/3 cup warm cherry mixture into each of eight dessert dishes. Top with 2 Tbsp. ice cream and garnish with a cookie.

Editor's Note: Save time and calories by making the delightful little cookies (shown in photo) instead of an entire pie crust for this dessert. These crispy toppers are so simple to whip up, yet make an impressive presentation.

Nutrition Facts: 1 serving equals 183 calories, 3 g fat (2 g saturated fat), 6 mg cholesterol, 59 mg sodium, 37 g carbohydrate, 1 g fiber, 2 g protein.

Oatmeal Cake With Caramel Icing

PREP: 30 min. BAKE: 20 min. + cooling
YIELD: 20 servings

SUMMER MARKS • LOUISVILLE, KENTUCKY

This tastes anything but light. The icing sets up quick, so frost the cake immediately after it cools.

- 1-1/4 cups boiling water
- 1   cup quick-cooking oats
- 1/4 cup butter, softened
- 1   cup packed brown sugar
- 1/2 cup sugar
- 2   eggs
- 1/4 cup unsweetened applesauce
- 1   tsp. vanilla extract
- 1-1/2 cups all-purpose flour
- 2   tsp. baking powder
- 3/4 tsp. ground cinnamon
- 1/2 tsp. baking soda
- 1/2 tsp. salt
- 1/4 tsp. ground nutmeg

ICING:
- 1/2 cup packed brown sugar
- 1/4 cup butter, cubed
- 1/4 cup fat-free milk
- 1/2 tsp. vanilla extract
- 1/8 tsp. salt
- 1-1/2 cups confectioners' sugar

1. In a small bowl, pour boiling water over oats; let stand for 10 minutes.

2. Meanwhile, in a large bowl, beat butter and sugars until crumbly, about 2 minutes. Add eggs, one at a time, beating well after each addition. Beat in applesauce and vanilla. Combine the flour, baking powder, cinnamon, baking soda, salt and nutmeg. Gradually add to creamed mixture. Stir in the oats. Pour into a 13-in. x 9-in. baking pan coated with cooking spray.

3. Bake at 350° for 18-22 minutes or until a toothpick inserted near the center comes out with moist crumbs. Cool completely on a wire rack.

4. For icing, in a small saucepan, combine brown sugar and butter. Bring to a boil over medium heat, stirring constantly. Cook and stir for 1 minute. Gradually whisk in milk. Return to a boil. Cook and stir 1 minute longer. Transfer to a small bowl. Stir in vanilla and salt. Gradually beat in confectioners' sugar until smooth. Immediately spread icing over cake. Let stand until set.

Nutrition Facts: 1 piece equals 216 calories, 5 g fat (3 g saturated fat), 33 mg cholesterol, 193 mg sodium, 41 g carbohydrate, 1 g fiber, 2 g protein.

Cranberry Pecan Bars F S C

PREP: 15 min. **BAKE:** 40 min. + cooling
YIELD: 1 to 1-1/2 dozen

BEVERLY MCCLARREN • FINDLAY, OHIO

I like to mix cranberries, coconut and a little orange peel into the filling of my rich pecan bars. Whenever I serve these at gatherings, people ask if I'll share the recipe with them.

    1   cup all-purpose flour
    1/2 cup finely chopped pecans
    1/2 cup packed brown sugar
    1/2 tsp. salt
    6   Tbsp. cold butter
FILLING:
    2   Tbsp. all-purpose flour
    1/2 tsp. baking powder
    2   eggs, beaten
    1   cup sugar
    1   Tbsp. milk
    1   Tbsp. vanilla extract
    1   cup fresh or frozen cranberries, chopped
    1/2 cup flaked coconut
    1/2 cup chopped pecans
  1-1/2 tsp. grated orange peel

1. In a large bowl, combine the flour, pecans, brown sugar and salt. Cut in butter until crumbly. Press onto a greased 9-in. square baking dish. Bake at 350° for 15-20 minutes or until edges are lightly browned.

2. Meanwhile, in a large bowl, combine the flour and baking powder. Combine the eggs, sugar, milk and vanilla; add to the dry ingredients. Fold in the cranberries, coconut, pecans and orange peel. Pour over the crust. Bake 25-30 minutes longer or until bars are set. Cool on a wire rack. Cut into the bars. Refrigerate any leftovers.

Nutrition Facts: 1 bar equals 200 calories, 10 g fat (4 g saturated fat), 34 mg cholesterol, 132 mg sodium, 26 g carbohydrate, 1 g fiber, 2 g protein.

Gluten-Free Almond Crispies F S C

PREP: 20 min. **BAKE:** 10 min./batch
YIELD: about 3 dozen

JEAN ECOS • HARTLAND, WISCONSIN

Here's a wonderful treat everyone in the family can enjoy. Ideal with milk or tea, these cookies impart hints of cinnamon and maple in every crunchy bite.

    1/3 cup maple syrup
    1/4 cup canola oil
    1   Tbsp. water
    1   tsp. almond extract
    1   cup brown rice flour
    1/2 cup almond flour
    1/4 cup sugar
    1   tsp. baking powder
    1   tsp. ground cinnamon
    1/8 tsp. salt
    1/2 cup finely chopped almonds

1. In a small bowl, beat the syrup, oil, water and extract until well blended. Combine the flours, sugar, baking powder, cinnamon and salt; gradually beat into the syrup mixture until blended. Stir in almonds.

2. Drop by rounded teaspoonfuls onto parchment paper-lined baking sheets; flatten slightly. Bake at 350° for 10-12 minutes or until bottoms are lightly browned. Cool for 1 minute before removing from pans to wire racks.

Editor's Note: Read all ingredient labels for possible gluten content prior to use. Ingredient formulas can change, and production facilities vary among brands. If you're concerned that your brand may contain gluten, contact the company.

Nutrition Facts: 1 cookie equals 54 calories, 3 g fat (trace saturated fat), 0 cholesterol, 18 mg sodium, 6 g carbohydrate, 1 g fiber, 1 g protein. **Diabetic Exchanges:** 1/2 starch, 1/2 fat.

GLUTEN-FREE ALMOND CRISPIES

Lemon Crumb Cake

PREP: 20 min. BAKE: 30 min. + cooling
YIELD: 20 servings

KATIE WOLLGAST • FLORISSANT, MISSOURI

I like to serve up this light, lip-smacking, lemony cake at any springtime brunch or dinner.

- 2 cups buttermilk
- 1 cup sugar
- 2 eggs
- 2 Tbsp. butter, melted
- 2 tsp. vanilla extract
- 3 cups all-purpose flour
- 1-1/4 tsp. baking powder
- 1 tsp. salt
- 1/2 tsp. baking soda
- 1 can (15-3/4 oz.) lemon pie filling

TOPPING:
- 1 cup all-purpose flour
- 2/3 cup sugar
- 1/3 cup cold butter, cubed
- 1/4 cup sliced almonds, toasted

Reduced-fat vanilla ice cream, optional

1. In a large bowl, beat the first five ingredients until well blended. In a small bowl, combine the flour, baking powder, salt and baking soda; gradually beat into buttermilk mixture until blended. Pour into a 13-in. x 9-in. baking pan coated with cooking spray. Drop pie filling by teaspoonfuls over batter.

2. In a small bowl, combine flour and sugar. Cut in butter until crumbly. Stir in almonds; sprinkle over batter. Bake at 350° for 30-35 minutes or until a toothpick inserted near the center comes out clean.

3. Cool for 10 minutes on a wire rack. Serve warm with ice cream if desired.

Nutrition Facts: 1 piece (calculated without ice cream) equals 295 calories, 7 g fat (3 g saturated fat), 62 mg cholesterol, 255 mg sodium, 53 g carbohydrate, 1 g fiber, 5 g protein.

Amaretto-Almond Bliss Cookies S C

PREP: 20 min. BAKE: 10 min./batch YIELD: 2-1/2 dozen

VERA DECKER • WINDSOR, NEW YORK

I trimmed down these sweet, chunky cookies, and now they're guilt-free and delicious!

- 1/3 cup butter, softened
- 1/2 cup sugar
- 1/3 cup packed brown sugar
- 1 egg
- 2 Tbsp. Amaretto
- 1/2 tsp. almond extract
- 1 cup all-purpose flour
- 1 cup oat flour
- 1 tsp. baking powder
- 1 tsp. baking soda
- 1/4 tsp. salt
- 3/4 cup miniature semisweet chocolate chips
- 2/3 cup sliced almonds, toasted

1. In a large bowl, beat butter and sugars until crumbly, about 2 minutes. Add egg; mix well. Stir in Amaretto and almond extract. Combine the flours, baking powder, baking soda and salt; gradually add to butter mixture and mix well. Stir in chocolate chips and almonds.

2. With lightly floured hands, shape into 1-in. balls. Place them 2 in. apart on baking sheets coated with cooking spray. Flatten balls slightly with a glass coated with cooking spray.

3. Bake at 350° for 7-9 minutes or until the tops are cracked and the bottoms are lightly browned. Remove to wire racks.

LEMON CRUMB CAKE

AMARETTO-ALMOND BLISS COOKIES

Editor's Note: As a substitute for 1 cup oat flour, process 1-1/4 cups quick-cooking or old-fashioned oats until finely ground.

Nutrition Facts: 1 cookie equals 106 calories, 5 g fat (2 g saturated fat), 12 mg cholesterol, 93 mg sodium, 15 g carbohydrate, 1 g fiber, 2 g protein. **Diabetic Exchanges:** 1 starch, 1 fat.

Honey Cheese Bars S

PREP: 25 min. BAKE: 30 min. + cooling YIELD: 16 bars

EDNA HOFFMAN • HEBRON, INDIANA

If you like cheesecake, you'll love this light dessert. Walnuts lend a subtle nutty taste to the crust, and honey and lemon make the creamy topping a pure delight.

    1   cup all-purpose flour
    1/3 cup packed brown sugar
    1/4 cup cold butter, cubed
    1/2 cup finely chopped walnuts

FILLING:
    1   pkg. (8 oz.) reduced-fat cream cheese
    1/4 cup honey
    2   Tbsp. milk
    1   Tbsp. lemon juice
    1/2 tsp. vanilla extract
    1   egg, lightly beaten
Additional honey, optional

1. In a small bowl, combine flour and brown sugar. Cut in butter until crumbly. Stir in walnuts. Press onto the bottom of an 8-in. square baking dish coated with cooking spray. Bake at 350° for 10-12 minutes or until lightly browned.

2. For filling, in a large bowl, beat the cream cheese, honey, milk, lemon juice and vanilla until blended. Add egg; beat on low speed just until combined. Pour

over crust. Bake 20-25 minutes longer or until set. Cool completely on a wire rack. Drizzle with additional honey if desired. Cut into bars. Refrigerate any leftovers.

Nutrition Facts: 1 bar (calculated without additional honey) equals 152 calories, 8 g fat (4 g saturated fat), 31 mg cholesterol, 88 mg sodium, 16 g carbohydrate, trace fiber, 4 g protein. **Diabetic Exchanges:** 2 fat, 1 starch.

Heavenly Chocolate Pie

PREP: 15 min. + chilling YIELD: 8 servings

DONNA ROBERTS • MANHATTAN, KANSAS

I rely on fat-free, sugar-free and reduced-fat products for my dessert. What a lovely way to satisfy chocolate cravings!

    1   cup fat-free vanilla frozen yogurt, softened
    2   cups fat-free milk
    1   pkg. (1.4 oz.) sugar-free instant chocolate pudding mix
    1   pkg. (1 oz.) sugar-free instant vanilla pudding mix
    1   carton (8 oz.) frozen reduced-fat whipped topping, thawed, *divided*
    1   reduced-fat graham cracker crust (8 in.)
Chocolate curls, optional

1. In a large bowl, whisk yogurt until soft and smooth. Gradually whisk in milk until blended. Add pudding mixes; whisk 2 minutes longer. Let stand for 2 minutes or until soft-set.

2. Fold in 1 cup whipped topping. Transfer to crust. Top with remaining whipped topping and chocolate curls if desired. Refrigerate for at least 4 hours.

Nutrition Facts: 1 piece equals 235 calories, 6 g fat (4 g saturated fat), 2 mg cholesterol, 433 mg sodium, 40 g carbohydrate, trace fiber, 5 g protein.

MAKEOVER
TRADITIONAL
CHEESECAKE

Makeover Traditional Cheesecake

PREP: 40 min. **BAKE:** 1-1/2 hours + chilling
YIELD: 16 servings

ANNE ADDESSO • SHEBOYGAN, WISCONSIN

Though softer than a full-fat cheesecake, this lightened-up dessert has all of the original's delectable flavor. It's sure to make any special event more festive.

1-3/4 cups graham cracker crumbs
  2 Tbsp. confectioners' sugar
  1/4 cup butter, melted

FILLING:
  1 Tbsp. lemon juice
  1 Tbsp. vanilla extract
  2 cups (16 oz.) 1% cottage cheese
  2 cups (16 oz.) reduced-fat sour cream, *divided*
  2 pkg. (8 oz. *each*) reduced-fat cream cheese
1-1/4 cups sugar
  2 Tbsp. all-purpose flour
  4 eggs, lightly beaten
  1 Tbsp. fat-free caramel ice cream topping
  2 Heath candy bars (1.4 oz. *each*), chopped

1. Place a 9-in. springform pan coated with cooking spray on a double thickness of heavy-duty foil (about 18 in. square). Securely wrap foil around pan.

2. In a small bowl, combine graham cracker crumbs and confectioners' sugar; stir in butter. Press onto the bottom and 1 in. up the sides of prepared pan. Place on a baking sheet. Bake at 325° for 18-22 minutes or until lightly browned. Cool on a wire rack.

3. Place the lemon juice, vanilla, cottage cheese and 1 cup sour cream in a blender; cover and process for 2 minutes or until smooth.

4. In a large bowl, beat cream cheese and sugar until smooth. Beat in the remaining sour cream. Add the flour and pureed cottage cheese mixture; mix well. Add the eggs; beat on low speed just until combined. Pour into crust.

5. Place springform pan in a larger baking pan; add 3/4 in. of hot water to larger pan. Bake at 325° for 1-1/2 hours or until center is just set and top appears dull. Remove springform pan from water bath. Cool on a wire rack for 10 minutes.

6. Carefully run a knife around the edge of the pan to loosen; cool 1 hour longer. Refrigerate overnight. Remove sides of pan. Garnish with caramel topping and chopped candy.

Nutrition Facts: 1 slice equals 311 calories, 15 g fat (9 g saturated fat), 93 mg cholesterol, 369 mg sodium, 32 g carbohydrate, trace fiber, 11 g protein.

Makeover Meringue Coconut Brownies §

PREP: 30 min. **BAKE:** 30 min. + cooling **YIELD:** 2 dozen

ELLEN AHO • SOUTH PARIS, MAINE

A chocolate-lover's dream, these bars have a rich, pleasant combination of flavors.

- 1/3 cup butter, softened
- 1/3 cup plus 3/4 cup packed brown sugar, *divided*
- 1/3 cup sugar
- 1 tsp. vanilla extract
- 2 cups all-purpose flour
- 1/2 tsp. baking soda
- 1/4 tsp. salt
- 1/3 cup fat-free milk
- 1 cup (6 oz.) semisweet chocolate chips
- 1 cup flaked coconut
- 1/2 cup chopped walnuts
- 3 egg whites
- 1/4 tsp. cream of tartar

1. In a small bowl, cream the butter, 1/3 cup brown sugar and sugar until light and fluffy. Beat in vanilla. Combine the flour, baking soda and salt; add to the creamed mixture alternately with milk, beating well after each addition. Press into a 13-in. x 9-in. baking pan coated with cooking spray. Sprinkle with chocolate chips, coconut and walnuts.

2. In a large bowl, beat egg whites and cream of tartar until soft peaks form. Gradually beat in remaining brown sugar, 1 tablespoonful at a time. Beat until stiff peaks form. Spread over the top. Bake at 350° for 30-35 minutes or until a toothpick inserted near the center comes out clean (do not overbake).

3. Cool on a wire rack. Cut into bars. Store in the refrigerator.

Nutrition Facts: 1 brownie equals 181 calories, 8 g fat (4 g saturated fat), 7 mg cholesterol, 92 mg sodium, 27 g carbohydrate, 1 g fiber, 2 g protein. **Diabetic Exchanges:** 2 starch, 1 fat.

Peanut Butter-Chocolate Chip Cookies F S C

PREP: 15 min. + chilling **BAKE:** 10 min./batch
YIELD: 4-1/2 dozen

MURIEL MABLESON • WINNIPEG, MANITOBA

I stir a few chocolate chips into the melted butters to give my cookie batter a little extra chocolate flavor.

- 1/2 cup butter, cubed
- 1/3 cup reduced-fat creamy peanut butter
- 1/4 cup unsweetened applesauce
- 3/4 cup sugar
- 3/4 cup packed brown sugar
- 2 eggs
- 1-1/2 tsp. vanilla extract
- 2-1/4 cups all-purpose flour
- 1/2 tsp. baking soda
- 1/2 tsp. ground cinnamon
- 1/4 tsp. salt
- 1/2 cup semisweet chocolate chips

1. In a small microwave-safe bowl, microwave butter and peanut butter until butter is melted; stir until smooth. Stir in applesauce.

2. Transfer to a large bowl. Beat in the sugars until blended. Beat in eggs and vanilla. Combine the flour, baking soda, cinnamon and salt; gradually add to peanut butter mixture and mix well. Stir in chocolate chips. Cover and refrigerate for at least 2 hours.

3. Drop by tablespoonfuls 2 in. apart onto baking sheets coated with cooking spray. Bake at 350° for 7-9 minutes or until lightly browned. Remove to wire racks. Store in an airtight container.

Nutrition Facts: 1 cookie equals 75 calories, 3 g fat (2 g saturated fat), 12 mg cholesterol, 47 mg sodium, 11 g carbohydrate, trace fiber, 1 g protein. **Diabetic Exchanges:** 1 starch, 1/2 fat.

MAKEOVER MERINGUE COCONUT BROWNIES

PEANUT BUTTER-CHOCOLATE CHIP COOKIES

Makeover Italian Cream Cake

PREP: 40 min. **BAKE:** 20 min. + cooling
YIELD: 16 servings

CHRISTY WHITE • OXFORD, MISSISSIPPI

Toasted pecans and coconut take this moist cake from good to great, but it's the cream cheese frosting that makes it truly extraordinary. Thank goodness it's a makeover, because you'll definitely want seconds!

1/3	cup butter, softened
1	cup sugar
2	eggs
1/3	cup unsweetened applesauce
1/2	tsp. vanilla extract
1-1/3	cups all-purpose flour
3/4	tsp. baking soda
1/8	tsp. salt
2/3	cup buttermilk
1/3	cup chopped pecans, toasted
1/4	cup flaked coconut, toasted

CREAM CHEESE FROSTING:

1	pkg. (8 oz.) cream cheese, softened
2	Tbsp. butter, softened
2	cups confectioners' sugar
1/2	tsp. vanilla extract
1/3	cup chopped pecans, toasted

1. Line two 9-in. round baking pans with waxed paper. Coat pans with cooking spray and sprinkle with flour; set aside.

2. In a large bowl, beat butter and sugar until crumbly, about 2 minutes. Add eggs, one at a time, beating well after each addition. Beat in applesauce and vanilla (mixture will appear curdled). Combine the flour, baking soda and salt; add to creamed mixture alternately with buttermilk. Fold in pecans and coconut.

3. Pour into prepared pans. Bake at 350° for 18-22 minutes or until a toothpick inserted near the center comes out clean. Cool for 10 minutes before removing from pans to wire racks to cool completely.

4. For frosting, in a large bowl, beat cream cheese and butter until fluffy. Add confectioners' sugar and vanilla; beat until smooth. Spread frosting between layers and over top and sides of cake. Sprinkle pecans over top of cake. Store in the refrigerator.

Nutrition Facts: 1 slice equals 297 calories, 15 g fat (7 g saturated fat), 56 mg cholesterol, 180 mg sodium, 38 g carbohydrate, 1 g fiber, 4 g protein.

Makeover Macaroon Cake

PREP: 20 min. **BAKE:** 65 min. + cooling
YIELD: 16 servings

GAYE ANDREE • ROCHESTER, NEW YORK

This is one of my husband's favorite recipes and now with it made over, he can really enjoy it, and even go back for seconds!

6	egg whites
4	egg yolks
2-1/4	cups sugar
1/2	cup unsweetened applesauce
1/4	cup canola oil
3/4	cup fat-free milk
1/2	tsp. almond extract
1-1/2	cups cake flour
1-1/2	cups all-purpose flour
1	cup flaked coconut
3	tsp. baking powder
1/4	tsp. salt
1/2	tsp. cream of tartar
1	tsp. confectioners' sugar

MAKEOVER MACAROON CAKE

MAKEOVER ITALIAN CREAM CAKE

RAISIN-NUT CHOCOLATE CAKE

1. Let the egg whites stand at room temperature for 30 minutes. In a large bowl, beat the egg yolks, sugar, applesauce and oil until well blended; beat in milk and almond extract. Combine the flours, coconut, baking powder and salt; gradually beat into the egg yolk mixture until blended.

2. In another bowl, beat egg whites and cream of tartar until stiff peaks form; fold into batter.

3. Gently spoon into an ungreased 10-in. tube pan. Cut through batter with a knife to remove air pockets. Bake on the lowest oven rack at 325° for 65-75 minutes or until cake springs back when lightly touched. Immediately invert pan; cool completely, about 1 hour.

4. Run a knife around side and center tube of pan. Remove cake to a serving plate. Sprinkle with confectioners' sugar.

Nutrition Facts: 1 slice equals 287 calories, 7 g fat (3 g saturated fat), 51 mg cholesterol, 155 mg sodium, 52 g carbohydrate, 1 g fiber, 5 g protein.

Raisin-Nut Chocolate Cake

PREP: 20 min. **BAKE:** 40 min. + cooling
YIELD: 16 servings

KAREN SUE GARBACK-PRISTERA • ALBANY, NEW YORK

My husband really enjoys this delightful cake. Eye-catching enough for a special occasion, this is so good you'll want it any day of the week.

1/3 cup butter, softened
1 cup packed brown sugar
2 eggs
1-1/2 cups unsweetened applesauce
1/2 cup plus 3 Tbsp. brewed coffee, room temperature, *divided*
2 cups all-purpose flour
1/4 cup plus 3 Tbsp. baking cocoa, *divided*
1-1/2 tsp. ground cinnamon
1 tsp. baking soda
1 tsp. ground allspice
1/2 tsp. salt
1/4 tsp. ground cloves
1-1/2 cups raisins
3/4 cup chopped walnuts
1-1/3 cups confectioners' sugar

1. In a large bowl, cream butter and brown sugar until well blended. Add eggs, one at a time, beating well after each addition. Beat in applesauce and 1/2 cup coffee. Combine the flour, 1/4 cup baking cocoa, cinnamon, baking soda, allspice, salt and cloves; gradually beat into creamed mixture until blended. Fold in raisins and walnuts.

2. Pour into a 10-in. fluted tube pan coated with cooking spray. Bake at 350° for 40-45 minutes or until a toothpick inserted near the center comes out clean. Cool for 10 minutes before removing from pan to a wire rack to cool completely.

3. In a small bowl, combine the confectioners' sugar and remaining baking cocoa and coffee; drizzle over the cake.

Nutrition Facts: 1 slice equals 284 calories, 8 g fat (3 g saturated fat), 36 mg cholesterol, 196 mg sodium, 51 g carbohydrate, 2 g fiber, 5 g protein.

MAKEOVER PEANUT BUTTER CUP CHEESECAKE

Makeover Peanut Butter Cup Cheesecake

PREP: 30 min. **BAKE:** 50 min. + chilling
YIELD: 16 servings

SHARON ANDERSON • LYONS, ILLINOIS

No one will ever guess this decadently rich, firmer-textured cheesecake has been lightened up!

3/4	cup graham cracker crumbs
2	Tbsp. sugar
2	Tbsp. butter, melted
3/4	cup creamy peanut butter

FILLING:

2	pkg. (8 oz. *each*) fat-free cream cheese
1	pkg. (8 oz.) reduced-fat cream cheese
1	cup (8 oz.) reduced-fat sour cream
3/4	cup sugar
2	eggs, lightly beaten
1-1/2	tsp. vanilla extract
3/4	cup hot fudge ice cream topping, *divided*
6	peanut butter cups, cut into small wedges

1. In a small bowl, combine the cracker crumbs, sugar and butter. Press onto the bottom of a 9-in. springform pan coated with cooking spray.

2. Place pan on a baking sheet. Bake at 350° for 10 minutes. Cool on a wire rack. In a microwave-safe bowl, heat the peanut butter on high for 30 seconds or until softened. Spread over the crust to within 1 in. of the edges.

3. In a large bowl, beat the cream cheese, sour cream and sugar until smooth. Add the eggs; beat on low speed just until combined. Stir in vanilla. Pour 1 cup into a bowl; set aside. Pour remaining filling over the peanut butter layer.

4. In a microwave-safe bowl, heat 1/4 cup fudge topping on high for 30 seconds or until thin; fold into the reserved cream cheese mixture. Carefully pour over filling; cut through with a knife to swirl.

5. Return pan to baking sheet. Bake for 50-60 minutes or until center is almost set. Cool on a wire rack for 10 minutes. Carefully run a knife around edge of pan to loosen; cool 1 hour longer.

6. Microwave remaining fudge topping on high for 30 seconds or until warmed; spread over cheesecake. Garnish with peanut butter cups. Refrigerate overnight.

Nutrition Facts: 1 slice equals 316 calories, 16 g fat (6 g saturated fat), 47 mg cholesterol, 361 mg sodium, 32 g carbohydrate, 1 g fiber, 12 g protein.

Citrus Cornmeal Cake ⓢ

PREP: 25 min. **BAKE:** 25 min. **YIELD:** 8 servings

ROXANNE CHAN • ALBANY, CALIFORNIA

Cornmeal adds a rustic quality to this delicate dessert flavored with citrus and almond. It's sure to be a staple in your recipe collection and also makes a perfect hostess gift.

1/2	cup lemon yogurt
1/3	cup honey
1/4	cup olive oil
1	egg
2	egg whites
1/4	tsp. almond extract
3/4	cup all-purpose flour
1/2	cup cornmeal
1	tsp. baking powder
1/2	tsp. grated orange peel
1	can (15 oz.) mandarin oranges, drained
3	Tbsp. slivered almonds

1. Coat a 9-in. fluted tart pan with a removable bottom with cooking spray. In a large bowl, beat the yogurt, honey, oil, egg, egg whites and almond extract until well blended. Combine the flour, cornmeal and baking powder; gradually beat into the yogurt mixture until blended. Stir in the orange peel.

2. Pour into a prepared pan. Arrange the oranges over the batter; sprinkle with almonds. Bake at 350° for 25-30 minutes or until a toothpick inserted near the center comes out clean. Cool on a wire rack for 10 minutes before cutting. Serve warm or at room temperature.

Nutrition Facts: 1 slice equals 240 calories, 9 g fat (1 g saturated fat), 27 mg cholesterol, 85 mg sodium, 36 g carbohydrate, 2 g fiber, 5 g protein.

Gluten-Free Brownies ⑤

PREP: 15 min. BAKE: 30 min. + cooling YIELD: 1 dozen

JEAN ECOS • HARTLAND, WISCONSIN

At parties, friends and family rarely realize that these fudgy, moist brownies are gluten-free, as well as flourless. What's more, they're usually shocked when I divulge the secret ingredient: garbanzo beans!

1-1/4 cups semisweet chocolate chips
    1 can (15 oz.) garbanzo beans or chickpeas, rinsed and drained
    3 egg whites
    1 egg
    2 Tbsp. instant coffee granules, optional
    2 Tbsp. canola oil
1-1/2 tsp. vanilla extract
  1/2 cup packed brown sugar
  1/2 tsp. baking powder
Dash salt
  1/2 cup chopped walnuts, optional

1. In a microwave, melt chocolate chips; stir until smooth. Cool slightly.

2. Meanwhile, place the garbanzo beans, egg whites, egg, coffee granules if desired, oil and vanilla extract in a food processor. Cover and process until the mixture is smooth.

3. In a small bowl, combine the brown sugar, baking powder and salt; add to bean mixture. Cover and process until combined. Gradually add the chocolate; process until blended.

4. Pour the batter into a 9-in. square baking pan coated with cooking spray. Sprinkle with walnuts if desired. Bake at 350° for 30-35 minutes or until a toothpick inserted near the center comes out dotted with moist crumbs (do not overbake). Cool completely on a wire rack.

Editor's Note: Read all ingredient labels for possible gluten content prior to use. Ingredient formulas can change, and production facilities vary among brands. If you're concerned that your brand may contain gluten, contact the company.

Nutrition Facts: 1 brownie equals 184 calories, 9 g fat (3 g saturated fat), 18 mg cholesterol, 100 mg sodium, 26 g carbohydrate, 2 g fiber, 4 g protein. **Diabetic Exchanges:** 1-1/2 starch, 1-1/2 fat.

Makeover Rum Cake

PREP: 15 min. BAKE: 40 min. + cooling
YIELD: 16 servings

CATHARINE SEMAN • PITTSBURGH, PENNSYLVANIA

Makeover Rum Cake is draped in a shiny glaze, and has only about half the calories and cholesterol as the original version. But it's still tender and as good with coffee in the morning as it is at the end of a special meal. Now that's definitely something worth celebrating.

  1/2 cup chopped pecans, toasted
    1 pkg. (18-1/4 oz.) yellow cake mix
  1/2 cup fat-free milk
  1/4 cup dark rum
  1/4 cup canola oil
  1/4 cup unsweetened applesauce
    2 eggs
GLAZE:
  1/2 cup sugar
  1/4 cup butter, cubed
    2 Tbsp. water
    2 Tbsp. dark rum

1. Coat a 10-in. fluted tube pan with cooking spray and sprinkle with flour; add pecans. In a large bowl, combine the cake mix, milk, rum, oil, applesauce and eggs; beat on low speed for 30 seconds. Beat on medium for 2 minutes.

2. Pour into prepared pan. Bake at 325° for 40-45 minutes or until a toothpick inserted near the center comes out clean. Cool for 10 minutes before removing from pan to a wire rack to cool completely.

3. In a small saucepan, combine glaze ingredients. Bring to a boil. Reduce heat; cook and stir for 4-5 minutes or until thickened. Drizzle over cake.

Nutrition Facts: 1 slice equals 251 calories, 12 g fat (4 g saturated fat), 34 mg cholesterol, 243 mg sodium, 34 g carbohydrate, trace fiber, 2 g protein.

MAKEOVER RUM CAKE

Taste-of-Summer Light Pound Cake

PREP: 20 min. BAKE: 35 min. + cooling
YIELD: 12 servings

JILL BELLROSE • PORTLAND, OREGON

This delicious, reduced-calorie pound cake brings the bright look and taste of summer to your table year-round.

- 1/2 cup butter, softened
- 1 cup sugar
- 2 egg whites
- 1 egg
- 1 Tbsp. lemon juice
- 1 tsp. lemon extract
- 1 tsp. vanilla extract
- 1-1/2 cups all-purpose flour
- 1 cup whole wheat pastry flour
- 2 tsp. baking powder
- 1/2 tsp. salt
- 1/4 tsp. baking soda
- 3/4 cup (6 oz.) fat-free lemon yogurt

GLAZE:
- 3/4 cup confectioners' sugar
- 4 tsp. lemon juice
- 1 tsp. grated lemon peel
- 1/3 cup dried apricots, finely chopped

1. In a large bowl, cream the butter and sugar until light and fluffy. Add the egg whites, then the egg, beating well after each addition. Beat in lemon juice and extracts. Combine the flours, baking powder, salt and baking soda; add to the creamed mixture alternately with yogurt.

2. Transfer to a 10-in. fluted tube pan coated with cooking spray. Bake at 350° for 35-40 minutes or until a toothpick inserted near the center comes out clean. Cool for 10 minutes before removing from the pan to a wire rack to cool completely.

3. For glaze, in a small bowl, whisk the confectioners' sugar, lemon juice and lemon peel until blended. Stir in apricots. Drizzle over cake.

Nutrition Facts: 1 slice equals 276 calories, 8 g fat (5 g saturated fat), 38 mg cholesterol, 267 mg sodium, 46 g carbohydrate, 2 g fiber, 4 g protein.

Makeover Hummingbird Cake

PREP: 25 min. BAKE: 25 min. + cooling
YIELD: 24 servings

SUE JERNIGAN • FREDERICKSBURG, VIRGINIA

With pineapple, bananas, nuts and just a hint of cinnamon, this cake gets raves at potlucks and parties!

- 2 cups mashed ripe bananas (3 to 4 medium)
- 1 can (8 oz.) unsweetened crushed pineapple, drained
- 3/4 cup unsweetened applesauce
- 1/3 cup canola oil
- 2 eggs
- 1-1/2 tsp. vanilla extract
- 3 cups all-purpose flour
- 1-1/2 cups sugar
- 1 tsp. salt
- 1 tsp. baking soda
- 1 tsp. ground cinnamon
- 1/2 cup chopped walnuts

ICING:
- 1 pkg. (8 oz.) reduced-fat cream cheese
- 1/3 cup reduced-fat butter
- 3 cups confectioners' sugar
- 1 tsp. vanilla extract
- 1/2 cup chopped walnuts

TASTE-OF-SUMMER LIGHT POUND CAKE

MAKEOVER HUMMINGBIRD CAKE

MAKEOVER SEMISWEET ESPRESSO CHEESECAKE

1. In a large bowl, beat the first six ingredients until well blended. In another bowl, combine the flour, sugar, salt, baking soda and cinnamon; gradually beat into banana mixture until blended. Stir in walnuts.

2. Pour into a 15-in. x 10-in. x 1-in. baking pan coated with cooking spray. Bake at 350° for 25-30 minutes or until a toothpick inserted near the center comes out clean. Cool completely on a wire rack.

3. For icing, in a large bowl, beat cream cheese and butter until fluffy. Add confectioners' sugar and vanilla; beat until smooth. Spread over cake. Sprinkle with walnuts. Refrigerate leftovers.

Editor's Note: This recipe was tested with Land O'Lakes light stick butter.

Nutrition Facts: 1 piece equals 290 calories, 10 g fat (3 g saturated fat), 28 mg cholesterol, 219 mg sodium, 47 g carbohydrate, 1 g fiber, 5 g protein.

Makeover Semisweet Espresso Cheesecake

PREP: 30 min. **BAKE:** 40 min. + chilling
YIELD: 16 servings

SONYA LABBE • SANTA MONICA, CALIFORNIA

With fabulous flavor and a firmer texture that cuts like a breeze, this dish has only half the saturated fat and cholesterol as my original.

- 2 cups crushed reduced-fat cream-filled chocolate sandwich cookies (about 20 cookies)
- 2 Tbsp. butter, melted
- 3 pkg. (8 oz. *each*) reduced-fat cream cheese
- 1 pkg. (8 oz.) fat-free cream cheese
- 1 cup sugar
- 2 eggs, lightly beaten
- 3 Tbsp. coffee liqueur
- 2 Tbsp. instant espresso powder
- 1 tsp. vanilla extract
- 2 oz. semisweet chocolate, melted and cooled

1. Place a 9-in. springform pan coated with cooking spray on a double thickness of heavy-duty foil (about 18 in. square). Securely wrap foil around pan.

2. In a small bowl, combine cookie crumbs and butter. Press onto the bottom of prepared pan. Place pan on a baking sheet. Bake at 325° for 10 minutes. Cool on a wire rack.

3. In a large bowl, beat cream cheeses and sugar until smooth. Add the eggs; beat on low speed just until combined. Stir in the coffee liqueur, espresso powder and vanilla. Remove 1-1/4 cups batter to a small bowl; stir in chocolate until well blended.

4. Pour plain batter over crust. Drop chocolate batter by tablespoonfuls over plain batter. Cut through batter with a knife to swirl. Place springform pan in a large baking pan; add 1 in. of hot water to larger pan.

5. Bake at 325° for 40-45 minutes or until center is just set and top appears dull. Remove springform pan from water bath. Cool on a wire rack for 10 minutes. Carefully run a knife around edge of pan to loosen; cool 1 hour longer. Refrigerate overnight. Remove sides of pan.

Nutrition Facts: 1 slice equals 272 calories, 14 g fat (8 g saturated fat), 61 mg cholesterol, 355 mg sodium, 29 g carbohydrate, 1 g fiber, 8 g protein.

EGG- AND LACTOSE-FREE CHOCOLATE CUPCAKES

ISAIAH'S PUMPKIN MUFFINS WITH CRUMBLE TOPPING

ANGEL FOOD TRIFLE

Treat Yourself

Eating right doesn't mean cutting out all of your favorite foods...and that includes luscious desserts and sweet treats! Turn here when you want a little indulgence that keeps your commitment to healthy living.

Angel Food Trifle F

PREP/TOTAL TIME: 15 min. YIELD: 8 servings

MERWYN GARBINI • TUCSON, ARIZONA

A creamy ricotta-vanilla "custard" cuts calories and boosts calcium in this light take on an English classic. Best of all, it's a no-bake delight that comes together easily with readily available ingredients!

    2 cups fat-free vanilla yogurt
    1 cup part-skim ricotta cheese
    1 cup fresh blueberries
    1 cup sliced fresh strawberries
    4 cups cubed angel food cake
  1/2 cup reduced-fat whipped topping

1. In a blender, combine yogurt and ricotta cheese; cover and process until combined.

2. In a small bowl, combine blueberries and strawberries. Place half the cake cubes in a 2-qt. glass bowl. Layer with 1 cup berries and half the yogurt mixture. Top with remaining cake cubes, 3/4 cup berries and the remaining yogurt mixture. Garnish with remaining berries. Top with whipped topping. Refrigerate leftovers.

Nutrition Facts: 3/4 cup equals 182 calories, 3 g fat (2 g saturated fat), 11 mg cholesterol, 248 mg sodium, 30 g carbohydrate, 1 g fiber, 8 g protein. **Diabetic Exchanges:** 1-1/2 starch, 1/2 fat-free milk, 1/2 fat.

Isaiah's Pumpkin Muffins With Crumble Topping

PREP: 25 min. BAKE: 25 min. YIELD: 1 dozen

SILVANA NARDONE • BROOKLYN, NEW YORK

These tender muffins have a subtle pumpkin flavor and sugary topping that make them special. They're an ideal snack for my son, Isaiah, who needs foods that are free of gluten. Fabulous warm, the muffins make a quick on-the-go breakfast your whole family will love.

1-3/4 cups gluten-free all-purpose baking flour
    1 cup sugar
    2 tsp. baking powder
    2 tsp. pumpkin pie spice
  3/4 tsp. salt

    2 eggs
    1 cup canned pumpkin
  1/2 cup canola oil
    3 tsp. vanilla extract

TOPPING:
  1/4 cup gluten-free all-purpose baking flour
  1/4 cup sugar
  1/4 cup packed brown sugar
  1/2 tsp. pumpkin pie spice
  1/4 cup shortening

Confectioners' sugar, optional

1. In a large bowl, combine the flour, sugar, baking powder, pie spice and salt. In another bowl, combine the eggs, pumpkin, oil and vanilla. Stir into dry ingredients just until moistened. Coat muffin cups with cooking spray or use paper liners; fill three-fourths full with batter.

2. For topping, combine the flour, sugar, brown sugar and pie spice; cut in shortening until crumbly. Sprinkle over batter. Bake at 350° for 25-30 minutes or until a toothpick inserted near the center comes out clean.

3. Cool for 5 minutes before removing from pan to a wire rack. Dust with confectioners' sugar if desired.

Editor's Note: Read all ingredient labels for possible gluten content prior to use. Ingredient formulas can change, and production facilities vary among brands. If you're concerned that your brand may contain gluten, contact the company.

Nutrition Facts: 1 muffin (calculated without confectioners' sugar) equals 306 calories, 15 g fat (2 g saturated fat), 35 mg cholesterol, 229 mg sodium, 42 g carbohydrate, 3 g fiber, 3 g protein.

> **Brown sugar** is a mixture of granulated sugars and molasses, with dark brown sugar containing more molasses than light brown. Light brown sugar has a delicate flavor while dark brown sugar has a stronger molasses flavor. They can be used interchangeably.

Egg- and Lactose-Free Chocolate Cupcakes

PREP: 20 min. **BAKE:** 20 min. + cooling
YIELD: 1-1/2 dozen

HEALTHY COOKING TEST KITCHEN

These super-chocolaty, moist cupcakes don't have eggs or lactose, but they don't lack a bit of flavor. A yummy treat that travels well and appeals to all ages, this is one recipe you'll keep handy year-round.

2	cups water
1-1/2	cups sugar
1/2	cup unsweetened applesauce
1/3	cup canola oil
3	tsp. vanilla extract
3	cups all-purpose flour
1/2	cup baking cocoa
1-1/4	tsp. baking powder
1	tsp. salt
1/2	tsp. baking soda

FROSTING:

1/3	cup lactose-free margarine, softened
2	cups confectioners' sugar
1/3	cup baking cocoa
2	Tbsp. water
3/4	tsp. vanilla extract

1. In a large bowl, beat the water, sugar, applesauce, oil and vanilla until well blended. In a small bowl, combine the flour, cocoa, baking powder, salt and baking soda; gradually beat into the sugar mixture until blended.

2. Fill foiled-lined muffin cups three-fourths full. Bake at 350° for 18-22 minutes or until a toothpick inserted near the center comes out clean. Cool for 10 minutes before removing from pans to wire racks to cool completely.

3. In a small bowl, beat margarine until fluffy. Add the confectioners' sugar, cocoa, water and vanilla; beat until smooth. Frost cupcakes.

EGG- AND LACTOSE-FREE CHOCOLATE CUPCAKES

Nutrition Facts: 1 cupcake equals 275 calories, 8 g fat (1 g saturated fat), 0 cholesterol, 234 mg sodium, 49 g carbohydrate, 1 g fiber, 3 g protein.

Poppy Seed Torte

PREP: 50 min. + chilling **BAKE:** 15 min. + cooling
YIELD: 16 servings

BRENDA PATTERSON • PULLMAN, WASHINGTON

I got this recipe from my grandmother; it's an old-fashioned dessert, but well worth the effort. My dad requests this cake every year for his birthday. I make it for church events and charity auctions, too. Everyone loves it!

3	eggs, *separated*
1/4	cup butter, softened
3/4	cup sugar blend
1/4	cup unsweetened applesauce
1-1/2	tsp. vanilla extract, *divided*
2-1/2	cups plus 1 Tbsp. all-purpose flour, *divided*
3	tsp. baking powder
3/4	tsp. baking soda
1/2	tsp. salt
1-3/4	cups buttermilk
1/4	cup poppy seeds
1	cup sugar
1	cup (8 oz.) reduced-fat sour cream
1/4	cup confectioners' sugar
1-1/2	tsp. baking cocoa
1-1/2	to 2 tsp. cold brewed coffee
1/4	cup chopped walnuts, toasted

1. Place egg whites in a small bowl; let stand at room temperature for 30 minutes. Coat three 9-in. round baking pans with cooking spray; line with waxed paper and coat the paper. Sprinkle with flour; set aside.

2. In a large bowl, beat butter and sugar blend until crumbly, about 2 minutes. Beat in applesauce and 1 teaspoon vanilla. Combine 2-1/2 cups flour, baking powder, baking soda and salt; add to creamed mixture alternately with buttermilk. Fold in poppy seeds.

3. Beat egg whites on medium speed until soft peaks form; fold into batter. Spread into prepared pans. Bake at 350° for 12-18 minutes or until a toothpick comes out clean. Cool for 10 minutes before removing from pans to wire racks to cool completely.

4. For filling, in a small saucepan, combine sugar and remaining flour. Stir in sour cream until smooth. Bring to a boil. Stir a small amount of hot mixture into egg yolks; return all to the pan, stirring constantly. Bring to a gentle boil; cook and stir 2 minutes longer. Remove from the heat. Stir in remaining vanilla. Transfer to a bowl; refrigerate until chilled.

5. Place one cake layer on a serving platter; top with a third of the filling. Repeat layers twice.

6. Combine the confectioners' sugar, cocoa and enough coffee to achieve a drizzling consistency. Drizzle over the cake. Sprinkle with nuts. Refrigerate until serving.

GRILLED FRUIT SKEWERS WITH CHOCOLATE SYRUP

Editor's Note: This recipe was tested with Splenda sugar blend.
Nutrition Facts: 1 slice equals 261 calories, 8 g fat (3 g saturated fat), 54 mg cholesterol, 288 mg sodium, 43 g carbohydrate, 1 g fiber, 6 g protein.

Cinnamon-Spiced Bananas S

PREP/TOTAL TIME: 10 min. YIELD: 4 servings

JANET HOMES • SURPRISE, ARIZONA

The whole family will adore this special treat that uses the microwave so it's ready in a flash. Plus, it's a delicious way to jazz up bananas and add more fruit to your diet.

- 3 large bananas, sliced
- 3 Tbsp. brown sugar
- 3/4 tsp. vanilla extract
- 1/4 tsp. ground cinnamon
- 1 Tbsp. butter
- 1 cup reduced-fat vanilla ice cream

1. Place the bananas in a small microwave-safe bowl. Top with brown sugar, vanilla and cinnamon; dot with the butter.

2. Cover and microwave on high for 1-2 minutes or until the sugar is melted, stirring once. Spoon the banana mixture into bowls; top with the ice cream. Serve immediately.

Nutrition Facts: 1/2 cup banana mixture with 1/4 cup reduced-fat vanilla ice cream equals 211 calories, 5 g fat (3 g saturated fat), 16 mg cholesterol, 50 mg sodium, 42 g carbohydrate, 3 g fiber, 3 g protein.

Grilled Fruit Skewers with Chocolate Syrup F S

PREP/TOTAL TIME: 25 min. YIELD: 8 servings

MELISSA BIRDSONG • GILBERT, SOUTH CAROLINA

With toasted angel food cake and chocolate syrup, this recipe makes fruit seem especially decadent. It's the perfect treat for a summer party.

- 2 cups cubed angel food cake
- 1 cup fresh strawberries
- 1 cup cubed fresh pineapple
- 1 cup cubed cantaloupe
- 1 large banana, cut into 1-in. slices
- 2 medium plums, pitted and quartered
  Butter-flavored cooking spray
- 1/2 cup packed brown sugar
- 8 tsp. chocolate syrup

1. On eight metal or soaked wooden skewers, alternately thread the cake cubes and fruits. Spritz each skewer with butter-flavored spray and roll in brown sugar.

2. Place skewers on a piece of heavy-duty foil. Place foil on grill rack. Grill, covered, over medium heat for 4-5 minutes on each side or until fruits are tender, turning once. Drizzle each skewer with 1 teaspoon chocolate syrup.

Nutrition Facts: 1 skewer equals 131 calories, 1 g fat (trace saturated fat), 0 cholesterol, 93 mg sodium, 30 g carbohydrate, 2 g fiber, 2 g protein. **Diabetic Exchanges:** 1 starch, 1 fruit.

BERRY-MARSHMALLOW TRIFLE

Berry-Marshmallow Trifle

PREP/TOTAL TIME: 25 min. **YIELD:** 10 servings

SHANNON ALDRIDGE • SUWANEE, GEORGIA

My guests say this is almost too pretty to eat! I like the way it can be made a day ahead for convenience, and neither taste nor appearance is compromised.

1-3/4	cups cold fat-free milk
1	package (1 oz.) sugar-free instant vanilla pudding mix
1	carton (8 oz.) frozen fat-free whipped topping, thawed, *divided*
1	loaf (10-3/4 oz.) frozen reduced-fat pound cake, thawed and cut into 1-in. cubes
3	cups fresh strawberries, halved
2	cups miniature marshmallows
3	Tbsp. sliced almonds

1. In a small bowl, whisk milk and pudding mix for 2 minutes. Let stand for 2 minutes or until soft-set. Fold in 2-1/2 cups whipped topping; set aside.

2. Place half of cake cubes in a 3-qt. trifle bowl; spoon half of reserved pudding mixture over the top. Top with half of strawberries and marshmallows.

3. Repeat layers. Top with remaining whipped topping; sprinkle with almonds. Chill until serving.

Nutrition Facts: 1 cup equals 230 calories, 6 g fat (1 g saturated fat), 18 mg cholesterol, 298 mg sodium, 40 g carbohydrate, 2 g fiber, 4 g protein.

Orange Cream Pops F S C

PREP: 5 min. + freezing **YIELD:** 10 pops

LAURIE PAYTON • COTTONWOOD, CALIFORNIA

Yogurt adds creaminess, calcium and a hint of tang to these frosty three-ingredient treats.

2	cups (16 oz.) plain yogurt
1	can (6 oz.) frozen orange juice concentrate, thawed
2	tsp. vanilla extract
10	Popsicle molds *or* paper cups (3 oz. *each*) and Popsicle sticks

1. In a small bowl, combine the yogurt, orange juice concentrate and vanilla. Fill each mold or cup with 1/4 cup yogurt mixture; top with holders or insert sticks into cups. Freeze.

Nutrition Facts: 1 pop equals 59 calories, 2 g fat (1 g saturated fat), 6 mg cholesterol, 23 mg sodium, 9 g carbohydrate, trace fiber, 2 g protein. **Diabetic Exchange:** 1/2 starch.

Poached Peaches with Cream Cheese Filling S

PREP: 25 min. + chilling **YIELD:** 4 servings

GREG FONTENOT • THE WOODLANDS, TEXAS

Chocolate chips and confectioners' sugar add to the natural sweetness of these perfectly poached peaches.

       4 cups water
       1 cup sugar
       1 tsp. vanilla extract
    1/4 tsp. ground cinnamon
       2 medium peaches
       3 oz. reduced-fat cream cheese
       2 Tbsp. confectioners' sugar
       2 Tbsp. miniature semisweet chocolate chips
       1 Tbsp. orange juice
Additional ground cinnamon

1. In a large saucepan, combine the water, sugar, vanilla and cinnamon; add peaches. Bring to a boil. Reduce heat; cover and simmer for 10-15 minutes or until peaches are tender. Remove peaches with a slotted spoon; cool to room temperature. Discard cooking liquid. Halve, pit and peel peaches; refrigerate until chilled.

2. In a small bowl, beat the cream cheese, confectioners' sugar, chocolate chips and orange juice until blended. Pipe or spoon into peach halves. Sprinkle with additional cinnamon.

Nutrition Facts: 1 stuffed peach half equals 135 calories, 6 g fat (4 g saturated fat), 15 mg cholesterol, 91 mg sodium, 18 g carbohydrate, 1 g fiber, 3 g protein. **Diabetic Exchanges:** 1 starch, 1 fat, 1/2 fruit.

Makeover Bread Pudding

PREP: 20 min. **BAKE:** 40 min. **YIELD:** 15 servings

APRIL TAYLOR • APO, AE

I used to feel guilty serving bread pudding, but this light take offers the same warm and cozy flavors as my original recipe.

       8 cups cubed day-old bread
       4 eggs
       1 cup egg substitute
    2-1/4 cups fat-free milk
    1-3/4 cups half-and-half cream
    1/2 cup sugar
    1/3 cup butter, melted
       3 tsp. vanilla extract
    1-1/2 tsp. ground cinnamon
CARAMEL SAUCE:
       1 cup packed brown sugar
       3 Tbsp. all-purpose flour
       1 cup fat-free milk
       2 egg yolks, lightly beaten
       2 Tbsp. butter

1. Place bread cubes in a 13-in. x 9-in. baking dish coated with cooking spray. In a large bowl, whisk the eggs, egg substitute, milk, cream, sugar, butter, vanilla and cinnamon. Pour evenly over bread.

2. Bake, uncovered, at 350° for 40-45 minutes or until a knife inserted near the center comes out clean.

3. For caramel sauce, in a small saucepan, combine brown sugar and flour. Stir in milk until smooth. Cook and stir over medium-high heat until thickened and bubbly. Reduce heat; cook and stir for 2 minutes.

4. Remove from the heat. Stir a small amount of hot mixture into egg yolks; return all to pan, stirring constantly. Bring to a gentle boil; cook and stir for 2 minutes. Remove from the heat; gently stir in butter. Serve with pudding. Refrigerate leftovers.

Nutrition Facts: 1 piece with about 2 tablespoons sauce equals 278 calories, 11 g fat (6 g saturated fat), 113 mg cholesterol, 262 mg sodium, 36 g carbohydrate, 1 g fiber, 8 g protein.

MAKEOVER BREAD PUDDING

POACHED PEACHES WITH CREAM CHEESE FILLING

Candy Bar Cupcakes

PREP: 30 min. BAKE: 20 min. + cooling
YIELD: 1-1/2 dozen

EDIE DESPAIN • LOGAN, UTAH

Everyone in my family loves cupcakes, so I experimented to create these treats that fit my family's tastes. I also tried to make them healthier. I hope you enjoy them as much as we do!

1	cup sugar
1	cup buttermilk
1/4	cup canola oil
1	tsp. vanilla extract
1-1/2	cups all-purpose flour
1/3	cup baking cocoa
1	tsp. baking soda
1/2	tsp. salt

FILLING:

6	oz. fat-free cream cheese
2	Tbsp. confectioners' sugar
1	egg
2	Snickers candy bars (2.07 oz. each), finely chopped

FROSTING:

1/3	cup butter, cubed
1/3	cup packed brown sugar
3	Tbsp. fat-free milk
1-1/2	cups confectioners' sugar

1. In a large bowl, beat the sugar, buttermilk, oil and vanilla until well blended. Combine the flour, cocoa, baking soda and salt; gradually beat into sugar mixture until blended.

2. For filling, in a small bowl, beat cream cheese and confectioners' sugar until light and fluffy. Add egg; mix well. Stir in the candy bars.

3. Fill paper-lined muffin cups one-third full with batter. Drop filling by tablespoonfuls into the center of each cupcake (cups will be about half full). Bake at 350° for 20-25 minutes or until a toothpick inserted in the filling comes out clean. Cool for 10 minutes before removing from pans to wire racks to cool completely.

4. For frosting, in a small saucepan, melt butter. Stir in brown sugar. Bring to a boil; cook for two minutes, stirring occasionally. Remove from the heat; stir in the milk, then confectioners' sugar. Cool until frosting reaches spreading consistency. Frost cupcakes.

Nutrition Facts: 1 cupcake equals 250 calories, 9 g fat (3 g saturated fat), 23 mg cholesterol, 248 mg sodium, 40 g carbohydrate, 1 g fiber, 4 g protein.

Strawberry Rhubarb Sauce F S

PREP/TOTAL TIME: 15 min. YIELD: 1-3/4 cups

MIA WERNER • WAUKEGAN, ILLINOIS

Try this easy, scrumptious sauce spooned over pound cake, ice cream, pancakes, waffles or just use it on top of toast. It's as good served cold as it is warm.

2	cups halved fresh strawberries
1	cup sliced fresh *or* frozen rhubarb
2/3	cup sugar
1	Tbsp. cornstarch
2	Tbsp. cold water

1. In a small saucepan, combine the strawberries, rhubarb and sugar. Bring to a boil over medium heat. Combine cornstarch and water until smooth; stir into fruit mixture. Cook and stir for 1-2 minutes or until thickened. Serve warm or chilled.

Editor's Note: If using frozen rhubarb, measure rhubarb while still frozen, then thaw completely. Drain in a colander, but do not press liquid out.

Nutrition Facts: 1/4 cup equals 96 calories, trace fat (trace saturated fat), 0 cholesterol, 1 mg sodium, 24 g carbohydrate, 1 g fiber, trace protein.

Makeover Chocolate Croissant Pudding

PREP: 25 min. BAKE: 55 min. + standing
YIELD: 12 servings

SONYA LABBE • SANTA MONICA, CALIFORNIA

My father is French, and I have a lot of family recipes that involve croissants. Thankfully, the "Healthy Cooking" Test Kitchen transformed my best-loved dessert into a delectable, slimmed-down version without sacrificing the croissants we all adore so much.

6	day-old croissants, split
2/3	cup semisweet chocolate chips
8	eggs
5	cups 2% milk
1	cup sugar
1-1/2	tsp. vanilla extract

CANDY BAR CUPCAKES

PEACH ALMOND CRISP

1. Place croissant bottoms in a 13-in. x 9-in. baking dish coated with cooking spray. Sprinkle with chocolate chips and replace croissant tops.

2. In a large bowl, combine the eggs, milk, sugar and vanilla; pour over croissants. Let stand for 10 minutes or until croissants are softened.

3. Bake, uncovered, at 350° for 55-60 minutes or until a knife inserted near the center comes out clean. Let stand for 10 minutes before cutting.

Nutrition Facts: 1 serving equals 326 calories, 14 g fat (7 g saturated fat), 166 mg cholesterol, 313 mg sodium, 41 g carbohydrate, 1 g fiber, 11 g protein.

Peach Almond Crisp S

PREP: 15 min. BAKE: 20 min. YIELD: 8 servings

LILY JULOW • GAINESVILLE, FLORIDA

This is delectable with any stone fruit, but especially peaches. It makes eight servings, though six people will eat it up faster than you can blink an eye!

- 2/3 cup sliced almonds
- 1/2 cup all-purpose flour
- 1/4 cup packed dark brown sugar
- 3 Tbsp. cold butter
- 1 Tbsp. sugar
- 1/4 tsp. ground cinnamon
- Dash ground nutmeg
- 8 medium peaches, peeled and sliced
- 3 Tbsp. thawed orange juice concentrate
- Reduced-fat vanilla ice cream, optional

1. In a food processor, combine the first seven ingredients. Cover and process until crumbly; set the mixture aside.

2. Place peaches in an 11-in. x 7-in. baking dish coated with cooking spray; drizzle with orange juice concentrate. Sprinkle with almond mixture. Bake at 400° for 20-25 minutes or until topping is golden brown. Serve warm with ice cream if desired.

Nutrition Facts: 3/4 cup (calculated without ice cream) equals 193 calories, 9 g fat (3 g saturated fat), 11 mg cholesterol, 33 mg sodium, 28 g carbohydrate, 3 g fiber, 4 g protein. **Diabetic Exchanges:** 2 fat, 1 fruit, 1/2 starch.

Berry Smoothie Pops F S C

PREP: 10 min. + freezing YIELD: 9 pops

LISA ROMAN • HONOLULU, HAWAII

Three types of good-for-you berries make these icy pops bright and tasty. What a fun snack on hot summer days!

- 1/2 cup orange juice
- 1 cup fresh blackberries
- 1 cup fresh raspberries
- 3/4 cup fresh blueberries
- 1 medium ripe banana, cut into chunks
- 1 Tbsp. sugar
- 9 Popsicle molds or paper cups (3 oz. *each*) and Popsicle sticks

1. In a blender, combine the orange juice, blackberries, raspberries, blueberries, banana and sugar; cover and process until blended. Fill each mold or cup with 1/4 cup berry mixture; top with holders or insert sticks into cups. Freeze.

Nutrition Facts: 1 pop equals 44 calories, trace fat (trace saturated fat), 0 cholesterol, trace sodium, 11 g carbohydrate, 2 g fiber, 1 g protein. **Diabetic Exchange:** 1/2 fruit.

Makeover Blueberry Whipped Topping Dessert

PREP: 30 min. + chilling **YIELD:** 20 servings

LAURA BAUDOIN • RACELAND, LOUISIANA

This lightened-up dessert is so yummy! It's like enjoying a taste of summer in every bite. Most importantly, no one will suspect this sweet surprise is on the light side of most desserts.

1	cup all-purpose flour
3/4	cup finely chopped pecans
6	Tbsp. butter, melted
1	envelope unflavored gelatin
1/2	cup cold water
2	pkg. (8 oz. *each*) fat-free cream cheese
2	cups confectioners' sugar
1	carton (8 oz.) frozen reduced-fat whipped topping, thawed
1	can (21 oz.) blueberry pie filling

1. In a small bowl, combine the flour, pecans and butter. Press onto the bottom a 13-in. x 9-in. baking dish coated with cooking spray. Bake at 350° for 10 minutes. Cool on a wire rack.

2. Meanwhile, in a small saucepan, sprinkle gelatin over cold water; let stand for 1 minute. Heat over low heat, stirring until gelatin is completely dissolved. Remove from the heat; set aside.

3. In a large bowl, beat cream cheese and confectioners' sugar until smooth. Beat in gelatin mixture until blended. Fold in whipped topping. Pour over crust. Spoon pie filling over top. Cover and refrigerate for at least 4 hours or until firm. Refrigerate leftovers.

Nutrition Facts: 1 piece equals 232 calories, 8 g fat (4 g saturated fat), 11 mg cholesterol, 152 mg sodium, 36 g carbohydrate, 1 g fiber, 5 g protein.

Strawberry Apple Cream Pops `F` `S`

PREP: 5 min. + freezing **YIELD:** 10 pops

BRITTNEY MUSGROVE • DALLAS, GEORGIA

Perfect on a hot summer's day, these super-yummy frozen bars couldn't be any simpler!

2	cups (16 oz.) strawberry yogurt
3/4	cup thawed apple juice concentrate
10	Popsicle molds *or* paper cups (3 oz. *each*) and Popsicle sticks

1. In a large bowl, combine yogurt and apple juice concentrate. Fill each mold or cup with 1/4 cup yogurt mixture; top with holders or insert sticks into cups. Freeze.

Nutrition Facts: 1 pop equals 84 calories, 1 g fat (trace saturated fat), 2 mg cholesterol, 31 mg sodium, 18 g carbohydrate, trace fiber, 2 g protein. **Diabetic Exchange:** 1 starch.

Makeover Raspberry Ice Cream `S`

PREP: 20 min. + chilling
PROCESS: 15 min./batch + freezing **YIELD:** 1-1/2 qt.

JEAN ECOS • HARTLAND, WISCONSIN

There's even more to love with my fruity ice cream since the "Healthy Cooking" pros made a few tweaks. With the original's creaminess and 30 percent fewer calories, this makeover is a stone-cold success!

1-1/2 cups half-and-half cream
1 cup whole milk
1-1/4 cups sugar, *divided*
1/8 tsp. salt
1 egg, beaten
1/2 cup fat-free sour cream
1 Tbsp. apple jelly
3 cups fresh raspberries
4-1/2 tsp. lemon juice

1. In a large saucepan, heat cream and milk to 175°; stir in 1/2 cup sugar and salt until dissolved. Whisk a small amount of the hot mixture into the egg. Return all to the pan, whisking constantly. Cook and stir over low heat until mixture is slightly thickened.

2. Remove from the heat. Cool quickly by placing pan in a bowl of ice water; stir for 2 minutes. Stir in sour cream and jelly. Press waxed paper onto surface of custard. Refrigerate for several hours or overnight.

3. Meanwhile, in a small bowl, gently combine raspberries with lemon juice and remaining sugar. Let stand for 2 hours, stirring occasionally. Mash raspberry mixture slightly; stir into custard.

4. Fill cylinder of ice cream freezer two-thirds full; freeze according to the manufacturer's directions. Refrigerate remaining mixture until ready to freeze. When ice cream is frozen, transfer to a freezer container; freeze for 2-4 hours before serving.

Nutrition Facts: 1/2 cup equals 169 calories, 4 g fat (3 g saturated fat), 36 mg cholesterol, 62 mg sodium, 29 g carbohydrate, 2 g fiber, 3 g protein. **Diabetic Exchanges:** 2 starch, 1/2 fat.

Rhubarb Raspberry Crumble [S]

Appv.

PREP: 20 min. **BAKE:** 35 min. **YIELD:** 8 servings

HEIDI FARNWORTH • RIVERTON, UTAH

The crumbly topping on this slightly sweet, slightly tart dessert really takes the cake. With slivered almonds, coconut and brown sugar, what's not to love?

3 cups chopped fresh *or* frozen rhubarb, thawed
2 cups fresh raspberries
2 tsp. lemon juice
1/2 cup sugar
1/2 cup reduced-fat plain yogurt
1/3 cup reduced-fat sour cream
1/4 cup all-purpose flour
1 egg

TOPPING:
1/2 cup quick-cooking oats
1/3 cup whole wheat flour
1/4 cup flaked coconut
1/4 cup packed brown sugar
1/2 tsp. ground cinnamon
3 Tbsp. cold butter
3 Tbsp. thawed apple juice concentrate
1/4 cup slivered almonds

1. In a large bowl, combine the rhubarb, raspberries and lemon juice. In a small bowl, combine the sugar, yogurt, sour cream, flour and egg. Pour over fruit mixture and stir gently to coat. Transfer to an 11-in. x 7-in. baking dish coated with cooking spray.

2. For topping, place the oats, flour, coconut, brown sugar and cinnamon in a food processor; cover and process until combined. Add butter and apple juice concentrate; process until crumbly. Stir in almonds; sprinkle over fruit mixture.

3. Bake, uncovered, at 350° for 35-45 minutes or until bubbly. Serve warm.

Editor's Note: If using frozen rhubarb, measure rhubarb while still frozen, then thaw completely. Drain in a colander, but do not press liquid out.

Nutrition Facts: 1 serving equals 264 calories, 9 g fat (5 g saturated fat), 42 mg cholesterol, 71 mg sodium, 42 g carbohydrate, 5 g fiber, 6 g protein.

MAKEOVER RASPBERRY ICE CREAM

RHUBARB RASPBERRY CRUMBLE

Chocolate Biscuit Puffs F C

PREP/TOTAL TIME: 20 min. YIELD: 10 servings

JOY CLARK • SEABECK, WASHINGTON

I know my favorite snack is fun for kids to make and eat because I dreamed it up at age 9! Pretty with the chocolate peeking out, the puffs could also be shaped to hide the chocolate within for a tasty surprise.

- 1 package (7-1/2 oz.) refrigerated flaky buttermilk biscuits
- 1 milk chocolate candy bar (1.55 oz.)
- 2 tsp. cinnamon-sugar

1. Flatten each biscuit into a 3-in. circle. Break candy bar into 10 pieces; place a piece on each biscuit. Bring up edges to enclose candy and pinch to seal.

2. Place on an ungreased baking sheet. Sprinkle with cinnamon-sugar. Bake at 450° for 8-10 minutes or until golden brown.

Nutrition Facts: 1 puff equals 78 calories, 2 g fat (1 g saturated fat), 1 mg cholesterol, 185 mg sodium, 14 g carbohydrate, trace fiber, 2 g protein. **Diabetic Exchange:** 1 starch.

Mother's Banana Sherbet F S

PREP: 15 min. PROCESS: 20 min. + freezing
YIELD: 2-1/2 cups

KATHY BARTON • HOMER, MICHIGAN

Here's a cool, creamy treat that's such a favorite with my family, I usually triple the recipe.

- 1 cup water
- 2/3 cup sugar
- 1/3 cup reduced-fat evaporated milk
- 1/3 cup orange juice
- 2 Tbsp. lemon juice
- 1 medium banana, cut into chunks

1. In a small saucepan, bring water and sugar to a boil. Cook and stir until sugar is dissolved; set aside to cool.

2. Place the evaporated milk, orange juice, lemon juice and banana in a blender. Add the sugar syrup; cover and process until smooth.

CHOCOLATE BISCUIT PUFFS

3. Fill cylinder of ice cream freezer; freeze according to manufacturer's directions. Transfer to a freezer container; freeze mixture for 4 hours or until firm before serving.

Nutrition Facts: 1/2 cup equals 149 calories, trace fat (trace saturated fat), 1 mg cholesterol, 19 mg sodium, 36 g carbohydrate, 1 g fiber, 2 g protein.

Strawberry Mango Sorbet F S

PREP: 20 min. + freezing YIELD: 1 qt.

SANDRA VACHON • SAINT-CONSTANT, QUEBEC

This is fresh, really simple and will keep in a freezer container—if you don't eat it all the first day!

- 3/4 cup sugar
- 1-1/2 cups water
- 1-1/2 cups chopped peeled mangoes
- 1-1/2 cups fresh strawberries, halved
- 1/4 cup lime juice

1. In a small saucepan, bring sugar and water to a boil. Cook and stir until sugar is dissolved; set aside to cool.

2. In a food processor, cover and process mangoes and strawberries until pureed. Transfer to a large bowl; stir in sugar syrup and lime juice. Pour into a 13-in. x 9-in. dish; cover and freeze for 45 minutes or until edges begin to firm. Stir and return to freezer. Freeze 2 hours longer or until firm.

3. Just before serving, transfer to a food processor; cover and process for 2-3 minutes or until smooth.

Nutrition Facts: 1/2 cup equals 103 calories, trace fat (trace saturated fat), 0 cholesterol, 1 mg sodium, 27 g carbohydrate, 1 g fiber, trace protein. **Diabetic Exchanges:** 1-1/2 starch, 1/2 fruit.

Zesty Lemon Granita F S

PREP: 15 min. + freezing YIELD: 2 cups

SONYA LABBE • SANTA MONICA, CALIFORNIA

A light dessert with a refreshing, icy texture, this full-flavored delight always hits the spot on hot summer days. What a great change of pace from regular ice cream and frozen yogurt.

- 1 cup water
- 2/3 cup sugar
- 2/3 cup lemon juice
- 2 fresh thyme sprigs
- 2 tsp. grated lemon peel

1. In a small saucepan, bring water and sugar to a boil. Cook and stir until sugar is dissolved. Remove from the heat; stir in lemon juice and thyme. Transfer to an 8-in. square dish; cool to room temperature.

2. Remove thyme sprigs. Freeze for 1 hour; stir with a fork. Freeze 2-3 hours longer or until completely frozen, stirring every 30 minutes.

3. Stir granita with a fork just before serving; spoon into dessert dishes. Garnish with lemon peel.

Nutrition Facts: 1/2 cup equals 140 calories, trace fat (0 saturated fat), 0 cholesterol, trace sodium, 37 g carbohydrate, trace fiber, trace protein.

ZESTY LEMON GRANITA

MOTHER'S BANANA SHERBET

STRAWBERRY MANGO SORBET

Orange Cranberry Torte

PREP: 20 min. **BAKE:** 55 min. + cooling
YIELD: 16 servings

BERTHA PALAMAR • FULTON, NEW YORK

About 45 years ago, a friend gave me this recipe around the holidays; it's been a favorite ever since.

1	cup sugar
1	cup buttermilk
1/2	cup unsweetened applesauce
1/3	cup canola oil
2	eggs
2-1/4	cups all-purpose flour
1	tsp. baking powder
3/4	tsp. baking soda
1/4	tsp. salt
1	cup chopped walnuts
1	cup fresh or frozen cranberries, coarsely chopped
1	cup chopped dates
4	tsp. grated orange peel

GLAZE:

1/2	cup confectioners' sugar
2	tsp. orange juice

1. Coat a 10-in. fluted tube pan with cooking spray and sprinkle with flour; set aside.

2. In a large bowl, beat the sugar, buttermilk, applesauce, oil and eggs until well blended. Combine the flour, baking powder, baking soda and salt; gradually beat into sugar mixture until blended. Stir in the walnuts, cranberries, dates and orange peel.

3. Pour into prepared pan. Bake at 350° for 55-60 minutes or until a toothpick inserted near the center comes out clean. Cool for 10 minutes before removing from pan to a wire rack to cool completely. Combine glaze ingredients; drizzle over cake.

Nutrition Facts: 1 slice equals 269 calories, 10 g fat (1 g saturated fat), 27 mg cholesterol, 147 mg sodium, 42 g carbohydrate, 2 g fiber, 5 g protein.

Dulce de Leche Rice Pudding

PREP: 15 min. **COOK:** 50 min. **YIELD:** 6 servings

CARLA CERVANTES-JAUREGUI • MODESTO, CALIFORNIA

Brown rice lends a wonderful nuttiness to this tasty treat. I'm sure your family will love this sweet and salty version of down-home comfort food.

2	cups water
1/2	cup uncooked brown rice
1/2	cup uncooked long grain rice

1/4 cup sugar

1-1/2 cinnamon sticks (3 in.)

1 Tbsp. butter

Dash salt

1 can (12 oz.) evaporated milk

8 caramels

1 Tbsp. coarse sugar

1/8 tsp. kosher salt

1. In a large saucepan, combine the first seven ingredients. Bring to a boil. Reduce heat; simmer, uncovered, for 30 minutes or until water is absorbed.

2. Stir in milk. Bring to a boil. Reduce heat; simmer, uncovered, for 12-16 minutes or until thick and creamy, stirring occasionally. Add caramels, stirring until melted. Discard cinnamon sticks.

3. Spoon into dessert dishes. In a small bowl, combine coarse sugar and kosher salt; sprinkle over pudding. Serve warm or cold.

Nutrition Facts: 1/2 cup equals 294 calories, 7 g fat (4 g saturated fat), 24 mg cholesterol, 166 mg sodium, 50 g carbohydrate, 1 g fiber, 7 g protein.

Chai-Chocolate Chip Biscotti F S

PREP: 30 min. + chilling **BAKE:** 30 min. + cooling
YIELD: 2-1/2 dozen

PAT RUNTZ • HUNTLEY, ILLINOIS

This crunchy cookie was made to be dunked! Enjoy it with a hot cup of coffee or cold glass of milk.

2-1/3 cups all-purpose flour

1 cup sugar

3/4 tsp. ground cinnamon

1/2 tsp. baking powder

1/2 tsp. baking soda

1/4 tsp. salt

1/4 tsp. ground allspice

1/4 tsp. ground cardamom

1/4 cup strong brewed chai tea, room temperature

1 egg

1 egg white

1 Tbsp. fat-free milk

1 tsp. vanilla extract

1/2 cup chopped walnuts

1/2 cup miniature semisweet chocolate chips

1. In a large bowl, combine the first eight ingredients. In a small bowl, whisk the tea, egg, egg white, milk and vanilla. Stir into dry ingredients just until combined. Stir in walnuts and chocolate chips. Divide dough in half. Wrap each portion in plastic wrap and refrigerate for 1 hour.

2. On a baking sheet coated with cooking spray, shape each half into a 10-in. x 2-in. rectangle. Bake at 350° for 20-25 minutes or until golden brown. Place pans on wire racks. When cool enough to handle, transfer to a cutting board; cut diagonally with a serrated knife into 3/4-in. slices. Place cut side down on baking sheets coated with cooking spray.

3. Bake for 6-9 minutes on each side or until firm. Remove to wire racks. Store in an airtight container.

Nutrition Facts: 1 cookie equals 93 calories, 3 g fat (1 g saturated fat), 7 mg cholesterol, 52 mg sodium, 16 g carbohydrate, 1 g fiber, 2 g protein. **Diabetic Exchanges:** 1 starch, 1/2 fat.

Mini Raspberry Mousse Parfaits S

PREP: 30 min. + chilling **YIELD:** 4 servings

HEALTHY COOKING TEST KITCHEN

These elegant parfaits make the perfect finish to a special meal. Busy hostesses can assemble them ahead.

1-3/4 cups fresh or frozen unsweetened raspberries, thawed

3 Tbsp. sugar

2 tsp. cornstarch

2 tsp. orange juice

1-1/3 cups whipped topping

1/3 cup cubed angel food cake (1/2-in. cubes)

1. Press raspberries through a strainer and discard seeds and pulp. In a small saucepan, combine sugar and cornstarch; stir in raspberry juice. Bring to a boil; cook and stir for 2 minutes or until thickened. Refrigerate until chilled.

2. Divide raspberry mixture in half. Stir orange juice into one portion; set aside. Place remaining mixture in a small bowl; fold in whipped topping.

3. Divide angel food cake among four small cocktail glasses or dessert dishes. Layer each with a scant Tbsp. of reserved raspberry-orange mixture and 1/3 cup creamy mixture. Refrigerate until serving.

Nutrition Facts: 1 parfait equals 143 calories, 4 g fat (4 g saturated fat), 0 cholesterol, 29 mg sodium, 24 g carbohydrate, 1 g fiber, 1 g protein. **Diabetic Exchanges:** 1 starch, 1 fat, 1/2 fruit.

CHAI-CHOCOLATE CHIP BISCOTTI

Mock Apple Strudel

PREP: 20 min. **BAKE:** 25 min. + cooling
YIELD: 12 servings

BETH DAUENHAUER • PUEBLO, COLORADO

On Saturdays, Mom would pack us five kids into the car, and we'd drive into the country looking for wild apple trees alongside the road. With the apples we picked, she'd bake this strudel, our traditional Sunday-morning breakfast in fall.

- 2 cups all-purpose flour
- 3 tsp. baking powder
- 2 Tbsp. plus 1/2 cup sugar, *divided*
- 1/2 tsp. salt
- 1/4 cup cold butter
- 3/4 cup fat-free milk
- 1 Tbsp. butter, melted
- 3 cups chopped tart apples
- 1 tsp. ground cinnamon

FROSTING:
- 1/2 cup confectioners' sugar
- 1 tsp. fat-free milk
- 1/4 tsp. vanilla extract

Chopped nuts, optional

1. In a large bowl, combine the flour, baking powder, 2 Tbsp. sugar and salt. Cut in butter until mixture resembles coarse crumbs. Stir in milk just until moistened. Turn onto a lightly floured surface; knead 8-10 times.

2. Roll out into a 14-in. x 10-in. rectangle. Brush with melted butter. Top with apples; sprinkle with cinnamon and remaining sugar. Roll up jelly-roll style, starting with a long side; pinch seams to seal. Place on a parchment paper-lined 15-in. x 10-in. x 1-in. baking pan. Bake at 425° for 25-30 minutes or until golden brown.

3. Remove from pan to a wire rack. In a small bowl, combine the confectioners' sugar, milk and vanilla; drizzle over warm strudel. Sprinkle with nuts if desired.

Nutrition Facts: 1 slice (calculated without nuts) equals 200 calories, 5 g fat (3 g saturated fat), 13 mg cholesterol, 239 mg sodium, 37 g carbohydrate, 1 g fiber, 3 g protein.

Wonton Sundaes F S C

PREP: 25 min. **BAKE:** 10 min. + cooling **YIELD:** 2 dozen

BETTY JO MORRIS • LITTLE ROCK, ARKANSAS

I created this recipe by combining two favorite treats. Set these sundaes on a dessert buffet and watch them disappear.

- 24 wonton wrappers
- Refrigerated butter-flavored spray
- 1 Tbsp. plus 1/4 cup sugar, *divided*
- 1 tsp. ground cinnamon
- 1 package (8 oz.) reduced-fat cream cheese
- 1 tsp. vanilla extract
- 1/4 cup miniature semisweet chocolate chips
- 1/4 cup chopped pecans
- 24 maraschino cherries with stems

1. Place wonton wrappers on a work surface; spritz with butter-flavored spray. Combine 1 Tbsp. sugar and cinnamon; sprinkle over wontons. Press into miniature muffin cups coated with cooking spray.

2. Bake at 350° for 4-5 minutes or until lightly browned. Immediately remove wonton cups to an ungreased baking sheet. Bake 2-3 minutes longer or until bottoms of cups are lightly browned. Remove to a wire rack to cool.

3. In a small bowl, beat the cream cheese, vanilla and remaining sugar until smooth. Stir in chocolate chips and pecans. Spoon into wonton cups. Top each with a maraschino cherry.

Nutrition Facts: 1 sundae equals 83 calories, 3 g fat (1 g saturated fat), 6 mg cholesterol, 74 mg sodium, 12 g carbohydrate, trace fiber, 2 g protein. **Diabetic Exchanges:** 1 starch, 1/2 fat.

Banana Strawberry Pops F S C

PREP: 10 min. + freezing **YIELD:** 10 pops

DEIRDRE DEE COX • MILWAUKEE, WISCONSIN

Strawberry and banana shine in these summery, refreshing pops with a pretty pink color.

MOCK APPLE STRUDEL

BANANA STRAWBERRY POPS

MOCHACCINO PUDDING

1/2 cup fat-free milk

1/2 cup orange juice

2 Tbsp. honey

1 pint fresh strawberries, hulled

1 medium ripe banana, cut into chunks

10 Popsicle molds *or* paper cups (3 oz. *each*) and Popsicle sticks

1. In a blender, combine the milk, juice, honey, strawberries and banana; cover and process until blended. Fill each mold or cup with 1/4 cup strawberry mixture; top with holders or insert sticks into cups. Freeze.

Nutrition Facts: 1 pop equals 42 calories, trace fat (trace saturated fat), trace cholesterol, 6 mg sodium, 10 g carbohydrate, 1 g fiber, 1 g protein. **Diabetic Exchange:** 1/2 fruit.

Mochaccino Pudding S

PREP: 15 min. COOK: 10 min. + chilling
YIELD: 6 servings

MARIA REGAKIS • SOMERVILLE, MASSACHUSETTS

I like to top this homey prize-winning pudding with chocolate-covered espresso beans and whipped cream. Pudding never tasted so elegant!

1 Tbsp. boiling water

2 tsp. instant espresso powder

3/4 cup sugar

1/4 cup baking cocoa

3 Tbsp. cornstarch

1/2 tsp. ground cinnamon

1/8 tsp. salt

3 cups 2% milk

3 egg yolks, lightly beaten

1 Tbsp. brandy, optional

1 tsp. vanilla extract

Whipped cream and chocolate-covered coffee beans, optional

1. Combine boiling water and espresso powder; set aside. In a large heavy saucepan, combine the sugar, cocoa, cornstarch, cinnamon and salt. Stir in milk until smooth. Cook and stir over medium-high heat until thickened and bubbly. Reduce heat to low; cook and stir 2 minutes longer.

2. Remove from the heat. Stir a small amount of hot mixture into egg yolks; return all to the pan, stirring constantly. Bring to a gentle boil; cook and stir 2 minutes longer. Remove from the heat. Stir in brandy if desired, vanilla and espresso mixture. Cool for 15 minutes, stirring occasionally.

3. Transfer to dessert dishes. Cover and refrigerate for 1 hour. Garnish with whipped cream and coffee beans if desired.

Nutrition Facts: 1/2 cup (calculated without optional ingredients) equals 212 calories, 5 g fat (2 g saturated fat), 112 mg cholesterol, 115 mg sodium, 37 g carbohydrate, 1 g fiber, 6 g protein.

General Recipe Index

This handy index lists every recipe by food category, major ingredient and/or cooking method, so you can easily locate recipes to suit your needs.

•*Table-ready in 30 minutes or less.*

Alphabetical Index

This handy index lists every recipe alphabetically, so you can easily find the dishes you enjoy most.
•*Table-ready in 30 minutes or less.*